THE GUINNESS BOOK OF CRIME

The Guinness Book of Crime

By
Brian Bailey

Reprint 10 9 8 7 6 5 4 3 2 1 0

Published in Great Britain by
Guinness Publishing Ltd,
338 Euston Road,
London, NW1 3BD.

Printed and bound in Great Britain by The Bath Press.

Editor: Caroline Chapman
Design and Page Make-up: Mitchell Associates
Cover Design: Design 23
Project Manager: Helen Weller
Project Assistant: Keith Jackson
Joint Publishing Directors: Ian Castello-Cortes and Michael Feldman

A catalogue record for this book is available from The British Library

ISBN 0-85112-559-X

Contents

Acknowledgments

THE AUTHOR's chief debt in any book of this scope is, of course, to his countless predecessors who have recorded, in books and newspapers, the criminal activities of the human race; endlessly debated the rights and wrongs of legislation and punishment; and tried to fathom some of the enduring mysteries of crime.

I have also to thank the Home Office and the governors of Barlinnie and Wakefield prisons for answering particular queries, and am grateful to Mrs Anne McQueen, Chief Librarian of *The Yorkshire Post,* and the Association of British Insurers, for supplying helpful information.

I am extremely grateful to Caroline Chapman, the book's editor, who has made many constructive comments and saved me from several ambiguities.

My wife's help has (as on so many occasions before) been invaluable in enabling me to complete the job on time.

I cannot omit to mention my indebtedness to Laura Norder, that ever-present muse so often invoked by radio and television journalists when reporting matters of crime and punishment. Without her, this book could not have been written.

Introduction

GLANCE AT THE BOOKS on 'True Crime' in any bookshop, and you will find that the vast majority of them are concerned exclusively with murder. Yet murder, especially in Britain, is among the rarest of crimes. Why is the public interest in murder so disproportionate to its actual occurrence? The question answers itself: it is the extreme nature and rarity of the crime that explains a large part of its fascination. But it is also, of course, partly due to a compelling curiosity about the darkest side of human nature. Murder is the gravest of crimes, and there is a perverse thrill in reading about the wicked and often gruesome acts committed by men and women whom we might have passed in the street, or sat next to on a bus and thought of as 'ordinary people'.

I have recognized the overwhelming pre-eminence of murder in the popular conception of 'true crime' by devoting by far the largest section of the book to it, as well as adding a section on assassination, which is only murder under a posh name. But there is a great deal more to the vast subject of crime than murder, and it is no less absorbing for not having a bloody corpse at the scene, as I hope to demonstrate. With a few exceptions, this book is confined to serious civil crimes, avoiding military crimes, political terrorism and war crimes.

For convenience, I have divided the subject-matter into three main sections, dealing with crimes against the individual, against property, and against the State. Some of the crimes covered, like murder, are universal crimes—against the law in every civilized society. Others, like witchcraft, are historical crimes, widespread once and causing as much fear and distress among the populace as the most heinous crimes of our own times. One or two, like body-snatching, are crimes that were more-or-less peculiar to Britain. There is inevitably some overlapping of subject matter. The line between murder and manslaughter, for instance, is a fine one—as between, say, treason and sedition.

My aim has been to make a wide-ranging survey of what have been seen at different times as the most serious criminal acts. The emphasis of the book is on Britain and the English-speaking world, but I have included cases from other countries when they show different aspects of the crimes under discussion. In some cases, the introductory pages to each crime may range over the whole of history, but I have restricted the detailed case histories to the modern world; that is, from the Tudor period to the present day.

Finally, there is a review of crime and punishment. Every human society must set up rules of behaviour in order to preserve itself from anarchy and ultimate destruction, and a criminal is one who breaks the rules of the society in which he or she lives. The punishment of crimes by the courts represents public denunciation of acts which are, by common consent, against the public interest. That is to say, crimes are acts which threaten the stability of society, and society has every right to reinforce its rules by punishing the criminal. In that sense, *all* crimes are crimes against the State, and the means used by different societies to protect themselves from the effects of crime are no less fascinating than the crimes themselves.

In view of the famous dictum that "every society gets the criminals it deserves", it is worth noting that in England and Wales there was a 44 per cent increase in the number of crimes recorded by the police in the six years 1987-92 inclusive. This was higher than in any other major developed country, the nearest rivals being Belgium and Portugal with 32 per cent. The increase in Scotland over the same period was 23 per cent. In the last two years before this book goes to press, the number of recorded crimes has fallen slightly.

It is perhaps hardly necessary to add that opinions expressed in the course of the text are my own, and not necessarily those of the publishers.

To Rita,
my accessory before, during and after the fact

Part one:
Crimes Against Individuals

Section 1: Murder

Truth will come to light; murder cannot be hid long.
William Shakespeare: *The Merchant of Venice*

ONE OF THE FIRST NOTABLE INCIDENTS in the history of the human race, according to the Old Testament, was an act of murder. Hardly had Adam and Eve raised their two sons, we are told, before one brother slew the other in a fit of jealous rage.

If it were true, it would seem a depressing debut for mankind to have on his conscience—the so-called Mark of Cain. But it is a picturesque tale, and laws against murder have nothing to do with religious myths. If Moses had slipped and broken his neck on the way down from Mount Sinai, "Thou shalt not kill" would still be a cardinal rule in all civilized societies, for obvious practical as well as moral reasons.

Nevertheless, the divine interdict against murder may have much to do with the perennial fascination that the most heinous of crimes holds for most people. For what manner of man (or woman) is it that dares to defy such an absolute prohibition, and risk the ultimate retribution of eternal damnation? Little wonder that in primitive societies murderers were subject to strict taboos. Another reason for the hold murder has on our imagination is that it is a comparatively rare event. Its very infrequency adds to the sense of startled disbelief with which we tend to view it.

The story of Cain and Abel was well founded by the Hebrew composers of the Book of Genesis.

Fact

Nearly four centuries separated the murders of two famous English playwrights, Christopher Marlowe and Joe Orton. Marlowe, born in Canterbury and author of Tamburlaine the Great *and* Edward II, *was stabbed by one Frizer or Frazer in a tavern brawl at Deptford on 1 June 1593, at the age of 29. Orton, born in Leicester, author of* Entertaining Mr Sloane *and* What the Butler Saw, *was battered to death by his homosexual flat-mate Kenneth Halliwell at Islington on 9 August 1967. Orton was 34. Halliwell committed suicide shortly afterwards. The work of both authors is much concerned with violent death. Marlowe was himself suspected of complicity in a murder in 1589, but was released after two weeks in prison.*

The most common type of murder in western societies is the killing of one individual by another in a domestic situation, in circumstances of extreme provocation, uncontrollable rage, drunkenness or temporary insanity. Around a third of murder victims in the UK are killed by their partners, and about three-quarters by relatives or people well known to them. Such murderers as these are unlikely to repeat their criminal acts, which are unreasoned responses, on the spur of the moment, to extreme stress. A considerable number of such murderers, in fact, commit suicide. These murders do not, as a rule, grab the mesmerized attention of the media like the more sensational kinds of homicide, such as mass or multiple murders. These are the rarer types of murder, although there has been a significant increase in the present violent century which is reflected in the cases included here.

It is perhaps necessary to define the terms used in this book since some writers carelessly confuse them. A mass murderer is one who kills several people at more-or-less the same time, as in a bomb explosion. A multiple murderer is one who kills several people at different times, as in a series of gangland killings. A serial killer is one who methodically murders a number of chosen individuals, one by one.

Murder is such a vast subject that, in the end, every book on the subject has to be highly selective and reflect the author's reactions and attitudes. The case histories in this section have been chosen to illustrate many different aspects of the crime of murder, as regards both motive and method. Some unsolved murders and miscarriages of justice are included. The cases also reflect common trends and periodic fashions in murder—the doctor with his poisons; the social conditions in which baby-farming flourished; the growth in sexual serial murders, etc. Many of the cases are classics of their kind; others less well known. I have drawn them chiefly, but not exclusively, from the last 250 years in Britain.

In his essay *Decline of the English Murder*, George Orwell considered that the golden age of murder in England was roughly between 1850 and 1925—the period of Dr Palmer, Jack the Ripper, Crippen and the 'Brides in the Bath'. But Orwell was writing in 1946, when the war had stemmed the flow of sensational cases in the Sunday papers. There was soon to be a revival, with the likes of Christie and Haigh, Ruth Ellis and Derek Bentley, that Orwell could not have anticipated.

Case Histories

The Aristocrat

Laurence Shirley, the 4th Earl Ferrers, was the descendant of an ancient and distinguished Leicestershire family, whose seat was Staunton Harold Hall, near Ashby-de-la-Zouch. He was a hard drinker and had a violent temper. His long-suffering wife had separated from him on grounds of cruelty after he had kicked her unconscious in front of their servants.

One day early in 1760, Lord Ferrers called a family retainer named Johnson into his presence. He had developed an unreasoning hatred for the old man. He ordered him down on his knees and shot him dead. The Earl was taken to Leicester Gaol and then to the Tower of London to await trial by the House of Lords in Westminster Hall. He was probably taken aback at being tried for his life for killing a mere servant. His feudal ancestors would have regarded servants as part of their property, to do with as they liked. But Lord Ferrers conducted his own defence, and used all his eloquence—and numerous witnesses—to try and convince his peers that he was insane. This was undoubtedly the plain truth of the matter, but it is a rather difficult task to get anyone to believe you are insane if you are able to present an argument lucidly. Their Lordships were not persuaded, and Lord Ferrers was convicted of murder and sentenced to death.

Huge crowds gathered to watch the execution at Tyburn on 5 May 1760. The Earl, arriving in his own landau, attended by his liveried servants and accompanied by an escort of cavalry and infantry, remarked: "I suppose they never saw a lord hanged, and perhaps they will never see another". He was right: Lord Ferrers was the only peer of the realm to be hanged for murder. The executioner was Thomas Turlis. There is no truth in the popular myth that the Earl was hanged with a silk rope. He had to make do with hemp like a common criminal.

Fact

Mary Lamb, co-author of the once-popular Lamb's Tales from Shakespeare, *was a murderess. Charles Lamb, the famous essayist and critic, spent most of his life as his sister's guardian. Mary, nine years older than Charles, inherited insanity from her mother, and in 1796 she suddenly stabbed her to death with a table-knife. She was committed to an asylum, but Charles withdrew from his imminent marriage and gave priority to looking after her, the authorities having accepted his undertaking of guardianship. He devoted the remaining 38 years of his life to Mary's care. In the last years, his own health was seriously affected by her increasing and prolonged attacks of mental derangement.*

The Midwife

Elizabeth Brownrigg was a midwife appointed to look after women in labour in St Dunstan's parish workhouse. She and her family lived in Fetter Lane, where she took in young girls from the parish as apprentices to help in her private practice. She habitually ill-treated them, whipping them at the slightest provocation and keeping them in a filthy and wretched condition. One girl ran away, returning to the Foundling Hospital from which she had come. She was replaced by a girl named Mary Clifford.

This 16 year-old girl quickly became the chief victim of Mrs Brownrigg's sadistic temperament. She was tied up naked and beaten mercilessly, sometimes with a cane, sometimes a horse-whip, and sometimes a broom-handle. She was made to sleep in a cold, dark coal-hole on a bed of straw and a sack, and was fed on bread and water for long periods. Once, when Mary broke open a cupboard in a desperate search for food, the fiendish Mrs Brownrigg determined to punish her with special rigour to deter the girl from repeating the crime. Mary was made to strip naked and was chained to a yard door. Then she was beaten repeatedly with the butt-end of a whip throughout the course of a whole day, before being returned to the coal-hole with her hands tied behind her back.

Mary Clifford and a girl named Mitchell were frequently horse-whipped whilst secured by a rope round their wrists to a hook in the kitchen ceiling. Brownrigg would whip them until blood ran down their bodies, and when she was tired, her eldest son John would take over. On

Fact

Among more recent eminent murder suspects have been Queen Victoria's grandson, Prince Albert, Duke of Clarence, thought by some to have been Jack the Ripper; Robert Graves, the poet and novelist, author of I, Claudius, *who was briefly suspected by police of the attempted murder of the American poet Laura Riding by pushing her out of a window; Jeremy Thorpe, politician and leader of the Liberal Party in the late 60s and early 70s, who was acquitted at the Old Bailey in 1979 of conspiracy to murder; and Terry Marsh, former world light-welterweight boxing champion, acquitted in 1990 of shooting his former manager, Frank Warren.*

one occasion, Mrs Brownrigg seized Mary Clifford's cheeks in her fingers and forced the skin down so violently that blood ran from the girl's eyes. When Mary complained to a woman lodger about the treatment she received, and the woman tried to intercede on her behalf, Mrs Brownrigg flew into a frenzy of rage and abuse, and, threatening to cut out the girl's tongue, succeeded in cutting it in two places with a pair of scissors.

Eventually it came to the notice of one of Mary's relatives that neighbours had often heard shrieks and moans from the Brownriggs' house, and law officers visited the premises. They did not find Mary Clifford, but they took away Mary Mitchell, who screamed with pain when her bodice, stuck to her wounds with coagulated blood, was removed. But when she was assured that she would not be sent back to Mrs Brownrigg, she described how she and Mary Clifford had been ill-treated. Mary Clifford was then produced from a cupboard, in a critical condition, by Mr Brownrigg. She was covered in ulcers and bruises, and could barely speak. She was taken immediately to St Bartholomew's Hospital, but died a few days later.

By this time, Mrs Brownrigg and her son had fled in disguise to a lodging-house in Wandsworth, where they were subsequently traced and arrested. James Brownrigg, his wife and son were indicted for murder. But while the barbaric midwife was convicted and sentenced to death, the charge in the men's cases was reduced to misdemeanour, and they each got away with six months imprisonment.

Elizabeth Brownrigg was hanged at Tyburn on 14 September 1767 by Thomas Turlis, amid the execrations of a large crowd that wished her eternal damnation. Her body was afterwards dissected at Surgeons' Hall, where her skeleton was kept for many years.

Neither public execration nor public execution had much deterrent effect. In 1829 Esther Hibner was hanged outside Newgate Gaol for an almost identical crime. She had killed a 10 year-old girl apprentice by flogging and starving her. Two other girls had also died whilst in her charge. A broadside circulated at her execution included the lines:

Since Mother Brownrigg's ancient doom,
Now sixty years and more,
Such treatment to poor infants
Was never heard before.

This was hardly true: child-killing was alarmingly common.

The Clergyman

The circumstances of the death of Martha Reay, mistress of John Montagu, 4th Earl of Sandwich and First Lord of the Admiralty, became a great *cause célèbre* in 1779. Although Miss Reay had been the Earl's mistress for 17 years, and was the mother of nine children by him, she had an affair with a young officer of the 68th Regiment of Foot, James Hackman, whom she met at the Earl's country seat near Huntingdon in 1774. But despite Hackman's passionate entreaties, she refused to leave the Earl and marry the soldier.

Early in 1779 Hackman left the army and was ordained as a deacon in the Church of England. He was still distracted with love for Martha Reay, and entertained strong hopes that she might change her mind. When it finally became clear to him that she would not, he went one night to the Theatre Royal, Covent Garden, knowing she was there. He was armed with two pistols. He waited outside until she came out, and shot her in the head as she stepped into her coach.

At his trial for her murder, Rev. Hackman claimed that he had gone to the theatre with the intention of committing suicide in front of her, but had been overcome by a sudden impulse and had taken the second pistol as a precaution in case the first misfired. He had, in fact, discharged the second pistol at himself after shooting Miss Reay, but succeeded only in wounding himself.

Most people, including the jury members, considered the possession of two pistols sufficient proof of murderous intent, and the passionate clergyman was convicted and sentenced to death. James Hackman was hanged at Tyburn on 19 April 1779. The executioner was Edward Dennis, who features in Dickens's *Barnaby Rudge*.

Fact

When Madge Oberhaltzer died, aged 28, in Indiana in 1925, her death was attributed to poisons she had swallowed in committing suicide. Nevertheless, a man was charged with her murder. The local Klu Klux Klan 'Grand Wizard', one Stevenson, had kidnapped and raped the young woman, and it was this event which drove her to kill herself. A court ruling stated that a murder charge may be brought against a felon whose criminal conduct had led to suicide.

The Labourer

Late one Saturday night in December 1811, a draper, Timothy Marr, sent his servant, 18 year-old Margaret Jewell, to buy oysters for the family's supper. The Marrs lived over the shop in Ratcliffe Highway, a sordid thoroughfare notorious for thieves' dens, brothels and the haunts of sailors and Irish stevedores in a dangerous neighbourhood behind the London Docks. When the girl returned, the house was locked and in darkness, and she could make no one answer her knocks and shouts. In some alarm, she went to a local watchman, but he could do nothing either, and eventually neighbours alerted to the scene managed to gain entry. Inside they found Timothy Marr and his 13 year-old shop-boy apprentice, John Gowen, lying dead in pools of blood. Their throats had been cut and their skulls battered in. On the floor lay the murder weapons—a ripping chisel and a heavy hammer. Upstairs, Timothy's wife Cecilia and their young child had been murdered in the same way. Nothing appeared to have been taken from the house or shop.

News of the slaughter spread like wildfire through the capital, and there was a great deal of understandable apprehension in the East End about this savage and seemingly motiveless killing of a whole family. But that was as nothing compared with the general air of terror and panic 12 days later when another mass murder occurred nearby, obviously committed by the same person. There was a crazed madman on the loose. This time the victims were living at the King's Arms tavern.

Fact

According to the law, killing a man in a duel is no different from premeditated murder. Duellists' seconds in such cases were deemed to be accessories to wilful homicide. In practice, however, juries tended to regard a duel as a legitimate way for a "gentleman" to defend his honour, and rarely convicted for murder. Aristocratic defendants in such cases would occasionally be convicted of manslaughter, but were more likely to be acquitted. In the mid-18th century, an officer in the Royal Navy, Captain Clarke, was convicted of murder and sentenced to death after killing a man in a duel, but was subsequently pardoned when it was pointed out that his dying victim had forgiven him. George Fitzgerald was hanged for killing his opponent in a duel in Ireland in 1786.

A lodger there, John Turner, had been disturbed during the night, and had seen a stranger bending over a body downstairs. Escaping through a bedroom window, he summoned a nightwatchman who broke into the premises. The publican and his wife, Mr and Mrs Williamson, and their maidservant, Bridget Harrington, lay with their throats cut and their skulls smashed. Bridget's head had been almost severed from her body. The Williamsons' 14 year-old grand-daughter remained alive upstairs. The killer had evidently been disturbed before he got to her. A sailor's maul bearing the initials 'JP' lay beside one of the corpses.

A reward for information was offered by the government, while many false arrests were made, and at length the maul was traced to a Swedish sailor named Petersen. He, however, had a perfect alibi – he was at sea when the murders were committed. But he regularly lodged at the same place when he was in London, and this led to the arrest of another man who lodged in the same house. He was a young Irish labourer named John Williams. He had been seen in the vicinity at night, and admitted that he frequented the King's Arms. He was taken to Coldbath Fields House of Correction, but a few days later, before being brought to face charges, he hanged himself in his cell.

The evidence that John Williams was the Ratcliffe Highway murderer was, at best, circumstantial, and no clear motive was adduced. But his suicide and the fact that there were no more such murders appeared to confirm his guilt. Several theories have been proposed about the Ratcliffe Highway murders. It has been suggested that Williams may have had an insane grudge against humanity due to syphilis. Or that he was framed by a sailor named Ablass, a man with a record of violence. Thomas De Quincey dealt with the case in an appendix to his essay *Murder Considered as One of the Fine Arts.*

To help quell public unrest, on 31 December 1811, the body of Williams was publicly exhibited by being drawn on an open cart through the neighbourhood. Then he was buried in quicklime at a nearby crossroads in accordance with the law for suicides, with a stake through his heart.

The Lodging-house Keepers

On the morning of 1 November 1828, a woman known as Ann Gray, who was staying with her husband and child in a cramped and squalid lodging in the Wester Portsburgh district of Edinburgh, looked on the floor around the bed and moved a pile of straw. To her horror, she found the naked corpse of an old woman, with blood about the mouth and head. Mr Gray, a former soldier, went off to the police office to report his suspicion of murder, despite being detained and entreated by two women in the house to say nothing about it. They said the old woman had died of drink. When Gray came back with a sergeant and a constable, the body was no longer there, but they saw blood on the bed and the straw. The sergeant questioned the landlord, William Burke, and one of the women, Helen McDougal, and got contradictory statements. He decided to take them into custody.

Next morning, Sergeant Fisher, acting on information received, and accompanied by Gray, went to 10 Surgeons' Square, the premises of a lecturer in anatomy and surgery, Dr Robert Knox, and found in a chest in the cellar the corpse of an old woman. Mr Gray recognised the body as that of the woman he had seen both dead and alive in Burke's house.

Gray and his common-law wife had lodged with Burke for a few days prior to these developments. But on 31 October, Burke had brought home a frail old Irish woman named Mary Docherty, who had apparently come to Edinburgh looking for her son. Burke told the Grays that she was related to his mother, and he wanted her to stay with him during her brief visit to the city. It would therefore be necessary for the Grays to move out temporarily but he would fix them up with a friend of his, named Hare. The Grays spent that night in Tanner's Close, the house of William Hare and his common-law wife Mary, but Ann Gray went back to Burke's house during the evening to get her child's clothes, and found Burke and his mistress McDougal, and the Hares, singing, dancing and drinking with Mary Docherty in a merry, not to say intoxicated, Hallowe'en party.

Next morning, Burke invited the Grays to return to his place for breakfast. They noticed that the old woman was no longer there, and enquired about her. Burke said that they had turned her out for impudence. After breakfast, Mrs Gray dressed her child and looked under the bed for some stockings. Burke, who was in the room, became very agitated and started deliberately splashing whisky about the room. This made her suspicious, and as soon as he went out she found the body of Mary Docherty under the straw. Helen McDougal had pleaded with the Grays not to report the matter, and said it would be worth £10 to them to keep quiet.

Shortly after the body was traced to Dr Knox's cellar, the Hares were also arrested. Burke and Hare had stuffed the woman's corpse into a box and hired a street porter to carry it to Knox's premises, where they had been paid £5 on account.

Doctors examining the corpse were unable to say with certainty that the woman had met her death by violence, and the Lord Advocate could not hope to get a conviction for murder with the circumstantial evidence he had. He accepted William Hare's offer to turn King's Evidence as the only chance he had of bringing *any* of the four to justice. Hare and his wife were granted immunity from prosecution in connection with any murder about which he testified. Gradually, the grisly story of the Burke and Hare murders was pieced together, based chiefly on Burke's confessions in prison.

Burke and Hare were Irish navvies who had come to Scotland to work on the Union Canal. Burke had left a wife and family in Ireland, and taken up with McDougal and they had moved into the Hares' slum tenement in Tanner's Close. This had several beds, and Hare took in lodgers for threepence a night, sometimes sleeping three to a bed. The squalid houses of Burke and Hare were like twin towns of Irish slaughter and destruction—Sod'em and Begorrah.

Fact

Lynching is murder by a mob (not necessarily by hanging). It has been common in the USA, where it originated (the word comes from Charles Lynch, a Virginian Quaker who led local people into taking the law into their own hands when there was little proper law enforcement in the state). Negroes who had raped white women were frequently victims of lynch mobs. There were 231 lynchings throughout the United States in 1892, the highest number in one year since records began. In 1913 Leo Frank, a Jewish factory manager in Georgia who had murdered a 14 year-old girl, was abducted from the jail and hanged from a tree when the local populace became incensed by the commutation of his death sentence to life imprisonment. A rare case of lynching in modern Britain occurred in Glasgow in December 1922 when two men named Caskie and Stevenson assaulted and killed Robert Stewart whom they thought was kidnapping a 5 year-old boy. Their trial for murder resulted in the Scottish verdict "Not proven".

Fact

The case which established the 'McNaghten Rules' in Britain is often referred to as an assassination, though in fact it was common murder. In 1843 a Scotsman, Daniel McNaghten, shot Edward Drummond, the Prime Minister's private secretary, evidently mistaking him for the Prime Minister, Sir Robert Peel. McNaghten was suffering from a delusion that he was being persecuted by the Tories. McNaghten was acquitted on grounds of partial insanity. There was much disquiet about this ruling, and the verdict was challenged in the House of Lords. After lengthy debate, the McNaghten Rules were brought into being. They laid down that, to establish a defence of insanity, it must be proved that at the time the offence was committed, the accused did not know the nature and quality of the act he was committing; or, if he did know it, did not understand that what he was doing was wrong. It was an imperfect formula, much criticized by psychiatrists in particular who argued that if a person's mind was diseased, it was wholly diseased, not partly diseased, as the rule implied. But it served the law in Britain for more than a century before the Homicide Act of 1957 sought to embrace some of the long-standing reservations about the McNaghten Rules by recognizing the plea of diminished responsibility.

One of Hare's lodgers in 1827 was an old soldier named Donald, who died owing Hare £4 in rent. According to Burke, he died of dropsy, and Hare had the idea of selling the body to a surgeon. He offered Burke a share of the proceeds in return for his help, and they took the old man's body out of its coffin which they filled with tanner's bark. Then they sought out an anatomist they had heard of, Dr Monro, but were directed instead by some self-serving students to Dr Knox's premises. Knox himself examined the corpse, and not only gave them £7.10s for it, but invited them to call again when they had another body to dispose of.

Clearly, this was a profitable enterprise. Teachers of anatomy needed all the corpses they could get, and the fresher they were, the better. Body-snatchers were at work in all parts of Georgian Britain, digging up newly-buried corpses from churchyards and burial grounds in the interests of medical science and the training of skilled surgeons. Burke and Hare lost no time in exploiting their inspirational one-upmanship. It seemed easy work compared with the nocturnal labours of the resurrection men.

Their second sale was the body of a destitute old woman named Abigail Simpson, whom Hare invited back to his place for a wee dram. She got drunk and spent the night in one of Hare's beds. The next morning the two men, fortified by their night's drinking, set about their business. Hare clapped one hand over the woman's mouth and held her nostrils closed with the other, while Burke threw his whole weight on top of her to prevent her from thrashing about and making a noise. As soon as she was dead, they stripped the body and bundled it into a box. When they delivered it to Dr Knox, he asked no questions and paid £10.

Among the next victims of the fiendish duo was a teenage prostitute, Mary Paterson. Knox was so pleased with this delivery that he preserved the corpse in spirits and invited an artist to draw the voluptuous body before he dissected it. Soon, Burke and Hare had an unwritten "contract" with Knox whereby they received £8 in summer and £10 in winter. Lecture courses took place mainly in autumn and winter, and bodies were in less demand during the summer months because of the problems of preservation.

Burke and Hare preyed chiefly on poor old women. In the Edinburgh slums, the destitute drank heavily to drown their miseries, and were easily enticed by free drink into accompanying one of the men to their lair. Their method of murder was always more or less the same: one held the body down while the other caused death by suffocation. There was little noise or blood, and no marks were left on the bodies. When the mouth and nose were kept shut a very few minutes, one of Burke's statements said, "they could make no resistance, but would convulse and make a rumbling noise in their bellies for some time; after they had ceased crying and making resistance, they left them to die of themselves; but their bodies would often move afterwards, and for some time they would have long breathings before life went away".

The murderers had a little more trouble with an 18 year-old mentally deficient youth named James Wilson, well known on the streets of Edinburgh as 'Daft Jamie'. He wandered about without shoes, and his feet were recognisably deformed. He was stronger than most of their victims, and struggled violently for his life before his killers managed to overpower him. It was alleged afterwards that Dr Knox had been sufficiently alarmed by the possibility of Jamie's corpse being recognised that he cut off the head and feet immediately, and used the body for demonstration with more than usual promptness.

Burke and Hare were the most prolific of the reliably-accounted for murderers in British history. Their known victims add up to 16, all murdered within a period of nine months. There may have been more. William Burke and Helen McDougal were brought to trial on Christmas Eve; Burke on three counts, and McDougal for the murder of Mary Docherty only. Hare's evidence predictably laid all the blame on Burke's shoulders, and Burke's defence counsel tried to discredit the evidence of this "squalid wretch", who had nothing to lose by adding Burke and McDougal to his catalogue of victims. But Burke was found guilty and sentenced to death. The case against McDougal was judged "not proven" by the jury of 15 men, who were told by one of their lordships on the bench that the case was "one of the most monstrous delineations of human depravity that has ever been brought under your consideration". There was a great deal of disquiet about the fact that Hare had escaped justice.

Burke was hanged in Edinburgh's Lawnmarket on 28 January 1829, before a vast and noisy crowd. His body was dissected by Professor Monro and exhibited to an eager stream of spectators, said to have numbered more than 20,000. His skeleton was preserved at Edinburgh University's Medical School, where it remains to this day.

Controversy has continued ever since about the role of Dr Knox in the affair, many people thinking he should have been in the dock alongside Burke. There can hardly be any reasonable doubt that he not only knew that the bodies he bought had not been buried, which should have alerted him to enquire more closely into their origins, but that he also gave encouragement to men he must at least have *suspected* of being murderers. But the Edinburgh elite closed ranks to protect him from prosecution as an accessory, and their class from ill-repute. The ordinary folk, however, had no doubt of his guilt by association:

Up the close and doon the stair,
But and ben wi' Burke and Hare.
Burke's the butcher, Hare's the thief,
Knox the boy who buys the beef.

Fact

In 1921, a 15 year-old Welsh boy, Harold Jones, killed 11 year-old Florence Little in a frenzied sexual attack after being acquitted only two weeks earlier of the rape and murder of an 8 year-old girl. In the nine years between the passing of the Homicide Act (1957) and suspension of the death penalty (1965), one boy under 14 was convicted of murder in England and Wales, and 24 between the ages of 14 and 17. In Scotland in the same period, no one under 14 was convicted, but there were 19 convictions of persons between 14 and 17, all of them male. Mary Bell, aged 11, was charged at Newcastle Assizes in 1968 with the murder of Martin Brown, aged 4, and Brian Howe, aged 3. Both boys had been found dead in a slum area of Newcastle. Mary's friend Norma Bell, two years older and not related, was also charged but acquitted. Mary, who suffered from a mental abnormality which impaired her responsibility for her actions, was convicted of manslaughter on both counts, and sentenced to detention for life. She was released in 1980.

The Gambler

John Parsons Cook, a 29 year-old solicitor, racehorse owner and inveterate gambler, died in November 1855 whilst staying at the Talbot Arms Hotel in Rugeley, Staffordshire. He had been in great pain and suffered vomiting and convulsions, and had been attended by an octogenarian doctor named Bamford, and also by Dr William Palmer, the dead man's former gambling companion. Cook's step-father,

Fact

The first murder committed on a train in Britain was that of Thomas Briggs on 9 July 1864. A German immigrant, Franz Müller, killed him in the furtherance of theft on a North London Railway train between Bow and Hackney Wick, throwing the body out of a carriage window. Müller, who left the train wearing Briggs's hat by mistake and leaving his own behind, was sentenced to death and hanged on 14 November 1864, in front of Newgate Gaol before a vast and disorderly mob which did much to persuade the government of the day to abolish public executions.

William Stevens, was immediately suspicious. He had seen Cook in London only a fortnight before his death when the young man had appeared perfectly fit and well and had, indeed, assured his step-father that he was. Mr Stevens insisted on an autopsy.

The manner of Cook's death was consistent with strychnine poisoning, but no strychnine was found in the body. There were, however, traces of antimony. It soon appeared that Dr Palmer stood to gain financially by Cook's death, and he was arrested and charged with murder. Whilst he was in Stafford Gaol awaiting trial, police exhumed the bodies of his wife, Annie, and his brother, Walter, both of whom had died rather mysteriously. Antimony was found in the stomach, liver and kidneys of Annie Palmer. Professor Taylor of Guy's Hospital considered that the poison had been administered in the form of tartar emetic. Palmer had heavily insured the lives of Annie and Walter, and the coroner's jury delivered a verdict in both cases of wilful murder by Dr Palmer.

William Palmer, born in 1824, had qualified as a doctor in London and set up in practice at Rugeley, his native town. He had married Annie Brookes, the daughter of an Indian Army officer, and might have been expected to settle down to a comfortable family life and a prosperous medical practice, especially as he had inherited a small fortune when he was 21 as a result of his father's death. But there was a fatal flaw in William Palmer's character: he had become an obsessive gambler after associating with the horse-racing fraternity of Liverpool, where he had been apprenticed to a firm of chemists after leaving school. His gambling debts had left him with a shady past. The company with whom he had insured his brother's life had refused to pay up because of their suspicions, and an attempt to insure an illiterate racing friend's life had been refused.

Palmer was widely suspected of having caused other deaths by poisoning over many years, including those of his own children. He was tried at the Old Bailey for the murder of John Parsons Cook. The Attorney-General, prosecuting, asserted that Dr Palmer had substituted strychnine in the form of pills for some pills prescribed for Cook by Dr Bamford. Strychnine, he said, being rapidly absorbed into the system, leaves no trace in the tissues. But there was much disagreement among the medical witnesses, and although it appeared that the doctor had acquired enough poison from local chemists to kill the entire population of Rugeley, he claimed to have required it only for use in his racing stables.

The evidence against William Palmer was entirely circumstantial, but the jury found him guilty as charged. The Lord Chief Justice, in passing sentence, said to the defendant: "Whether this be the first and only offence of this sort which you have committed is certainly known only to God and your own conscience". A question-mark remains about his alleged crimes, though perhaps few would go so far as Robert Graves who said in his book *They Hanged My Saintly Billy* that Dr Palmer "never killed nobody". The generally accepted view is that he probably poisoned as many as 14 victims.

Palmer was hanged at Stafford in June 1856 before a massive crowd which was estimated to include around 20,000 visitors who had come to town especially for the event. Dr Palmer shook hands with the executioner, George Smith from Dudley, as he mounted the scaffold, and died quickly, much to the annoyance of the mob which always felt cheated if there was not a bit of a struggle. Mr Smith sold the rope to souvenir hunters at a shilling an inch.

There is a nice story that the people of Rugeley, not wishing their town to live on in infamy, thought to change its name, and their representatives appealed directly to the Prime Minister. "By all means, gentlemen", he said, "as long as you name it after me". But Rugeley it remains to this day. If they had taken the statesman's hint, the town would be known as Palmerston!

Sister Constance

During the morning of 30 June 1860, a search for a missing child at the Kent family's household at Rode on the Somerset/Wiltshire border near Trowbridge, ended when the child's body was found in a disused outside privy. Three year-old Francis Kent's throat had been cut so deeply that his head had been all but separated from his body, and there was a severe stab wound in his chest.

There was nothing to suggest that an intruder had entered the house during the night, nothing had been stolen, and there seemed to be no motive for such a cruel killing. The coroner's jury returned a verdict of murder by a person or persons unknown. Some suspicion fell on a member of the household, the child's nursemaid, Elizabeth Gough, and she was arrested, but released for lack of evidence. Local police then asked Scotland Yard for assistance, and soon the officer in charge of the case arrested the victim's 16 year-old half-sister, Constance. But she, too, was released because of insufficient evidence.

Local folk suspected that the child's father, Samuel Kent, had committed the crime, and the local atmosphere of gossip and innuendo became so intolerable that he decided it was best for them all to move away. He sent Constance to a convent in France, while he and the rest of the household went to Wales.

Five years later, Constance Kent, having returned to England to join a convent in Brighton, suddenly confessed to the murder under the pressure of her religious conscience. She said she had killed the boy with a razor she had taken from her father's wardrobe. The motive was a mixture of jealousy and revenge. Constance was the ninth of Samuel Kent's 10 children by his first wife. After her mother's death, her father had married the children's governess, Mary Pratt, who had given him three more children. Mary had shown little affection for her step-children, and often abused them.

Constance was brought to trial at Salisbury, pleaded guilty, and was condemned to death, but because of her age the sentence was commuted to life imprisonment. She served 20 years, and on her release in 1885, at the age of 41, went to Australia. There, under the name Ruth Kaye, she trained to be a nurse and became a matron, working at hospitals in

Fact

The first murderer to be convicted partly on the evidence of a fingerprint expert was Alfred Stratton, who was arrested with his brother Albert for the murder of Thomas Farrow and his wife Ann in Deptford. The brothers—young hooligans with previous convictions for housebreaking and burglary—had forced their way into Mr Farrow's shop in order to rob him, and Alfred Stratton's thumb print was identified at the scene of the crime. The Strattons were convicted in May 1905 and executed by hanging. The first large-scale murder hunt relying on fingerprints was carried out in 1948, when more than 46,000 sets of prints—those of almost the entire adult male population of Blackburn, Lancashire—were examined to track down 22 year-old Peter Griffiths as the killer of 3 year-old June Devaney, whom he had abducted from Queen's Park Hospital after leaving his prints on a bottle beside the child's cot. Mentally subnormal, he had raped the child and beaten her head against a wall to stop her crying. Griffiths was hanged at Walton Prison, Liverpool, on 19 November 1948.

Fact

The first murderer to be hunted with the aid of television was William Pettit, a mentally-ill man who killed his mistress, Mrs Agnes Brown, in September 1953. Police used TV to show pictures and broadcast a description of the man they wanted to interview. But Pettit was already dead. His body was found on a London bomb-site. A post-mortem examination led to the conclusion that he had died from natural causes.

Sydney, Perth and elsewhere. 'Miss Kaye' retired in 1936 at Maitland, north of Sydney, and died in 1944, a frail and much respected spinster of 100 years.

The 'Priory' Mystery

Charles Bravo, a prosperous 30 year-old barrister, died at his home in Balham on 21 April 1876, after suffering agonies for several days. Two days earlier he had flung open his bedroom door and screamed, "Florence! Hot water! Hot water!" His wife, to whom he had been married only five months, had brought in no less than seven doctors, but they were unable to save him. A post-mortem examination carried out at St Thomas's Hospital determined that Mr Bravo had died as a result of an irritant poison, antimony. The immediate conclusion of many was that Charles Bravo had committed suicide. Florence Bravo's middle-aged companion, a widow named Jane Cox, said that when she had gone to Mr Bravo's assistance on the night he had cried out (Mrs Bravo being asleep), he told her that he had taken poison. But there appeared to be no sufficient reason for Charles Bravo to kill himself, and besides, it was unlikely that anyone intent on suicide would employ antimony for the purpose.

The inquest jury returned a verdict of death from the effects of poison, adding "we have not sufficient evidence to show under what circumstances it came into his body". This, of course, satisfied no one, and speculation mounted whilst further investigations were carried out, leading to the exhumation of Bravo's remains and a second inquest lasting nearly a month. This found that Charles Bravo was wilfully murdered by the administration of tartar emetic, "but there is not sufficient evidence to fix the guilt upon any person or persons". That remains the situation to this day.

The chief suspect, of course, was Florence Bravo. She was an attractive and wealthy young widow when she had met Charles, and the mistress of a Malvern doctor, James Gully. She had promised Charles that she would not see the doctor again, but did not keep her word. She had suffered three miscarriages, and began to drink too much. She was extravagant with money, and this and her consumption of alcohol had caused some domestic strife. Various motives have been suggested for Florence Bravo wanting her husband out of the way. She wanted to return to Dr Gully; or she saw an unhappy future for herself, unable to cope with her husband's sexual appetite, and suffering further miscarriages; or she had realised that Charles had married her only for her money. It was even rumoured that she had murdered her first husband, Captain Alexander Ricardo, by the same method. None of these theories stands up to serious examination.

The other principal suspect was Dr Gully. James Manby Gully was 67 at the time of Charles Bravo's death, and had been retired for four years. He had been a well-known practitioner in Malvern for 30 years, pioneering hydropathic treatment for various illnesses. His patients had included Charles Dickens, Benjamin Disraeli, George Eliot, Thomas Carlyle and Alfred, Lord Tennyson. There had been some local surprise when Dr Gully had let it be known that he would be retiring to London. Some suspected that, hopeful of winning back Florence Bravo's affections and marrying her, he had supplied the poison which was fed to Charles either by Florence herself or by Mrs Cox. But there is no evidence to support this theory, and it seems unlikely that such an intelligent and reputable man of nearly 70 would go so far as to refuse to accept that he had lost his former lover and enter into a murder conspiracy against her husband. Nevertheless, the case ruined his reputation as well as the good name of Florence Bravo.

The remaining suspect was Mrs Cox. She had been employed as Florence's companion since 1842, and supported three sons. She must have feared that the Bravo marriage would leave her redundant, particularly as Charles was notoriously careful with money. He *did* resent the cost of keeping her on, and Jane Cox knew that her security was at stake.

After the second inquest, Mrs Cox returned to Jamaica, where she had once lived. Florence Bravo, 33, died of alcoholism at Southsea in September 1878. Dr Gully died in 1882. It remains a legitimate question whether *anyone* murdered Charles Bravo. No one has proved beyond any possible doubt that he did not administer the poison to himself.

Fact

A murder victim in the UK – especially a female – is much more likely to have been killed by someone related or known to him or her than in the USA, where murder by a complete stranger is more common.

The Hypochondriac

Edwin Bartlett, a prosperous grocer, was found dead in his rented apartment in Pimlico on the first day of 1886. A post-mortem examination revealed that he had died as a result of swallowing a large dose of liquid chloroform. Bartlett's wife, Adelaide, and her 'friend', Rev. George Dyson, were arrested and charged with his murder.

Although it was proved that Dyson, a Wesleyan Methodist minister, had purchased chloroform in small amounts from various chemists in south London, and handed it over to Mrs Bartlett, no evidence was offered against him in court because he shamefully sought to preserve his own life by turning prosecution witness against Mrs Bartlett, and the trial was concerned wholly with her conduct.

The Bartletts had been married for nearly 11 years. The same period also separated their ages. Adelaide de la Tremoille, the attractive illegitimate daughter of a French mother and an English father, was only 19 when she was married to the ambitious shopkeeper, who sent her to school to continue her education. He had said that he wanted their relationship to be platonic, and it seemed they had consummated their marriage only once. They had always appeared content with each other, and neither an antagonistic father-in-law nor a still-born baby had apparently done anything to damage Adelaide's devotion to her husband.

They met Dyson in 1885, and it was Edwin Bartlett, rather than

Fact

Before the Homicide Act of 1957, all criminally responsible persons convicted of murder were, by law, sentenced to death. The Homicide Act distinguished certain types of murder (murders of policemen, murders in the course of theft, etc.) as capital murder, and others as non-capital murder, but the creation of two degrees of murder produced many anomalies and proved unsatisfactory. Suspension of the death penalty in 1965 made life imprisonment the mandatory sentence for all convicted murderers.

Adelaide, who cultivated the young minister's friendship and urged him to take on his wife's further education. Dyson certainly became more than a mere teacher to Adelaide. She was seen sitting at his feet with her head on his knee, and Dyson would kiss her in Edward's presence. He even wrote love poems to her. Whether she actually became his mistress is uncertain—the landlady saw the curtains at their window securely pinned shut one day after Dyson had visited her—but in any case, Edwin Bartlett did not object. He not only encouraged their friendship, but positively threw them together, and made it perfectly clear that, in the event of his death, he wanted Dyson to marry Adelaide.

She had asked Dyson to get her the chloroform after her husband had suffered an unpleasant and depressing illness arising partly from rotting stumps of teeth which an incompetent dentist had left in his gums, and which made his breath foul. Adelaide said that she had wanted it as an anaesthetic for her husband, who had recently shown an unwelcome resurgence of sexual desire, and had a supply of contraceptives in his possession. But instead of inhaling the vapour, wafted under his nose on a handkerchief by his wife, Edwin Bartlett appeared to have drunk the bottle of liquid. The chloroform was in his stomach. If it had been poured down his throat while he slept, it would have been in his lungs and windpipe as well. The Crown's allegation was that Mrs Bartlett had first used the chloroform to render her husband unconscious, and had then poured the remaining liquid down his throat. But Edward Clarke, defending, elicited expert medical opinion that, whilst it was *possible* that this could be done, it would need great expertise to achieve it without waking the victim. Furthermore, if Bartlett had inhaled the vapour before the liquid had entered his stomach, his heart and brain would have shown signs of it. But if he had drunk it whilst conscious, it should have caused vomiting and roars of agony which others in the house must have heard, and left traces in his mouth. None of these effects had, in fact, occurred.

Clarke presented to the court an image of a virtuous woman married to a hypochondriac who had become eccentric to the point of insanity. There was evidence that Edwin had, not long before his death, swallowed a pill he had found without having the least idea what it was, or what it was intended for. Adelaide had, Clarke proposed, showed her husband the bottle of chloroform, and told him frankly why she had it. Edwin had swallowed it—perhaps out of an overwhelming sense of frustration and resentment—while his wife dozed in a chair by his bedside.

The Old Bailey jury decided that there was insufficient evidence to show how the chloroform had got into Mr Bartlett's stomach, or who had administered it. Adelaide Bartlett was acquitted of murder.

The celebrated remark of the surgeon Sir James Paget—"Now it's all over she should tell us, in the interests of science, how she did it"—perhaps represented the view of the majority, that Adelaide Bartlett was a wicked scheming adulteress who had got away with murder. But there can hardly be any doubt that the jury made the right decision on the evidence with which it was presented, particularly when some of that evidence came from her probable lover who was prepared to send her to the gallows if it would save his own skin.

The Physician

Early in 1887, at Dripsey in County Cork, Laura Cross, the 40 year-old wife of a retired army surgeon, began to suffer from attacks of an illness which her husband diagnosed as typhoid. She experienced repeated vomiting, diarrhoea and an unquenchable thirst. Her condition deteriorated until at last, one morning in June, Philip Cross informed the servants that his wife had died during the night. He signed the death certificate himself, specifying typhus as the cause of death.

After the funeral, Dr Cross left for London, and on 17 June he married Effie Skinner, his children's governess, at St James's Church, Piccadilly, where 18 years earlier he had married Laura Marriott. Within a month of Laura's death, Effie, who was 20 years old, had been installed as the new mistress of Dr Cross's home in Ireland, Shandy Hall.

Not surprisingly, the unseemly haste of all this led to much local gossip and eventually to enquiries by the police. When the remains of Mrs Cross were exhumed, arsenic and strychnine were found, and Philip Cross was arrested and charged with her murder.

Dr and Mrs Cross had five children, two of whom were epileptic, and they had engaged Effie Skinner in 1886. But it seems that in no time at all Effie had become the father's mistress as well as the children's governess, and in due course Mrs Cross had insisted on Miss Skinner's dismissal. Dr Cross had complied at once, but followed Effie to Dublin on the pretext of business and stayed with her in a hotel for a few days. It was then that Laura Cross had begun to feel ill.

Philip Cross, arrogant and apparently indifferent to his fate, was found guilty and, when asked if he had anything to say before sentencing, made one of the longest speeches on record in such circumstances. He was executed at Cork by the English hangman James Berry. Ireland was not a safe place for English executioners, and Berry returned poste haste to England without waiting for the official inquest, as he was required to do. The coroner twice adjourned the proceedings, insisting on Berry's attendance, but Berry refused to go back to Ireland unless he was paid £10 and his travelling expenses. The upshot of all this was that the inquest on Dr Philip Henry Eustace Cross remains technically adjourned to this day, and he is not officially dead.

Fact

The longest trial for murder in British history lasted for a little more than seven months, from 11 November 1976 to 17 June 1977. It resulted from the discovery of two bodies. One was a male torso found near Rainham, Essex and identified as that of William Moseley, and the other that of Michael Cornwall, found near Hatfield, Hertfordshire. Both men were members of a criminal gang. Seven people were arrested in connection with the murders. Reginald Dudley and Robert Maynard were convicted of both murders and sentenced to life imprisonment. Two other defendants were sentenced to terms of imprisonment for conspiracy to cause grievous bodily harm.

Jack the Knife

The fascination of the Victorian Whitechapel murders for succeeding generations of people, not only in Britain but throughout the world, is due not so much to the number of victims, which was relatively small, or to their peculiar horror, but to the enduring mystery. We do not know who 'Jack the Ripper' was, nor why he committed the murders. And those gaps in our knowledge stimulate a curiosity which ensures the Ripper's survival as the epitome of serial killers. Christie and Sutcliffe and their like are closed cases—history. But on Jack the Ripper, the

Fact

More books have been written and more films and TV programmes made about Jack the Ripper than about any other murderer in history. The Ripper even features in an unfinished opera, Alban Berg's Lulu, *based on the play* Pandora's Box, *by Frank Wedekind, first staged in 1905.*

public mind, if not the police file, remains open and unsatisfied. Man's nature abhors a vacuum.

The series of macabre killings started, in all probability, with Mary Ann Nicholls, a 42 year-old prostitute, sometimes known as 'Polly'. In the early hours of the morning of 31 August 1888, a carter named George Cross was walking along Buck's Row on his way to work when he made out in the dim gaslight a bundle lying in a gateway. He crossed the road for a closer look, and saw that it was the body of a woman. She was lying on her back with her skirt and petticoats up round her thighs. Cross thought at first that she was an unconscious rape victim, and he and another passer-by went to find a policeman. PC Neil examined her a little more carefully, and found that she had been murdered. Her throat had been cut and the body was still warm. But it was only when the corpse was properly examined in the mortuary that the full extent of her injuries was realised. Her death had apparently been caused by severing of the carotid artery (although it is believed by some experts who have studied the evidence that Jack the Ripper strangled his victims before cutting their throats). She had also been savagely mutilated about the abdomen. There was no obvious motive for the killing.

Eight days later, another body was found in the back yard of a lodging house in Hanbury Street, only a short distance from Buck's Row. This time the woman was identified as Annie Chapman, a 47 year-old prostitute. Her head had been almost separated from her body by two savage slashes, and she had been disembowelled. Pieces of skin and small intestines lay about the body, and some of the internal organs had been removed and taken away.

The next murder was discovered at the end of September, three weeks later. A hawker drove his pony and cart into a yard in Berners Street at the back of a club where he also worked as a steward. As he did so, his pony shied at something lying in the yard. He got down and lit a match. The cause of the pony's nervousness was a woman's body. It was identified as that of Elizabeth Stride, a 44 year-old prostitute. Her throat had been cut and the body was still warm. There were no mutilations. It seemed that the murderer had been disturbed and made off. The time of the discovery was about an hour after midnight.

If the murderer had been frightened off before completing his operations on the body, he left unsatisfied with his night's work. At 1:45 a.m., another body was found by a policeman in Mitre Square, a little farther west in the City of London. The victim was another prostitute, 43 year-old Catherine Eddowes. Her throat had been cut and she had been disembowelled. Entrails were draped over the corpse, and the uterus and a kidney had been cut out and taken away. This woman had been released from the police station in Bishopsgate, where she had been detained for being drunk and disorderly little more than half an hour before she was killed.

General alarm at the news of these murders spread rapidly throughout the capital, but in the East End it amounted to near panic. Whitechapel was a squalid area of overcrowded slums, common lodging houses, brothels, sweat-shops and slaughter-houses, in which Queen Victoria's loyal subjects lived in conditions of extreme poverty, depravity and drunkenness. Crime and vice were part of everyday life. The area accommodated large numbers of dock-labourers and Jewish refugees from eastern Europe. Police estimated that there were 1,200 prostitutes of the lowest class in Whitechapel. Public meetings were held, and petitions got up to urge the police to do more to find this savage murderer. Vigilantes began to patrol the dark and narrow streets and alleys at night.

On 3rd October the newspapers—eager as ever for every lurid detail—published a letter addressed some days earlier to the Central News Office, and temporarily withheld by the police. It said that the writer was "down on whores" and would clip the next victim's ears off and send them to the police. It was signed 'Jack the Ripper'. No one knows whether this letter was genuine or a hoax, but it provided a nickname for the Whitechapel murderer by which he has been known ever since.

In the middle of the month, George Lusk, chairman of the Whitechapel Vigilance Committee, received a small parcel in the post containing an unpunctuated note and part of a human kidney in a cardboard box. The note read:

> *Sor I send you half the kidne I took from one woman prasarved it for you tother piece I fried and ate it was very nise I may send you the bloody knif that took it out if you only wate a whil longer.*
> *Signed Catch me when you can Mishter Lusk.*

Some believe this note to be the only genuine one among several, but there is no proof that it was. Twenty-four days after it was received, the last and most horrific of the five murders safely attributable to Jack the Ripper occurred. In the middle of the morning of 9 November, a tradesman sent his shop assistant to a house he owned in Dorset Street to collect the rent from the tenant of room 13, a prostitute named Mary Kelly. The entrance to this part of the house was in a passage at the side, called Miller's Court. Getting no answer to his knock at the door, the messenger peered inside through a broken window, and got the shock of his life. It was not long before police and doctors were on the scene and curious bystanders were thronging the street outside.

Mary Kelly, 24 years old and three months pregnant, was the only victim of Jack the Ripper to be killed indoors, and with less risk of interruption he had had time to do his ghastly work more thoroughly. He had cut the woman's throat, almost severing the head, then carried out the most savage and appalling acts of butchery ever encountered in a murder case in Britain. The thighs had been stripped of skin and the left arm almost severed from the body. He had slashed and gutted the body, dumping the severed breasts on a bedside table and the liver at the foot of the bed on which his victim lay. Some entrails lay on the bed and other parts had been taken away. It was estimated that the maniac must have taken about two hours to wreak such havoc on a human body. But although it was clear that the man known as Jack the Ripper had some knowledge of human anatomy, there is no evidence that he was a skilled medical man, as has sometimes been suggested.

Fact

The eminent artist Walter Sickert has been implicated in the Ripper case ever since he apparently claimed to know the identity of the killer. Sir Osbert Sitwell wrote that Sickert often introduced the Ripper into his conversation, and once – according to the landlord – lodged in a room whose previous occupant had been the Ripper. It has even been suggested by recent writers that Sickert was himself involved in the Whitechapel murders.

Fact

Montague John Druitt forms a curious link, not previously noted as far as I know, between Jack the Ripper and Burke and Hare. Druitt's father, William, was the leading surgeon at Wimborne, in Dorset. His uncle, Robert, was also a doctor and his cousin, Lionel, was sometime assistant house surgeon at a hospital in Edinburgh. When the notorious Dr Robert Knox died in 1862, it was Robert Druitt, Montague's uncle, who wrote what has been called an "admirable" obituary of Knox in the Medical Times & Gazette, *of which he was editor.*

Police entertained suspicions about several men at the time, and amateur criminologists ever since have been tempted into laying the crimes at the doors of many others, including Edward VII's eldest son, the Duke of Clarence, and assorted Russian, Polish and Jewish residents of Whitechapel at the time. Another distinguished and unlikely name which has cropped up is that of Sir William Gull, one of the royal physicians, who was also one of the doctors who attended Charles Bravo on his death-bed.

When George Chapman, whose real name was Severin Klosovski, a former surgeon's apprentice from Poland, was arrested in 1902 for the murder of his 'wife', Maud Marsh, whom he had married bigamously, Chief Detective-Inspector Abberline, who had worked on the Whitechapel murders, remarked to the arresting officer, Chief Inspector Godley, "You've caught the Ripper, then?" Chapman was convicted of murdering three women, and was hanged in April 1903. He was living and working in Whitechapel at the time of the Ripper murders. But the overwhelming argument against identifying Chapman as Jack the Ripper is his murder method. Chapman poisoned his victims with arsenic, and it is inconceivable that a man possessed by a sadistic and frenzied sexual mania could later turn himself into a patient and calculating poisoner.

One of the favourite suspects, both at the time and since, has been Montague John Druitt, an unsuccessful barrister from a medical family who had possibly studied medicine himself for a time before turning to a career in law. His body was found floating in the Thames on the last day of 1888. Druitt's mother, Anne, had gone into a private mental home in Chiswick in July 1888, a month before the first murder, and he feared for his own sanity. He committed suicide by loading his pockets with stones and drowning himself. He was 31 years old. It happened about a month after the murder of Mary Kelly, and no more murders clearly committed by the Ripper occurred after that time. The case against Druitt, as with those against all other suspects, is based on speculation and circumstantial evidence. For what it is worth, however, it still seems to the present writer, despite all the ingenious theories of recent years, that the strongest probability is that Druitt was the Ripper. And apart from all other considerations, he is the only suspect whose real name provides any logic for the apparently self-given soubriquet 'Jack'. Why not 'Ben the Ripper' or 'Dick the Ripper'?

The most recent entrant in the line-up of suspects is Francis Tumblety, an Irish-American quack doctor who was in London at the time of the murders. As with all serious suspects in this affair, the case against him is replete with circumstantial evidence.

Nevertheless, the plain fact of the matter is that, despite the unceasing efforts of contemporary professionals and modern armchair detectives to solve the mystery of Jack the Ripper, his identity is not known and, almost certainly, never will be known.

The 'White Stuff'

On 13 October 1891, Ellen Donworth, a 19 year-old London prostitute, collapsed in agony in Waterloo Road, and died on the way to hospital. She had managed to gasp to a man who came to her aid that she had drunk some "white stuff" from a bottle given to her by a client, a tall cross-eyed gentleman wearing a silk hat.

A post-mortem revealed strychnine poisoning. Meanwhile, various people began to receive letters accusing them, or individuals known to them, of having committed the murder, and demanding money on assorted pretexts. The coroner at the inquest received a letter from 'A. O'Brien, Detective', offering to expose the killer for £300,000. The newsagents and stationers, W.H. Smith, received a letter from 'H. Bayne, Barrister', offering legal help to the member of the Smith family he accused of the murder. William Broadbent, a fashionable doctor in Portman Square, received a letter from 'M. Malone', demanding money in return for the writer's silence.

At the end of April 1892, two more young prostitutes, Emma Shrivell and Alice Marsh, died in hospital after suffering violent convulsions. Both managed to say that they had been visited at their Stamford Street brothel by a doctor called Fred, who had given them some white pills. They were found to have died from strychnine poisoning.

This led police to exhume the corpse of another prostitute who had died after being found writhing in agony in a Lambeth brothel a week after Ellen Donworth's death. Twenty-six year-old Matilda Clover's demise had been attributed to alcoholism, but she was now found to have been poisoned with strychnine. She had also claimed that a man named Fred had given her some pills. An acquaintance had seen her with a man wearing a cape and a tall silk hat.

Whilst police were working on the case, and the press was speculating about the identity of the 'Lambeth poisoner', a certain Dr Neill, who lived in Lambeth Palace Road, complained to a Scotland Yard detective that he was being followed by police who wanted to interview him about the deaths of Matilda Clover and Louise Harvey. He accused a medical student, Walter Harper, of being responsible for these murders, and wrote to Harper's father, a doctor in practice in Barnstaple, Devon, threatening to provide evidence of his son's guilt to the coroner unless he was paid £1,500.

Police had no murder victim by the name of Louise Harvey, however. She was still alive. This led to 'Dr Neill' being charged with murder after he had been arrested for attempted extortion. He was really Thomas Neill Cream, born in Glasgow. He had qualified as a doctor in Canada, where his parents had emigrated, but had turned to a life of crime, and had been given a life sentence in the United States after conviction for the murder of his mistress's husband. He had been released after serving 10 years, and had then returned to Britain.

Dr Cream was tried at the Old Bailey for the murder of Matilda Clover, and among the witnesses against him was Louise Harvey, whom he had carelessly assumed to be dead. She described how this tall, well-dressed, cross-eyed man had picked her up at the Alhambra Theatre and

Fact

Thomas Ley, convicted in London of the 'Chalkpit Murder' of John Mudie in 1947, was a former Minister of Justice for New South Wales. He had left Australia under suspicion of corruption in 1929. Ley was declared insane after being sentenced to death, and was sent to Broadmoor where he died a month later from a stroke. He was said to have been Broadmoor's richest-ever inmate.

Fact

The infamous St Valentine's Day Massacre, which occurred in a Chicago garage in February 1929, was undoubtedly carried out on the orders of Al Capone, the leading Chicago gangster. Seven men were shot dead by a gang armed with machine-guns, two of them disguised as police officers. The killings wiped out a large part of the rival gang to Capone's, run by George 'Bugs' Moran. But Moran himself was not among the victims—he arrived late. No one was ever tried for the murders, which remain officially unsolved.

spent the night with her, and met her again the following evening when he had given her pills for some spots on her face. She had pretended to swallow them, but had thrown them into the Thames.

Neill Cream was convicted and sentenced to death for the murder of Matilda Clover, and hanged at Newgate on 15 November 1892. James Billington, the executioner, claimed afterwards that as the trap-door fell, Cream had begun to say, "I am Jack the... ", but failed to complete the sentence. No one else present at the execution heard it. If Cream *did* try to say this, such a dramatic statement would have been in keeping with his customary, fatal and probably insane exhibitionism. At the time of the Ripper murders Dr Cream was, in fact, confined in Joliet Prison, Illinois.

Hatchet Job

In August 1892, the maid at the Borden household in Fall River, Massachusetts, was woken from a nap by a voice shrieking, "Bridget! Come down quick! Someone's killed father!" In fact, someone had killed mother, too. The bodies of Andrew Borden, 69, and his second wife, Abby, 42, were found hacked to death with blows from an axe or hatchet in what had clearly been a frenzied attack.

The voice which had summoned the maid was that of Andrew Borden's youngest daughter by his first wife. Miss Lizzie, 32, was a Sunday School teacher and secretary of the Christian Endeavour Society. She had immediately sent the maid, Bridget Sullivan, for the local doctor to attend to her father, and when a neighbour, Mrs Churchill, came with Dr Bowen, she asked Lizzie where her mother was. "I'm sure I don't know", Lizzie replied, then added: "But I don't know perhaps that she isn't killed also..." Mrs Churchill then found the body of Abby Borden. It was established that she had died an hour and a half before her husband.

Suspicion fell on Lizzie, who was known to hate her step-mother and also to resent her father's puritanical meanness with money. Her elder sister, Emma, was away staying with friends, and neighbours had seen no one arriving or leaving the house. Lizzie Borden was arrested for murder.

Police found that Mr and Mrs Borden had suffered from severe stomach pains and vomiting the day before their deaths, and that Lizzie had attempted, though unsuccessfully, to purchase prussic acid the day before that. They also found an axe-head, recently cleaned, with the handle burnt off.

Lizzie Borden made various contradictory statements during her trial. The prosecution alleged that the motive for the murders was money since Mr Borden, a retired banker, would probably leave half a million dollars to his wife who was barely older than her step-daughters. But the jury was challenged by the defence to say that this respectable woman, prim and proper in pince-nez, who had fainted in the courtroom, was a fiend. They acquitted her. She bought a large house in Fall River on the proceeds of her father's fortune. After a short period in which Emma lived with her there, Lisbeth, as she now preferred to be known, lived alone until her death in 1927.

Since Lizzie was the only suspect, no one else was ever brought to trial for the murders of Andrew and Abby Borden. The idea that a maniacal intruder had broken in and killed them was discounted because of the time that separated their deaths. One modern theory is that Lizzie committed the crimes whilst suffering from epilepsy during a menstrual period. The popular belief was always that Lizzie had done it:

Lizzie Borden took an axe
And gave her mother forty whacks.
When she saw what she had done,
She gave her father forty-one.

Fact

Several murder trials in which the defendant has pleaded guilty have occupied less than a minute of court time. The trial of a man named Cawley at Winchester on 14 December 1959, took 30 seconds.

Tender Loving Care

Bargemen working on the River Kennet near Reading in March 1896 fished out of the water a parcel wrapped in brown paper. It contained the corpse of a baby girl, who had been strangled, and a brick to weight the parcel down. A length of tape used to strangle the child was still round the neck. Police found on the brown paper the faint name 'Mrs Thomas' and the address 'Piggott's Road, Lower Caversham'. Although no longer at that address, 'Mrs Thomas' was traced to a house in Reading. She turned out to be Amelia Dyer, a baby-farmer who used the name Thomas, among others, as an alias. Meanwhile, police dragged the Kennet and the Thames in the vicinity and found more bodies. Six were recovered in addition to the bargemen's discovery—all corpses of strangled infants.

Mrs Dyer was charged with the murder of Doris Marmon, the four month-old child in the original parcel. The girl was the illegitimate daughter of a Cheltenham barmaid, who had paid a 'Mrs Harding' £10 to take her baby off her hands after replying to an advertisement in a Bristol newspaper. She had thought her baby was going to a good foster-home, and collapsed with grief when she was told of its fate. 'Mrs Harding' had written to her that she was "dearly fond of children. I have no child of my own. A child with me will have a good home, and a mother's love and care..."

Distraught mothers in various parts of England were soon contacting police about babies they had handed over to women whom they now suspected of being Mrs Dyer. There was little doubt that she was responsible for the murders of all seven of the children lately recovered from the river near Reading, but she had practised baby-farming for 20 years, and no one knew how many infants she might have killed. She told police that they would know hers by the tape round their necks.

Fact

The age group most at risk as victims of homicide in Britain is that of children under one year old. Infanticide, which may qualify as murder or manslaughter according to the circumstances, is a woman's crime. In 1983 ten women were convicted; in 1992, six.

Amelia Dyer had originally come from Bristol, but had lived at various addresses, including a recent one in Willesden where the landlord had removed a fireplace and stacked the spare bricks at the back of the house. Mrs Dyer tried to kill herself with a pair of scissors whilst in custody at Reading police station. Having failed in that attempt, she then tried to throttle herself with a boot-lace.

She was tried at the Old Bailey, and pleaded insanity. Her daughter Mary became the prosecution's chief witness. Evidence was presented that Amelia Dyer had been in asylums at Gloucester and Wells, and that her mother had died in an asylum. But prosecution experts denied that she was insane, and the jury preferred to believe them, taking only five minutes to find her guilty of murder. She was hanged at Newgate on 10 June 1896. She was 57, and the oldest woman to be executed in Britain since 1843. In fact, no older woman was to be hanged before the abolition of the death penalty nearly 70 years later.

This notorious case did have a beneficial side-effect: dominating the nation's headlines, it helped to reduce the incidence of baby-farming. After all, who could be sure that there was not another foster-mother "dearly fond of children" profiting from infanticide? It was a period when baby-farming had become a thriving business. Poor young mothers with unwanted babies handed them over to working-class women who were prepared to take them, for a suitable regular payment, until their mothers claimed them back. Often, they never did. For a substantial one-off payment, mothers could dispose of their babies for good. Amelia Dyer was by no means alone among baby-farmers in murdering her charges. A mid-century analysis of coroners' returns showed an average of 226 infant deaths a year by foul play in London alone. Hundreds of corpses of babies were recovered from the Thames. Many unwanted children were murdered by their parents, of course, but there were plenty of cases of murder by baby-farmers. Mrs Dyer was merely the most notorious.

Annie Walters and Amelia Sach were hanged together at Holloway on 3 February 1903 for murdering their infant charges. This was the first execution carried out at Holloway Prison. Rhoda Willis was hanged at Cardiff on 14 August 1907. She had relieved an unmarried mother of her one day-old baby for a payment of £6, and then smothered the baby on a train. Henry Pierrepoint took part in the executions of all three of these women—as assistant to William Billington at Holloway, and as hangman at Cardiff, with his brother Thomas as assistant.

The Wandering Jew

One evening in 1908, a few days before Christmas, Helen Lambie, the young maid and companion of an elderly spinster, returned to the first-floor flat in Queen's Terrace where they lived in West Princes Street, Glasgow, after going out to buy a newspaper. A neighbour, Arthur

Adams, was standing outside the door, agitated by loud noises he had heard coming from inside. When Miss Lambie unlocked the door and went in, a man appeared, calmly walked past her and Mr Adams, who was still standing outside, and then shot down the stairs and out of the building "like greased lightning", almost knocking down a girl named Mary Barrowman in the street as he fled. Inside the flat, which was well protected with spring-locks and bolts, Marion Gilchrist lay dying in the dining room, her head having been savagely battered in by repeated blows, apparently with a chair. There was blood all over the place. By the time a doctor arrived she was dead.

Miss Gilchrist had a collection of jewellery worth several thousand pounds, but the only item that was missing—according to Helen Lambie—was a crescent-shaped diamond brooch. A box containing Miss Gilchrist's private papers had been broken open and its contents scattered about, but only the dead woman herself would have known if anything had been stolen from it.

Police took sketchy and contradictory descriptions of the man, provided by the three people who had seen him so briefly, and issued a statement in the hope that someone might come forward with information. Someone did. On Christmas Day, a local bicycle-dealer told police that a man at a club in India Street had been hawking a pawn ticket for a diamond brooch. He was a German Jew known as Oscar Slater. When police went to Slater's flat in St George's Road, he had gone. They soon discovered that he had sailed for New York with his mistress on the *Lusitania*, and that his real name was Oscar Leschziner. The brooch, which he had pawned more than a month before the murder, was not Miss Gilchrist's. But Oscar Slater was the only suspect the police had in the case, and they pursued him across the Atlantic, taking Mr Adams, Helen Lambie and Mary Barrowman to New York to identify him. He denied murdering Miss Gilchrist, and said that he knew nothing of her or her jewels. Police were on the point of seeking his extradition when he agreed to return to Britain voluntarily to clear his name.

These actions resulted in one of the most deplorable trials for murder in British judicial history. It began at the High Court of Justiciary in Edinburgh on 3 May 1909. The Lord Advocate, prosecuting, painted a damning picture of the defendant which was not challenged adequately by the defence, even though it included misleading allegations such as that Slater had fled to America as soon as his description had been published in the press. In fact he had planned to go early in December, had booked his passage quite openly, and his name and description had not been published until he was already at sea.

Mr Adams, who was short-sighted and had not been wearing his spectacles when the man had emerged from the flat, was hesitant about identifying Slater, but the young woman and the girl were not. Lambie, who had previously said that she had not seen his face, and only recognised him by his walk, now said that she *had* seen his face. Barrowman, after being shown photographs of the dark Jewish suspect, was asked to pick him out from an identity parade made up of Slater, nine Scottish policemen and two Glasgow railway workers.

Fact

In Britain, male murder victims are most likely to be killed by stabbing; female ones by strangulation. An injury causing death cannot be murder if death occurs more than one year and a day after the injury was inflicted.

Fact

The worst case of multiple child-murder in recent years was the killing of four young patients at the Grantham and Kesteven General Hospital in Lincolnshire. Beverley Allitt, a 24 year-old nurse, was convicted in May 1993 of murder, attempted murder and grievous bodily harm, after causing four deaths and near-fatal injuries to other children. (Her crimes were also responsible for the suicide of a ward sister, Jean Saville.) Some of the victims were injected with overdoses of insulin. Sentenced to life imprisonment, Allitt was found to be suffering from Munchausen Syndrome, a rare personality disorder, and was committed to Rampton, the secure psychiatric hospital in Nottinghamshire.

A small tack-hammer found among other common household tools in Slater's possession was identified as the probable murder weapon, although in fact it was a quite *improbable* cause of Miss Gilchrist's death. The defence did manage to elicit from the doctor who had performed the post-mortem that he would have expected a *heavier* weapon. But the doctor who had originally been called to the flat, and thought she had been killed with a heavily blood-stained chair, was not called to give evidence.

Oscar Leschziner had come to England from Germany as a young man and lived in London for a time, but had been in Glasgow before, as well as Edinburgh and New York, and had been involved in running gambling clubs. He had also lived off immoral earnings and his mistress was a prostitute. The Lord Advocate said that the defendant's record of low life made it possible to say without hesitation that the man in the dock was "capable of having committed this dastardly crime". He added: "He may be, and probably is, the worst of men; but he is entitled to as fair a trial as if he was the best of men". The judge, in summing up, said: "The Lord Advocate finds the prisoner's admittedly abandoned character a point in support of the Crown. He is entitled to do so because a man of that kind has not the presumption of innocence in his favour..." Oscar Slater was found guilty of murder by a majority verdict of nine to six, and sentenced to death. He cried out, "You are convicting an innocent man!" His execution was fixed for 27 May.

There was an immediate public reaction against the conviction. A petition containing over 20,000 signatures was presented to the Scottish Secretary on the grounds that the evidence was insufficient to justify the verdict, and that it was improper that the jury's decision had been influenced by remarks about the defendant's immoral character. Two days before the execution date, Oscar Slater was reprieved, and sentenced instead to penal servitude for life.

Several eminent men, chief among whom was Arthur Conan Doyle, took up the case on Slater's behalf. The famous advocate Edward Marshall Hall asked questions in the House of Commons about a possible miscarriage of justice. The case became world-famous. The next event was that the conscience of a police officer, John Trench, got the better of him. He informed the Scottish Secretary that Helen Lambie had *named* the man she saw leave the flat. That name had been suppressed. Glasgow police denied this, and Trench was dismissed from the constabulary for communicating police information to someone outside the force. In all subsequent documents, the man allegedly named by Miss Lambie was referred to as 'A.B.' No one knows who he was, but he was not Oscar Slater.

Fifteen years had passed when the writer Edgar Wallace drew public attention in the *Morning Post* to the obvious conclusion that Helen Lambie had *known* the man she saw. She had not screamed, or feared for Miss Gilchrist when she saw him, but let him pass without comment, which could only mean that she was not surprised to see him there. No questions were asked of Lambie, Wallace added, that were "in any way inconvenient to the prosecution", and nothing was said of the bloodstained chair "because it did not fit in with the case that had been manufactured against Slater".

It was equally clear that Miss Gilchrist herself not only knew her murderer, but was expecting him, for she had let him in to the locked flat while Lambie was out getting a newspaper. No one could gain access to the flat without a pre-arranged signal. It turned out that it was not a habit of Lambie's to go out each evening for a paper, but that Miss Gilchrist sometimes sent her out on trivial errands when she was expecting a male visitor. In an interview with an *Empire News* reporter, Helen Lambie confirmed that she had recognised the man, and said that police had refused to accept her story and bullied her into identifying Oscar Slater.

Mary Barrowman, now a grown-up married woman, made a statement to the *Daily News* to the effect that she had been bullied by the Procurator Fiscal into saying that Slater was the man who had run past her in the street, and that the police had made her rehearse her evidence every day for a fortnight before the trial.

At last, on 14 November 1927, Oscar Slater was released from Peterhead Prison, where he had spent almost 19 years, and Conan Doyle was instrumental in having the case referred to the Scottish Court of Criminal Appeal, which had not existed at the time of Slater's conviction. By this time, some witnesses who might have been called to give evidence were dead, including the doctor who had first gone to the flat when Miss Gilchrist was murdered, and Trench, the former policeman. Lambie had married a man named Gillon and emigrated to the United States. She refused to come back to testify, no doubt fearing a perjury charge.

In addition to all the other accumulated evidence, it was revealed that Sir Bernard Spilsbury was prepared to say that Miss Gilchrist's death could not have been caused with the tack-hammer, but this testimony was not admitted since Spilsbury had not seen the body and was only basing his opinion on photographs and descriptions. On a technicality, however, the conviction of Oscar Slater was unanimously quashed by the five appeal judges. He was compensated to the tune of £6,000, accepting this offer from the Secretary of State for Scotland—unwisely, perhaps—without reference to his legal advisers. There was then a dispute about who was to pay the costs, and the man who ended up footing most of the bill was Sir Arthur Conan Doyle, towards whom Slater showed little in the way of gratitude for his unceasing efforts to have him cleared.

Oscar Slater lived quietly at Ayr for the rest of his life, and died in January 1948, aged 74. 'A.B.', whoever he was, was never brought to justice. Conan Doyle always believed him to be a nephew of Marion Gilchrist.

Fact

The number of convictions for murder in England and Wales in 1965 was 57; 99 in 1975; 168 in 1985; 215 (latest reliable figures) in 1992. In the 11 years 1983-93 inclusive, 14 persons convicted of homicide in England and Wales had previous convictions for murder. This number is out of a total of 7,152 cases of homicide recorded by police in the same period.

Fact

The first murderer to be traced in Britain with the aid of a police Identikit portrait was 21 year-old Edwin Bush, hanged in 1961 for the murder of Elsie Batten, an assistant in a London antique shop which Bush was attempting to rob.

Dangerous Liaisons

There was nothing particularly unusual, even in 1915, about a man who preyed on comfortably-off and gullible women in order to profit from their savings or life insurance. What was novel about George Smith was his method of getting rid of them. He was, by general consent, one of the most contemptible of British murderers in the first half of the 20th century.

George Joseph Smith was a native of London's East End, and had a record of petty crime stretching back to the age of nine. He grew up to become a vulgar scoundrel variously known as a baker, an art-dealer, a land agent and a junk-shop owner. He married a woman in Leicester in 1898, but they separated two years later, and his wife went to Canada. After that, Smith set out on a course of relationships under false names in order to cheat women out of their money. He seems to have had a magnetic attraction for certain women. More than one of them referred to his hypnotic eyes. It is not known with certainty how many women he seduced, and then vanished after securing their property in his own name. But on three occasions when he resorted to bigamous marriages, he murdered his 'brides'.

He killed Beatrice Mundy, a 31 year-old woman who knew him as Henry Williams, at Herne Bay, Kent, in July 1912. Then he killed Alice Burnham, a nurse whom he had married under his real name at Blackpool in December 1913. Finally, he killed Margaret Lofty, who knew her husband as John Lloyd, at Highgate in December 1914. Smith had sat at the harmonium in the sitting room of their lodgings, playing "Nearer, my God, to Thee", whilst Margaret Lofty lay dead in the bath upstairs and water leaked through the ceiling.

Smith's brides all died in their baths, and were found lying on their backs with their heads under the water. The inquests, separated by time and space, all resulted in verdicts of death by misadventure. But Alice Burnham's father, living in Buckinghamshire, saw the report of Margaret Lofty's death in the *News of the World*, and drew the attention of police at Aylesbury to the similarity between her death and his daughter's.

The Home Office pathologist, Bernard Spilsbury, said at Smith's trial that he believed the deaths to have been caused by the sudden lifting of the victims' feet out of the water, resulting in suffocation by drowning. The jury was treated to a dramatic demonstration. A volunteer nurse in a bathing costume got into one of the baths brought to court as an exhibit, and her feet were pulled upwards by a police officer, submerging her head. The nurse showed great distress and had to be revived by artificial respiration.

Despite having the celebrated Edward Marshall Hall to defend him, Smith was found guilty of murder and sentenced to death. "It's a disgrace to a Christian country, this is!" he shouted during the judge's summing-up. "I am not a murderer, though I may be a bit peculiar". That was an understatement. At Herne Bay, Smith had bought a zinc bath from an ironmonger whom he talked into knocking down the price by half-a-crown but, refusing to pay for it there and then, returned it later as soon as he had finished with it, and paid nothing at all.

George Joseph Smith was hanged at Maidstone Prison by John Ellis on Friday, 13 August 1915, his terror so great that he had to be half-carried to the scaffold and held up by warders on the trap doors while Ellis and his assistant prepared him for the drop.

Fact

William Whiteley, the millionaire owner of London's first department store, who liked to call himself the 'Universal Provider', was shot dead in his office in January 1907 by a young man named Horace Rayner. The trial revealed that Whiteley, who posed as a man of great virtue, practised three-at-once intercourse with Rayner's mother and aunt, and Rayner believed he was Whiteley's illegitimate son. Convicted of murder and sentenced to death, Rayner was subsequently reprieved.

Superman

In the morning of Christmas Eve, 1919, the body of a young woman was found on sandhills on the Lancashire coast, between Blackpool and Lytham St Anne's. It had three bullet wounds. The victim was an attractive young brunette, Kathleen Breaks. Among the items found on or near the body was a letter signed 'F.R. Holt'.

It led that same day to a former army officer who was staying at Lytham's Clifton Arms Hotel. Lieutenant Frederick Rothwell Holt had been invalided out of the army during the war, suffering from depression and amnesia, or what was then called "shell-shock". He had met Kathleen Breaks at Lytham. She came from Bradford, and was separated from her husband. She and Holt had been living together for more than a year when she was killed.

There was never the slightest doubt that it was he who had killed her. His revolver was found next day by a boy playing on the beach. Holt had also left his gloves at the scene, to say nothing of his footprints in the sand. But what was the motive? Why would a well-groomed and apparently respectable ex-officer murder a vivacious young woman who was clearly in love with him? Her letters were read out during his trial at Manchester Assizes to prove it. "I want to put my arms round your neck and kiss you when you are away. You are a dear good pal. I love you ever so much". And Holt had told her: "You are the only person in the whole world for me". Another of her letters ended: "Write me again, superman". But this infatuated girl he called Kitty had never tumbled to the fact that her hero had a double life.

Sir Edward Marshall Hall tried to convince the jury that Holt was out of his mind. Mentally unbalanced as a result of his war experiences, and insanely jealous of other men in Mrs Breaks's life, he had, Hall insisted, killed her on an uncontrollable impulse. But the jury was more impressed by the Crown's evidence that Kathleen had insured her life for £5,000 at Holt's instigation, and that this woman in her mid-twenties had made a will in Holt's favour one week before her death. He was a playboy who had been living beyond his means, and had tired of her, seeing her murder as an answer to all his problems.

Holt was found guilty and sentenced to death. He showed remarkable indifference to his fate. He was reported to have shrugged his shoulders when sentenced and, shoving his hands into his trouser pockets as he was taken down, said, "Well, that's over. I hope my tea won't be late". Marshall Hall always maintained that Holt was mad,

Fact

Jesse James, the 35 year-old American gangster, was murdered in cold blood in 1882 when Bob Ford, a member of James's own gang, shot him in the back while he was standing on a chair to straighten a picture on the wall. Ford and his brother had made a deal with the Governor of Missouri, Thomas Crittenden, to kill James for a reward of $10,000, but popular outrage at the crime cost Crittenden his political career.

and in the present author's opinion, for what it is worth, he was right. There was mental illness in his family—close relatives had been committed to asylums. "I feel so strongly that he is now mad", Marshall Hall wrote, "and, as a man, contemplate with horror the idea of executing a madman..." The image of a "cold-blooded, calculated, long-deliberated and resolved" murder for profit, painted by the Attorney-General and accepted by the jury, does not tie in very well with a man who made no attempt whatever to conceal his crime, leaving the murder weapon and other incriminating evidence at the scene in a very public place at the seaside. But even if he was medically insane, he would hardly have satisfied the requirements of the McNaghten Rules.

Frederick Holt was hanged at Strangeways Prison on 13 April 1920, by the local man, Ellis, who replied to a reporter when asked how Holt had met his death, "Oh, aw reet, tha knows!"

The Italian Job?

On 15 April 1920, an armed attack on a payroll delivery in Braintree, Massachusetts, left two employees of Slater & Morrill, shoe manufacturers, dying in the street. They were Frederick Parmenter, the company's paymaster, and Alessandro Berardelli, an armed guard. The two men who shot them got away with the money in a car with three other men in it. The attackers were described as "foreign-looking", and one of them had a moustache.

Three weeks later, a police officer arrested two Italian immigrants on a streetcar, and held them on a charge of possessing firearms without a permit. Both anarchists, they were questioned about a hold-up in December of the previous year, and one was charged and convicted, being sentenced to 15 years imprisonment. His companion had a safe alibi. But by the time the convicted man had been sent to prison, both of them had also been charged with the Braintree payroll murders.

After a trial lasting seven weeks, Bartolomeo Vanzetti, a 32 year-old fish-pedlar, and Nicola Sacco, a 29 year-old shoemaker, were convicted in July 1921 of murder in the first degree. The evidence was almost entirely circumstantial. A ballistics expert testified that Sacco's pistol had fired the fatal shots. This evidence was challenged by defence witnesses, but widespread hostility to the two men on account of their political opinions ensured their conviction. The trial judge, Webster Thayer, was alleged to have referred to them in private as "dagos" and "anarchist bastards".

A series of legal arguments for a new hearing and pleas for clemency now commenced, culminating in an appeal before the Supreme Court of Massachusetts in January 1926. In the meantime, an Italian under sentence of death for another murder confessed that he had taken part in the Braintree attack, and exonerated Sacco and Vanzetti. But the Supreme Court stated that any decision about a retrial was a matter for the trial judge, and he, Judge Thayer, had refused it on the grounds that the confession was merely a device for delaying the man's own execution. On 9 April 1927, Sacco and Vanzetti were sentenced to death by the same judge. Both men spoke bitterly of the cruelty they had suffered. Vanzetti told the court: "I am not only innocent of these two crimes, but I never commit a crime in my life. I have never steal and I have never kill..."

Pleas for clemency arrived from all over the world, and there were many public demonstrations. Albert Einstein and George Bernard Shaw were among those who argued that the convictions were unsafe. It was widely recognised that American intolerance of radical politics had prejudiced a fair trial. The executions, originally set for 10 July, were postponed for a month to allow further legal representations, and then, at the last minute, for a further 12 days. But on 23 August 1927, Nicola Sacco and Bartolomeo Vanzetti were executed by electric chair, after more than six years on death row.

Fact

London's Adelphi Theatre was the scene of a murder in December 1897 when the much-loved actor-manager William Terris, a handsome and debonair star of classic plays and popular melodramas, was stabbed to death at his own stage door by Richard Prince, an unsuccessful Scottish actor. Prince was paranoid and killed Terris in a fit of jealous rage. He was committed to a mental asylum.

Femmes Fatales

The customary likening of Henri Landru, the French multiple murderer, to the legendary Bluebeard, has one important drawback: in the story, the bodies of all Bluebeard's wives are found in his castle. The Landru case was remarkable for the fact that none of his victims was ever found at all.

In 1917, the family of a Madame Anna Collomb, who had lost touch with her, wrote to the mayor of Gambais, a village near Paris, asking if he could help them to locate her. It was at Gambais that she had last been seen by her sister some months earlier in the company of a Monsieur Cuchet, whom she planned to marry. Through the mayor, the family contacted another family which was missing one of its members, Madame Celestine Buisson. She was also known to have visited Gambais, seeing a Monsieur Fremyet. The disappearances of these two middle-aged widows were reported to the police, who searched the Villa Ermitage, the house at Gambais where both women had stayed. They found nothing at first, but issued a warrant for the arrest of the tenant, Henri Désiré Landru. He was arrested in Paris in April 1919. A notebook in his pocket contained notes about 283 women, and efficiently filed correspondence in the house enabled police to trace all the women alive except for 10. The notebook revealed that when Landru had brought certain women from Paris to Gambais, he had purchased one return and one single ticket, thus saving himself a franc each time. The garden of the Villa Ermitage was dug up, but only the corpses of three dogs were found. In the house, however, were many articles of women's clothing. Furthermore, it was found that Landru had bought a new stove on moving into the villa. People in the village had seen—and smelt—black smoke coming from his chimney, but had minded their own business. Detectives found hundreds of fragments of bone in the ashes.

Fact

Most readers of the newspapers during the 1950s confidently expected the conviction for multiple murder of Dr John Bodkin Adams, an apple-dumpling figure of a man whose patients in Eastbourne all appeared to be rich elderly widows who left him legacies in their wills and then died, it seemed, from his drug prescriptions. He was finally charged with the murder of Mrs Edith Morrell, who left him – among other things – a Rolls Royce. But Dr Adams was acquitted, mainly due to faulty evidence from prosecution witnesses, and the Director of Public Prosecutions declined to proceed with other charges.

Landru, who was married and had several children, remained stubbornly uncooperative, but long and careful investigation gradually pieced together the story of 11 murders which he evidently believed could not be proved without a single body being discovered.

Landru had turned to crime early in life and had been imprisoned several times for fraud. It seems that he committed his first murders in 1914, when he had an affair with Jeanne Cuchet, a widow with a teenage son. Landru murdered them both, profiting from Mme Cuchet's money, jewellery and other property. His next victim was Thérèse Laborde-Line. He met her in June 1915, and before the month was out, she had disappeared, her money going to the man she thought was going to marry her.

Using a variety of names, Landru was placing advertisements for prospective wives in Paris newspapers, and one of them brought Marie Angélique Guillin to his house at Vernouillet. She was a wealthy 51 year-old widow, and soon she vanished like the others. Landru then rented the Villa Ermitage at Gambais under the name Dupont, although his first victim there, Mme Héon, knew him as 'M Petit'. She was last seen there in December 1915, and it was then that Mme Buisson moved in.

Mme Collomb came next, and then—somewhat out of character for Landru—19 year-old Andrée Babelay, who was a servant girl and had no money or property. Landru's motive for getting rid of her remains a mystery. His next known victims followed the usual pattern—widows by whose deaths he could profit. Mesdames Jaume, Pascal and Marchadier replied to his advertisements and knew him either as M Forest or M Guillet. Mme Marchadier brought her pet dogs to Gambais with her.

When Landru was arrested, he had already spent two years with his latest 'fiancée', Fernande Segret. She, like Mademoiselle Babelay perhaps, may have had some more genuine relationship with him, but who knows if she might have become yet another victim?

Landru was convicted of the murders of 10 women and the youth, André Cuchet, and sentenced to death. He was publicly executed on 25 February 1922, when a multitude of spectators watched the murderer walk barefooted between two warders across the cobblestones from the prison to the guillotine where the executioner Anatole Deibler awaited him. They saw the falling blade sever the 52 year-old head. The body, spurting blood, was rolled into a large wicker basket and the head tipped into it from the smaller basket into which it had dropped. Then the remains were quickly taken away in a horse-drawn van. There was no doubt about how Landru died, but his refusal to admit anything during his trial left two unsolved mysteries— how he had killed his victims, and how he had disposed of them with such thoroughness and efficiency.

Taken in Adultery

Whilst middle-aged widows were falling for the charms of the French Bluebeard, a young English woman in Ilford, Essex, was having an affair with her youthful lodger. Edith Grayson had been married to Percy Thompson, a shipping clerk, in 1916, but their love was short-lived. She was sensual and imaginative, given to romantic dreams and fantasies, but he was a dull and disagreeable character who sometimes ill-treated her. There were no children. For many years she had known a youth named Frederick Bywaters, nine years her junior, who was a ship's writer on a P & O liner, and during one of his spells on leave he stayed with the Thompsons at their Ilford home. A flirtation grew into a passionate love affair. On one occasion Bywaters interfered in a quarrel between the Thompsons when he saw Percy strike his wife, and afterwards left the house.

Edith Thompson was employed as a book-keeper and buyer by a London milliner, and took the opportunities presented by commuting to the City to meet Freddy whenever he was on leave. When he was at sea, they kept up a regular and voluminous correspondence.

Shortly after midnight on the morning of 4 October 1922, Percy and Edith were walking home in Ilford after a visit to a London theatre. Suddenly Bywaters appeared and, pushing Edith out of the way, fought briefly with Thompson in the street before stabbing him several times. Edith screamed, "Oh, don't! Oh, don't!" As Bywaters ran off, Edith tried to help her husband and then ran to get a doctor, but by the time he arrived, Percy Thompson was dead.

Mrs Thompson and Bywaters were arrested and charged with his murder, and their joint trial began at the Old Bailey on 6 December. The police had an open and shut case against Bywaters. He admitted that he had stabbed Thompson, but claimed that he had done so in self-defence when Thompson had threatened to shoot him—a claim that was neither supported by the evidence nor believed by the jury.

Edith Thompson was charged as a principal in the first degree. That is, she was accused of being an accessory before and during the fact, having incited Bywaters to commit the crime and assisted him in doing so. She denied absolutely that she had had any knowledge of her lover's intentions on that fatal night.

Mrs Thompson had destroyed the letters which Bywaters had written to her, but he had kept all of hers, and it was on the strength of letters admitted in evidence that she was convicted. Some passages in them were interpreted as references to a plot to murder her husband, and she occasionally enclosed newspaper cuttings describing murders by poisoning. Her defending counsel, Sir Henry Curtis-Bennett, did his best to persuade the jury that references to poisons and powdered glass being administered to Percy Thompson were mere products of a vivid imagination, and that neither she nor Bywaters took them seriously. And indeed, Sir Bernard Spilsbury testified that, having performed an autopsy on the exhumed corpse of Thompson, he had found no trace whatever of any poison or powdered glass. But after a disgracefully misleading and damning summing-up by Mr Justice Shearman, who failed to mention Spilsbury's significant evidence and left the jury in no doubt about his utter disgust at the couple's illicit love affair, Edith Thompson was pronounced guilty and, like Bywaters, sentenced to death. She cried out, "I am not guilty; oh, God, I am not guilty!" There

Fact

The last person to be executed in Britain for the murder of a policeman was Guenther Fritz Podola, a German immigrant who shot Detective Sergeant Raymond Purdy whilst under arrest in a block of flats in Onslow Square, London. Podola was hanged at Wandsworth on 5 November 1959 under the Homicide Act. He qualified in three of the categories of murder for which the death penalty could still be imposed: murder by shooting; murder of a police officer; murder for the purpose of resisting arrest.

Fact

The youngest persons to be convicted of murder in the UK in the 20th century were Robert Thompson and John Venables, accused of abducting and murdering James Bulger, aged 2, at Bootle, Merseyside, in February 1993. Both boys were 11 years old when convicted. There have been numerous cases of illegal killing by children, some of them below the age of criminal responsibility. In the 1790s, Ann Mead, 14 years old, was hanged for poisoning one of her employer's children. In more recent times, those over 10 years old who have been charged with murder have generally been convicted of manslaughter and ordered to be detained during His or Her Majesty's pleasure.

can hardly be any serious doubt, though, notwithstanding the tens of thousands of words that have been written deploring Edith Thompson's conviction that—fantasy or not—her letters encouraged Bywaters to dwell on the benefits of having Percy Thompson out of the way. She knew not what she did.

Bywaters, 20 years old, was hanged at Pentonville on 9 January 1923. Edith Thompson, 29, was hanged at Holloway at the same time. She was the first woman to be executed in Britain for 15 years. It has been widely felt since that Edith Thompson was, in effect, hanged for adultery. Moreover, the circumstances of her execution were particularly harrowing. She had been made insensible with brandy and had to be carried to the scaffold. The prison chaplain had a nervous breakdown, prison staff were much affected, and the executioner, John Ellis, who later described the job as the most nerve-wracking experience he ever had, attempted suicide in the following year. Questions were asked about the case in the House of Commons.

Twelve years after the executions of Thompson and Bywaters, a murder occurred at Bournemouth which bore many similarities to the earlier case. Alma Rattenbury, a bored middle-class housewife of 38, whose husband was her senior by 25 years, took on George Percy Stoner, 18, as a live-in chauffeur and handyman, and they were soon lovers. In March 1935, police were called to the house when Francis Rattenbury was found savagely battered about the head with blood splashed all over the bedroom. Mrs Rattenbury was drunk and hysterical, but said that she had killed her husband, and was arrested. In fact, he was not yet dead, but died from his injuries four days later. Stoner then admitted that it was *he* who had attacked Mr Rattenbury while he was asleep, using a mallet. The two were tried for murder, the Crown alleging a plot between them. Stoner was convicted and sentenced to death, but in this case the woman in the affair was declared not guilty. Who can say to what extent the jury was deterred by memories of the Thompson case from sending another woman to the gallows? Stoner's sentence was commuted to life imprisonment, but Mrs Rattenbury never knew her lover's life was spared. Three days after her acquittal, Alma Rattenbury, branded, like Edith Thompson, as an adulteress, and stricken with grief, stood at the riverside at Christchurch and stabbed herself repeatedly in the chest with a knife, piercing her heart three times. There has rarely been a more frenziedly determined case of suicide.

Blood and Thunder

For gruesome horrors, few cases of murder in 20th century Britain can rival the one committed in 1924 in—of all places—the sedate Sussex resort of Eastbourne. It was the most sensational case between the two world wars. In the course of the trial, four jurors became ill and had to be replaced.

At the end of April of that year, Mrs Jessie Mahon consulted a friend of hers, a former railway policeman, about a Waterloo Station cloakroom ticket which she had found in one of her husband's pockets. She was suspicious about his recent activities and absences from home, and wanted to know what he had deposited at Waterloo. The former officer went there and retrieved a Gladstone bag. It contained a knife and blood-stained female clothing. The bag was returned to the cloakroom and police waited to interview whoever arrived to claim it. Patrick Mahon turned up during the following morning.

At Scotland Yard, Mahon—a soda-fountain salesman—was questioned about the bag and its contents. He said at first that he had taken meat for his dogs home in it, but soon volunteered a long statement in which he described how he had quarrelled and fought with his mistress, 37 year-old Emily Kaye, who had thrown an axe at him in her fury. She had died accidentally, he said, after hitting her head on a coal-scuttle as she fell. Then he had bought a meat-saw and a cook's knife and dismembered the body. This had all taken place in a bungalow he rented at the Crumbles on Pevensey Bay.

Detectives travelled to the bungalow to investigate this story. There was blood all over the place, as well as the stench of putrefaction. There were fragments of bone in a pile of ashes outside, and charred remains in the fireplaces. The detectives then found in a bedroom a large trunk with the letters 'EBK' on it. They broke the lock and raised the lid to reveal the quartered torso of a woman. The head and limbs were missing. The heart and other internal organs were found in separate containers. A saucepan contained boiled flesh. They dug up the garden in search of the missing head and limbs, but in vain.

When Patrick Mahon was charged with the murder of Emily Beilby Kaye, he said: "It wasn't murder, as my statement clearly shows". But Sir Bernard Spilsbury, the Home Office pathologist, stated that the woman could not have received fatal injuries from falling on the coal-scuttle. He also established that she had been pregnant.

Mahon's trial at Lewes, before an all-male jury, began on 15 July. A crowd had gathered outside the building. As the gory details were disclosed, on the second day two jurors were taken ill and replaced. Then another fainted, and another asked to be excused. Two more were sworn in, and counsel had to repeat the prosecution's case for the benefit of the newcomers.

Mahon, a well-dressed and respectable-looking man, related how he had cut off Emily Kaye's head and legs in order to get her body into the trunk. He had also cut off the arms and burnt them. The attempt to dispose of the corpse had taken place over several days at Easter, during which he had met another lover, Ethel Duncan, at Eastbourne and gone up to London with her before going home to his wife. Returning to Eastbourne, according to his account he had put Emily's head on the sitting-room fire—together with the legs and feet—during a thunderstorm; the heat of the fire caused the eyes to open just as lightning flashed and he fled from the room. But, persisting in his efforts, he threw some boiled pieces, packed in a brown bag, out of a train in London.

Fact

The youngest female murderer in Britain was Sharon Carr, convicted at Winchester in March 1997 of the murder in 1992 – when she was 12 years old – of Katie Rackliff, an 18 year-old hairdresser.

Fact

Although Ruth Ellis was the last woman to be executed for murder in Britain, in 1955, a 66 year-old woman named Mary Wilson was sentenced to death at Leeds in 1958. She was convicted for the murder by poisoning of two of her three husbands. The sentence was commuted to life imprisonment, presumably on account of her age.

During his evidence, lightning lit the court and there was a clap of thunder. Mahon shuddered and went pale; sweat poured from him under cross-examination, and he broke down in tears more than once and almost fainted.

It became clear that Emily Kaye, a comfortably-off spinster, had been induced by Mahon, with a promise of marriage, to part with her savings. He had told her that they would start a new life together in South Africa. It was proved that he had bought the knife and saw in London *before* going to Eastbourne to meet her. Mahon had a criminal record, and had earlier received a five-year prison sentence for robbery with violence. Patrick Mahon was hanged on 9 September 1924. A young Yorkshire lad named Albert Pierrepoint, visiting his aunt in Bradford, was told that his Uncle Tom was in London, "doing that Mahon at Wandsworth".

Newspaper cuttings about the Mahon case were found among the possessions of Norman Thorne, a Sunday School teacher and chicken-farmer at Crowborough, Sussex, who went to his death at Wandsworth in April 1925, seven months after Mahon. Thorne had murdered Elsie Cameron to whom he had been engaged for nearly two years. She had tried to pressurize him into marrying her by pretending that she was pregnant. Police found her remains under a chicken-run at the farm. Thorne had killed her with blows to the head and dismembered her body with a hacksaw. The head was found buried in a biscuit tin, and the other parts in pieces of sacking.

The Salesman

The early hours of 6 November would not normally be a surprising time to find a bonfire burning in England. And it was only mild curiosity that led William Bailey and Alfred Brown, who were walking home after a Guy Fawkes dance, to take a closer look at a blaze they saw near the village of Hardingstone in Northamptonshire. But as they approached, a man scrambled from a ditch and hurried away, saying: "It looks as if someone has had a bonfire!" What was burning, in fact, was a car. Bailey was the village constable's son, and the two young men decided they had better report the matter to him at once.

When the flames were extinguished, the charred remains of a man were found lying across the front seats of the Morris Minor; the licence plate remained clearly legible—MU1468. The vehicle was traced to a 36 year-old commercial traveller named Rouse, whose address was in Finchley, north London. When police called, Mrs Rouse said she had last seen her husband at about one o'clock that morning, when he had left on business. At first sight, it seemed as if a fatal accident had occurred.

The story about the man in the ditch, however, made Northampton police suspicious, and they issued a description of Rouse which soon produced a result from Wales. They intercepted a man as he alighted from a Cardiff coach at Hammersmith, and asked if he was Alfred Arthur Rouse. He said he was, and that he was glad it was all over. Bailey and Brown identified him as the man they had seen clambering out of the ditch.

It appeared that no one, including Rouse, knew the identity of the man in the car. But Rouse was charged with murder, and his trial began at Northampton Assizes in January 1931, with Norman Birkett, KC, leading the prosecution.

The story which gradually unravelled was of a philanderer and bigamist who had countless illegitimate children and was staggering under the weight of the costs of his other homes and the maintenance orders made against him. His legal wife Lily, loyal to the end, knew about some of his affairs, and took a job as a shop assistant to help pay for his defence. She believed that his personality had been affected by a war wound to his head.

Rouse claimed that he had picked up a hitchhiker on the Great North Road near St Albans. At Hardingstone he had given him a cigar and asked him to fill the car's petrol tank from a reserve can while Rouse went to relieve himself. Suddenly the car had burst into flames, and when he had seen the two men approaching, he had panicked. But the smooth-talking salesman was over-confident. Sir Bernard Spilsbury testified that the victim had probably been unconscious but still alive when the fire started, and that part of his clothing had been soaked in petrol. When Birkett suggested that Rouse had thrown the unconscious victim face-downwards across the front seats before setting fire to the car, Rouse bridled at the implication: "Most decidedly not. I should not throw a man. If I did a thing like that I should not throw him forwards. I should think where I put him, I imagine".

Birkett: *You would imagine what?*
Rouse: *Hardly that I should throw him down like nothing. That is absurd.*
Birkett: *If you rendered him unconscious, would you have a delicacy about his posture?*
Rouse: *No, but I think if I had been going to do as you suggest, I should do a little more than that.*
Birkett: *Would you?*
Rouse: *I think I have a little more brains than that.*

Rouse was convicted of murder and sentenced to death. He confessed afterwards that he had planned the whole thing with great care, choosing a victim who welcomed the offer of a free ride to the Midlands and who would not be missed. He expected the incinerated man, whom he had strangled, to be identified as himself, and he would then be free to start a new life. The only thing that had gone wrong was the unforeseeable coincidence of the two men coming along and seeing him at the scene. Rouse was hanged by Thomas Pierrepoint at Bedford Prison on 10 March 1931. The victim's identity was never established.

Almost exactly one year *before* the Rouse case, a man's body had been found in a burnt-out car near Regensburg in Germany. The corpse was

Fact

Tony Teare, a 22 year-old man convicted in 1992 at Douglas, Isle of Man, of the murder of Corinne Bentley, was the last person in the British Isles to receive a death sentence. It was commuted to life imprisonment. Later the same year the Isle of Man became the last part of the British Isles to abolish the death penalty for murder.

Fact

One of the most curious of unsolved murders in recent years is the killing in March 1984 of Hilda Murrell, a well-known 78 year-old rose grower. Miss Murrell was stabbed and left to die in a wood a few miles from her home in Shropshire. It was believed at first that she had disturbed a burglar when she returned home from a shopping trip, but the case soon began to assume more sinister tones. No valuables had been stolen from the cottage, but some of Miss Murrell's papers were missing. The Labour MP Tam Dalyell alleged that her death may have been connected with the sinking of the Argentinean ship Belgrano *during the Falklands War, and other conspiracy theories were also mooted. The truth remains hidden.*

at first assumed to be that of the vehicle's owner, Erich Tetzner. But Tetzner was still alive, and subsequently confessed to the murder of a hitchhiker he had killed in order to fake his own death and defraud his insurers. Tetzner was executed on 2 May 1930 for the murder of the unidentified hitchhiker.

Blue Murder?

When Alice Thomas died in Plymouth City Hospital on 4 November 1930, having been admitted suffering from violent stomach pains and vomiting, a post-mortem examination revealed arsenic in the body. Enquiries showed that on the day in October when Mrs Thomas had first become ill, she and her farmer husband, William, had been for a day out to Bude, the Cornish resort about 15 miles from their home at Lewannick, near Launceston. They had taken their neighbour with them. She was Sarah Ann Hearn, a widow who had become rather lonely since the death of her sister Lydia a few months earlier. Mrs Hearn had provided sandwiches of tinned salmon for the trip.

While police pursued their enquiries, local rumour had it that Annie Hearn and William Thomas were a bit too friendly, and fingers of suspicion began to point to Mrs Hearn. The troubled widow then wrote to William Thomas (addressing him as "Dear Mr Thomas") saying: "I am *innocent, innocent,* but she is dead and it was my lunch she ate... When I'm dead they will be sure I am guilty and you at least will be cleared". Shortly afterwards, a woman's hat and coat, found on a cliff top at Looe, were identified as Mrs Hearn's. The jury at the inquest on Alice Thomas returned a verdict of murder by a person or persons unknown, and the remains of Mrs Hearn's sister, Lydia Everard, were exhumed. Traces of arsenic were also found in *her* remains.

Then it was discovered that Sarah Hearn, so far from having committed suicide, was working as a housekeeper in Torquay under an assumed name. She was arrested and brought to trial at Bodmin Assizes in June 1931, charged only with the murder of Alice Thomas. She pleaded not guilty and was defended by Norman Birkett. The matter of Lydia Everard's death was admitted in evidence but speedily dealt with. She had suffered for many years from chronic gastric catarrh, and that was the cause of her death. The soil in Lewannick churchyard, where she had been buried, contained the exceptionally high level of arsenic normally found in tin-mining areas, and this could have accounted for the arsenic in the remains, especially as the organs removed from the body had been in containers in the churchyard, open to contamination, for over an hour.

Birkett next turned to the matter of the supposedly lethal salmon sandwiches. The Crown had established that four years earlier Mrs Hearn had once purchased weedkiller, containing arsenic and dyed blue as was customary. But if this had been used in sandwiches, Mr Birkett suggested to Dr G. Roche Lynch, the Home Office analyst, it would surely have stained the white bread blue. Dr Lynch at first thought it unlikely, but had not tried it, whereas Sir Sydney Smith (advising Birkett), had.

Birkett: *If you have sandwiches in two piles of three each, assume for the moment that the topmost sandwich in one of these piles contains arsenic. Am I right in assuming that the sandwich with the blue weedkiller would stain downwards?*
Lynch: *Yes.*
Birkett: *The white bread…would make the stains instantly discernible?*
Lynch: *I agree, and the white bread being more localized, the blue would come through in spots and stains.*

Clearly, no one in her right mind would have willingly eaten blue sandwiches, and the only thing left for Birkett to do was to clear up the question of motive. The prosecution had alleged that Mrs Hearn had murdered Mrs Thomas because she had been emotionally involved with Mr Thomas and wanted to marry him.

Birkett: *Is there a word of truth in that?*
Hearn: *Not an atom.*
Birkett: *Did you ever conceive a passion, guilty or otherwise, for Mr Thomas?*
Hearn: *No.*

The jury acquitted Sarah Hearn of murder. No one, as far as I am aware, ever asked William Thomas if *he* had conceived a passion for *her*, and the death of Alice Thomas remains officially unsolved to this day.

Fact

When the headless torso of Stanley Setty, a London racketeer and car-dealer, was washed up on the Essex marshes in 1949, Brian Donald Hume was arrested for his murder. He had dropped parcels into the English Channel from a light aircraft, and the parcels contained Setty's dismembered corpse. Hume claimed that three unidentified gangsters had bribed him into disposing of the remains for them. The jury could not agree on a verdict and Hume was acquitted of murder but sent to prison as an accessory. After his release eight years later, he boasted that he had murdered Setty. Then he murdered a man in Zurich during the course of a bank robbery, and was imprisoned for life in Switzerland. In 1976, he was declared insane and was returned to Britain and committed to Broadmoor.

The Butcher and the Vampire

In the years between the world wars, the German cities of Hanover and Düsseldorf experienced the terror of two of Europe's most prolific and repulsive serial killers. Their lives had some curious parallels, but their multiple murders were driven by one important difference: the butcher of Hanover was homosexual; the vampire of Düsseldorf was not.

Fritz Haarmann, one of a large ill-assorted family, turned to petty crime early in life and served prison terms for larceny, smuggling and indecent assaults on children. He was in prison during WWI, and came out to find Germany broken and in chaos. Hanover was crawling with swindlers and profiteers on the one hand, and refugees and starving people on the other. Haarmann set himself up as a trader in meat and second-hand clothing.

In September 1918, a teenage boy named Friedel Rothe was reported missing. He had been seen in Haarmann's company, but when police

Fact

Cannibalism as a concomitant of murder is not such a rarity as might be thought. Many cases are recorded. Among the most notorious of cannibal murderers was Albert Fish, a 64 year-old house painter who abducted 12 year-old Grace Budd from her home in New York in 1928. It was six years before he was arrested–after he had written to the girl's mother to describe the pleasure he had from eating little girls. Fish was executed in the electric chair at Sing Sing Prison in January 1936.

made a cursory search of his premises and found nothing, he heard no more about it. Haarmann took to picking up boys who arrived at the railway station as refugees. He had an accomplice, a younger man named Grans, who helped him to lure boys and young men to his home.

Over the next few years, police in Hanover received more and more reports of missing teenagers. They remained suspicious of Haarmann, but had nothing more than circumstantial evidence to go on. Neighbours had noticed boys going into the apartment and had not seen them coming out. A woman had seen Haarmann carrying a bucket of blood downstairs, but had thought nothing of it as he was a meat-dealer. A suspicious customer was assured by a police doctor that some meat she had bought from Haarmann was pork.

In the spring of 1924, two skulls and a sackful of human bones were found on separate occasions along the local river banks. And on 22 June, under pressure from mounting public anxiety, police arrested Haarmann as he accosted a boy at the Bahnhof. When they went to his premises in the Rothe Reihe, officers found heaps of boys' clothing and walls splashed with blood. A coat worn by the landlady's son was recognised by the mother of one of the missing boys.

Haarmann confessed, and Grans was also arrested. Their trial began on 4 December, and the blood of those in court almost froze as they listened to the ghastly recital of Haarmann's deeds. The two men were accused of killing 27 boys between the ages of 12 and 18, but the real number was almost certainly higher. It was clear that Haarmann had done the killing on his own. Grans acted as a procurer. Haarmann claimed that he had murdered the victims by biting through their necks, and had then cut up their bodies and sold them as meat, disposing of the inedible parts in the river. He said that when police had searched his rooms in the Cellarstrasse in 1918, the head of the boy Friedel Rohe had been behind the stove, wrapped in newspaper.

Haarmann, aged 45, was sentenced to death, and on the morning of 20 December 1924, he was executed by beheading. Grans was sentenced to life imprisonment, but this was later reduced to 12 years.

Meanwhile, 250 miles away in Düsseldorf, Peter Kürten, born four years after Haarmann, and also from a large (and somewhat psychopathic) family, had recently married and appeared to be a respectable citizen, well-dressed and charming in manner. But Kürten had a secret life which even his wife knew nothing about. Like Haarmann, he had a long record of imprisonment for theft, fraud and arson. He also had an insatiable blood-lust. Blood and fire were sexual stimuli to this seriously deranged man.

Kürten's attacks on women had started before he settled with his wife in Düsseldorf, living in Mettmännerstrasse and going to work in a factory where he became involved in trade union activities. But from 1925 to 1929 the city experienced a sense of panic akin to that in London's East End at the time of Jack the Ripper. The sadistic German killer's reign of terror left a bloody trail of murdered men, women and children, to say nothing of animals. He was said to have cut the head off a swan and drunk its blood. But most of his crimes were sexual attacks on women, whom he afterwards stabbed or strangled.

Kürten was eventually brought to justice after confessing to his wife that he was the notorious 'Monster of Düsseldorf'. It seems he wanted her to have the reward offered for information leading to the arrest of the 'monster', and the shocked Frau Kürten duly went to the police. Nearly a million people had already been interviewed throughout Germany, police acting on the slightest clues and information which they could not afford to ignore, and calling in detectives from the Alexanderplatz, Berlin—the German equivalent of Scotland Yard—to assist in the manhunt.

Kürten's trial took place in April 1931. He had confessed to 68 crimes, and was charged with nine murders and seven attempted murders. It became perfectly clear that this man was a sadistic sexual maniac. His perversions were reminiscent of the 15th century French mass murderer, Gilles de Rais. Kürten said that he had drunk blood from some of his victims. It goes without saying that his defence was insanity, but this was dismissed. He was found guilty on all counts and sentenced to death. Dr Karl Berg, the police doctor who got to know Kürten better than anyone after his arrest, said that Kürten anticipated his own execution with a sense of pleasure, hoping he would be conscious just long enough to hear the blood spurting from his neck as his head dropped into the basket. He was executed in the prison in Cologne on 2 July 1931.

Fact

The only 'fact' that can be inserted here about Behram, the Hindu thuggee devotee in India, and Sawney Bean, the 17th-century Scottish cannibal–each of whom is reputed to have murdered around 1000 people–is that the numbers are not substantiated. Indeed, it is probable that Bean and his notorious family never existed at all.

Lovers' Quarrel

When police were summoned to a fashionable mews house near London's Knightsbridge on the last day of May 1932, they found the body of 24 year-old Scott Stephen who had died from a gunshot wound in his chest. The woman who owned the property was hysterical, but said that the shooting was an accident. She was Elvira Dolores Barney, the 26 year-old daughter of wealthy titled parents who lived close by in Belgrave Square. Mrs Barney, née Mullens, was separated from her husband, an American cabaret singer who had gone back to the United States. Stephen had been her lover. His full name was William Thomas Scott Stephen, but for some reason he was known to everyone as Michael. Long-suffering neighbours were used to noisy quarrels between the couple, who entertained friends late into the night and drank heavily, but it seemed on this occasion that Mrs Barney, a young woman of highly-charged emotions, had been heard screaming that she was going to shoot someone. She had apparently tried before. According to a neighbour, about 10 days earlier she had leaned out of a bedroom window and fired a shot at Stephen as he stood in the mews below. They had made it up, as usual, but now the young man had lost his life. Elvira Barney was arrested and charged with murder.

Her story was that they had come home in the early hours of the morning from a night out on the town, and had quarrelled about a

Fact

When Jael, the Biblical wife of Heber, hammered a nail into the head of Sisera, who had sought refuge in her tent, the killing was considered justifiable homicide in the eyes of the Semitic race, since vengeance for a crime was not merely a right, but a legal obligation for the victim's nearest kinsman. Sisera was captain of the Canaanite army, and had "mightily oppressed the children of Israel".

woman Michael was fond of. He had threatened to leave Elvira, who had retaliated by threatening suicide. He had then attempted to take away the loaded revolver she kept. They had struggled for possession of the weapon, and it had gone off accidentally.

Mrs Barney was defended at her trial in the Central Criminal Court by Patrick Hastings, whose chief task was to discredit the evidence of prosecution witnesses. Bernard Spilsbury testified that Stephen could not have fired the shot himself, and thought Mrs Barney's account very improbable. (No one had suggested to him that Stephen *had* shot himself.)

Robert Churchill, the firearms expert, testified that the revolver in question was a safe weapon which required "considerable pressure" to pull the trigger, implying that it could hardly have been fired accidentally. Hastings pointed the unloaded weapon at the ceiling of the court and pulled the trigger several times. "It doesn't seem to require any terrific muscular strength", he observed, as click followed click in the otherwise silent courtroom.

Whilst the defendant herself was in the witness box, Hastings had the revolver placed on the shelf in front of her, and suddenly ordered her to pick it up. She instinctively did so with her right hand. The neighbour who alleged that she had fired at Stephen from the bedroom window had said that she was holding the gun in her *left* hand. This hostile witness confirmed that she had seen a puff of smoke as the shot was fired. Hastings invited her to demonstrate the size of the puff with her hands, which she did.

Hastings: I suppose you didn't know that Mrs Barney's revolver contained cordite cartridges?'
Witness: No.
Hastings: And I suppose you don't know either that cordite cartridges don't make any smoke?

Mrs Barney's version of the incident was that she had fired a shot *inside* the room to make Stephen think she had killed herself, then looked out of the window to observe his reaction. And indeed, a bullet mark had been found on the bedroom wall.

Hastings pointed out to the jury that Spilsbury's evidence did not prove that the young man's death "could not have been caused in the way that Mrs Barney has always said it was". The judge, Mr Justice Travers Humphreys, reminded the members of the jury in his summing up that a verdict of manslaughter was one of their options. But if they believed the defendant's story was demonstrably false, they must find her guilty of murder.

The jury was out for nearly two hours, at the end of which the foreman pronounced Mrs Barney not guilty of murder, and not guilty of manslaughter. Elvira Barney walked free from the Old Bailey, to applause from the crowd outside. But she could not escape her unhappy lifestyle: in 1936 she was found dead in a Paris hotel room.

Down Under

The fascination of spectators watching a shark in a Sydney aquarium in April 1935 suddenly turned to horror and revulsion when the creature, only recently captured by two fishermen, vomited a human arm. By the fingerprints and a tattoo on it, police were able to identify the arm as that of a man listed as missing—James Smith, a former boxer who had worked in a billiard hall. A length of rope was tied to the wrist suggesting murder or possibly suicide. Experts reckoned that the arm had been in the shark's stomach for at least a week, and the only reason for its remarkable state of preservation was that the creature's digestive processes had been disturbed by the change of environment.

Searches of beaches and the sea-bed failed to reveal other parts of Smith's body, and when the shark died, it was dissected but no other human remains were found. For some time police thought they were dealing with a case of suicide. Then pathologists concluded that the arm had not been bitten off by the shark, but had been cut off at the shoulder after his death. Various items missing from a cottage rented for a fishing holiday led to the conclusion that Smith's body had been dismembered, packed up and dumped at sea.

Smith's widow told police that he had left home a fortnight earlier to go on a fishing holiday with a friend. She did not know who the friend was, but enquiries led to a man named Patrick Brady, known to police as a forger. Smith's employer at the billiard hall, Reginald Holmes, accused Brady of killing Smith and disposing of the corpse. Brady, who denied knowing anything about Smith's death, was charged with murder.

On the day prior to the coroner's inquest, Holmes, who was to be the chief prosecution witness against Brady, was shot dead in his car under Sydney Harbour Bridge. The Australian Supreme Court then ruled that a severed arm was not proof that Smith was dead. The inquest was stopped, and at his trial for murder, Brady was acquitted for lack of evidence. For the rest of his life, he denied killing Smith. He died in 1965 at the age of 72. Two men accused of murdering Holmes were also acquitted.

Sir Sydney Smith, the Scottish pathologist, who happened to be in Australia at the time and gave police some help with the case, remarked afterwards on the extraordinary coincidence that of the thousands of sharks which infest the coastal waters of Australia, the one that was caught and exhibited in the Coogee Aquarium was the one which had swallowed Smith's arm.

Fact

Giuseppe Baretti, secretary of the Royal Academy and author of A Dictionary and Grammar of the Italian Language, *was tried in London in 1769 for the murder of Evan Morgan, a ruffian whom he had stabbed during an affray. Baretti was acquitted, the killing being judged an act of self-defence. Morgan had attacked Baretti after the Italian had struck a prostitute who had obscenely accosted him in the street. Dr Johnson, Edmund Burke, David Garrick and Sir Joshua Reynolds were among those who testified to Baretti's good character.*

Forensic Evidence

This classic case is interesting chiefly for the advances in forensic science which led to a conviction, rather than for the murder itself.

On 29 September 1935, a woman saw a human arm lying on a bank

Fact

The first murderer to be apprehended with the aid of wireless telegraphy was Hawley Harvey Crippen, the American doctor who killed his wife Cora and buried her dismembered remains under the cellar floor of their London home. Crippen fled the country with his mistress, Ethel le Neve, but they were recognised by the captain of the SS Montrose *in mid-Atlantic who telegraphed the ship's owners. Scotland Yard detectives crossed the Atlantic in a faster ship and arrested Crippen on 31 July 1910.*

in a gully near Moffat, Dumfriesshire (known afterwards, with grim Scots humour, as the 'Devil's Beef Tub'). Police soon uncovered a large number of other human remains, including two heads, and it was established that they were the bodies of two persons, thoroughly dismembered and disfigured by someone with a knowledge of anatomy. One set of remains was of a young woman. The others, thought at first to be those of a man, were those of a middle-aged woman. The inventory of recovered bundles of remains included items such as "part of a cotton sheet containing 17 pieces of flesh", and "a pillowslip enclosing two arm bones, two thigh bones, two lower leg bones, and nine pieces of flesh". Some pieces of flesh were wrapped in a newspaper—the *Sunday Graphic* —which was identifiable as an edition circulated in the Morecambe and Lancaster area. Police in Lancashire, meanwhile, were investigating the disappearances from their Lancaster home of Isabella Ruxton, a woman who passed as the wife of a local doctor, and Mary Rogerson, nursemaid to their children. It was not long before police in Scotland and Lancashire put two and two together.

Dr Buck Ruxton was a Parsee, whose original name was Bukhtyar Rustomji Ratanji Hakim. He had qualified as a doctor in Bombay, and changed his name by deed poll when he came to England. After studying at London University he had set up in general practice in Lancaster. His partner Isabella Van Ess (née Kerr) was divorced from her Dutch husband.

Circumstantial evidence that Ruxton had murdered the two women was overwhelming. Blood-stained clothes and carpets were found on his premises, human debris was found in the drains, and a blouse in which some remains had been wrapped was identified as belonging to Mary Rogerson. A local newsagent told police that a copy of the *Sunday Graphic* in question had been delivered to Dr Ruxton's house.

Ruxton was arrested and charged with the murder of Mary Rogerson and, later, of his wife. The prosecution case was that Ruxton had killed his wife in a fit of jealous rage because he thought she was seeing another man, and then murdered the nursemaid because she had either witnessed or discovered the crime. "That", said the doctor, "is absolute bunkum, with a capital B..." But the doctor's violent temper was already well-known to local police.

Among other anatomical remains found in the gully was a cyclopean eye. It was stated categorically by the pathologist Sir Sydney Smith that this was from an animal and not human, but Ruxton had once taken an interest in opthalmology, and if it could have been proved that he had owned this rare specimen, it would have aided the prosecution's case considerably.

Positive identification of the two bodies was made after skilled and patient work by Professor J. C. Brash of Edinburgh University and Professor John Glaister of Glasgow University. Seventy separate items, badly decomposed, were cleaned of maggots and carefully reconstructed as far as was possible to establish beyond reasonable doubt that the two murdered women were indeed Mrs Ruxton and Miss Rogerson, even though the murderer had gone to extreme lengths to prevent them from being identified. He had, for example, removed the eyes of the younger woman. Mary Rogerson had had a squint in one eye. Photographs of the living women's heads were superimposed on prints of the skulls made to the same size and at the same angles, and were shown to match. And fingerprints and a palm print were obtained from the remains which matched prints found in the Ruxton house.

Ruxton was tried at Manchester Assizes in March 1936 for the murder of Isabella Van Ess. He consistently denied the charge, saying that the two women had left to visit Edinburgh on 15 September and he had not seen them since. Norman Birkett, defending, told the jury that even if they were completely satisfied that the remains found near Moffat *were* those of the two women, that did not prove that Ruxton had murdered them. But the jury was convinced that he had, and he was sentenced to death and hanged at Strangeways Prison on 21 May 1936. It was not long before the street-wise kids of Lancashire were singing a variation on the song, 'Red sails in the Sunset':

Red stains on the carpet, red stains on your knife.
Oh Doctor Buck Ruxton, you murdered your wife.
The nursemaid she saw you, and threatened to tell,
Oh Doctor Buck Ruxton, you killed her as well.

Fact

In July 1873, in Brussels, the French poet Paul Verlaine, who was drunk, shot his fellow-poet and homosexual partner, Arthur Rimbaud, in the wrist, after Rimbaud had threatened to leave him. Verlaine was convicted of attempted murder, and sentenced to two years hard labour at Mons.

War Crimes

One day in March 1944, during the German occupation of Paris, Jacques Marcais, a resident in the rue Lesueur, complained to police about acrid black smoke coming from the chimney of a neighbouring house. He and other local residents had found it offensive before, but now it was intolerable. A card on the door of the house directed enquiries to the owner's medical practice in the rue Caumartin, and when a gendarme telephoned, Dr Marcel Petiot said that he would come at once. In the meantime, the fire brigade had been called, and firemen broke into the house to deal with a serious fire hazard. They found the stove which was the source of the trouble in the cellar. But that was not all they found. The floor was littered with human remains—many parts of dismembered corpses.

When Dr Petiot arrived, he showed no signs of agitation, and when the senior policeman present told him that he would have to arrest him, the doctor took him aside and informed him confidentially that the place was an execution chamber used by the French Resistance. The corpses were those of Nazi sympathisers and collaborators. The gendarmes, supporting the resistance movement and no doubt flattered to be parties to this privileged information, allowed him to leave.

However, they did not let the matter drop without looking into it more thoroughly, and gradually the story of Marcel Petiot was pieced together. Born in 1897, he had begun a criminal career early in life, and had been convicted of petty theft on several occasions. But he had qualified as a doctor at Villeneuve, and in 1928 he became the town's

Fact

A Ministry of Health insurance card helped to trace the murderer of Max Kassell, an international crook known as 'Red Max', whose corpse was found near St Albans, Hertfordshire, in January 1936. His killer was Robert Vernon, a French criminal who had escaped from Devil's Island. After his conviction for murder, he was sent back to French Guiana.

mayor. Over the following years, three women disappeared, and they were all linked to him. One was his pregnant young housekeeper, another a patient, and the third a woman who had accused him of supplying illegal drugs to her daughter. But there was no evidence to justify any action being taken against Dr Petiot. In 1941 he bought the house in Paris and got builders in to make some alterations. He had a courtyard wall increased in height so that neighbours could not overlook it. He also had a sound-proofed triangular room constructed, without windows, and a new incinerator installed in the cellar.

In the spring of 1943, Gestapo officers trying to trace wanted Jews found a trail leading to Dr Petiot. Suspecting at first that he was a resistance worker smuggling them out of France, they arrested him and held him for some months, but then released him. It seems probable that they let him go because they realised he was doing their work for them—killing Jews and anti-Nazis.

Paris police now suspected him of being an agent of the Gestapo. Forensic experts had pieced together 27 bodies from the remains in the cellar, and found meticulously-kept records in the house of more than 60 people who had gone there and disappeared. But when they called to interview him, Petiot had fled Paris.

He was finally caught in November 1944, a little over two months after the liberation of Paris by the Allies. His trial began in March 1946, and the truth about this despicable mass-murderer was revealed. He was an agent of neither the French Resistance, as he claimed, nor the Gestapo, but a private operator killing for profit. He took in Jews and others with good reason to leave German-occupied France—frightened people who came to him on the understanding that he could get them safely out of the country. They brought their money and valuables to the house in rue Lesueur. They were taken to the triangular room where they were given lethal injections, probably on the pretence of inoculating them against disease. Petiot disposed of the bodies by burying them in quicklime or cutting them up and burning them.

Petiot admitted to sixty-three killings, claiming the victims were all German soldiers or Nazi collaborators. But their possessions were found in trunks, suitcases and parcels on his premises, and it was estimated that he had made hundreds of thousands of pounds from plundering his victims. Charged with twenty-seven murders and convicted of twenty-four, Dr Marcel Petiot was executed by guillotine on 26 May 1946.

Strange Death at Lower Quinton

On St Valentine's Day in 1945, the body of an old man was discovered in a field at Lower Quinton, Warwickshire, a few miles south of Stratford-on-Avon. He was pinned to the ground with a hay-fork driven through his neck and six inches into the soil, and his flesh had been slashed cross-wise with a trouncing hook which remained in one of his wounds. The man was Charles Walton, a 74 year-old hedge-cutter. The only thing apparently missing was his valueless tin watch, and robbery was quickly dismissed as a motive for the murder.

Warwickshire police called in Scotland Yard. Soon rumours were heard of witchcraft, and it was said that the murder was an evil-eye killing. Local people were distinctly reluctant to discuss the crime. A policeman drew Scotland Yard's attention to a local murder case in 1875 when a youth named Haywood had killed an old woman named Ann Turner. Haywood had said at his trial: "Her was a proper witch. I pinned her to the ground before slashing her throat with a billhook in the form of a cross". He had pinned her with a hayfork. This murder had occurred at Long Compton, further south—a place long associated with witchcraft.

There appeared to be no clear motive for the killing of the old man, although he was suspected by some of being a warlock, and despite police taking thousands of statements, his murderer was never identified. The officer in charge of the case, Chief Inspector Robert Fabian, was probably the best-known detective of his time, but this case demonstrated once again that real detectives, unlike fictitious ones, do not always get their man. Fabian wrote afterwards that the death of Charlie Walton was clearly the "ghastly climax of a pagan rite". All that can be said with certainty is that *someone* murdered Charles Walton, and it is possible that someone still alive knows who.

Fact

When Sjef Rijke was convicted of murdering two former girlfriends at Utrecht in The Netherlands in 1971, he said that he had not meant to kill anyone, but enjoyed watching women suffer. He had put rat poison in their food. He was given a life sentence for each murder.

The Body on the Bombsite

Two boys crossing a bombsite in Cumberland Street, Manchester, came across the body of a woman on the Sunday morning of 20 October 1946. She had been killed by savage blows to the head, and close to her body lay the murder weapon, a blood-stained hammer. She was fully dressed, and among the belongings found on her were a ten-shilling note and her identity card. She was Olive Balchin, a prostitute who had only recently come to Manchester.

The licensee of a public house nearby in Deansgate told police that he had seen a man and woman arguing near the murder site on the Saturday night, around midnight. He had had a clear view of both of them. He was taken to the mortuary, where he identified the dead woman as the one he had seen. He described the man as being between 30 and 35 years old, about 1.7 m (5 ft 7 inches) in height, with dark hair, clean-shaven and tidily dressed in a blue suit. Then a shopkeeper at Ardwick recognized the hammer from a photograph: it was a leather-dresser's hammer. He said he had sold it at about 5:30 p.m. on the Saturday evening to a man between 28 and 30 years old, 1.7 to 1.72 m (5 ft 7 or 8 inches), clean-shaven and respectably dressed in a dark suit and raincoat.

A police hunch led them to a man named Walter Rowland, 38, who had been demobilized from the army four months prior to the murder. He had a record of violence. Before the war, he had been serving a life

Fact

"When we want to read of the deeds that are done for love, whither do we turn? To the murder column." George Bernard Shaw: Preface to Three Plays for Puritans.

sentence at Strangeways for the murder of his infant daughter in 1934, and before that, he had done a stretch in a Borstal institution for trying to strangle his girlfriend.

When they found Rowland at the Services Transit Dormitory a week after the murder, he said, "You don't want me for murdering that bloody woman, do you?" They did indeed, and they soon had enough evidence to charge him with the killing. His trouser turn-ups contained particles consistent with his having been on the bombsite; hairs on his jacket were identical with Olive Balchin's; and the shopkeeper identified him as the man who had bought the hammer.

Rowland was over-talkative when arrested and cautioned, but admitted that he had known Olive Balchin for about two months and that he had been with her on the Friday night. He thought (wrongly) that he had contracted venereal disease from her. He denied killing her, but said: "If I had been sure it was her I would have strangled her... If she gave it to me she deserved all she got". Rowland was tried for her murder at Manchester Assizes in December.

He gave accounts of his movements on the Saturday night. He had been at his mother's house, 15 miles away, then caught a bus to Stockport where he had a few drinks in a public house called The Wellington, then moved on to Ardwick, where he bought fish and chips before seeking a lodging-house where he spent the night. Rowland's mother and the landlord of the lodging-house confirmed the earlier and later parts of this alibi, and there was convincing evidence that he had been in The Wellington. Enough time was left unaccounted for to enable him to have met Olive Balchin in Manchester, but according to the licensee, Olive Balchin was still alive at midnight, and the lodging-house landlord had confirmed what Rowland had claimed. He had arrived there at about 11:15 p.m. and was there when he had locked up for the night about half an hour later. Above all, perhaps, no trace of blood could be found on Rowland's 'demob suit'—the only one he owned—although a doctor testified that whoever killed the woman could hardly avoid being splashed with her blood. Nevertheless, the licensee thought Rowland was the man he had seen, and the shopkeeper was in no doubt that he was the man who had bought the hammer.

The jury found Walter Graham Rowland guilty of murder and he was sentenced to death. He told the court: "Somewhere there is a person who knows that I stand here today an innocent man. The killing of this woman was a terrible crime, but there is a worse crime being committed now, my lord, because someone with the knowledge of this murder is seeing me sentenced today for a crime which I did not commit... The day will come when this case will be quoted in the courts of this country to show what can happen to a man in a case of mistaken identity". Notice was given that he would appeal.

On 22 January, a man in prison in Liverpool for theft confessed to the murder of 'Olive Balshaw', a name which had been mistakenly printed in some newspapers. He said that he had picked her up in Manchester and taken her to a cinema before they found a dark spot near Piccadilly, where he had killed her with a hammer he had bought earlier to use in a robbery. While they were close to each other he had realised that she was going through his pockets, and after he had killed her in a rage and run away, he realised that a ten-shilling note was missing from a pocket in his trousers. He had given himself up for robbery as a cover-up for the murder. The prisoner's name was David John Ware, and he was 39.

This evidence was brought to the notice of the Court of Criminal Appeal, but an enquiry into Ware's confession—which he later withdrew—came to the conclusion that there had been no miscarriage of justice. Rowland's appeal was dismissed, and he was hanged at Strangeways on 27 February 1947.

Four years later in Bristol, a man walked into a police station and said: "I have killed a woman. I don't know what is the matter with me. I keep having an urge to hit women on the head". The woman, who survived the attack, was a prostitute. The man was David John Ware. He was convicted of attempted murder, but pronounced insane and sent to Broadmoor. He committed suicide there in 1954 by hanging himself.

Fact

When Honora Parker was killed in a New Zealand park in June 1954, her own daughter and her friend, both teenagers, were arrested for her murder. Pauline Parker and Juliet Hulme had a lesbian relationship, which Mrs Parker had been determined to put an end to. The defence claim that both girls were insane failed, and they were sentenced to be detained during Her Majesty's pleasure. They were, however, freed four years later.

Summoned by Bells

One morning in October 1947, a passenger was reported missing from the Union Castle liner *Durban Castle,* bound for England from Cape Town. The ship was then 150 miles off the coast of west Africa, and the missing person was a 21 year-old actress, Eileen Isabella Gibson, better known by her stage-name, Gay Gibson. The captain had the ship turned around in case she had fallen overboard and could be spotted and rescued, but there was no sign of her in the shark-infested waters. Meanwhile, it appeared that Miss Gibson had summoned a steward to her cabin in the early hours of that morning, but a watchman who answered the call had been intercepted by a deck steward, James Camb, who had told him that everything was all right. Captain Patey had the cabin sealed until the ship arrived at Southampton where Camb was interviewed by police.

James Camb, 31, said at first that he had gone to Gay Gibson's cabin on the night before her disappearance to see if she wanted some lemonade. Then he stated that she had invited him to her cabin, and during sexual intercourse, she had suddenly had a fit, foaming at the mouth, and had died in spite of his attempts at artificial respiration. He had panicked, and pushed her body through the cabin's porthole into the sea.

The trouble with this story was that Camb had long scratches on his wrists and shoulders, which he tried to dismiss as a heat rash; and he could not explain how the bell calling for a steward had been pressed. He was charged with murder and tried at Winchester Assizes. The prosecution's case was that Camb had strangled Gay Gibson because she had rejected his advances. Dr Donald Teare, the Crown pathologist, said that blood, saliva and urine stains found on the cabin's bed-sheets were consistent with strangulation. The defence produced medical witnesses who testified to these stains being equally consistent with a fit.

Fact

A murder trial jury at Winchester in 1942 startled the judge by returning a verdict of manslaughter after he had directed that there were no grounds for such a verdict in the case. Edward Lee, a young naval rating, had killed his lover, Vera Bicknell, during a quarrel, but the jury accepted the defence argument that he had not intended to kill her. Mr Justice Charles sentenced the defendant to 14 years penal servitude, and dismissed the jury with the remark, "You are not fit to be there".

But Camb could not explain satisfactorily why he had disposed of the body which would have confirmed his story, nor why he had failed to call for assistance in an emergency.

Camb was almost certainly under the impression that a prosecution for murder could not succeed without a body as evidence. He was found guilty, and escaped the death penalty only because Parliament was then debating the abolition of capital punishment. He was sentenced to life imprisonment. It turned out that he had previously assaulted other women on board the *Durban Castle*, but none of them had reported him.

Telltale Gallstones

When Constance Lane went to Chelsea police station in February 1949, to report the disappearance of her friend Olivia Durand-Deacon, she took with her a man named Haigh, who had said he might be able to help. It was Haigh who had first aroused Mrs Lane's concern when he told her that Mrs Durand-Deacon had failed to turn up for a business meeting he had arranged with her.

The woman police officer who interviewed the couple, Sergeant Lambourne, felt an immediate distrust of Haigh, and soon discovered that he had a criminal record as long as her arm. He had spent a good deal of his life in prison for crimes such as theft and deception. John George Haigh was a dapper Yorkshireman, the son of a colliery foreman. His parents were Plymouth Brethren, and had brought him up in the strict isolation of that oppressive sect. When the boy broke free of this regime in his later school years, he had gradually turned to crime.

Now, when police suspicions had turned up enough circumstantial evidence to justify arrest, Haigh suddenly volunteered that Mrs Durand-Deacon no longer existed. "I have destroyed her with acid", he told Detective Inspector Webb. "You will find the sludge which remains in Leopold Road. Every trace has gone. How can you prove murder if there is no body?" (James Camb could have told him.)

Leopold Road was in Crawley, Sussex, where Haigh had the use of part of the premises of a manufacturing company. He had referred to it as his factory when he had got into conversation with Mrs Durand-Deacon at a London hotel and had taken a flattering interest in a little business scheme she had in mind. Police visited these premises and found in an unsurfaced yard a mass of sludge and a large steel drum. In a storeroom there were three carboys of sulphuric acid, stirrup pumps, rubber gloves, traces of blood, and a leather hat-box containing a revolver and ammunition.

When Dr Keith Simpson, the Home Office pathologist, was called in to examine this evidence, he promptly identified a human gallstone in the sludge. Later, in the laboratory, he was able to identify other gallstones and bone fragments from which—even without pieces of a handbag and a lipstick case also found—he was able to say that the remains were those of a well-built elderly woman. The discovery of a set of dentures established beyond doubt that the remains were, indeed, those of Olivia Durand-Deacon.

Haigh, so far from denying her murder, confessed to others, carried out in a similar fashion. His motive in all cases was financial gain—his victims were all wealthy. But he told police that he had drunk the blood of his victims, whom he had shot before immersing them in vats of acid. He said he had disposed of Donald McSwann and his parents in 1944/5, and Dr Archibald Henderson and his wife in 1948. And for good measure, he added three other victims as well, though these were almost certainly fictitious. He said that in between dumping Mrs Durand-Deacon's body in the vat and pumping in the acid, he had popped round to a café in the town for a cup of tea and a poached egg on toast. And he asked Detective Inspector Webb: "Tell me frankly, what are the chances of anyone being released from Broadmoor?"

He was never to find out, for the jury took less than 20 minutes to decide—despite the proposition that he presented a classic case of paranoia, acting under the delusion that a divine force made him drink the blood of his victims—that he was shamming insanity and was guilty of murder as charged. He was sentenced to death. But if John George Haigh was not out of his mind, then surely, as Dr Henry Yellowlees said in a different context, hardly anybody is. It was simply that he did not fall within the legal requirements of the McNaghten Rules. The 'Acid Bath Murderer', as he became known to posterity, was hanged at Wandsworth Prison by Albert Pierrepoint on 10 August 1949. "It isn't everyone", the exhibitionist Haigh had written to his parents, "who can create more sensation than a film star".

Fact

In 1984 at the Old Bailey, a man was sentenced to life imprisonment twice in two weeks. Kiernan Kelly, an Irish vagrant, got his first sentence for the murder of a man at Clapham, and his second for killing another vagrant in a police cell whilst awaiting trial.

Crime Passionnel

On 11 August 1951, Dr Pierre Chevallier, 42 year-old Mayor of Orléans and a local resistance war hero, was appointed Secretary of State for Technical Education, Youth and Sport in the government of France. Next morning, he returned home from Paris and was shot dead by his wife, Yvonne.

There was never any doubt about the plain facts of the killing. It was Madame Chevallier who called the police, took them upstairs to the bedroom where the blood-soaked body of her husband lay, and gave them the automatic pistol she had bought three days earlier after obtaining a gun licence from the local police station. She had fired five shots, and five bullets were recovered from her husband's body. She was arrested and charged with his murder.

Public feeling in Orléans was running so high against Yvonne Chevallier that her trial was held at Rheims, where it opened at the Palais de Justice on 5 November 1952. The story that unfolded was of a respectable Catholic working-class girl, Yvonne Rousseau, who had married the doctor son of a rich industrialist, and been left behind both sexually and socially in the course of her husband's ambitious career in

Fact

A Glasgow policeman, James Robertson, was hanged for murder at Barlinnie Prison in December 1950. He had knocked Catherine McCluskey unconscious in the street and then run over her body twice in a stolen car. Miss McCluskey was an unmarried mother with two children, one of whom had been fathered by Robertson. Married with two children himself, he had killed her in a desperate bid to end their relationship.

politics. Her reluctance to appear in the limelight, and his long absences from home, led to the inevitable breakdown of their marriage. Poison-pen letters informed Madame Chevallier that her husband did not sleep alone when he was in his Paris flat. His mistress was Jeanne Perreau, a frivolous young married woman who had often been a guest, with her husband, at the Chevalliers' home.

The point came when the miserable Yvonne could stand the situation no longer. When Pierre came home after his government promotion, she challenged him over his affair, and the arrogant doctor cruelly dismissed her. When she said that she wanted to kill herself, he snapped that it would be the first sensible thing she had done in her life. She took out her gun and killed *him* instead.

The woman in the dock was clearly very distraught. She had been brought up to believe in Christian moral principles, and the worry and unhappiness of the last few years had reduced her to a neurotic condition. But she had killed a man who was, whatever his faults, a successful doctor, a popular town mayor, and a new cabinet minister.

Nevertheless, when the jury returned to the court after three quarters of an hour, they declared Yvonne Chevallier not guilty. She walked from the court a free woman. There was great surprise at the jury's decision. For this to be a classic case of a *crime passionnel*, the five shots would have had to be fired in an uncontrollable momentary rage. But it was proved that Madame had begun by firing four shots, and had then been interrupted by her young son coming into the bedroom to see what was happening. She had calmly ushered the boy out of the room and handed him over to the care of her housekeeper, then gone back to the bedroom and fired one more bullet into her husband's body.

Although French juries have traditionally refused to convict in cases of homicide committed in the heat of passion, the law does not officially recognize sexual jealousy or provocation as mitigating circumstances. There is no such defence in French law as a *crime passionnel*.

Nevertheless, a French jury would almost certainly have acquitted Ruth Ellis, who was sentenced to death and executed in England less than three years later for the murder of her former lover, David Blakely, after suffering a miscarriage.

A State of Mind

John Thomas Straffen, a mentally defective 21 year-old man, was convicted at Taunton in 1951 of the murder of two children near Bath. He had strangled five year-old Brenda Goddard and nine year-old Cicely Batstone. Neither girl was sexually assaulted, and Straffen had made no attempt to conceal the bodies. After the first murder, he had gone to a cinema, and after the second, queued up for fish and chips. Judged unfit to plead, he was sent to Broadmoor "until His Majesty's pleasure be known".

Straffen was there only six months before he escaped. Whilst on a cleaning job, he climbed on to the roof of a lean-to shed against the perimeter wall, scaled the wall and jumped free. Within half an hour he was chatting to a woman in her garden at Crowthorne whom he had asked for a drink of water. He then moved on to Farley Hill where he was seen by several people, including the mother of five year-old Linda Bowyer who was riding her small bicycle in the road in front of her home.

Shortly afterwards, officers from Broadmoor spotted Straffen talking to some children, and he was quickly caught. He had been out for about four hours, but in that time he had killed Linda Bowyer. Her body was found in a field at dawn the next morning. She had been strangled. She had not been sexually assaulted and no attempt had been made to conceal the crime. Her bicycle had been left nearby.

When police interviewed Straffen at Broadmoor, he said: "I did not kill her", before anyone had mentioned anything about murder, and when pressed to explain what he meant, he said: "I did not kill the little girl with the bicycle". He was charged with the murder, and tried at Winchester in July 1952. It was the first time that an escaped Broadmoor inmate had been tried for an offence committed whilst at large.

This time, Straffen was not treated as unfit to plead, and he pleaded "not guilty". It was up to his defence counsel to plead insanity, which he did. There was little dispute about the facts of Straffen's escape and subsequent actions. The trial hinged on the question of whether or not he was insane at the time he committed the murder. Straffen's acts of strangulation were likened, controversially, to the act of squeezing an orange—as far as his understanding perceived it. Expert witnesses testified that although he was mentally defective and had a mental age of 10 or 12, he was not insane and understood the difference between right and wrong. The jury took less than an hour to find Straffen guilty of murder, and he was sentenced to death.

As a result of a report by psychologists, however, the Home Secretary, Sir David Maxwell-Fyfe, decided on a reprieve, but Straffen was sent to prison rather than to Broadmoor, and there he remains—the longest-serving reprieved murderer in Britain this century.

There has been a great deal of controversy about the medical evidence during Straffen's trial. It has been argued, among other things, that a mentally defective person cannot recover, and that if Straffen was unfit to plead in 1951, he could not have been fit to plead in 1952.

Fact

"If once a man indulge himself in murder, very soon he comes to think little of robbing; and from robbing he next comes to drinking and Sabbath-breaking, and from that to incivility and procrastination." Thomas De Quincey: Murder Considered as One of the Fine Arts

Man and Boy

The interest of this case lies not so much in the murder itself as in the injustice perceived by a great many people in the outcome. Derek Bentley, 19, and Christopher Craig, 16, were seen breaking into a warehouse in Croydon in November 1952. When police arrived, Craig and Bentley hid on the roof, and the attempt to arrest them led to Craig

Fact

Two rattlesnakes, named Lethal and Lightning, were the unusual weapons employed in a murder bid by Robert James in Los Angeles in 1935. He had procured them specially to bite his wife, Mary, and he and his accomplice held her down, having got her drunk on whisky, while the deadly reptiles did their stuff. But Mary James did not die as quickly as expected, and James finally drowned her in the bath. He was sentenced to death, and became the last man to be executed by hanging in the state of California, which henceforth carried out its executions by gas chamber.

opening fire with a revolver, wounding a detective who was already holding Bentley, and killing a uniformed constable, Sidney Miles. Craig and Bentley were both convicted of the murder of PC Miles. Bentley, who was mentally subnormal, was sentenced to death and hanged by Albert Pierrepoint at Wandsworth on 28 January 1953. Craig was too young to be sentenced to death, and was detained at Her Majesty's pleasure, being released in 1963.

The trial judge, Lord Chief Justice Goddard, who seemed to represent the Establishment's determination to make an example of these two young criminals, made many interjections during the trial which were harmful to the cause of the defendants. He made a remark during his summing-up about the efforts of the defence to save "Bentley's precious skin", and challenged the jury to say that the police officers, whom he had praised for their gallantry and resolution, were lying when they testified that Bentley had shouted out, "Let them have it, Chris!" Much has been made of this ambiguous exclamation which, if it *was* made, could arguably have meant "give them the gun".

The execution of Bentley raised many disturbing questions and added fuel to the abolitionist cause. He was hanged for a murder he did not commit, and which was committed a quarter of an hour after his arrest. Two hundred Members of Parliament protested at the refusal of the Home Secretary, Sir David Maxwell-Fyfe, to advise the exercise of the Royal Prerogative of Mercy which had been recommended by the jury.

The Wastrel

One day early in November 1952, whilst Craig and Bentley were in prison awaiting trial, two bodies were discovered on a beach below the cliffs at Carlyon Bay, near St Austell in Cornwall. The middle-aged man and woman had been battered to death with blows to their heads and dumped over the cliff-edge. A trail of blood marked the route, leading back through a copse and the back garden of a house called 'Carrickowl', the home of Charles Giffard, clerk at the local magistrates' court, and his wife and son. A half-hearted attempt had been made to clean up the scenes of the murders—the garage and kitchen of the house. The family car and 26 year-old Miles Giffard were missing.

Police in Cornwall had reason to believe that Miles might be in London, and they notified the Metropolitan Police, describing a Triumph car which was quickly located outside a house in Tite Street, Chelsea. Police were waiting there for Giffard when he brought his girlfriend home later that night.

He was taken back to Cornwall and committed for trial at Bodmin Assizes, where he pleaded not guilty of murder by reason of insanity. Miles Giffard had been diagnosed as schizophrenic while still in his teens, but had never received treatment. His mental condition was considered to be due largely to a sadistic nanny who had habitually beaten him as a child and locked him in a dark cupboard. Dr Roy Craig, a Devon psychiatrist, had warned Charles Giffard in 1941 that "the door is slowly closing on this boy's sanity". Nevertheless, it appeared that he had killed his parents with calculated deliberation. Although good at sport (he had played cricket for Cornwall), he had become a wastrel, unsuccessful in a variety of attempts to earn an honest living, and entirely dependent on his father for money which he frittered away. So when Charles Giffard forbade him to go to London, where he had fallen for 19 year-old Gabrielle Vallance, and threatened to withdraw his allowance, Miles rebelled against his parents' authority in an extreme manner. He had written to Gabrielle a few days before the murder: "I am dreadfully fed up as I was looking forward to seeing you. Short of doing him in, I see no future in the world at all". He had killed them with a length of iron pipe, and taken them one by one from the house to the cliff-edge in a wheelbarrow, which he had tipped over after them. His mother may have been still alive when she was thrown over. He had also stolen some of his mother's jewellery to sell in London.

The jury of Cornish businessmen, hardly at home with complicated psychiatric evidence, did not accept that he was insane in any legal sense, and he was convicted and sentenced to death. Miles Giffard was hanged at Bristol on 24 February 1953.

Fact

When human remains were found by potholers in a disused lead mine at Brandy Cove, Glamorgan, in November 1961, they were identified as those of Mamie Stuart, a chorus girl who had vanished in 1919. Suspicion fell on George Shotton, who in 1920 had been sentenced to 18 months hard labour for committing bigamy with Miss Stuart. Although discovery of the body 41 years later enabled police to satisfy themselves that Shotton had murdered her, he was no longer available to answer charges, having died in 1958 at the age of 78.

Rillington Place

In March 1953, Mr Beresford Brown, a West Indian tenant of a flat at 10 Rillington Place in London's Notting Hill district, set about fixing brackets to hold a radio in the kitchen. But when he tapped the wall, it sounded hollow. He pulled off a strip of wallpaper to reveal a boarded-up alcove, and shining a torch into it, found himself looking at the back of a woman's naked body. He ran off to fetch the police.

The corpses of three young women were found in the alcove. They were identified as Rita Nelson, Kathleen Maloney and Hectorina MacLennan. All three were prostitutes, and they had been strangled. Further searching revealed another corpse under the floorboards in the front room of the flat. This was the body of Ethel Christie, the wife of a former tenant, who had left only recently. She, too, had been strangled. Police announced to the press that they were anxious to interview John Reginald Halliday Christie, whom they believed might be able to help them with their enquiries. Meanwhile, they dug up the garden and uncovered two skeletons, later identified as those of Ruth Fuerst and Muriel Eady. Whilst the women in the house had died within the previous three months, the two in the garden had been there for some years. Police also found a tobacco tin on the premises containing four specimens of pubic hair, which had obviously been kept as trophies.

Christie was arrested on Putney Bridge a few days later, and admitted responsibility for all six deaths. His statements to police were vague and unreliable, but it seemed that he had murdered the two women buried in the garden during the war, strangling them whilst

Fact

Velma Barfield, who was executed by lethal injection in North Carolina in November 1984, was the first woman to be executed in the USA for 22 years. She was 52 years old, and had been convicted of poisoning her fiancé, Stuart Taylor, six years earlier. She had also murdered her second husband, her mother, and two other people.

having sexual intercourse with them. It was not clear why he had murdered his wife (he tried to make out that it was a mercy killing), but it was probably because she was a hindrance to his bizarre compulsion to murder other women during, or possibly before, having sexual intercourse with them. He had devised a method of making them drowsy with the carbon monoxide in the domestic gas supply before he attempted to penetrate them, but none of them had died as a result of gas poisoning. Clearly the only possible defence for Christie was a plea of insanity. It failed, and he was sentenced to death and hanged at Pentonville on 15 July 1953.

This might have been the end of a sordid tale of a sexual and probably necrophilic serial killer of the sort that naturally dominates the headlines of the time. But the Christie case created a sensation for another reason: three years earlier, Christie and his wife had been prosecution witnesses at the trial of another man charged with murder, Timothy John Evans, who had been accused of the murder of his wife and daughter, both of whom had been strangled. Convicted of the murder of the child, Geraldine, Evans had been hanged on 9 March 1950. He and his family had lived in the upstairs flat at 10 Rillington Place!

A great deal of public disquiet was caused by the fact that, firstly, Evans had been convicted partly on the testimony of a man who had already murdered two women and subsequently murdered four more, and secondly, that the nation was being asked to believe that there were two murderers living in the same house at the same time, killing women by the same method. Evans had accused Christie of murdering his wife and daughter, and Christie subsequently confessed to the murder of Beryl Evans, though he denied killing the child. Both men were mentally abnormal, however, and habitual liars. A serious miscarriage of justice seemed a distinct possibility. Numerous books were published about the case, most notably Ludovic Kennedy's *Ten Rillington Place*. Official enquiries were undertaken, and eventually Timothy Evans was granted a posthumous free pardon in 1965.

No one has proved conclusively that Evans was innocent of murder. What is certain, however, is that no jury would have convicted him knowing what was subsequently known about Christie. The case undoubtedly had some influence on the decision to abolish the death penalty in Britain. Rillington Place no longer exists. It was demolished and rebuilt as Ruston Mews. But argument about whether one or two murderers lived at 10 Rillington Place still continues.

Deadman's Hill

On the night of 22 August 1961, Michael Gregsten and his lover, Valerie Storie, were sitting in a car at the edge of a cornfield at Dorney Reach, near Maidenhead, when there was a tap on the driver's window. As Gregsten wound down the window, a man thrust a gun at him saying that he was a desperate man on the run, and if they did as they were told, they would be all right.

He got into the back seat, and they remained in the field for two hours, during which time the man took money and wrist watches from the couple, then ordered Gregsten to drive away. After stops for petrol and cigarettes, the car reached the village of Clophill on the A6 south of Bedford, and a little further on, the man ordered Gregsten to pull into a lay-by at the top of Deadman's Hill. It was now about 3 a.m. The man said he needed to sleep, but would have to tie the couple up first. He tied Valerie Storie's hands together and told Gregsten to pass him a duffle bag which was in the front of the car. As Gregsten turned to do so, the man suddenly shot him twice in the head, killing him instantly. Valerie Storie screamed and shouted at him to get a doctor, but the man retorted: "Be quiet will you, I'm finking". He then raped Miss Storie in the back of the car, and made her help him drag out Gregsten's body. Then he shot her five times while she was on the ground weeping, and drove off. The body of Michael Gregsten, and Valerie Storie—lying almost unconscious and paralyzed in both legs—were found by a passing farm worker almost three hours later.

A description of the man based on Miss Storie's statement to police in Bedford General Hospital the same day, was issued to the press and all police forces in Britain. The case was promptly christened the 'A6 Murder'. The blood-spattered car was found abandoned in a street at Ilford, Essex, on the evening of the crime. The murder weapon, a loaded revolver, was found on a London bus during cleaning at the Peckham depot on the following day.

Nearly three weeks later the manager of the Vienna Hotel at Maida Vale found two cartridge cases in one of the rooms. Scotland Yard experts soon realised that the bullets had been fired from the revolver used in the A6 murder. One man who had stayed at the hotel for one night after the murder, using the name Durrant, had already been interviewed by police and released. His real name was Peter Alphon. A few days later he was reported to the manager of the Alexandra Court Hotel at Finsbury Park by a permanent guest in the next room who had been kept awake at night by the noise he made, pacing the room and opening and shutting wardrobe doors.

A nation-wide manhunt was set in motion for Alphon, who was now the chief suspect. On the night of 22 September, Alphon walked into Scotland Yard and gave himself up, declaring that he had had nothing whatever to do with the murder. When he was lined up in an identity parade at Guy's Hospital, where Valerie Storie had been transferred from Bedford, she failed to pick him out and he was again dismissed from the enquiry.

Police turned their attention to another man who had stayed at the Vienna Hotel on the night *before* the murder, under the name Ryan. He was quickly identified as James Hanratty, a man with a record of petty crime, and he was arrested in Blackpool on 11 October. Hanratty was charged with the murder of Gregsten and taken to Bedford. Two days later, he was lined up in an identity parade at Stoke Mandeville

Fact

If television had existed in the 17th century, it would certainly have had countless field days with a high society murder case involving the most powerful families in the land. Frances Howard, daughter of the Earl of Suffolk and wife of Robert Devereux, Earl of Essex, wanted a divorce in order to marry Robert Carr, Viscount Rochester and later Earl of Somerset. But Sir Thomas Overbury, the only person who knew of the secret liaison between Carr and Frances Howard, did all he could to prevent it, so Frances had him poisoned, and eventually married her lover. King James I was a guest at the wedding. The truth only came to light two years later, and the Earl and Countess of Somerset were convicted of murder. Both were sentenced to death, but were reprieved by the King, and spent the rest of their lives under house arrest.

Fact

In 1927, the well-dressed defendant in a murder trial at Winnipeg, Canada, was said to have interested himself in various religious sects, and to have given blood when his wife was in hospital needing a transfusion. But Earle Nelson was convicted of the murder of Emily Patterson and sentenced to death. He is also believed to have committed at least 21 other murders in Canada and the United States, all of them women and girls. Most of the women were middle-aged landladies, whom he also raped. Nelson had a primitive-looking facial structure, with a receding forehead and protruding lips, and became known as the 'Gorilla Murderer'. He was hanged at Winnipeg in 1928.

Hospital, where Valerie Storie was by now being treated for her spinal injury. Taken up and down the line in a wheelchair, she asked the men to say, one by one, "Be quiet will you, I'm thinking". Then she picked out James Hanratty.

Hanratty's trial at Bedford Assizes in January and February of 1962 lasted 21 days, becoming the longest murder trial in English history up to that time. The jury considered the evidence for over nine hours before pronouncing Hanratty guilty. He was sentenced to death and hanged at Bedford Prison on 4 April, one of the last half-dozen men to be executed in Britain. The executioner was Harry Allen.

This was by no means the end of the A6 affair, however. Hanratty's alibi was that he had been in Rhyl when the murder was committed, and after his execution several witnesses claimed to have seen him there. Furthermore, Peter Alphon, who was inclined to pronounce 'th' as 'f' when he was excited, subsequently confessed repeatedly to the murder, though with inconsistencies and a degree of fantasy. It seemed, in certain respects, like the Rowland case of 1946 all over again. Alphon was undoubtedly mentally unbalanced, but there appeared to be no logical motive for the man in the car to kill Gregsten. It is well known that certain psychological types are drawn to confess to murders they did not commit. The Home Office revealed that it had received two other confessions to the A6 murder—as well as Alphon's—after Hanratty's execution. And Alphon tended to become hysterical and withdraw his confessions whenever anyone in authority showed signs of taking them seriously.

Several books were published disputing Hanratty's guilt. The arguments were less convincing to most people, perhaps, than those in the case of Timothy Evans in the previous decade, but the circumstances were sufficiently disquieting to draw the nation's attention once more to the fact that innocent men had almost certainly been hanged in the past and could be hanged again in the future. The case added momentum to the growing campaign against the death penalty.

Family Values

When the Polish film-maker Roman Polanski, director of *Repulsion* and *Rosemary's Baby*, left his rented home in Los Angeles to make a film in Europe in 1969, he arranged for a friend, Voytek Frykowski, and Voytek's girlfriend, Abigail Folger, to move in with his pregnant wife, the film actress Sharon Tate, while he was away. On the evening of 8 August, as well as these three and the house-boy, William Garretson, two visitors were at the house—Jay Sebring, a friend and former lover of Sharon's, and a young man named Stephen Parent, who had called to see Garretson.

When Stephen Parent left in his car, he saw some dark figures moving about in the garden. He pulled up and asked them what they were doing. A man instantly put a revolver to the 18 year-old's head and pulled the trigger, then fired more bullets into him. The man and two women then broke into the house, leaving another woman outside to keep watch, and carried out a bloody massacre of shooting and stabbing. Before they left, one of the women daubed the word 'Pig' on the hall door, using a towel dipped in Sharon Tate's blood. The killers, as well as some of the victims, were high on the drug LSD. The house-boy, Garretson, playing records in another part of the house, heard nothing, and was the only one to remain alive. The bodies were found early next morning when the housekeeper arrived.

The murderers were Charles Watson, Susan Atkins and Patricia Krenwinkel, followers of the psychopathic Charles Manson, leader of a hippie commune who had ordered the killings. On the following night, Manson himself entered the home of businessman Leno LaBianca with a gun, tied up LaBianca and his wife Rosemary, then went out and ordered three people waiting in their car to go inside and kill the couple. The murderers this time were Watson, Krenwinkel and Leslie Van Houten. Mr and Mrs LaBianca were slashed and stabbed many times in an orgy of bloodlust. The difference between fantasy and reality was blurred, if not blotted out altogether, by the killers' use of LSD. They left several mindless slogans written in blood about the house, including the word 'war' slashed on Mr LaBianca's body.

Within a few days Manson and 24 others were arrested in a police raid on the commune, but it was no more than an attempt to clamp down on crimes such as car-stealing and the use of drugs. All the detainees were soon released for lack of evidence. A few days later a man was murdered at the ranch where Manson and his 'family' were living, 30 miles from Los Angeles.

It was December before charges of murder were made against anyone. On 30 March 1970, Manson, Krenwinkel, Atkins and Van Houten were convicted and sentenced to death. Linda Kasabian, the girl left outside at the Sharon Tate home, turned State's evidence. Charles Watson had crossed the state line and was resisting extradition, but he was brought to trial in 1971 and also sentenced to death. However, while the five on death row were awaiting their appointments in the gas chamber in February 1972, the Supreme Court of California abolished the death penalty, and the sentences were commuted to several terms of life imprisonment.

In 1975, Lynette Fromme, one of Manson's tribe known as 'Squeaky', approached President Gerald Ford with the intention of shooting him at close range to draw public attention to the Manson credo, but she failed to fire a shot.

Since the death penalty has been restored in California, many murderers have gone to their deaths for crimes less heinous than those of Manson, the sinister bearded dwarf driven by resentment, and the adoring harem of teenage dropouts for whom he was a father figure. Manson has sometimes been credited with a tender feeling for children. It is invariably reported that five people lost their lives at the Polanski house, but there were six victims that night—Sharon Tate had been pregnant for over eight months.

Fact

The Suicide Act of 1961 repealed the law which made it a criminal offence to commit or attempt to commit suicide, which had been treated as a felony since the Middle Ages. But a person who survives a suicide pact, having aided someone else to commit suicide, can be charged with manslaughter, and if it can be shown that he or she intended to survive, may be liable to a charge of murder.

Fact

"It is forbidden to kill; therefore all murderers are punished who kill not in large companies or to the sound of trumpets." *Voltaire:* Philosophical Dictionary.

White Magic

Early one morning in June 1971, a house on a hillside above the port of Castries, capital of the Caribbean island of St Lucia, was seen by startled neighbours to be in flames. They raised the alarm, but firemen could not save the building. Inside the smouldering shell they found two charred corpses. They were identified as the remains of James Etherington and his wife, Marjorie, the owners of the house. The bodies were seen by a local police surgeon and by a Caribbean government pathologist, but no one suspected foul play, and the remains were buried in a churchyard on Barbados.

When a professional sceptic—an insurance company investigator—visited the burnt-out house, however, he literally smelt trouble. Poking about among the debris, he put his nose to the end of a plastic hosepipe which was draped over a window sill. It smelt of petrol, and he traced the hose from the house to the garage, where a car remained with its petrol tank open and the filler cap on the floor. The insurance man called the police, who asked for assistance from Scotland Yard.

Detectives were flown out next day, and soon established that the fire was a case of arson. The island's police commissioner had three well-known local criminals brought in for questioning on the grounds, he said, that if they had not done it they would know who had. Meanwhile, Professor Keith Simpson, the Home Office pathologist, had flown out to conduct post-mortem examinations on the exhumed remains of James and Marjorie Etherington. Both had died as a result of asphyxiation by inhaling fumes from the fire. But the man had been struck on the head with a blunt instrument, shattering the skull, and the woman had the remains of a plastic clothes line between her teeth, showing that she had been gagged. It seemed that the couple had been tied up and left to burn alive.

The three men held by police, named Florius, Faucher and Charles, were charged with murder. They admitted they had gone to the house and robbed the Etheringtons, tying them up whilst they did so, but denied using violence or setting fire to the house. But during the course of the trial, Faucher stated that Florius, the trio's leader, had insisted that they should burn the victims as the British police had a new method of making the dead talk. He apparently believed that electronic recordings could be made on tape of dead people's thoughts! The three were convicted of murder and executed by hanging.

Industrial Injuries

In the summer and autumn of 1971, a strange illness affected staff at John Hadland Ltd, a company making specialized photographic equipment at Bovingdon, near Hemel Hempstead in Hertfordshire. Several people suffered from stomach pains, vomiting and diarrhoea, and numbness in their limbs. They naturally suspected chemicals used on the premises, or contamination of the water supply. On 19 November, Frederick Biggs, a 60 year-old departmental manager, died in hospital. David Tilson, a clerk, and Jethro Batt, a storeman, were also admitted to hospital. David Tilson's hair began to fall out. Others were so ill that they could not work and had to stay at home. Alarm spread through the company as about 70 people went down with the symptoms, and some of the workers handed in their notice. They had not forgotten that five months earlier Robert Egle, the firm's chief storeman, had died in St Albans hospital from what had been certified as broncho-pneumonia and polyneuritis. He had suffered from nausea and diarrhoea, backache, and loss of feeling in his fingers.

The management organized a full medical investigation, and a meeting of the workforce was arranged in the canteen so that the doctor in charge could reassure everyone about the safety of the chemicals used in the company and try to allay the mounting panic. At this meeting, a voluble young trainee storeman asked the doctor if he thought the symptoms of the mysterious illness were consistent with thallium poisoning.

This man, 23 year-old Graham Young, had been taken on by the company in May, two months before Mr Egle had died. He had been at the funeral, and had taken the opportunity to show off to the managing director his keen interest in chemistry and related subjects. Now, his over-enthusiastic questioning of the medical officer aroused suspicion, and the police were called in. Bob Egle's remains were exhumed for analysis, and both he and Fred Biggs were found to have died from thallium poisoning. As soon as Young's background had been checked, he was arrested for murder, and was found to have thallium in his possession on the premises.

Young, it turned out, had been released from Broadmoor only weeks before applying for the job at Hadland's. He had been committed in 1962 to the institution for the criminally insane when he was 15, after poisoning several members of his family, one of whom—his stepmother—had died. He had been declared guilty but insane, and the judge had recommended that he should stay in Broadmoor for at least 15 years. But after nine years he had been released, having made what was described as an "extremely full recovery".

Graham Young was tried at St Albans for the murders of Robert Egle and Frederick Biggs. He pleaded not guilty. But various toxic substances had been found in his bed-sitting-room in Hemel Hempstead, as well as a diary containing incriminating entries such as his administration of "a fatal dose of the special compound to F..." Young claimed these entries were merely notes for a novel he was planning to write. But fellow-workers testified that Young, who talked a lot about Hitler and Dr Palmer, was always very obliging in bringing them tea or coffee, and that it sometimes tasted bitter. One storeroom employee, who had been ill for a month, had often left his tea after a couple of sips, and Bob Egle had sometimes drunk the rest, as well as his own.

Young was convicted in July 1972 of murder, attempted murder and administering poisons, and sentenced to life imprisonment. He eventually died of a heart attack in Parkhurst Prison.

Fact

One of the most appalling cases of multiple child murder occurred in China in 1951, when more than 2,000 children died at an orphanage in Canton. Most of them had been brought to the Holy Child Orphanage for medical treatment, but few survived, and some of those who did were sold. Five French-Canadian nuns who ran the orphanage were convicted of murder. Three were simply deported and the other two, Germain Gravel and Antoinette Couvrette, got a mere five years jail sentence.

Fact

Among the most intriguing unsolved murders of recent times was the brutal killing of Sandra Rivett in London's Belgravia in November 1974. Sandra was nanny to the children of Richard Bingham, 7th Earl of Lucan, and his wife Veronica. Lady Lucan had been attacked in her home, and rushed out covered in blood to tell the police that her husband had attacked her. When they went to investigate, Mrs Rivett's body was found in the basement. No motive was known, and it was assumed that she had been killed in mistake for Lady Lucan, who had been separated from her husband for two years. Lord Lucan disappeared, and has never been seen since. He had telephoned his mother and told her that he had come into the house and interrupted a man who was attacking his wife. A car used by Lord Lucan was found abandoned at Newhaven, with blood stains matching both his wife's group A and Sandra Rivett's group B. The inquest jury on Sandra Rivett concluded that she had been murdered by Lord Lucan, and a Red Alert was put out to Interpol. But the questions remain unanswered: did Lord Lucan murder Sandra Rivett, and is he alive or dead?

Alter Ego

John Wayne Gacy, born in 1942, was named after his parents' favourite film star, and this tenuous link with show-business was developed into something a little more substantial when he became a local celebrity in Chicago for his clowning act at children's parties and other social gatherings. He even came to the notice of President Jimmy Carter, whose wife had her photograph taken with Gacy, for as well as being a popular entertainer, he was also a successful businessman who made contributions to Democratic Party funds.

He was not a successful husband, however. Married in 1967, he was divorced two years later. He married again in 1972, and this time it lasted four years. Gacy, who had been dominated by his mother and elder sister in his formative years, was homosexual, and had two convictions for sexual assaults on young men. Chicago police had his name on their files as a suspect in the cases of several missing youths, and in December 1978, after he had been seen with 15 year-old Robert Piest, who had also disappeared, they arrested him and began a search of his luxury home and landscaped garden in the Norwood Park suburb of the city. They dug up the remains of 28 young men and boys, and raised five more from the bed of Des Plaines river. The youngest body found was that of a nine year-old boy.

For at least three years, Gacy had been in the habit of abducting young drifters at the Greyhound Bus station and the notorious gay rendezvous known as 'Bughouse Square'. He took his victims home and brutally raped them before murdering them with a garotte and disposing of their bodies.

Gacy pleaded insanity at his trial in 1979, but this cut no ice with the jury and the 'Killer Clown' was convicted of murder and subsequently sentenced to death. Following a series of appeals, he was taken from death row, where he had spent 14 years, and executed by lethal injection in May 1994.

This case is included here as representative of an epidemic of serial killings, mostly sexual, in the United States during the 1970s. Other murderers of this period included Theodore Bundy, responsible for the deaths of 23 young women in Washington State and Utah; Dean Corll, who committed 27 homosexual murders in Texas; Juan Corona, 25 murders in California; Paul Knowles, 18 in Florida and Georgia; Herbert Mullin, 27 in California; Wayne Williams, 28 in Atlanta; Donald Harvey, 67 in Kentucky and Ohio; Randy Knight, 16 in California; Jeffrey Dahmer, 16 in Wisconsin.

Dingoism

There was a curious echo in the 1980s of the antipodean mystery of the shark, half a century earlier, in another murder case involving wild life, when the nine week-old daughter of Michael and Alice Lynne Chamberlain disappeared from a camp site in the shadows of Ayers

Rock. Again the question arose—was the killer animal or human?

Lindy Chamberlain claimed that her daughter had been snatched from their tent by a dingo, the species of predatory wild dog that roams the Australian outback. She said she had seen one walking away from the camp before she realised that her baby was missing, but could not say if it held anything in its jaws. Police began to shoot dingos in the vicinity in the hope of proving the fact by dissecting the right dog. But this effort produced no results, and some days after the child's disappearance, her bloodstained clothing was found. Could a dingo take the clothes off a baby without leaving traces of flesh? By the time the inquest was held at Alice Springs in February 1981, various rumours were flying about, but the coroner's verdict was that Azaria Chamberlain's death had been caused by a dingo. Later that year, however, continuing doubt and circumstantial evidence led police to re-open their investigations, and when Professor James Cameron of the London Hospital Medical College found neither teethmarks nor saliva on the baby's stretchsuit, and described bloodstains as suggesting that blood had flowed down it from above (i.e. the baby had been killed in an upright position), Lindy Chamberlain was charged with murder and her husband as an accessory. The prosecution alleged that the woman had cut the baby's throat in the front seat of their car, where bloodstains had also been found.

After a trial lasting seven weeks, the jury found the Chamberlains guilty as charged. Lindy was sentenced to life and Michael was given an 18 months suspended sentence. In April 1983, Lindy's appeal was rejected by the Federal Court, and by the High Court of Australia in the following February.

There was much public disquiet about the case, however, particularly when it became generally known that a dingo had dragged another child from a car near Ayers Rock. Furthermore, no one had produced a convincing motive for a happily married mother, with two other children and pregnant during her trial, to murder her daughter. In February 1986, Lindy Chamberlain was released on the grounds that she had served her debt to society, and in 1987, she was pardoned. An enquiry by Mr Justice Morling had concluded that the evidence did not rule out the possibility of the child having been taken by a dingo.

Fact

Baron Dieter von Schauroth was shot dead by his own bodyguard in South Africa. Marthinus Rossouw admitted that he had done it, but claimed that his employer had not only asked him to kill him, but had paid him to do so and handed him the firearm. The baron had been depressed about his failing marriage and money matters. Nevertheless, Rossouw was convicted of murder and hanged in Cape Town in 1962.

The Mission

Wilma McCann, a 28 year-old prostitute, was found dead by a milkman at the edge of a playing field in Leeds on 30 October 1975. She had been savagely battered about the head and stabbed many times. The murder would not, in isolation, have excited the attention of the media, or particularly alarmed the general public, but Wilma McCann's death proved to be the first of a frightening series.

The second victim was Emily Jackson, a 42 year-old prostitute whose body was found in an alley in the Chapeltown district on 20 January

Fact

In January 1837, a human head was found blocking a lock-gate on the Grand Union Canal in Stepney. It turned out to be that of Hannah Brown, whose other remains had been found in various parts of London. James Greenacre, her former lover, was arrested for her murder. He had killed her when he found she had not the money he had expected to come to him if he married her. He had been a prominent tradesman and politician at Southwark, and was visited at Newgate by Members of Parliament and, it is said, noblemen. But Greenacre had to pay for his crime, and was hanged in the year of Queen Victoria's accession to the throne.

1976. Her injuries were similar, the multiple stab-wounds being cross-shaped as if made with a screwdriver of the Phillips type. A year passed before the man, who was quickly dubbed the 'Yorkshire Ripper', killed anyone else. The third victim was found in Roundhay Park on 8 February 1977. She was 28 year-old Irene Richardson, another prostitute. But in the meantime, the killer had attacked another woman who got away. In May 1976 a West Indian girl had been picked up on Chapeltown Road and taken to Soldier's Field at Roundhay. As they got out of the man's car, he attacked her with a knife, but her screams frightened him off and she survived, though she needed more than 50 stitches in her wounds. Police did not associate this attack with the 'Ripper' because of the different weapon used.

After the murder of Irene Richardson, the killings gathered pace and the scene widened. The next victim was murdered in her flat in Bradford: 32 year-old Patricia Atkinson, who died in April 1977, was the only victim of the Yorkshire Ripper to be killed indoors. At the end of June, he struck again: 16 year-old Jayne Macdonald was walking home in Leeds after an evening out with her boyfriend, when she was attacked and killed. It happened in the Chapeltown area, but Jayne was no prostitute. Women in Leeds and Bradford were feeling justifiably nervous as the murderer continued his reign of terror. It was to last for five years.

Bradford was the scene of another attack two weeks later. A woman was severely injured after accepting a lift from a stranger. But she escaped with her life and described her attacker. Police were building up a picture of the man they wanted, and the car he drove, and in October they had another lead. The killer had crossed the Pennines this time: the body of 21 year-old Jean Jordan was found on a disused allotment at Chorley, near Manchester. Her murderer had made an attempt to sever the victim's head, but his trademarks were recognizable. In Jean's handbag a new £5 note was found. The serial number led police to a bank at Shipley, a Bradford suburb, where the manager told them that the note, issued only a few days earlier, had probably been in a local company payroll. Police interviewed more than 6,000 people in an abortive effort to trace its original owner.

A prostitute picked up in the Chapeltown area of Leeds in December, and attacked on some waste ground to which she had been driven by her assailant, survived to describe him as a man with a beard and a drooping moustache, like 'Jason King', she said—a character played by Peter Wyngarde on television.

Meanwhile, the murders continued. Two more prostitutes were murdered in Bradford and Huddersfield in January 1978, and a third at Manchester in May. Then there was another gap of nearly a year before 19 year-old Josephine Whitaker was murdered in Savile Park in Halifax in April 1979 . West Yorkshire police then received a cassette tape on which a man—whose accent was pinned down by Professor Stanley Ellis of Leeds University to a western area of Sunderland—taunted George Oldfield, the Assistant Chief Constable who was leading the manhunt. The man said that he would probably strike again in September or October. "At the rate I'm going I should be in the book of records", he added, calling himself 'Jack the Ripper'. When the body of 20 year-old student Barbara Leach, who had been killed with a hammer and stabbed several times with a large Phillips-type screwdriver, was found in the back yard of a house in Bradford on 3 September, the nation was made aware that police were looking for a man with a Geordie accent.

In August 1980, Marguerite Walls, who was 47, was walking home in Pudsey when she was attacked in the street. A former WRAC, Miss Walls fought for her life, but the man dragged her to the driveway of a house and into a wooded area, where he strangled her. Although the body had been partly stripped, like the other victims, police again failed to connect this murder with the Ripper because of the method of killing.

Nearly five years had passed since the murder of Wilma McCann. The hunt for the killer had become a multi-million-pound enquiry—the most expensive single police investigation in British history. Police had visited 26,000 houses, interviewed a quarter of a million people, and taken no less than 32,000 statements. But the murderer was still at large. In November he killed again. The victim this time was 20 year-old Jacqueline Hill, another student, who was walking home in Headingley when she was attacked near the modern shopping centre of the fashionable Leeds district.

Public demands for more action mounted, and there was widespread criticism of police methods. A week after the murder of Jacqueline Hill, Assistant Chief Constable Oldfield was replaced as head of the investigation by James Hobson, head of Leeds CID, who was put in charge of a so-called 'super squad'.

A few weeks later, three days into the new year, two policemen in a patrol car stopped to investigate a car parked in a tree-lined avenue in Sheffield. The man sitting in it said that he was Peter Williams, and that the woman with him was his girlfriend. But he did not know her name. When the officers found that the car's number plates were false, they arrested him and his companion. The man's real name was Peter William Sutcliffe. It did not take Sheffield police long to realise that there was more to this suspect than a motoring offence. The woman was a local prostitute. She had almost certainly been within minutes of becoming the fourteenth victim of the Yorkshire Ripper.

Sutcliffe was no Geordie. The police had been led on a massive wild-goose chase by the hoax cassette tape. More than 3,000 calls had been taken from people who had heard it and claimed to have recognized the voice.

Peter Sutcliffe was born at Bingley in 1946. After leaving school he had gone through a variety of jobs, but his favourite occupations had been as a grave-digger at the local cemetery and as a mortuary attendant. People who had known him at that time testified to his macabre habits. In August 1974 he had married a young schoolteacher, Sonia Szurma, whose parents had come to Britain as refugees from eastern Europe. Two years before their marriage, while Sutcliffe had been courting her, Sonia had suffered a period of mental illness, apparently believing that she was the Christ of the Second Coming. The Sutcliffes lived in Bradford, and had been married for just over a year when he killed Wilma McCann. Since being sacked from his grave-digging job (for bad time-keeping), he had been employed as a driver of heavy goods vehicles, and was among those interviewed in 1977 in

Fact

One of the longest-running stage productions around the turn of the century, in both London and New York, was the musical Floradora. *But one of its Broadway chorus girls, Nan Patterson, soon upstaged the show by being charged with murder. The pretty 22 year-old was the mistress of Frank Young, a wealthy socialite, and she was accused in June 1904 of shooting him in the back of a cab during a quarrel. She claimed that Young had shot himself. Ballistics experts said this was impossible. The trial had to be stopped because a juror died. The second jury failed to agree on a verdict. A third trial was held, and again the jury became deadlocked. Miss Patterson was then discharged and declared immune from further prosecution.*

Fact

Eugene Aram, a scholar and schoolmaster in Yorkshire, was charged in 1758, along with his crony William Houseman, with the murder 14 years earlier of Daniel Clark, a shoemaker. Clark's remains had been found in a cave on the River Nidd at Knaresborough. Houseman turned King's Evidence, and described how they had killed Clark to rob him of £200. Aram made a long and ingenious speech during the trial suggesting that the skeleton found was not Clark's but that of a hermit or anchoress who had lived in the cave centuries ago. No one believed this theory, and after attempting to commit suicide in prison, Aram was hanged and his body suspended in chains. Thomas Hood wrote his famous poem The Dream of Eugene Aram *about the case.*

connection with the £5 note found on Jean Jordan. He had also been interviewed by police on other occasions.

Sutcliffe was charged with 13 murders and seven attempted murders. His legal advisers were prepared to enter an admission of manslaughter on grounds of diminished responsibility, but the judge ordered the case to go to trial. The trial of Peter Sutcliffe took place in London at the Old Bailey. A consultant psychiatrist, Dr Hugo Milne, who had interviewed him in Armley Gaol, Leeds, said that Sutcliffe was suffering from paranoid schizophrenia. He believed that he had a mission from God to kill prostitutes. He said a voice had first come to him from a cross over a grave. "It was an echoing voice, vague and distant..."

The prosecution pointed out that several of his victims were *not* prostitutes, but perfectly respectable young women. Besides, Sutcliffe had been interviewed six times after his arrest before mentioning any divinely-inspired mission, and had said at one point that he thought his urge to kill women had been caused by a motor-cycle accident when he had struck his head on a telegraph pole and been knocked unconscious. Furthermore, it was alleged that he had been overheard telling his wife during a prison visit that if he could prove he was a 'loony', he would get away with 10 years.

The jury rejected the suggestion of insanity, in spite of the unanimous testimony of three psychiatrists that he was a paranoid schizophrenic. Sutcliffe was sentenced on 22 May 1981 to life imprisonment for each of the 13 counts of murder, and the judge recommended that he should serve at least 30 years before any question of his release be considered. He was sent to Parkhurst Prison on the Isle of Wight. He had been there nearly three years when it was announced that he was being removed to Broadmoor. His deteriorating mental condition had made him a potential danger to prison staff and other inmates. Doctors at both Parkhurst and Broadmoor had diagnosed Sutcliffe as a paranoid schizophrenic.

The Hillside Strangler

In the fall of 1977, a series of rapes and murders occurred in California: nine young women and girls were found dead in the hills above Los Angeles and at other sites in the city. The murderer was promptly dubbed the 'Hillside Strangler', but forensic tests told police that the women, whose bodies were left bound and naked, had been raped by two men. The youngest victim was a 12 year-old schoolgirl, Dolores Cepeda. The last victim of the year, a call-girl named Kimberley Martin, had been heard screaming by Kenneth Bianchi, a tenant in the apartment block she was visiting. In February 1978, a car which had been pushed over a cliff-edge was found to contain the body of another victim, a young waitress called Cindy Huspeth.

Then Kenneth Bianchi turned up again near the Canadian border at Bellingham in Washington state. Two girls were murdered there after being hired as caretakers, and the man who had hired them was Bianchi. Although he denied any connection with the girls when police interviewed him, clear evidence linked him with them and he was arrested as a murder suspect.

Bianchi, who was 26 years old, then claimed that he was suffering from a split personality. His alter ego was called 'Steve', and it was he who committed crimes over which Kenneth had no control. The claim was supported by psychologists. A hearing in October 1979, however, declared that Bianchi was sane, and his assumed mental illness just a sham. Bianchi was faced with the distinct possibility of a death sentence in Washington for two murders he had committed alone. As police in Los Angeles suspected him of involvement in the 10 murders there, he opted to accept immunity from a capital conviction in return for testifying in California against his partner in crime there, his cousin Angelo Buono.

Buono was 17 years older than Bianchi, and a brutal drunkard. The two had gone into partnership as pimps, and graduated to rape and murder, descending deep into sexual depravity until Buono had tired of Bianchi and persuaded him to go back to his common-law wife in Washington.

The trial of Angelo Buono lasted for two years, ending in 1983, and was the longest criminal trial in US history. It cost millions of dollars, and involved 400 witnesses. Bianchi himself spent five months in the witness box. Buono's defence attorney accused Bianchi of committing all the murders himself, and only implicating his cousin in order to secure immunity from the death penalty. Bianchi then withdrew his confession to even the Bellingham murders, and protested that he was completely innocent.

Buono was convicted and sentenced to nine terms of life imprisonment. Bianchi was judged to have violated the terms of his plea bargain, and was returned to Washington state to serve life imprisonment where the climate, as well as the prison regime, is less comfortable than in sunny California.

Fact

The youngest person to suffer the death penalty in Britain in the years immediately before abolition was Francis Forsyth, leader of a gang of four who attacked and fatally injured a man in the so-called 'Hounslow Footpath' murder in 1960. Two of the gang - Forsyth and Norman Harris - were executed, at Wandsworth and Pentonville respectively, on 10 November 1960. Harris was 28, Forsyth 18. Terence Lutt, 17, was too young to be sentenced to death, and Christopher Darby, 20, was not convicted of 'capital' murder under the terms of the 1957 Homicide Act. James Farrell, who murdered his 14 year-old girl-friend, was also 18 when he was hanged in March 1949. Of the twenty-nine persons executed in England and Wales in the nine years between the passing of the Homicide Act (1957) and suspension of the death penalty (1965) four were between the ages of 18 and 20 inclusive.

Unlucky Find

When two peat-cutters working at Lindow Moss, near Wilmslow, Cheshire, uncovered the partly decomposed head of a middle-aged woman on Friday 13 May 1983, police thought that the riddle of a person who had gone missing nearly 23 years earlier had probably been solved. They reported the find to Mr Peter Reyn-Bardt, a former BOAC executive at Manchester's Ringway airport, now living in London, whose wife Malika had vanished in 1960. Faced with this discovery, he confessed to her murder. He had strangled her, hacked her body to pieces with an axe, and buried the remains in the grounds of a cottage he lived in at the time at Wilmslow. He had married Malika Maria de Fernandez to hide his homosexuality. He was tried at Chester, convicted, and sentenced to life imprisonment. But the head dug up in the peat-bog was not Mrs Reyn-Bardt's.

After his confession, Reyn-Bardt was taken to the site to point out to police exactly where he had buried his wife. But a search failed to reveal

Fact

John Ellis, who executed 18 year-old pantry-boy Henry Jacoby at Pentonville in June 1922, for the murder of Lady White at Spencer's Hotel, was reported to have said afterwards: "I saw t'poor lad the day before his death. He was nobbut a child. It was t'most harrowing sight I ever saw in my life. And I 'ad to kill him t'next day.' The jury had made a strong recommendation for mercy at Jacoby's trial.

more remains, and the skull was then sent to Oxford University for radiocarbon dating. The laboratory reported that the head was that of a woman aged between 30 and 50, and that she had died around 410 AD during the last years of the Roman occupation.

In the following year, a more complete corpse, this time male, was found in the same vicinity, preserved in the peat like bodies in other parts of northern Europe. This one was more clearly a victim of violence. There was evidence of blows to the head having split the skull, as well as a stab wound, and there was a garotte round the neck in the form of a knotted thong. The man may have been killed as a ritual sacrifice. 'Pete Marsh', as he was whimsically nicknamed, had died around 300 BC. Lindow Moss had yielded Britain's earliest known murder victim, and Reyn-Bardt had confessed to murder on the discovery of a prehistoric corpse.

Summer Madness

Patrick Henry Sherrill, a 44 year-old former US Marine, had been working part-time at the post office in Edmond, near Oklahoma City, for about a year and a half when he arrived there on the morning of 20 August 1986. At a few minutes past 7 a.m., all hell broke loose as he suddenly shot a supervisor with a pistol, and then continued shooting his fellow-workers. By the time he stopped firing, 14 men and women were dead and several others wounded. It had all taken less than 10 minutes.

Police marksmen surrounded the post office and a trained negotiator attempted to talk the killer into surrendering, but Sherrill refused to listen. When police finally stormed the building, Sherrill shot himself through the head.

He had gone to the post office that morning with the deliberate intention of killing the people there. He had taken three guns and plenty of ammunition, and locked the doors when he got inside so that no one could escape. Sherrill was a solitary individual whom neighbours and colleagues had identified as someone with a violent temper and a mental problem. He was also known as a peeping tom. On the previous day, he had been threatened with dismissal for not pulling his weight. "They'll be sorry", he had told a young woman, "and everyone's gonna know about it".

This type of mass murder with firearms is a peculiarly American problem. Cases in other countries—like that of Michael Ryan who went on an armed rampage through Hungerford in Berkshire in the following year, killing 16 people—are exceedingly rare. North America had already suffered the recent case of James Huberty, who shot 20 people dead in California in 1984; and it was not long after Sherrill's crime before Ronald Simmons, formerly of the US Air Force, shot 16 in Arkansas in 1987. Then came Marc Lepine in Canada, shooting 14 students at Montreal University in 1989, and George Hennard, who took a record 22 lives in a Texas cafeteria in 1991.

Society should clearly be wary of men—especially ex-servicemen—with a consuming interest in firearms, particularly during the summer months. The mass murders by Huberty, Sherrill and Ryan were all committed in July or August. It was also August when Charles Whitman, a former Marine, shot 17 people at Austin, Texas in 1966; and July when Christian Dornier shot 14 in France in 1989. It seems that these eruptions of violence are triggered off by the pressure of guilt, arguably sexual in origin, in men who are usually loners. Such men whose reason suddenly snaps are likely to begin their killing sprees with close relatives before turning their weapons on strangers. Whitman, Ryan and Dornier all shot their mothers. Whitman also shot his wife, as did Simmons, along with his children and grandchildren. Dornier also shot his sister.

Another September massacre has occurred in France. Eric Borel, 16 years old, shot dead eight innocent people and seriously wounded several others at Cuers, near Toulon, on 24 September 1995. He went on a rampage through the village, armed with a rifle, after beating three members of his family to death. True to type, he ended by killing himself. Death toll: 12, and expected to rise. On 13 March 1996, Thomas Hamilton shot dead a teacher and 16 pupils at the County Primary School in Dunblane, Scotland; and a few weeks later, on 28 April, Martin Bryant, 28 years old, killed 35 people in a shooting massacre at Port Arthur, Tasmania.

Ryan, Lepine and Hennard, as well as Sherrill, and Hamilton, all ended by shooting themselves. Whitman and Huberty were shot by police. Dornier was found insane and unfit to stand trial. Only Simmons and Bryant were brought to trial and convicted of murder. Simmons was executed by lethal injection in June 1990.

Fact

In Anglo-Saxon England, every man had his Wergild, *or life-value. If he were killed, his murderer had to pay this amount in compensation, either to the victim's master (the lord of the manor) if he were a serf; or to his next of kin if he were a free man.*

Cromwell Street

On 26 February 1994, police in Gloucester began searching a three-storey terraced house and its garden in Cromwell Street, the home of Frederick West, a 52 year-old builder, and his wife Rosemary. By 6 March they had found the remains of six young women and girls. Over the next few days, further remains were being unearthed at the rate of one a day, and it was reported that other sites, in the city and elsewhere, were also to be searched. At 25 Cromwell Street, three sets of remains were recovered from the garden, one from the ground-floor bathroom, and five from the cellar. Press speculation included stories of strangulation and dismemberment, and the case seemed reminiscent of the discoveries at 10 Rillington Place in London more than 40 years earlier. Police were aided in their search of the Gloucester premises by a seismic radar scanner which had been developed to locate buried mines after the Falklands war of 1982.

West was charged early in March with the murders of three women whose remains had already been identified. One of them was his daughter Heather, born to Rosemary in 1970, two years before they were married. The girl had vanished when she was 16 years old. Several other young women who had disappeared from the region over the past quarter of a century were soon feared to be among the victims being

Fact

When an ageing German prostitute, Marie Hermann, was tried at the Old Bailey in 1894 for the murder of 70 year-old cab-driver Henry Stevens, her conviction seemed a foregone conclusion. Stevens's battered corpse had been found in a trunk in her possession, and £50 was missing from his pockets. But Frau Hermann was represented by a young barrister conducting the defence in a murder trial for the first time. His name was Edward Marshall Hall, and he persuaded the jury that Stevens had forced himself on his client without paying, as she had claimed, and then attempted to strangle her. She had struck him with a poker in self-defence. Marie Hermann was convicted of manslaughter, and given a short prison sentence.

unearthed. Among them were West's first wife, Catherine, and their daughter, Charmaine.

The task of identifying the remains was in the hands of Bernard Knight, Professor of Forensic Pathology at the University of Wales Medical College in Cardiff. Professor Knight employed the relatively new technique of DNA profiling, using bone marrow to establish the age, sex and physical characteristics of the victims. On 10 March, Frederick West was charged with five more murders.

Police investigations moved on to a house in Midland Road, Gloucester, where the Wests had lived before moving to Cromwell Street, and a field near the village of Much Marcle in Hereford and Worcester, where West had once lived. The number of bodies recovered grew to 12, and it seemed a reasonably safe bet that the name of Frederick West, who was being held on remand at Birmingham's Winson Green prison, was soon to be added to the list of Britain's most prolific convicted multiple murderers, only giving way in recent history to Dennis Nilsen and Peter Sutcliffe. But on New Year's Day, 1995, it was announced that Frederick West had been found hanged in his prison cell.

Rosemary West, who had denied any knowledge of, or involvement in, the crimes for which her husband had been charged, was herself charged with 10 murders. Her trial opened at Winchester Crown Court in October 1995 and lasted nearly eight weeks. Fred and Rose West were a couple with excessive and perverted sexual appetites, and Rose was bisexual. They picked up their victims together and subjected them to appalling sexual assault and torture. One of the first prosecution witnesses was a woman who described how, as a teenager in 1972, she had been subjected to a terrifying sexual assault by the Wests, and afterwards went to the police. The Wests were charged with indecent assault and actual bodily harm on that occasion, but not with rape, and they got off with fines of £50 imposed by a local magistrate.

The court heard tape recordings of Frederick West being interviewed by police, in which he said that his wife had no part in any of the murders. But Charmaine West had been murdered in 1971, when Fred was in prison for theft. Rosemary had dumped the body in the coal cellar of the house in Midland Road so that Fred could deal with it when he was released.

The jury retired to consider its verdicts on 20 November. Next day, Rosemary West was unanimously declared guilty of three murders—those of her 16 year-old daughter Heather, 8 year-old stepdaughter Charmaine, and Shirley Robinson, an 18 year-old lodger who was pregnant by Fred West. The remains of the eight month-old foetus were found buried beside Shirley's dismembered remains at Cromwell Street. Rosemary West had denied even knowing Shirley, but her diary entries were found noting, "Shirley paid rent". By lunch-time on 22 November, the jury had convicted her of the remaining seven murders with which she was charged.

In sentencing Rosemary West to life imprisonment on each count, Mr Justice Mantell told her: "If attention is paid to what I think, you will never be released". The Home Secretary informed Rosemary West in 1997 that she would spend the rest of her life in prison.

The West murders comprised the most horrific case in Britain of sexual serial killing involving children since the notorious Moors murder trial nearly 30 years earlier. Questions were immediately asked about whether police and social services in Gloucester might have prevented many of the deaths if only they had shown more curiosity and sagacity about missing girls who were known to have visited the house in Cromwell Street which was occupied by convicted sex offenders. Television discussions also evinced some startlingly naïve disbelief among female journalists and others that a woman could descend to such evil.

Britain's most Prolific Murderers

Name	Motive	Method	Known victims	Fate of murderer and year
Thomas Hamilton	Crazed rampage	Firearm	17	Committed suicide before arrest, 1996
Burke and Hare	Financial gain	Suffocation	16	Burke hanged, 1829; Hare released after turning King's Evidence
Michael Ryan	Crazed rampage	Shooting	16	Committed suicide before arrest, 1987
Dr William Palmer	Financial gain	Poison	? 14	Executed by hanging, 1856
Mary Ann Cotton	Financial gain	Poison	? 14	Executed by hanging, 1873
Peter Sutcliffe	Sexual murders of women	Bludgeoning and stabbing	13	Life imprisonment, 1981
Dennis Nilsen	Homosexual murders	Strangulation or drowning	? 12	Life imprisonment, 1983
Frederick West	Sexual murders of young women & girls	Strangulation	? 12+	Committed suicide before trial, 1994
Rosemary West	As above	As above	10	Life imprisonment, 1995
Peter Manuel	Sadistic pleasure	Shooting or strangulation	9	Executed by hanging, 1958
'Jack the Stripper' (The 'Thames Nudes' murderer)	Sexual murders of prostitutes	Asphyxiation	8	Unsolved - chief suspect committed suicide, 1965
John Christie	Sexual murders of women	Strangulation	6	Executed by hanging, 1953
Gordon Frederick Cummings	Sexual murder and robbery of women	Strangulation	? 6	Executed by hanging, 1942
John George Haigh	Financial gain	Shooting	? 6	Executed by hanging, 1949
Jack the Ripper	Sexual murders of women	Strangulation	? 5	Unknown (1888)
Ian Brady and Myra Hindley	Sadistic killing of children	Bludgeoning and strangulation	5	Life imprisonment, 1966
Jeremy Bamber	Murdered own family to inherit fortune	Shooting	5	Life imprisonment, 1986

Note: It is certain that Amelia Dyer (see case history) should rank high among the most prolific British murderers, but as we do not know how many babies she killed, she cannot be included in the table with any confidence. Mary Ann Cotton is sometimes credited (if that is the word) with up to 20 murders, but she was convicted of only one, and there is no certainty about the true number of her victims.

Some Prolific Multiple Murderers in Countries of the Western World

(Note: these are noted examples of multiple murder, not necessarily national records)

Men

Country	Name	Victims	Motive	Method	Fate of murderer and year
Ecuador	Pedro Alonzo Lopez	? 300	Sexual murders of young girls	Strangulation	Life imprisonment, 1980
USA	Herman Mudgett (H.H. Holmes)	100 +	Financial gain and sadistic pleasure	Gas	Executed by hanging, 1896
France	Gilles de Rais	? 120	Sexual murders of children	Stabbing	Executed by strangulation, 1440
Germany	Bruno Ludke	? 85	Sexual murders	Stabbing or	Died in hospital (Vienna), 1944 strangulation
Russia	Andrei Chikatilo	55 +	Sexual killing of young people of both sexes	Strangulation	Executed by firearm, 1994
Australia	Martin Bryant	35	Crazed rampage	Firearm	Life imprisonment
Poland	Lucian Staniak	26	Teenage girls for sexual purposes	Stabbing or strangulation	Sentenced to death, but committed to asylum on being found insane, 1967
Hungary	Bela Kiss	23 +	Financial gain	Garotting	Reported killed in action (1916) but believed still alive in 1932. Never traced
Norway	Arnfinn Nesset	22 +	Elderly patients in nursing homes, for embezzlement	Poison	Imprisoned for 21 years, 1983
Austria	Max Gufler	? 18	Murdered women for financial gain	Drugging and drowning	Life imprisonment, 1961
Canada	Clifford Olsen	11 +	Sexual killing of young people	Stabbing or strangulation	Life imprisonment, 1982
Women					
Hungary	Elizabeth Bathory	? 600	Vampirism on young women	Bloodletting	Died in captivity, 1614
USA	Bella Gunness	? 100	Financial gain	Axe	Killed by farm hand, 1908
Germany	Anna Maria Zwanziger	? 85	Revenge	Poison	Executed by beheading, 1811
Romania	Vera Renczi	35	Murdered husband and lovers as she tired of them, and kept corpses in cellar	Poison	Life imprisonment. Died in prison, early 20th century
Belgium	Marie Becker	11	Mostly women for financial gain	Poison	Life imprisonment, Died in prison 1936.
France	Jeanne Weber	? 11	Children for sadistic pleasure	Strangulation	Committed to asylum, 1908
Austria	Martha Marek	6	Financial gain	Poison	Executed by beheading, 1938

Section 2: Assassination

Assassination is the extreme form of censorship.
George Bernard Shaw: *The Shewing-up of Blanco Posnet*

ASSASSINATION IS A DANGEROUS WORD; it lends to acts of murder overtones of dignity, and even virtue, to which they have no entitlement. By glamorizing certain murders or attempted murders, it doubtless increases its appeal to some disturbed individuals who set out to shed VIP blood.

Assassination is perhaps best distinguished from common murder as a form of illegal homicide by regarding it as an act carried out by, or at the behest of, one or more people acting from political or religious motives. By far the most common targets of assassins are heads of state. Kings and emperors are potential sacrificial targets because of what they *are* (as are republican heads of state as royal surrogates), whereas mere politicians become targets because of what they *do*.

Assassins usually maintain, rightly or wrongly, that they are acting in the interests of the people. Thus the assassins of Julius Caesar claimed that they had eliminated a dictator for the sake of Rome's future and the liberty of its citizens. But assassination has been proved over and over again throughout the centuries, except in a few cases of tyrannicide, to be a mistaken concept, often resulting in precisely the opposite effect to that planned. "Assassination", Disraeli said, "has never changed the history of the world". This is a debatable assertion, but it is true that assassination has never changed the world in the way the assassins intended. The short-term result of Caesar's assassination was civil war, and the long-term one was that Rome succumbed under the emperors to greater tyranny, bloodshed, vice and corruption than ever before. Brutus, Cassius and their fellow-conspirators had mistaken the man for the movement, and thought that by killing the individual they would kill the idea he represented. It has been a common error of assassins throughout the ages.

Great Britain is not notable for assassination, but one of the world's most famous instances of it occurred here in December 1170 when the Archbishop of Canterbury, Thomas Becket, was murdered in Canterbury Cathedral. Becket, formerly the close friend of Henry II, had become the king's opponent in disputes between Church and State. He exasperated the king to such an extent that Henry's temper finally exploded into the famous incitement, "Will no one rid me of this turbulent priest?" Four barons took the hint, and Becket died horribly under the blows of their swords and an axe. There was a storm of protest throughout Christendom. The king acknowledged that his unguarded outburst had been the cause of the murder, and did public penance. The assassination helped to secure the supremacy of Canon over Common Law in England for more than four centuries.

The incidence of assassination throughout the world increasing with the growing availability of firearms. The musket used to kill the Earl of Moray, Regent of Scotland, in 1570, and the pistol used in an attempt on

Fact

Queen Victoria was the target of several assassination attempts. Gladstone told the Queen that whereas assassins in other countries had political motives, in England they were always madmen. There was some justification for this view, though it cannot have been particularly comforting for the Queen. Margaret Nicholson and James Hadfield, failing in separate attempts to kill George III, had both been declared insane, and John Bellingham, the man who shot Spencer Perceval, the only British Prime Minister to be assassinated, was undoubtedly out of his mind, though he was hanged for it. The two most serious would-be assassins of Queen Victoria were Edward Oxford and Roderick Maclean, both committed to Broadmoor after attempts on her life in 1840 and 1882 respectively.

the life of William of Orange in 1582, were the precursors of a new method of assassination challenged in effectiveness only by the increasing use of terrorist bombs in the 20th century. The gun culture of America makes firearms the universally favoured means of assassination there. The tables in the following pages show attempted assassinations in the USA compared with notable cases in the rest of the world during a similar period.

Fact

The world record for assassination plots against a modern head of state dates from the years 1944-66, when no less than 31 plots were hatched against the French president, Charles de Gaulle. Most of the plots were on behalf of the Algerian FLN (Front de la Libération Nationale). Between 1961 and 1965, 17 attempts were made on his life. Not all the other plots resulted in actual attempts to kill him, but over the years bombs, grenades, dynamite, machine-guns, high-powered rifles, revolvers, cyanide pellets and booby-trapped dogs were employed in attempts to eliminate the President, who dismissed worries about his safety with the order to his police: "I am doing my job. You do yours. De Gaulle is not going to be kept in a glass case".

Case Histories

Jean Paul Marat

Modern history is often said to begin with the French Revolution, and the murder of Jean Paul Marat may therefore be called the first famous assassination of modern times. Marat, the Jacobin hero of the people and champion of universal suffrage, had contracted a painful and putrefying skin disease called prurigo whilst hiding in cellars and sewers during the turmoil in Paris which led to the declaration of the republic. His body was covered in running sores and gave off a repellent stench of decay. He could obtain relief only by sitting in a warm bath, covered in towels.

On 13 July 1793 he was in his bath at his residence, 44 rue de l'Ecole, when a Madame d'Armans was admitted into his presence. She had come, she told his servants, to bring him information about the treasonable activities of the Jacobins' political opponents, the Girondists. Citizen Marat began to make notes as his visitor spoke, and as he did so, Madame d'Armans drew a knife and plunged it into his chest, piercing a lung and severing the aorta. "A moi, chère amie!" Marat cried, and the assailant was quickly overpowered by those who rushed to his aid, but they were too late to save Marat.

The assassin was Marie Anne Charlotte Corday d'Armans, a Girondist. She was 25 years old. She claimed that she had "killed one man to save a hundred thousand; a villain to save innocents; a savage wild beast to give repose to my country". But she was mistaken. It was a symbolic sacrifice which achieved nothing, and probably did more harm than if Marat had been left alive. He was seen henceforth as a martyr of the revolution, and his murder contributed to the unleashing of the Terror, which resulted in the deaths of tens of thousands.

The woman who became popularly known as Charlotte Corday, the 'angel of the assassination', was executed by guillotine in the Place de la Revolution four days after the killing.

Abraham Lincoln

The 16th President of the United States and his wife, Mary, decided to spend the evening of Good Friday, 14 April 1865, at Ford's Theatre in Washington, to see a performance of *Our American Cousin*, a play by Tom Taylor. The theatre visit was in the nature of a celebration. The President had begun his second term of office six weeks earlier, and on 9 April, the Civil War had ended with the surrender of the Confederate forces under General Robert E. Lee.

Major Henry Rathbone and his fiancée Clara Harris were Mr and Mrs Lincoln's guests for the occasion, and they sat at the front of the box, with the President and his wife behind them. Lincoln's bodyguard, John F. Parker, a police officer on the White House staff, was supposed to be sitting in the foyer outside the door of the President's box, but he deserted his post and went to the bar for a drink during the third act of the comedy. During his absence a man opened the door, stepped into the box, and shot the President in the head with a Derringer pistol at point blank range. Major Rathbone tried to overpower the assailant, but was seriously wounded in his arm by a slash from a knife. As the performance stopped, amid great commotion, the assassin cried *"Sic semper tyrranis!"* (Thus die tyrants!), and leapt on to the stage, but caught a spur in the curtain as he jumped and crashed to the boards fracturing an ankle. Nevertheless, in all the shock and confusion, he succeeded in making his escape.

People in the theatre were screaming. The President, unconscious but still alive, was carried to a house across the street to await the arrival of doctors. The ball had penetrated his brain and lodged behind his right eye. He survived for some hours, but died just after 7 a.m. the next morning. He was 56.

The assassin was John Wilkes Booth, an actor. His father had acted at Covent Garden and Drury Lane before emigrating to America, and his brother, Edwin Booth, was the first American actor to gain an international reputation as a tragedian. But there was a history of mental illness in the family. Booth claimed that he was avenging the Confederacy, and appeared to believe that Lincoln intended to proclaim himself king, having rigged the voting to get himself re-elected. Booth did not act alone, but was the instigator of a conspiracy to kill Vice-President Andrew Johnson and Secretary of State William Seward, as well as Lincoln. But Booth's associates were a motley crew of malcontents, and the other two planned assassinations were botched.

After a pursuit by Union troops, Booth was shot dead in a barn 12 days later. It is not known for certain whether he was killed by his own hand or by a soldier. Four others were hanged, and three more sentenced to hard labour for life, including Dr Samuel Mudd, whose only connection with the affair was that he had treated Booth's injured leg during his bid for freedom.

Fact

More often than not, assassination is murder in public, and several modern assassination attempts have been captured on film and seen on television. Film of the killing of President Kennedy, taken by a spectator, Abraham Zapruder, has featured largely in debates about what actually happened. The first assassination to be filmed was that of King Alexander of Yugoslavia in Marseilles in 1934. A newsreel cameraman recorded the whole scene, in which the French Foreign Minister, M Barthou, was also killed.

Fact

In 1917, a feeble plot was made to assassinate the British Prime Minister, Lloyd-George, by three conscientious objectors who held him responsible for the enormous loss of life during the war. Alice Wheeldon, a suffragette from Derby, and her daughter Winnie and son-in-law Alfred Mason, planned to kill him with curare, injected by means of nails in his shoes or pins in his hat, whilst he was playing golf. They were each sentenced to 10 years penal servitude for conspiracy to commit murder.

The Phoenix Park Murders

In May 1882, Lord Frederick Cavendish, the newly-appointed Secretary of State for Ireland, walked through Dublin's Phoenix Park in the company of the Permanent Under-Secretary, Thomas Burke, en route for the official residence, the Viceregal Lodge. Entirely unprotected, they walked into an ambush. Suddenly, four men leapt out of hiding and one of them drove a long abbatoir knife into Mr Burke's back. Another then cut his throat. Lord Cavendish tried to come to Burke's aid, and he, too, was stabbed to death. Both men were savagely mutilated with surgical knives.

The killers were Irish nationalists calling themselves Invincibles, and Mr Burke had been the principal target of their attack. He was an Irish Catholic loyal to the Crown's representative at Dublin Castle, and was known as a 'castle rat'. But the murder was an example of an entirely counter-productive terrorist assassination. It served only to harden the attitude of the English towards the Irish. A £10,000 reward was offered for information leading to the apprehension of the killers, and it was made known that any participant in the conspiracy who informed on the others would be granted immunity from prosecution.

Long and painstaking investigation by police eventually led to the arrests of 27 men, three of whom turned informers. The man who stabbed Burke, one Brady, and the one who cut his throat, named Kelly, were hanged, along with three others named Curley, Fagan and Caffrey. The other conspirators received long terms of imprisonment. One of the informers, the prosecution's chief witness, was James Carey who had been leader of the gang. He was shipped to South Africa after the trial for his own safety, but was soon shot dead there by an Irish nationalist named O'Donnell.

Archduke Franz Ferdinand

The Archduke Franz Ferdinand, Habsburg heir to the Austro-Hungarian throne, was on an official visit to Sarajevo, the capital of Bosnia, in the course of attending army manoeuvres. The Archduke was Inspector-General of the empire's armed forces. He was accompanied by his wife, Sophie von Chotkova, Duchess of Hohenberg. The date was 28 June 1914.

Franz Ferdinand hated the claustrophobic attention of personal bodyguards. Security arrangements were practically non-existent as the Archduke and Duchess made their way to the town hall for a reception. Suddenly, a grenade was thrown at their open carriage, but it missed the target and exploded under the car behind, wounding three officers and several spectators. The unharmed Archduke, showing great courage, insisted on stopping and supervising the attention to the wounded. Then he resumed his programme, and was greeted at the town hall by a ridiculously inappropriate speech of welcome from the Lord Mayor.

The next stage of the progress was supposed to be an official lunch, but the Archduke first insisted on visiting a badly injured officer in hospital. Sophie was equally insistent that she would go with him. For safety's sake, there was a change to the planned route, but some confusion about the new plan led the Archduke's chauffeur to take a wrong turn. He reversed in order to resume the correct route, and as he did so, a man stepped forward and fired two shots with a Browning revolver. The first bullet hit the Duchess, passing through the bodywork of the car. The second hit Franz Ferdinand in the neck and passed through his jugular vein into his spine. He, more concerned for his wife, told his aides, "It is nothing", and managed to gasp, "Sopherl! Sopherl! Don't die! Keep alive for our children!" But blood spurted from his mouth, and both he and his wife were dead within a few minutes.

The assassin was Gavrilo Princip, a 19 year-old student. Having achieved his aim, he attempted to shoot himself, but failed. He claimed at first that he had acted alone, but eventually admitted to a conspiracy. He saw the Archduke as a personification of the hated Habsburgs who held the Serbs in subjection, but he had not intended to kill the Duchess.

Princip and his young friends, who wanted the union of Serbs and Croats in an independent nation, had been financed and supplied with their arms and ammunition by a secret organisation known as the Black Hand. The Austrians thought the Serbian government had instigated the plot, and declared war on Serbia a month after the assassination, believing that Russia would not interfere on Serbia's behalf. They were wrong. Russia and Germany aligned themselves with the opposing sides, mobilized their forces, and WWI was set in motion.

The assassination of Archduke Franz Ferdinand was not the *cause* of the war; it merely provided an excuse for the first shots in a political situation that was leading to war in any case. The Habsburg Empire was brought to an end, and Yugoslavia was brought into being after the war.

Princip did not live to see it. He was sentenced to 20 years hard labour because he was too young for the death penalty to be imposed, but he died in Theresienstadt prison near Vienna in April 1916, having contracted tuberculosis. Three older conspirators were hanged, and several younger ones imprisoned.

Princip had predicted that he would become a national hero, and the old Latein Bridge over the River Miljacka in Sarajevo was renamed after him. But hardly had the assassins' dream of union between Serbs and Croats been realised before the Croats began to demand independence from the Serbs, and the consequences of the affair have lasted throughout the 20th century.

Fact

Julius Caesar may have been warned by a Roman soothsayer to beware the Ides of March, but it would appear that November is the month in modern times when VIPs should be most on their guard against assassins. Among those assassinated during November have been Sir Lee Stack Pasha, Governor General of Sudan, in 1924; Prime Minister Hamaguchi of Japan in 1930; the king of Afghanistan in 1933; Ngo Dinh Diem, President of South Vietnam, and President John F. Kennedy, in 1963; General Vaidya, Indian Chief of Staff, in 1986; President Moawad of Lebanon in 1989; and Itzhak Rabin in 1995. The first attempt on Hitler's life occurred in Munich in November 1939, and an attempt was made on the life of Pope Paul VI in November 1970. Mrs Indira Gandhi, Prime Minister of India, was killed on the last day of October, 1984.

Leon Trotsky

Lev Davidovich Bronstein became world-famous under his alias, Trotsky, as a founder with Lenin of the USSR, and creator of the Red Army. He was a powerful and influential revolutionary theorist, and

Fact

Among the most tragic of political assassinations was that of William, Count of Nassau and Prince of Orange, known to history as William the Silent. He was the heroic leader of The Netherlands' fight for freedom from Spanish domination. Balthazar Gerard, a fanatical French Catholic, shot him at Delft on 10 July 1584, having inveigled himself into the Prince's service by pretending to be a loyal Calvinist. William had given him money to buy himself shoes and clothing, but instead he bought two pistols from one of the Prince's own guards. Gerard was executed, but Philip of Spain rewarded his parents for their son's deed. The killing achieved nothing. The architect of the Dutch Republic was mourned by a grieving nation. "As long as he lived," the historian J.L. Motley wrote, "he was the guiding star of a whole brave nation, and when he died the little children cried in the streets."

president of the first Soviet in St Petersburg. But after the death of Lenin in 1924, Trotsky fell foul of Stalin in the latter's ruthless bid for power, and was ousted from the politburo and exiled. He moved from country to country for several years, agitating against Stalin, until in 1937 he settled with his wife in Mexico.

Trotsky's secretary, Erwin Wolf, was murdered in Spain in that year, and in 1938, the headless corpse of Rudolf Clement, secretary of Trotsky's Fourth International, was dragged out of the Seine in Paris. Trotsky's son, Lev, also died in suspicious circumstances in hospital. Well aware that he himself was a marked man, Trotsky built a veritable fortress, with high enclosure walls of concrete, at Coyoacán near Mexico City. Here he continued to write widely-read and influential attacks on Stalin's regime.

Stalin, having made the mistake of putting Trotsky beyond his reach, feared that his old rival would become the focus of a concerted effort from abroad to displace him. It is virtually certain that he ordered Beria, the chief of the secret police (NKVD) to have Trotsky eliminated by any means possible.

One day in May 1940, an assault party of 20 men forced their way into Trotsky's house. They burst into his bedroom with sub-machine-guns and sprayed the sleeping figure on the bed with bullets, after cutting telephone and alarm wires, and quickly made their escape, throwing a few incendiary bombs for good measure. But Trotsky was not under the bed covers. Ever alert to danger, he had heard an unusual scuffle downstairs, and had quickly stuffed bedding under the blankets and hidden in a wardrobe.

On 20 August, Trotsky was in his garden chatting to a friendly journalist, Frank Jacson, and after a few minutes they went indoors to discuss an article Jacson had written. As the 61 year-old revolutionary sat reading at his desk, Jacson, standing behind him, drew a mountaineer's ice-axe from beneath the trench-coat he had kept over his arm, and brought the steel head crashing down on Trotsky's skull.

Trotsky screamed out and rose from his chair, grasping at Jacson and biting his hand as his wife and aides rushed in. The guards would have killed Jacson instantly if the blood-drenched Trotsky had not forbidden it. He wanted this man to talk. Rushed to hospital, Trotsky, who believed he had been shot, was operated on immediately, but the blow had caused massive brain damage and he died the following day.

The man called Frank Jacson was, in fact, a fanatical 26 year-old Spanish Communist whose real name was Ramón del Rio Mercader. He was Beria's agent in an alternative plot to assassinate Trotsky. He had planned his task, it seems, with infinite skill and patience.

He had begun by seducing an American girl, Sylvia Ageloff, in Paris where she was on holiday. She too was a Communist, and her sisters, Hilda and Ruth, worked for Trotsky in Mexico. Mercader followed Sylvia to America, letting her believe he was in love with her, and then prevailed on her to go with him to Mexico and introduce him to her sisters and, of course, to Trotsky. Then he worked patiently at gaining Trotsky's trust by posing as a journalistic disciple who could be helpful to him in his work.

Mercader served nearly 20 years in prison in Mexico for his crime, during which he was made a Hero of the Soviet Union by Stalin in his absence. On his release he went first to Cuba, courtesy of Fidel Castro, then to Czechoslovakia, apparently settling in Prague.

This is the generally accepted version of Trotsky's assassination. Much doubt has been cast on the story over the years, not least because Mercader seems to have been an almost incredible choice as a potential assassin. When he killed Trotsky, he had a loaded revolver in his pocket and a dagger sewn into the lining of his coat, but chose to strike with an ice-axe which did not kill the victim at once, saying afterwards: "I took it in my fist and, closing my eyes, I gave him a tremendous blow on the head". Stalin's hired killer had to *close his eyes* to carry out his task? Well, truth—as many pages in this book surely prove—is often stranger than fiction.

Fact

The word 'assassin' is a European version of the Arabic hassasin, *the plural of* hassas, *meaning 'hashish-eater'. The name was originally given to a sect of Shi'ite Muslim fanatics who carried out the secret elimination of the sect's enemies during the period of the Crusades. They were reputed to be doped with hashish when they set out on their murderous missions.*

Mahatma Gandhi

Just after 5 p.m. on Saturday, 30 January 1948—four days after the first anniversary of India's Independence—Mohandas Gandhi, the father of modern India, walked across the lawn of Birla House in Delhi where he was staying to attend an open-air prayer meeting. Crowds surged around him as he walked slowly, his frail figure supported by two young women. The 78 year-old Mahatma was recovering from one of the fasts which had brought him close to death.

A young man stepped forward into Gandhi's path and raised his joined hands in Hindu greeting, and Gandhi responded in like manner. Then the man pulled a revolver from his clothing and fired three shots, hitting Gandhi in the abdomen, chest and groin. Gandhi gasped, *"He Ram! He Ram!"* (Oh God! Oh God!) as he fell, joining his hands in a gesture of prayer. Within half an hour he was dead.

The first reaction to the event was that the man Hindus called 'Bapu' (Father) had been murdered by a Muslim. The Governor General of India, Lord Mountbatten, heard a man shout out that a Muslim had done it, and had the presence of mind to retort that it was a Hindu, even before he knew the facts. It was as well for India and Pakistan that he proved to be right. The assassin was Nathuram Vinayak Godse, a Brahman newspaper editor from Poona. Police had to rescue him from the shocked and outraged crowd and from an Indian Air Force sergeant, who proposed to shoot him dead on the spot.

Godse said that he had killed Gandhi for agreeing to the partition of India, which gave away part of the country to the Muslims. He was also deeply offended by Gandhi's expression of sympathy for Muslims subjected to Hindu violence in Delhi. He denied at first that he had any part in a conspiracy, but the existence of a plot was already known to the police. Only 10 days earlier a bomb had been thrown at Birla House, but no one had been injured. One Hindu fanatic was already in custody. The Mahatma had refused police advice and offers of protection.

Fact

The most frequently targeted religious leaders have been the Popes of Rome. John VIII in 882; Stephen VI in 897; Leo V in 904; John X in 929; Benedict VI in 974; John XIV in 984 and Urban VI in 1389 were undoubtedly victims of assassination, and several others have died in suspicious circumstances, even in modern times. Pope John Paul II was seriously wounded in an attempt on his life in 1981, when a Turkish terrorist, Mehmet Ali Agca, shot him in Rome.

"Cut me in little pieces", the chillingly unrepentant Godse exclaimed, "and I will still maintain I did right". Godse and a schoolmaster, Narayan Apte, were hanged. Gandhi would not have wished the State to take such revenge for his death. Several other extremists involved in the conspiracy were imprisoned. They included Godse's brother, Gopal. He and Vishnu Karkare, the two chief conspirators besides Nathuram Godse and Apte, remained in prison for 16 years. Many other Hindu fanatics were assaulted and one killed in revenge attacks following the Mahatma's death. But it is frightening to contemplate the scale of slaughter that would certainly have ensued if a Muslim had killed Gandhi.

John F. Kennedy

The most widely discussed and written-about assassination in history occurred in Dallas, Texas, on 22 November 1963. The killing of President John Fitzgerald Kennedy is the best-documented assassination of all time, but after 30 years, argument and speculation about the true identity of the killers and their motives still goes on.

As it appeared at the time, the President was shot in the head and neck by a high-powered rifle whilst travelling in a motorcade, and died before he reached hospital. The shots were identified as coming from the 6th floor of the Texas School Book Depository as the President's car passed the building. An hour and twenty minutes after the shooting, Lee Harvey Oswald was arrested after shooting and killing a police officer, J.D. Tippit, who had tried to detain him. Two days later, as Oswald was being transferred from the Dallas city gaol to the county gaol, he was shot dead by a local night-club owner, Jack Ruby. Ruby was convicted of murder in March 1964 and sentenced to death. But in October 1966, the Texas Court of Criminal Appeals overturned the conviction and ordered a fresh trial. Before it began, Ruby, who had attempted suicide three times, died of cancer. Thus the two men who could possibly have told us most about the Kennedy assassination were both dead.

Within days of Kennedy's death, the new President, Lyndon Johnson, appointed a commission to enquire into the assassination. It was headed by Chief Justice Earl Warren and the members included Gerald Ford, a future president, and Allen Dulles, former Director of the Central Intelligence Agency. The commission concluded that there was no evidence whatever to suggest that the President had been the victim of a conspiracy, and that Oswald was the sole assassin, acting entirely alone.

Scepticism about this conclusion was immediate and widespread. Oswald had no reputation as a crack marksman, and no apparent personal motive for wanting to kill Kennedy. One of the major points of dispute concerned the number of shots fired and the direction they had come from. Gradually a barrage of criticism was built up against the

Warren Report, which was seen either as a deliberate cover-up or as an incompetent "rush to judgement". Theories involving the CIA, the KGB, Fidel Castro and the Mafia were among those which assumed the existence of a conspiracy to murder the President.

The blaze of publicity that surrounded the assassination and its aftermath undoubtedly stimulated fantasies, and possibly imitative ambitions, in America's mentally-disturbed individuals. An adolescent boy "gave himself up" to the FBI, "confessing" that he had paid Oswald to do the job.

After 13 years, such was the pressure of public doubt and dissatisfaction with the Warren Commission's conclusions that Congress set up a House of Representatives Select Committee on Assassinations, which turned the tide in official attitudes towards the killing of Kennedy by finding that he was "probably assassinated as a result of a conspiracy"; that *two* gunmen had fired at the President; and that the Warren Commission had suppressed vital evidence.

As "nature abhors a vacuum", so the mind of man is intolerant of unsolved puzzles, and the fascination of the mystery about Kennedy's killers seems destined for a long life, perhaps rivalling Jack the Ripper as a lasting challenge to compulsive seekers of solutions.

Fact

The murderer of pop-star and former Beatle John Lennon, who was gunned down on a New York street in December 1980, had been a born-again Christian at one stage of his wildy anarchic career. Mark David Chapman was an example of the well-known phenomenon of a mentally deranged character seeking recognition by killing someone famous. He was evidently much influenced by J.D. Salinger's acclaimed novel of disaffected youth, The Catcher in the Rye.

Olof Palme

A 1970 Supplementary Report to the National Commission on the Causes and Prevention of Violence (set up in 1968 by President Johnson after the murder of Senator Robert Kennedy), discussed reasons for the virtually non-existent history of assassination in modern Sweden. Way back in 1792, King Gustavus III had been shot dead in Stockholm, but there was no tradition of political violence, and the kings of Sweden had become willing figureheads instead of personal rulers. There had also been strict control over the use of firearms. (A Swedish nobleman, Count Folke Bernadotte, had been assassinated in 1948, but that occurred in the Middle East where Bernadotte was a UN mediator between Jews and Arabs in Palestine.) So much greater, therefore, was the national sense of shock when, in 1986, the Prime Minister, Olof Palme, was murdered in a Stockholm street.

Palme, 58, was the charismatic leader of the Social Democratic Party. A radical and controversial figure, he had become internationally famous when he offered asylum in Sweden to young Americans who refused to serve in the Vietnam War. More recently, he was the founder of the International Nuclear Disarmament Commission, and United Nations mediator in the Iran-Iraq war.

On 28 February 1986, Palme and his wife, Lisbeth, went to the cinema with their son and his girlfriend. Palme had dismissed his bodyguards. When they left the cinema, Mr and Mrs Palme parted from the younger couple and were walking home when a man suddenly stepped out and fired two shots at Palme with a revolver, at point blank range, and ran

ATTEMPTED ASSASSINATIONS OF US PRESIDENTS AND OTHERS

(Victims of successful attempts in capitals)

Target	Date	Place	Method	Assassin(s)	Fate of Assassin(s)
Andrew Jackson	1835	Washington	Firearm	Richard Lawrence	Committed to mental institution
ABRAHAM LINCOLN	1865	Washington	"	John Wilkes Booth	Shot dead before trial
JAMES GARFIELD	1881	Washington	"	Charles Guiteau	Executed by hanging
WILLIAM MCKINLEY	1901	Buffalo	"	Leon Czolgosz	Executed by electric chair
Theodore Roosevelt	1912	Milwaukee	"	John Schrank	Committed to mental institution
Franklin D. Roosevelt	1933	Miami	"	Guiseppe Zangara	Executed by electric chair
Harry S. Truman	1950	Washington	"	Collazo and Torresola	Torresola shot dead before trial; Collazo sentenced to death but reprieved
JOHN F. KENNEDY	1963	Dallas	"	?Lee Harvey Oswald	Shot dead before trial
DR MARTIN LUTHER KING	1968	Memphis	"	James Earl Ray	Life imprisonment
SEN. ROBERT KENNEDY	1968	Los Angeles	"	Sirhan Bishara Sirhan	Sentenced to death but reprieved due to abolition of death penalty. Life imprisonment
Gov. George Wallace	1972	Laurel, Maryland	"	Arthur Bremer	Life imprisonment
Gerald Ford	1975	San Francisco	"	Sara Moore	Imprisonment
Ronald Reagan	1981	Washington	"	John Hinckley	Committed to mental institution

SOME CONTEMPORANEOUS ASSASSINATION ATTEMPTS IN OTHER PARTS OF THE WORLD

(Victims of successful attempts in capitals)

Target	Date	Place	Method	Assassin(s)	Fate of Assassin(s)
Emp. Franz Josef	1853	Vienna	Stabbing	Janos Libényi	?
Emp. Napoleon III	1858	Paris	Bomb	Count Orsini et al	Executed by guillotine
TSAR ALEXANDER II	1881	St Petersburg	Bomb	'People's Will' terrorists	Executed by hanging
PRES. CARNOT OF FRANCE	1894	Lyon	Stabbing	Santo Caserio	Executed by guillotine
EMP. ELIZABETH OF AUSTRIA	1898	Geneva	Stabbing	Luigi Lucheni	?
KING UMBERTO OF ITALY	1900	Monza	Firearm	Gaetano Bresci	Life imprisonment (committed suicide in prison)
King Alfonso of Spain	1906	Madrid	Dynamite	Matteo Morales	Committed suicide before capture
GRIGORI RASPUTIN	1916	St Petersburg	Poison, shooting & drowning	Prince Yussoupov et al	No punishment
WALTER RATHENAU	1922	Berlin	Grenade	Kern and Fischer	Shot in suicide pact before trial
KING ALEXANDER OF YUGOSLAVIA	1934	Marseilles	Firearm	Vlada Chernozamsky	Shot dead before trial
LEON TROTSKY	1940	Mexico City	Bludgeoned with ice axe	Ramón del Rio Mercader	20 years imprisonment
Adolf Hitler	1944	Rastenburg	Bomb	Col. von Stauffenberg	Executed by firing squad
DR HENDRIK VERWOERD	1960	Johannesburg	Stabbing	Dimitrio Tsafendas	Committed to mental institution
PRES. TRUJILLO OF DOMINICAN REPUBLIC	1961	Santo Domingo	Firearms	Military ambush	Tortured and executed
Pres. Charles de Gaulle	1962	Paris	Firearms	Lt-Col Bastien-Thiry and others	Bastien-Thiry executed by firing squad
Shah of Iran	1965	Teheran	Firearm	Abadi	Shot dead before trial
KING FAISAL OF SAUDI ARABIA	1975	Riyadh	Firearm	Prince Faisal (nephew)	Executed publicly by beheading
ALDO MORO	1978	Rome	Firearm	Red Brigade terrorists	Life imprisonment
EARL MOUNTBATTEN	1979	Mullaghmore	Bomb	Thomas McMahon	Life imprisonment
MRS INDIRA GANDHI	1984	Delhi	Firearms	Beant Singh and Satwant Singh	Beant shot dead before trial; Satwant executed by hanging.

off. There were other people about, who heard the shots, but neither they nor Lisbeth Palme got a clear look at the killer. Olof Palme was rushed to Sabbatsbergs Hospital, but died almost at once. One of the bullets had penetrated his aorta.

Despite the detention of various suspects, and an offer by the Swedish government of a reward equivalent to more than $8 million for information leading to the solution of the murder, police failed to identify the killer. Mounting criticism of their handling of the case led to resignations in both police and government offices. No individual or group has ever claimed responsibility for the killing. This is an unusual circumstance because assassins desire, above all, to draw public attention to their causes.

The authorities were desperate for a scapegoat, and in 1989 one Christer Pettersson, an unemployed labourer known as 'the bayonet man', was identified by Lisbeth Palme as the man who had shot her husband, and sentenced to life imprisonment for the murder. He had a history of mental instability and violent crime, but all his previous convictions had involved the use of a bayonet, not a firearm. Three months later, the sentence was overturned by the appeal court on the grounds that the evidence used to convict Pettersson was insufficient.

Meanwhile, rumours of bribery and corruption began to circulate. Palme had been in India a month before his death as a guest of his friend the Prime Minister, Rajiv Gandhi. A contract was then awarded by India to the ailing Swedish arms company, Bofors, in the face of strong competition from other countries, including Britain, France and the United States. Palme was posthumously awarded India's Nehru Prize for the promotion of peace and non-violence. There were allegations that Bofors had paid millions of pounds into Swiss bank accounts held by Indian politicians. There was also speculation that Palme had been doing arms deals with Iran even whilst on his UN peace mission during the Gulf War, and suspicions fell heavily on an Iraqi plot. All this remains mostly unproven, and it is uncertain whether Olof Palme was assassinated for political reasons, or murdered by some lone lunatic killer.

Palme's friend Rajiv Gandhi was himself assassinated in India in May 1991, apparently by Tamil separatists, whilst campaigning for re-election.

Fact

On 4 November 1995, Itzhak Rabin, Prime Minister of Israel and winner of the Nobel Peace Prize, was shot by a Jewish extremist in Tel Aviv, dying in hospital shortly afterwards while surgeons fought to save his life. Mr Rabin had been one of the architects of the long-hoped-for Middle East peace process.

Fact

In 1926 a firm named Cory Brothers of Bridgend, Glamorgan, was prosecuted for manslaughter when a young miner was killed by an electric fence which surrounded the premises. The fence had been erected to prevent the theft of coal by local pilferers. Brynmor John, 18, was out ratting with his mates in drizzly rain when he slipped and fell, instinctively grasping the wire in trying to break his fall, and at the same time falling with his other hand on a sheet of corrugated zinc which lay on the ground. One of his friends who attempted to pull him away from the fence by his damp clothes also received a shock. The company was initially represented by Sir Edward Marshall Hall, but he died before the case came to trial at Cardiff Assizes, and the defence was taken over by Norman Birkett. Sir Bernard Spilsbury testified that it was highly exceptional for a fit young man to be killed by an electric current of such low voltage, and that an unusual combination of circumstances had led to his death by misadventure. The company was acquitted of manslaughter.

Section 3: Manslaughter

Human blood is heavy; the man who has shed it cannot run away.
African proverb

MANSLAUGHTER IS ILLEGAL HOMICIDE in which a charge of murder cannot be sustained. It can be intentional, with malice aforethought, where a charge of murder is reduced to one of manslaughter because of extreme provocation or diminished responsibility; or involuntary, where death is caused through negligence, dangerous driving, etc. In Scotland, what English law labels manslaughter is called culpable homicide.

An example of the first type was the trial in 1984 of Peter Hogg, whose wife Margaret had disappeared in 1976. Her body was discovered accidentally in Wastwater in Cumbria whilst police were searching for another missing person. Hogg, an airline pilot, had married Margaret in 1963, and killed her 13 years later after she had openly flaunted her affair with another man. An angry row between husband and wife ended in a physical brawl during which he strangled her. He then drove through the night from their home in Cranleigh, Surrey, to the Lake District, and dumped his wife's body, weighted with concrete, into the lake from a dinghy. Charged with her murder, eight years later, he was judged to have acted under provocation which resulted in sudden loss of self-control, and was found guilty of manslaughter. Hogg was sentenced to four years imprisonment.

Such mitigating circumstances were not *always* taken into account in English law when someone was being charged with homicide. Sir William Blackstone wrote in his famous *Commentaries on the Laws of England:* "All homicide is presumed to be malicious, until the contrary appeareth upon evidence". In other words, you were guilty of murder until proved innocent.

Unintentional manslaughter embraces various types of homicide that fall short of murder. A builder working on scaffolding, who carelessly dropped a brick or a plank which killed someone walking below, would be charged with manslaughter. A surgeon whose patient died on the operating table through his negligence might be guilty of manslaughter. In neither case had the hypothetical defendant *intended* to kill the victim.

A charge of corporate manslaughter can be brought against a company or organisation which causes death by neglect. Charges of corporate manslaughter were brought—but subsequently dropped—against Townsend Thoresen, operators of the 'roll on, roll off' ferry *Herald of Free Enterprise,* which capsized in Zeebrugge harbour on 6 March 1987, with the loss of 188 lives. Of the 543 passengers on aboard the ferry, many were hurled into the icy North Sea in the worst peacetime shipping disaster in the English Channel. Although it was the company's employees on board the ship who had failed to close the bow doors before sailing, allowing water to enter the vehicle deck, the company's management was accused by the enquiry judge of "staggering complacency" in not ensuring that the ship's safety regulations were complied with. The company was ordered to pay the enquiry costs of £400,000.

Case Histories

Death in Tinsel Town

When an inquest in San Francisco considered the circumstances of 25 year-old model and aspiring actress Virginia Rappe's death from peritonitis in September 1921, the jury decided that Roscoe Arbuckle was "criminally responsible" for her death, and recommended that he should be charged with manslaughter.

Virginia had been at a party at the St Francis Hotel when guests had heard screams from a bedroom and found her undressed and moaning, "I'm dying, I'm dying". She did die three days later, after a great deal of pain and periods of unconsciousness. An autopsy showed that she had a ruptured bladder.

Roscoe Arbuckle, who had been chasing Miss Rappe without success for years, had forced her into the bedroom, torn off most of her clothes and apparently leapt on her with his full weight of 101.6 kg (2 cwt) whilst she had a distended bladder. His trial began in November.

The defendant was famous—known to the world as 'Fatty' Arbuckle, the Hollywood contemporary of Charles Chaplin and Buster Keaton. The chief prosecution witness was Henry Lehrman, who had directed Chaplin's first film. The court was told that the outsize but cherubic movie star, dressed in pyjamas and a bathrobe, had grabbed Miss Rappe during the noisy drinking party and winked at his friends, saying: "This is what I've been waiting for". When her screams had attracted attention and the hotel manager had been called, Arbuckle had appeared and shouted at her, "Shut up, or I'll throw you out of the window".

Arbuckle's lawyers suggested that Virginia Rappe was hardly better than a common prostitute, and denied that their client had harmed her in any way. The jury failed to reach agreement, and a retrial was ordered. The jury at the second trial was also unable to arrive at a unanimous verdict, and yet another trial had to be arranged. Arbuckle was finally acquitted of manslaughter in April 1922, saying outside the courthouse that his innocence had been proved. He believed naïvely that he could now resume his career. But Fatty Arbuckle's stardom had already been ended by the scandal. Stark reality had descended like a heavy curtain between the public and its illusions. Arbuckle was now seen not as a clown but rather as a monster. He started drinking heavily, and died of a heart attack in 1933, aged 46.

Fact

Two famous 18th-century actors were convicted of manslaughter and sentenced to be burnt in their hands. James Quin, generally regarded as the finest actor in England until he was eclipsed by Garrick, killed a fellow actor during a trivial quarrel. On another occasion, James Macklin, a celebrated Irish actor noted for his Shylock, also killed a fellow actor during a quarrel. Both men were committed to Newgate on charges of murder, but verdicts of manslaughter were brought against them. Macklin went on to live past his 100th birthday.

Fact

An unusual case of manslaughter occurred in Germany in 1981 when Klaus Grabowski, 35, was tried at Lübeck for the murder of 7 year-old Anna Bachmeier. Grabowski, who had a history of child-molesting, had strangled her. He admitted killing the girl, but pleaded guilty to manslaughter, not murder. On the fourth day of the trial, Anna's mother, Marianne, shot Grabowski dead in the courtroom. The 'Avenging Mother' was herself convicted of manslaughter, and sentenced in March 1983 to six years imprisonment. She was released after serving two years and three months.

Fact

Egon Krenz, the last Communist leader of East Germany, was sentenced by a Berlin court on 25 August 1997 to six and a half years imprisonment for manslaughter. Two other members of the former Politburo got three years each. They were held responsible for the killing of four youths who were shot dead while attempting to escape across the Berlin Wall between 1984 and 1989, and were the final defendants in the long process of bringing to justice those who both ordered and carried out the Cold War shoot-to-kill policy.

Poisonous Cooking Oil

In 1981 an illness of epidemic proportions struck people in Madrid and other parts of central Spain. Thousands were brought down with abdominal pains, respiratory problems and weight loss. For many, the long-term effects were serious disabilities and premature ageing, and the victims were mainly poor people. The weak and elderly among them died. The cause of the trouble was identified as cooking oil. Scientists and medical experts traced the origin of the illness to a brand of oil, sold as olive oil, which in fact contained reprocessed industrial-grade rapeseed oil, which was unfit for human consumption.

The subsequent investigations and judicial enquiries dragged on for years, whilst the death toll mounted. By the time charges had been brought and the accused faced trial in 1987, the number of deaths had reached around 600.

The chief defendants, charged with fraud as well as unlawful killing, were Juan and Fernando Bengoechea, brother directors of Rapsa, a firm dealing in imported oil; and Ramón and Elias Ferrero, brother directors of Raelco, the company which had bought oil from Rapsa and sold it as cooking oil. There were 34 other defendants, who all sat behind bullet-proof screens in the courtroom for their protection. There were frequent public demonstrations outside, and relatives of the victims screamed "Killers!" and other abuse at the accused.

Defence testimony tried to shift the cause of the poisoning on to pesticides, but the five trial judges rejected this theory, and although it was acknowledged that the toxic element had not been identified in laboratory tests, they decided that the deaths and injuries had been caused by the industrial rapeseed oil.

Juan Manuel Bengoechea was convicted and sentenced to 20 years imprisonment, and Ramón Ferrero to 12 years. Eleven other defendants were sentenced to shorter terms of imprisonment, but released on parole. The remaining accused were acquitted. The trial lasted for nearly 15 months, ending on 28 June 1988—the longest trial in Spain's history.

Fact

Edward Southwell Russell, 26th Baron de Clifford, was acquitted of manslaughter in December 1935, after his car had been involved in an accident near Kingston-on-Thames in which a man was killed. Lord de Clifford was the last peer of the realm to be tried by his peers in the House of Lords. The right of peers to be tried by the Lords for treason or felony was established by Magna Carta in 1215, and abolished by the Criminal Justice Act of 1948.

Killing for Sport

In 1985, Liverpool FC reached the final of the European Cup, and on 29 May met the other finalists, the Italian club Juventus. The match was staged at the Heysel Stadium in Brussels. Before the kick-off, however, Liverpool fans began taunting the Italian supporters and throwing missiles. As tempers rose, they charged across the terraces, smashing the old stadium's inadequate barriers and causing many Juventus fans to make for the main exit in panic. In the ensuing chaos, many fans were crushed and trampled. The match started an hour and half later than scheduled while Belgian police struggled to restore order, and medical teams attended to hundreds of people caught in the crush. Thirty-nine people were killed, most of them Italian.

Many Liverpool supporters were arrested and charged with assault, and eventually brought to trial at the Palais de Justice in Brussels in

1988, along with a few Belgian and French defendants, including the police chief in charge of security at the ground and the former head of the Belgian football association. The trial lasted for over five months.

At the end of April 1989, 14 Liverpool supporters were convicted of manslaughter and sentenced to three years imprisonment and fines of £1,000 each. The Belgian football and police chiefs received suspended sentences of nine and six months respectively for criminal negligence. The convicted fans had half their jail sentences suspended and, having spent six months in prison awaiting trial, were allowed to return home.

The riot resulted in English football clubs being banned from taking part in European competitions for four years, but although this was the aspect of the disaster that preoccupied the British sports media in the aftermath, it was a triviality compared with the tragedy of lives destroyed and families devastated by the brainless acts of English criminal elements.

Sport of another kind resulted in the death of 74 year-old Edna Condie in Leeds in August 1995. She was walking along the street with her husband and daughter when a slab of concrete fell on her from the roof of a block of flats, and she was killed instantly. A 10 year-old boy was subsequently charged with manslaughter. Two other boys were released after questioning by police.

Children had turned the roof of the Grayson Heights block at Kirkstall into an unofficial and highly dangerous adventure playground during the school holidays. *The Yorkshire Post* reported a story that children had been swinging 30.5 m (100 ft) above the ground from a plank resting on the roof parapet, and residents said that children threw bricks, iron bars and rubbish from the upper floors into the street below. The boy charged, who was 11 by the time of his trial, was convicted of manslaughter in May 1996 at Leeds Crown Court, and sentenced to a three-year supervision order.

Fact

The matron of a nursing home in Worthing was brought to trial at Lewes in 1951 for the murder of a 76 year-old patient, Mrs Parkinson. A young nurse reported to a doctor how the matron had suffocated the woman with a pillow, then told the nurse to say nothing to anyone. It transpired that the old woman had been particularly objectionable on the evening of her death, spitting out her sleeping pills, abusing matron and other nurses, and struggling against attempts to restrain her. Counsel for the prosecution said that matron had committed a "deliberate, intentional, cruel act", but the judge, Travers Humphreys, went along with the defence of provocation. Convicted of manslaughter, the matron was sentenced to three months imprisonment.

Fact

When Paul Getty, teenage grandson of the oil multi-millionaire Jean Paul Getty, was kidnapped in Italy in 1972, his captors—members of the Calabrian Mafia—sent one of his ear lobes in the mail to his mother as a sign that they would carry out their threat to kill the boy if the ransom was not paid. He returned home, otherwise safe, when his grandfather paid 2 billion lire for his release.

Fact

Daphne, the wife of Rolf Schild, a British electronics engineer, and their 15 year-old daughter Annabel, were kidnapped from their holiday villa near Palau in northern Sardinia, in August 1979. In St Peter's Square, Rome, on 16 March 1980, Pope John Paul II announced that Mrs Schild had been freed. She had, in fact, been released two months earlier, but the news had been withheld by the media at the family's request. The Pope's appeal to the kidnappers was successful in obtaining the release of Annabel on 21 March.

Section 4: Kidnapping and Abduction

Wherever anyone is against his will, that is to him a prison.
Epictetus: *Discourses*

In English law kidnapping is the stealing or forcible carrying-off of any person against his or her will. The crime can be punished by life imprisonment. The closely-related crime of abduction is the seizure of a woman against her will or of a girl without her parents' consent. It can be punished by long terms of imprisonment. Abduction is often carried out for sexual purposes; kidnapping to extort a ransom or for some political objective. The word 'kidnap' entered the language from an old slang expression for snatching a child—nabbing a kid—and probably originated in the slave trade in the 17th century.

The holding of hostages for ransom has a very long history. King Richard I of England was ransomed for £100,000 by his countrymen in 1194 after being seized and held captive for more than a year by Leopold of Austria. In 1533 the Incas of Peru paid a vast ransom in gold and silver to the Spanish Conquistadors under Pizarro for the release of their monarch Atahualpa. (The Conquistadors executed him *and* kept the gold and silver.)

The abduction of an heiress by Edward Gibbon Wakefield is outlined in a following case history, and this crime was not especially uncommon at one period. Wakefield's case is merely one of the most famous. Captain James Campbell, the Earl of Argyll's brother, abducted Mary Wharton, a 13 year-old girl worth £50,000, from her home in London in November 1690, and married her against her will. Campbell's accomplice in the crime, Sir John Johnson, was subsequently hanged, but Campbell himself appears to have escaped to the continent.

Nevertheless, kidnapping and abduction have never featured largely in Britain, although British subjects have often been kidnapped abroad, mostly from political motives. Geoffrey Jackson, the British ambassador in Uruguay , was kidnapped by Tupamaro guerrillas in 1970 and held for eight months in a small, dark and filthy cage below a factory lavatory in Montevideo. The long ordeals of Terry Waite, the Archbishop of Canterbury's envoy captured in Beirut, and those of John McCarthy and other contemporary victims of Islamic extremists in the Middle East, are well known. In the past, the danger of being kidnapped for ransom by bandits or brigands, particularly in what we now call Third World countries, made travelling a hazardous undertaking for Europeans.

In domestic crime, those involved with kidnapping or abduction frequently end up being charged with something else as well. Kidnapping for ransom often ends in murder, and two case histories in this section have been chosen because it was the kidnapping that initially captured the headlines, even though murder was the end result. One of the most common forms of abduction in modern times occurs when one parent in a dissolved marriage takes away a child who is legally in the custody of the other parent.

CASE HISTORIES

The Pursuit

Edward Gibbon Wakefield, later to become a celebrated colonial statesman, a critic of transportation and author of *View of the Art of Colonisation*, was in 1825 a widower of 29 with two children. With his younger brother William, he put into action a plan to abduct and marry an heiress, Ellen Turner, the 15 year-old daughter of the High Sheriff of Cheshire. She was taken from her school in Liverpool on the pretext that her mother was seriously ill at the family home, Shrigley Hall near Macclesfield, and wished to see her urgently. But the messenger took her to a Manchester hotel, where the elder Wakefield presented himself and said that the real reason for her being fetched from school was that her father was on the verge of bankruptcy, and wished her to join him at Kendal where he had stopped on his journey to the Scottish border, with sheriff's officers hot on his heels. Arriving at Kendal, with no sign of her father, Miss Turner was persuaded by Wakefield that only she—with his help—could save her father from ruin. If Ellen were to marry him, her father's property could be transferred to her, and it would then be safe as the legal property of her husband. Falling for this desperate measure, Ellen accompanied Wakefield to Gretna Green where they were married by the blacksmith. Wakefield then invented elaborate reasons for taking her at once to France.

Meanwhile, the abduction was discovered after communication between the school and Ellen's parents, and her uncle, with a solicitor and a Bow Street runner in tow, crossed to Calais in pursuit. There her uncle saw her walking on the pier with Wakefield, and after some argument between the two men, and consultation with the town's mayor, Ellen protested that she was not Wakefield's wife, that he had carried her off "by fraud and stratagem", and that she never wanted to see him again. At this point, Wakefield gave up, and Ellen returned to England and her family.

William Wakefield was arrested at Dover and Edward soon gave himself up. They were both held at Lancaster Gaol to await trial, charged with having "carried away Ellen Turner, spinster, then a maid and heir apparent unto her father, for the sake of the lucre of her substance; and for having afterwards unlawfully and against her will married the said Ellen Turner".

The brothers were convicted in March 1826 and both were sentenced to three years imprisonment. Edward served his time at Newgate, and William at Lancaster. The marriage was annulled by Act of Parliament. Ellen Turner was later married to a member of the Leigh family of Lymm Hall, Cheshire. Edward Gibbon Wakefield went to Australia, where he pursued his ideas of controlled colonialism, and became chiefly responsible for the commencement of British colonization of New Zealand.

Fact

The ERP (People's Republican Army) of Argentina took to kidnapping important foreign businessmen in a big way during the early 1970s. Among their victims were Jan van de Panne, the head of Philips, for whom they got half a million dollars; Victor Samuelson of Exxon, whose company paid $14.2 million for his safe return; John Thompson, vice-president of the Firestone Tyre & Rubber Company; and employees of Coca Cola, Kodak and other companies. Most of these hostages were released when the ransom demands were met, but Oberdan Sallustro, president of Fiat Argentina, was found shot dead in a house on the outskirts of Buenos Aires after his company was prevented from paying the ransom by the country's ruling military junta.

Fact

When Australian Muriel McKay disappeared from her London home a few days after Christmas in 1969, her husband Alick, deputy chairman of the News of the World, *received a telephone call demanding £1 million for her safe return. The kidnappers' spokesman, who spoke with a West Indian accent and said he represented the 'Mafia, M3', said their original intention had been to kidnap the wife of the newspaper's chairman, Rupert Murdoch. Over the next few weeks Mr McKay received various ransom notes as well as pleading letters from his wife. But his efforts to recover her by following the kidnappers' instructions for a first delivery of £500,000 were foiled on two occasions by a mixture of bad luck and police incompetence. At length police arrested Arthur and Nizamodeen Hosein, brothers who lived on a farm near the village of Stocking Pelham in Hertfordshire. No trace of Mrs McKay could be found, but the brothers were convicted of murder as well as kidnapping and blackmail. It was only the third time in half a century that a conviction for murder had been obtained without a corpse. Arthur Hosein got life imprisonment plus 25 years, and his younger brother, whom he dominated, got life plus 15 years. Speculation has led to the widespread but unproven belief that Mrs McKay's body was dismembered and fed to the farm pigs.*

The White Slave Case

W.T. Stead, the campaigning journalist and editor of the *Pall Mall Gazette*, began a crusade in 1885 to expose child prostitution in Victorian London (and, incidentally, increase his circulation figures). The age of consent for sexual intercourse at the time was 12, and all attempts to get it raised had foundered. It was repeatedly argued that, as the age at which a woman could marry—according to common law—was 12, then that must obviously be the age of consent. Stead had the idea that if it could be proved beyond doubt that there was a thriving trade in young girls, the age of consent would be raised to protect children from being abducted and sold, often abroad. There were many English girls in Belgian brothels, but Victorian polite society preferred not to know about such things.

Stead proposed to obtain his proof by 'buying' a child himself, incognito, to demonstrate how easily it could be done. He set up a plot whereby a Salvation Army woman, Rebecca Jarrett, who had been a child prostitute herself and thus knew the ropes, would act as his agent in procuring a child by seeking out a poor couple willing to sell their daughter for immoral purposes. Rebecca announced that she had found a family in Marylebone named Armstrong, whose 13 year-old daughter Eliza could be obtained for a mere £3. Stead paid up and the child was duly delivered to him.

Eliza was taken to a brothel run by a Madame Mourez, who ascertained that the girl was a virgin. Then Stead had her taken, drugged with chloroform, to a house in Poland Street and put to bed, making sure that the landlady had every opportunity to note the girl's tender age and see Stead in the same room with her. He then had Eliza examined by a doctor who certified that she had not been interfered with while she was in his hands. His mission thus accomplished, he sent Eliza to Paris for a while, in the care of the Salvation Army, to keep her well out of the way while he published his revelations of how easily the girl could have been sold into slavery, vanishing for ever from her family and country. He warned his readers in advance that "all those who are squeamish, and all those who are prudish, and all those who prefer to live in a fool's paradise of imaginary innocence and purity, selfishly oblivious of the horrible realities which torment those whose lives are passed in the London Inferno, will do well not to read the *Pall Mall Gazette* of Monday and the three following days".

Under the title *The Maiden Tribute of Modern Babylon*, Stead reprinted his *Gazette* exposé in the form of a pamphlet. His revelations caused outrage. An MP asked the Home Secretary in the House of Commons if there were any means of "subjecting the author and publisher of these obscene articles in a paper called the *Pall Mall Gazette* to a criminal prosecution". Stead had not made it clear that the story was not a real-life tragedy but a put-up job in which the girl had come to no real harm, and the stunt backfired on him. Rival journalists tracked down the family and discovered that Mr Armstrong had not given Rebecca Jarrett his permission to take Eliza away, and that the girl's mother had thought she was being taken into service.

Stead's action was construed as taking the girl away from her parents fraudulently, and he was arrested and charged with abduction, along with Rebecca Jarrett, Louise Mourez, an assistant named Sampson Jacques, and the Salvation Army's Bramwell Booth. Booth was acquitted, but Jacques got a month's imprisonment, Stead got three months, and Jarrett and Mourez six months. Stead's articles were described by the judge as "a disgrace to journalism". Stead spent two months of his sentence in Holloway Prison, where he was made comfortable with a blazing fire, an armchair and a "cosy little tea table".

Many doubts were expressed about the purity of Stead's motives, and later even his sanity was brought into question, but there is no doubting the dramatic success of his actions. The Criminal Law Amendment Bill, introduced to the Commons hot on the heels of the case, proposed raising the age of consent to 16 and making procuring a crime. After Stead's sensational propaganda, no MP dared to vote against it, and the Bill was carried without a division before Stead was released from prison.

William Thomas Stead was among the victims of the *Titanic* disaster in 1912.

One Way Street to Oblivion

In between Moody and Sankey in the 19th century, and Billy Graham in the second half of the 20th, the burden of American evangelical crusading was carried by Aimée Semple McPherson, who seduced her adoring followers down what she called the "one-way street for Jesus".

She was born Aimée Kennedy near London, Ontario, into a Salvation Army family, and married Robert Semple, a Pentecostal missionary. After his early death, she married Harold McPherson, whom she divorced after a few years. Meanwhile, she had embarked on her career as a flamboyant and increasingly famous evangelist, travelling across Canada and the United States, as well as in Britain, Australia and New Zealand, and building up an enormous following at her revivalist meetings. She preached the literal truth of the Bible story in every detail, persuading multitudes of sinners to come forward to be saved, and founded the Foursquare Gospel Movement in Los Angeles. She was able to raise $1.5 million from her admiring followers to build the Angelus Temple, and she had her own radio station. She published best-selling books such as *Divine Healing Sermons* and *The Second Coming of Christ*. She successfully converted Christianity into showbiz, with herself as the star performer.

Then suddenly, in May 1926, Sister Aimée disappeared. She had gone to the beach for a swim and vanished. A huge search was mounted. Her devoted multitude was frantic. Some of her followers were drowned while swimming along the coast looking for her. Two despairing people committed suicide. Thousands of dollars were raised for a memorial to her.

Fact

An attempt was made to kidnap Princess Anne in 1974. If it had succeeded, it would undoubtedly have been one of the most sensational crimes of its kind ever committed. On 20 March, a man driving a white Ford Escort blocked the path of the royal chauffeur-driven limousine in the Mall as the Princess and her then husband, Captain Mark Phillips, were returning to Buckingham Palace from a charity function in the City. The man got out and opened fire with a pistol on the limousine, wounding the chauffeur. Princess Anne's personal bodyguard, Inspector James Beaton, managed to fire one shot, but was himself seriously wounded. A uniformed policeman and a journalist on the scene were also injured. Princess Anne, Captain Phillips and a lady-in-waiting were unhurt, despite the assailant struggling to haul the Princess out of the car. A ransom letter was found during the investigation that followed the incident, demanding £3 million, and it was clear that the attacker, Ian Ball, had prepared his rented house at Fleet, Hampshire, to hold the Princess as a prisoner. The attempt occurred a month after the well-publicized kidnapping of Patty Hearst in the USA (see case history). Ball was committed to a mental hospital for an indefinite period.

Fact

One of the largest ransoms of modern times was paid to the left-wing Monteneros in Argentina in 1975. These urban guerillas kidnapped Juan and Jorge Born, wealthy brothers and business partners in Buenos Aires. The kidnappers made various demands, but released the brothers when a ransom of 1.5 billion pesos ($60 million) was paid. It has been estimated that in the five years from 1971 to 1975 inclusive, kidnappers in Latin America profited to the tune of $80 million in ransom money for hostages.

Fact

In 1983 there were 131 cases of kidnapping in England and Wales, and 81 cases of abduction. In 1993 there were 1,051 cases of kidnapping, and 354 of abduction.

Five weeks after her disappearance, a woman at Agua Prieta, just over the US border in Mexico, answered a knock at her door to find a woman who said she had been kidnapped. It was Aimée McPherson. She claimed that she had been kidnapped by two men and a woman, and had managed to escape from a shack in the desert where they had kept her, and had walked 20 miles to safety. She pressed the police to find the kidnappers, whom she could identify only as 'Steve', 'Jake' and 'Rose'. But no ransom demand had been made, and no evidence could be found on which to base an indictment.

Suspicions were soon being voiced in the press that Aimée had not been kidnapped at all, but had been having a clandestine relationship with one Kenneth Ormiston, a married man who had also been mysteriously absent from his home and work, and had been seen with a woman at places along the Californian coast. At length, Aimée was charged with conspiracy to obstruct justice. Evidence was accumulated against her from hotel registers and staff, and a woman who had been a witness on Aimée's behalf confessed that she had been paid by Aimée to say that *she* had been the woman seen with Ormiston. At the end of the longest hearing in California's legal history, the District Attorney had the case against Aimée Semple McPherson dismissed. Rumour had it that he had been bribed.

Aimée resumed her travelling and lecturing, but no longer attracted the massive audiences she was used to, although thousands still held her in veneration. She married a man named Hutton, but it was a disaster. Aimée became embroiled for years in litigation against her for debt, slander and breach of contract. She died in 1944, aged 53, from an overdose of sleeping pills.

The Lindbergh Affair

In the late 1920s Charles Augustus Lindbergh was one of the world's most famous men. In 1927, he had made the first non-stop solo flight across the Atlantic, piloting his tiny monoplane, *Spirit of St Louis,* from New York to Paris in 33 hours. He claimed the prize of £25,000 which had been offered to the first man to do it, and was promoted to colonel in the US Army. He was also awarded the Congressional Medal of Honour and was fêted everywhere he went. Soon afterwards, he married Anne Morrow, daughter of an American diplomat.

Less than five years after his famous achievement, Col. Lindbergh was again in the world's headlines. On 1 March 1932, his 19 month-old son Charles was kidnapped from the family's home in New Jersey, and a ransom of $50,000 was demanded. The ransom note was left on a windowsill of the child's bedroom. It read: "Dear sir, Have 50000$ ready 25000$ in 20$ bills 15000$ in 10$ bills and 10000$ in 5$ bills After 2-4 days we will inform you were to deliver the money We warn you for making anyding public or for notify the police The child is in gut care..." The note clearly indicated a German of low education. (In a subsequent note, he again wrote 'good' as 'gut', as well as putting 'aus' for 'out'.)

A few days later, a retired schoolmaster, John Condon, became an intermediary and made contact with the kidnapper through the advertisement columns of a local newspaper. A month after the kidnapping, Condon handed over $50,000 to the kidnapper, who called himself John, in a Bronx cemetery, and was told that the child was on a boat named *Nelly*, anchored off Martha's Vineyard, Massachusetts. But no such boat was found.

Distress turned into nightmare. A maid employed by Col. Lindbergh's mother-in-law committed suicide after police questioning. The Lindberghs received thousands of letters offering help, advice and solutions. Many were hoaxes, and no one knew what to believe. Al Capone volunteered to get the baby back if he were released from prison. On 12 May, young Charles Lindbergh's body was found in a shallow grave in a wood a few miles from his home. He had died from blows to the head, and had been dead for at least two months. He had probably been killed on the night he had been kidnapped. The kidnapping had turned into a murder enquiry.

It was two and a half years after the kidnapping before anyone was charged with the crime. In September 1934, a man with a German accent called at a Manhattan filling station, and paid for his gasoline with a $10 gold certificate. The certificates had been withdrawn from circulation in 1933 when President Roosevelt had taken the USA off the gold standard and they had ceased to be legal tender. But the attendant accepted the certificate and noted the man's car number as a precaution. A bank clerk then recognised the note as part of the Lindbergh ransom money. The vehicle license bureau quickly led police to the Bronx home of Bruno Richard Hauptmann, a carpenter with a criminal record in his native country who had entered the United States illegally. In his garage police found nearly $15,000 of the ransom money.

Hauptmann was convicted of the kidnapping and murder of Charles Lindbergh Jnr, and—after various legal delays—executed by electric chair on 3 April 1936 at Trenton State Prison, New Jersey. Some people felt that his guilt had not been proven beyond reasonable doubt. Lindbergh, convinced of Hauptmann's guilt and disgusted at what he saw as political interference in American justice, left the country, becoming an admirer of Nazi achievements and using his fame and influence to try to prevent the USA from entering the war against Germany. After Pearl Harbour, however, he supported the American war effort. He died in 1974.

Fact

James Strange and Garret Byrne, Irish squireens, were hanged in 1779 for abducting two teenage sisters, Ann and Catherine Kennedy, the daughters of a wealthy family. The men seduced and married the girls, who were aged 14 and 15 respectively, but they were soon rescued and their abductors convicted.

Fact

Susannah Lamplugh, 25, who worked for a London estate agent, appears to have been a victim of kidnapping, and probably of murder. She has not been seen since 28 July 1986, when she left her office to show a 'Mr Kipper' a vacant house in Hammersmith. A massive search was launched by police when Miss Lamplugh was reported missing, but only her car was found a mile away from the house to which she had gone.

The Red Light Bandit

When Caryl Chessman was executed in the gas chamber at San Quentin prison in 1960, after 12 years on 'death row' and appeals for clemency from such figures as Albert Schweitzer, Pablo Casals and the Queen

Fact

The Lindbergh case (see case history) was the most famous of many child kidnappings in the USA in the 1920s and 30s, when the 'snatch racket' reached epidemic proportions. A similar epidemic struck Italy in the 60s and 70s. The 1975 kidnapping in Milan of Cristina Mazzotti, an 18 year-old schoolgirl, was Italy's 161st case of kidnapping for ransom within a period of 15 years. Cristina was found dead after the ransom had been paid. In the same year Aldo Moro, a former prime minister, was kidnapped by Red Brigade terrorists in an ambush in which five bodyguards were shot dead. Moro was murdered by his captors and his body, riddled with 11 bullets, was left in the boot of a car in a street in Rome. His funeral was presided over by his lifelong friend, Giovanni Montini, Pope Paul VI.

Mother of Belgium, shock waves reverberated throughout the civilized world.

Many people old enough to remember the Chessman furore are still under the impression that he was a dangerous murderer. But he did not kill anyone. He was convicted by the Los Angeles County Superior Court in 1948 on eight counts of robbery, four of kidnapping, and other charges of attempted rape and sexual perversion. Under Californian law at the time, kidnapping for the purpose of robbery involving physical harm to the victim was a capital offence. Chessman was given two death sentences, one life sentence and imprisonment for 60 years.

Carol Whittier Chessman ('Caryl' was a later affectation) already had a long criminal record when he was arrested and charged with the crimes identified with the so-called 'Red Light Bandit'. The most serious of these charges was that, in the course of prowling lovers' lanes, using a car with a red spotlight and armed with a pistol and a flashlight, and robbing the young couples in parked cars, he had on two occasions taken women away from the cars and forced them to submit to "unnatural sex acts". He had taken $5 from one of these women. This was construed by the court as kidnapping and causing physical harm to the victim in the course of robbery—hence the death penalty. Chessman was consigned to cell 2455 at San Quentin prison to await execution.

He then set about a long course of delaying tactics by making himself an expert on the law, reading thousands of books, and becoming a best-selling author himself. For a time he became the world's most famous prisoner. His major appeals revolved round the disputed accuracy of the transcript of his trial. The court reporter, Ernest Perry, had died before completing the transcription of his shorthand notes, and the job had been completed by a replacement reporter. When the trial judge, Charles Fricke, certified the transcript at a hearing in 1949, he refused Chessman permission to be present. In 1957, nine years and six stays of execution after he had been sentenced, the US Supreme Court ruled that Judge Fricke's denial had violated Chessman's constitutional rights. More than 2,000 changes were subsequently made to the transcript. Chessman then challenged the revised version and obtained another stay of execution.

Meanwhile, the California State Governor, Edmund Brown, was receiving letters which showed a ratio of ten to one in favour of sparing Chessman's life. But it was all to no avail. There was never any real doubt about Chessman's guilt, and in spite of his knowledge of the law and his mastery of foreign languages whilst in prison, he remained an arrogant and self-centred criminal. One of his victims had been in a mental hospital for nearly as long as he had been in prison. According to psychiatrists, her illness had been brought on by the ordeal she had suffered at Chessman's hands.

After a further 60-day reprieve had been granted in February 1960—because of fears that President Eisenhower's imminent visit to Uruguay would be marred by demonstrations—the law was allowed to take its course. A new date was fixed for Chessman's execution, and this time it was carried out, on 2 May 1960.

The Heiress

Patty Hearst, the attractive blonde 19 year-old granddaughter of the American press magnate William Randolph Hearst, was having a shower in her flat in Berkeley, California, one day in 1974 when two men and a woman burst in, knocked her fiancé unconscious and carried off the naked girl. The men were black; the woman white. They were members of the 'Symbionese Liberation Army', whose demands were concerned with the distribution of food to the San Francisco poor.

The kidnapping shocked American high society. After many weeks of negotiation, Patty's father eventually acceded to the kidnappers' demands for a ransom of millions of dollars to be paid in the form of food in a distribution programme over the next nine months. By this time, however, the victim had been converted by her captors. She sent abusive tapes to her parents attacking their reluctance to pay up and criticizing the poor quality of the first food to be handed out. Finally she accused them of "stalling for time—time which the FBI was using in their attempts to assassinate me and the SLA elements which guarded me...", and said that she was joining the SLA to fight for the "freedom of all oppressed people". Not surprisingly, her distraught parents were convinced that she had been brainwashed.

Some weeks later, at Easter, the SLA carried out a bank raid in San Francisco, wounding two people and getting away with $10,000. The bank's security cameras showed one of the raiders, a girl with a gun, to be Patty Hearst wearing a black wig. A warrant was issued for the arrest of the girl now described as "armed and dangerous".

She was arrested after an armed police raid on a house in Los Angeles in which most of her comrades were killed. When she was put on trial for armed robbery, her own story was that she had been coerced by her captors. But she was really just a confused and impressionable victim. Sentenced to seven years imprisonment, she was pardoned by President Jimmy Carter after serving nearly two years. She subsequently married her bodyguard.

Fact

A man named Peter Manyfeld was brought before an ecclesiastical court in London in 1489 for carrying away "by stealth and violence and against her will, a certain Alice Burle from her parents' house and kept her in his room for a long time, committing with her the crime of fornication, and after he was tired of her, he sold her..."

The Trail of Red Tape

One morning in January 1975, Dorothy Whittle realized that her 17 year-old daughter Lesley was missing from home in the village of Highley, near Bridgnorth in Shropshire. Messages on red plastic Dymo-tape left in the house made it obvious that the girl had been kidnapped during the night. They demanded £50,000 and threatened death if the police were brought in. The Whittles, nevertheless, did inform the police and Scotland Yard was asked for assistance.

Later on the day of Lesley's disappearance, a security guard at a container depot in Dudley, West Midlands, was shot several times by a man he had approached for loitering suspiciously outside. Experts examining the spent cartridges realised that they came from a gun used

Fact

The Canadian government launched an all-out attack on terrorism when Jasper Cross, the British trade commissioner, and Pierre Laporte, a Liberal Party politician, were kidnapped from their homes in Montreal within four days of each other in October 1970. The kidnappers were members of the Québec separatist movement, the FLQ, and they were demanding the release of political prisoners. The Prime Minister, Pierre Trudeau, invoked war measures which allowed police to arrest and search without warrants, and 1,000 parachute troops were drafted in to the province of Québec to aid the Royal Canadian Mounted Police in finding the missing men. Nearly 2,000 houses were raided in the first month after the kidnappings. When Pierre Laporte was found dead in the boot of a car, having been strangled, it was the first political assassination in the Dominion's 103-year history. Jasper Cross was released after two months in return for the kidnappers' safe passage to Cuba.

in armed robberies on sub-post offices in the Midlands and north of England. The man they were looking for was the 'Black Panther', so-called because eye-witnesses had consistently described the raider as wearing a black hood over his head with a slit for his eyes. When detectives traced a car used by the man who had shot the security guard, they found red plastic Dymo-tape strips bearing instructions for handing over a ransom. The armed robber had added kidnapping to his repertoire. Lesley Whittle's slippers were also in the car, as well as a tape-recorded message from her saying: "There's no need to worry, Mum. I'm OK. I got a bit wet but I'm quite dry now. I'm being treated very well".

The Black Panther was a dangerous criminal who had shot dead three sub-postmasters and wounded several other people, as well as the security guard. Irresponsible journalists put Lesley's life at risk by publishing news of the kidnapping. The BBC broadcast the story on television without taking the precaution of checking it with police. Efforts to pay the ransom and ensure Lesley's safety were hindered by the presence of reporters and members of the public flocking to the area, and by hoax telephone calls from crooks pretending to be the kidnapper in order to get their hands on the ransom money.

One of the Dymo-tape instructions led Lesley's elder brother, Ronald, to take the ransom to Bathpool Park, a common at Kidsgrove, Staffordshire, which had formerly been the site of a coal-mine. The journey was abortive, as others had been, but police interest in Bathpool Park was again alerted when a local schoolboy handed in a strip of Dymo-tape saying "DROP SUITCASE INTO HOLE", which he had found in the area. Another boy found a torch wedged into an iron grille covering a ventilation shaft.

Police with tracker-dogs began a search of the land, and at the bottom of another ventilation shaft they found the body of Lesley Whittle, suspended by a wire round her neck from the shaft's iron ladder. It was 7 March, nearly two months after her disappearance.

The Black Panther was not caught until the end of the year. Two policemen at Mansfield Woodhouse, in Nottinghamshire, managed to overpower a man who ordered them at gunpoint to drive him to Blidworth. Among his possessions were two black hoods.

He was Donald Neilson, 39, a jobbing carpenter from Bradford, and was a married man with a daughter of his own. Among weapons, ammunition and other evidence found at his home was a Dymo-tape machine. Brought to trial at Oxford in June, Neilson was sentenced to life imprisonment for each of the three murders of sub-postmasters, and 21 years for the kidnapping and murder of Lesley Whittle. Gerald Smith, the security guard he had shot at Dudley, had died in March 1976, just too late for his death to be classified as murder.

Section 5: Defamation

Slander,
Whose edge is sharper than the sword, whose tongue
Outvenoms all the worms of Nile, whose breath
Rides on the posting winds and doth belie
All corners of the world.
William Shakespeare: *Cymbeline*

THE LAWS OF DEFAMATION are meant to protect the reputations of individuals from improper attack. A person can be defamed in English law by a libel or a slander. A libel is a statement in durable form, such as a written or printed document or a broadcast. A slander is a verbal statement. Scottish law does not distinguish between the two. Slanderous remarks about a person's sexual morals were formerly matters for the ecclesiastical courts, which frequently had to deal with small matters such as one woman calling another a whore during a quarrel. A rather extreme instance occurred at Kingarth in Scotland in 1664, when Margaret Fleming complained that Allan M'Conochie had not only called her a "runagate whoore", but said that "the crops of hir toes was cutte of in Irland for hir whooredome, and that he knew not what dogge was hir father and what bitche hir mother..."

In the Tudor period, you could have your ears cropped for slander, and your hand cut off for libel. However, neither a libel nor a slander is necessarily a criminal offence, and most libel suits are brought to court as civil actions for damages by persons whose good reputations have allegedly been undermined by unfair remarks in the media. A *criminal* prosecution can result from a statement which is liable to cause a breach of the peace or which could render the individual attacked, if true, liable to imprisonment. In modern times, a criminal libel can be punished by up to two years imprisonment as well as a fine.

If a man takes you to court in a civil action for calling him a fraud in public, and you can prove that he *is* a fraud, that is a complete defence. Otherwise you might be liable for damages. If he is suing you for slander, as opposed to libel, he has to prove *what* you said, as well as satisfying the jury that you damaged his reputation. But if a *criminal* prosecution were to be brought against you, then it would be no defence to prove the truth of the statement unless the statement were judged to be in the public interest. In this book, we deal only with criminal libel. (Seditious, blasphemous and obscene libels are different matters, not connected with the laws of personal defamation dealt with here.)

The law of criminal libel has been much criticized in recent times for being archaic. It has sometimes been used in purely personal squabbles. A report by the Law Commission in 1985 recommended abolition of criminal libel and the substitution of a new crime called 'criminal defamation'.

Fact

One of the most famous cases of criminal libel occurred in 1813, when the poet and essayist Leigh Hunt was prosecuted, with his brother John. They were joint editors of The Examiner, *a Sunday paper in which they published an article in March 1812 on the Prince Regent in which appeared the words: 'This Adonis in loveliness is a corpulent man of fifty... a libertine over head and ears in debt and disgrace, a despiser of domestic ties, the companion of gamblers and demireps, a man who has just closed half a century without one single claim on the gratitude of his country or the respect of posterity'. The Hunt brothers were sentenced in February 1813 by Lord Chief Justice Ellenborough to two years imprisonment as well as fines of £500 each. Whilst John served his sentence at Ilchester, Leigh Hunt did his time at the Surrey County Gaol in Southwark, where he received visits from Lord Byron and Charles Lamb, and cheerfully carried on his literary work from his cell.*

Fact

Not surprisingly, newspaper editors have frequently fallen foul of the law of criminal libel. In 1789, the editor of The Times, *John Walter, was prosecuted after suggesting that three sons of George III—the dukes of York, Gloucester and Cumberland— were less than sincere in their apparent joy at the king's recovery from his serious illness. Walter was sentenced to a year's imprisonment, a £50 fine, and an hour in the pillory at Charing Cross. In the event, he was excused the public pillorying, but was prosecuted again for similar libels on the Prince of Wales and the Duke of Clarence, and fined a further £200 and given an additional term of imprisonment. He was released at the instance of the Prince of Wales after serving 18 months in Newgate.*

Case Histories

The Cleveland Street Affair

In 1889, Victorian society was shocked by revelations about a male brothel at 19 Cleveland Street which involved teenage telegraph boys. It was allegedly patronized by men in the highest ranks of society. When the trial of those responsible for running the brothel came up, the names of these aristocratic customers were suppressed. But some time later, the *North London Press* named names. The paper identified Lord Arthur Somerset, a major in the Royal Horse Guards and an equerry to the Prince of Wales; and Henry Fitzroy, Earl of Euston. It added for good measure that 'a far more distinguished and more highly placed personage' was also involved.

Lord Arthur Somerset had already fled the country, but the Earl of Euston promptly prosecuted Ernest Parke, the paper's editor, and he was tried at the Old Bailey in January 1890. The Earl admitted that he had once visited the house in Cleveland Street, but said that it had been due to a misunderstanding. He had been led to believe that *poses plastiques* could be seen there—naked girls posing as classical figures. Immediately he had realised that there were no women there—only boys—he had left.

Defence witnesses told a different story, and a male prostitute claimed that he had been in bed with Lord Euston at Cleveland Street. But there were several contradictions in the testimony of witnesses, and the Earl's story was accepted. The *North London Press* had also rashly stated in its article that the Earl had fled to Peru, which was clearly untrue. Parke was convicted of criminal libel and sentenced to a year's imprisonment.

Regina v Queensberry

The intimate friendship between Oscar Wilde and Lord Alfred Douglas began in 1891, when Wilde was 36 and Douglas 21. It was a source of constant distress and agitation to Lord Alfred's father, John Sholto Douglas, 8th Marquis of Queensberry. The Marquis, well known in sporting circles, had given his name to the 'Queensberry rules' governing boxing, and was an arrogant, coarse and malicious individual given to fits of violent temper, and undoubtedly mentally unbalanced. He carried on a campaign of threats and ultimatums against his son and Oscar Wilde, and when these failed to have the desired effect, he went one day in February 1895 to the Albemarle Club and left a card for Wilde on which he wrote: 'For Oscar Wilde posing as Somdomite'(sic). Wilde had Queensberry arrested and charged with criminal libel.

The trial opened at the Old Bailey on 3 April 1895, before Mr Justice Collins. Counsel for the prosecution was Sir Edward Clarke, QC. Queensberry was defended by Edward Carson, QC. Carson had been a fellow-student of Wilde's at Trinity College, Dublin, and Wilde remarked characteristically: "No doubt he will perform his task with all the added bitterness of an old friend". The Marquis pleaded not guilty to the charge of false and malicious libel, claiming that the statement was true and its publication in the public interest.

Oscar Wilde, described by *The Star* as looking 'ponderous and fleshy' in court, was capable of being extremely serious when he chose, but he made the mistake of thinking that the wit and verbal dexterity for which he was renowned in the theatre and in society would serve him just as well in a court of law, and many of his replies under cross-examination were flippant. But Carson relentlessly pursued his aim of putting Wilde's sexual inclinations under a magnifying glass to show that there was justification for Lord Queensberry's accusation. He explored Wilde's relationships with a number of young men who, apart from those who were unemployed, included an office boy, a valet, a groom and a bookie's runner. When Carson asked Wilde about his intimacy with a lad named Alphonse Conway who, he said, sold newspapers on the pier at Worthing, Wilde replied: "It is the first I have heard of his connection with literature". When Wilde admitted to drinking champagne (against his doctor's orders), and Carson snapped, "Never mind your doctor's orders, sir!'", Wilde answered, "I never do".

Wilde consistently denied any improper conduct, but Carson's *coup de grâce* came when he asked Wilde about a young man named Walter Grainger, a waiter:

Carson: *Did you ever kiss him?*
Wilde: *Oh dear, no. He was a peculiarly plain boy.*
He was, unfortunately, extremely ugly. I pitied him for it.

Carson leapt on this answer, repeatedly asking Wilde if it was because Grainger was ugly that he had not kissed him. Wilde's self-assurance eventually faltered under Carson's barrage of questions as to why he had added that the boy was ugly. At last Wilde managed to say: "You sting me and insult me and try to unnerve me; and at times one says things flippantly when one ought to speak more seriously. I admit it".

Shortly afterwards, Carson began his long opening speech for the defence, but before he finished, Sir Edward Clarke withdrew the prosecution on Wilde's behalf. Queensberry was found not guilty of libel, the plea of justification having been proved and the jury satisfied that the statement was made for the public benefit.

The verdict led to the prompt arrest of Oscar Wilde and the savage sentence, after two trials, of two years imprisonment with hard labour for seven counts of gross indecency. It ruined not only a brilliant career, but also his life.

Fact

In 1879, the editor of a periodical called Town Talk *got 18 months in prison for suggesting that the Prince of Wales was having an affair with the actress Lillie Langtry. In 1913, the editor of* The Liberator *got two years for accusing the King, George V, of having committed bigamy in 1893. The law was not designed exclusively for the protection of the royal family, however, as these case histories show. In 1949, the editor of the Daily Mirror, Silvester Bolam, was given three months for publishing a headline immediately after the arrest for murder of John George Haigh: 'Vampire will never strike again'.*

Fact

In 1720 a clergyman, the Rev. Lawrence Howell, was prosecuted for publishing a pamphlet in which he denounced the King, George I, as a usurper. He was sentenced to three years imprisonment, whipping and a fine of £500. But Howell died in Newgate before the whipping was carried out.

Rex v Douglas

Lord Alfred Douglas, who had urged Oscar Wilde to prosecute the Marquis of Queensberry, was himself prosecuted for criminal libel in 1923, when he accused Winston Churchill, who had been First Lord of the Admiralty during WWI, of manipulating news of the Battle of Jutland in order to depress the value of English shares on the American Stock Exchange. Churchill, Douglas alleged, had thus enabled Sir Ernest Cassel to make an enormous profit for which Churchill had been amply rewarded.

Churchill was at first advised by the Attorney General to ignore the allegation. But Douglas repeated it in a pamphlet he published and circulated, and taunted Churchill for not instituting proceedings. 'If Mr Churchill were editing a paper and if he printed in his columns about one-half, one-quarter, one-fifth of what I printed about him, I would have him round at Bow Street with his nose hanging over the edge of the dock to answer a charge of criminal libel within 24 hours...'

This time Churchill took action. Douglas was tried at the Old Bailey in December 1923. His plea was justification, but his allegations were based on hearsay and were soon shown to be totally without foundation. He was found guilty of libel and sentenced to six months.

Goldsmith v 'Private Eye'

The long-running vendetta between the satirical journal *Private Eye* and the multi-millionaire industrialist Sir James Goldsmith came to a head in 1976 when the editor of *Private Eye*, Richard Ingrams, its publishers, Pressdram Ltd, and the chief distributors, Moore-Harness Ltd, were prosecuted for criminal libel.

Goldsmith had numerous civil actions pending against the paper, which had suggested, among other things, his involvement in an alleged conspiracy to pervert the course of justice in the Lord Lucan affair, as well as an involvement with the northern industrialist T. Dan Smith, who was then serving a jail sentence for corruption. *Private Eye* also questioned Goldsmith's fitness to be chairman of Slater Walker Industries. The serious Lucan allegation led Goldsmith to leave his civil actions in abeyance and institute criminal proceedings.

Goldsmith's alleged chairmanship of a meeting at which the murder of Sandra Rivett was discussed by Lucan's friends the day after it happened, was easily disproved. Goldsmith had been in Ireland at the time, making a speech to the Institute of Chartered Accountants. Solicitors for *Private Eye* wrote to Goldsmith's legal advisers to say that their clients now recognized that there was no truth in the suggestion that Mr Goldsmith was involved in an attempt to obstruct justice, and offered a public withdrawal and apology. Goldsmith declined to settle, and sought an injunction to prevent *Private Eye* from publishing anything else about him, but failed.

Meanwhile, Goldsmith was knighted in Prime Minister Harold Wilson's resignation honours.

The trial of Richard Ingrams and his associates began at the Central Criminal Court on 16 May 1977. Prior to its commencement, however, an apology from *Private Eye* was published in the *Evening Standard*, and a contribution of £30,000 made to Sir James's costs, as well as an agreement to desist from pursuing a campaign against him. Goldsmith accepted these terms. No evidence was offered against the defendants, and they were acquitted. The litigation was said to have cost Sir James Goldsmith £250,000, and *Private Eye* £85,000. Sir James afterwards regretted that he had agreed to a settlement in the case.

Fact

The libel action brought by the fast food chain, McDonalds, against two environmental campaigners, David Morris and Helen Steel, turned out to be the longest trial in British legal history. It ended on 13 December 1996 after two and a half years. The actual number of days in court was 314. Judgement was delivered on 19 June 1997 in favour of the plaintiff. Although some of the accusations made by the defendants were upheld, they had libelled the company in the more serious charges, and McDonalds were awarded damages of £60,000. On 1 November 1996, this trial overtook the famous Tichborne case (see under Fraud) as the longest-ever trial in Britain.

Section 6: Other Crimes

Rape

Any man or boy above the age of 14 can be found guilty of rape if the court is satisfied that he had sexual intercourse with a woman or girl without her consent, or if he forced a woman or girl to have sexual intercourse against her will by physical strength, intimidation or trickery. It is not necessary to prove completion by ejaculation. Partial penetration is all that is necessary to constitute rape.

There has been much public disquiet in recent years about the derisory sentences for rape handed down by judges, who sometimes appear to represent a sort of judicial misogyny. But rape has in the past been regarded in some male-dominated societies as a kind of legitimate sport, even in peacetime conditions. (The wholesale rape of women by troops in a conquered country has often been regarded the world over as a just reward for the soldiers' victory.) Even in the Victorian period, when rape could be punished by transportation, it is recorded that in 1849 at Willenhall, Staffordshire, townsfolk of both sexes and all ages gathered to 'enjoy the spectacle' when four young men gang-raped a girl on an open space in the town.

At the other extreme, the United States executed more than 300 convicted rapists between 1940 and 1967, when the death penalty for rape was abolished. Among the countries where a rapist can still be sentenced to death is the Philippines, which reintroduced capital punishment in 1993 after a six-year period without it, following the fall of the Marcos regime.

English law was not always so equivocal about punishing a man for rape: Romans and Saxons punished it with death; Normans by castration. But in the early medieval period, rape was not a crime at all,

Fact

In England and Wales 1,334 cases of rape were recorded by police in 1983. By 1993 the number had risen to 4,589. This represents an average annual increase in this crime of 13.2 per cent—the highest increase in any serious crime in Britain during this period. But it is important to remember that increasing awareness of sexual offences and greater sympathy towards rape victims has undoubtedly led to a higher proportion of rapes being reported to the police. Since 1992, it has been possible for a man to be convicted of raping his wife.

being regarded merely as a misdemeanour akin to trespassing. Rape has, of course, often been relegated by events to a mere secondary consideration, when men have been convicted of murder or manslaughter in the course of raping their victims. John Price, a London executioner, was himself hanged for murder in 1718 after killing Elizabeth White, a watchman's wife, whilst attempting to rape her in Moorfields one night.

Sometimes in the past, accused rapists would be brought before the ecclesiastical courts when unmarried women had to answer for their pregnancies. Joan Somers explained at Downham, Essex, in 1590, that she was looking after her mistress's cattle in a ploughed field when one Ryce approached her and said that "she mighte now crye her harte owte, before anie body colde heere her cris, and...he did violentlye abuse her bodye and committed fornication with her".

The extremely cautious attitude of the law towards charges of rape is probably due to a double hangover from earlier times. Firstly, the male domination of society and the low status of women; secondly, justified wariness of false accusations which might lead an innocent man to the gallows. A man hanged for raping a woman in London in 1749 was declared innocent two years later when another admitted the offence. Eight black youths were sentenced to death in Alabama in 1931 for raping two white girls. The executions were not carried out, but they served several years in prison, even though medical checks proved that the girls had not been raped and one of them admitted afterwards that she had lied.

The difficulties of securing convictions also help to account for the fact that many cases of rape go unreported to the police. It was fairly useless in the past for a parlourmaid or any other young female to accuse her master of raping her. The jury would always take the master's word against the servant's unless there were very exceptional circumstances, such as grievous bodily harm. When a milliner named Sarah Woodcock accused Lord Baltimore of raping her in 1764, after keeping her captive for three days at his country seat in Surrey, the judge directed the jury to acquit his lordship as it was only Sarah Woodcock's word against that of an aristocrat.

Among those accused of rape have been Sir Thomas Malory, the 15th-century author of the great English romance *Le Morte d'Arthur,* who was charged with having twice broken into the house of one Hugh Smyth and 'feloniously raped Joan, wife of the said Hugh'. Others, more recent, have included Colonel Valentine Baker, former Commanding Officer of the 10th Hussars, who in 1875 propositioned 22 year-old Rebecca Dickinson, a passenger on a train between Midhurst and Waterloo; Errol Flynn, the film star, who was acquitted in 1942 after being tried on four charges of Statutory Rape in the USA; and Mike Tyson, the former heavyweight boxing champion who was sentenced to six years imprisonment in 1991. In Colonel Baker's case, it turned out that what he had actually done was put his arm round Miss Dickinson's waist and kissed her. This was afterwards described by an MP as "one of the most scandalous and atrocious crimes ever committed".

One of the more notorious cases in recent years was the series of rapes committed on dozens of victims, ranging from schoolgirls to middle-aged women, in the Spokane district of Washington State between 1978 and 1981. The rapist turned out to be Frederick Coe, son of the editor of a local newspaper which had offered its own reward for the capture of the criminal. Convicted on four counts, Coe was sentenced to life imprisonment for each one.

In 1982, a man named Pollard was sentenced at Leeds to four and a half years imprisonment for the rape of a 40 year-old spinster, Zoe Wade, in Bradford. Pollard was released after serving only 16 months, and in June 1984 he visited the same woman again and raped and killed her. This time he was given 10 years for rape and life imprisonment for murder.

In 1983, a 28 year-old man serving a minimum of 20 years in Illinois for rape was released after only six years when his victim confessed that she had invented the story. Mrs Cathy Webb stated that she had picked Gary Dotson from police photographs after saying that she had been raped to hide from her foster parents that she—then 16 years old—was pregnant by her boyfriend. But the judge who presided over the trial of Dotson not only refused to quash the conviction but sent him back to prison, and his decision was upheld by the state governor, James Thompson. It was maintained that the original conviction had been safe, and it was not known why Cathy Webb was now recanting her evidence. Public opinion, however, forced Governor Thompson to commute the sentence to the six years Dotson had already served, and he was freed.

In December of the same year, Judge Victor Pyle aroused huge controversy in South Carolina by telling three convicted men, who had raped and tortured a 23 year-old woman, that they could choose between a 30 year prison sentence and castration. Defence lawyers called the sentence 'barbaric', but one of the men, Roscoe Brown, had little hesitation in opting for castration, saying that "to be isolated and not able to contribute to the world would be more damaging to me than to undergo castration".

Fact

Between 1982 and 1986 around 26 murders committed in London were associated with the so-called 'Railway Rapist'. The bodies of the victims were invariably found near railway lines, their hands tied behind their backs with a type of string used almost exclusively by British Rail. John Duffy, a railway carpenter, was eventually arrested and charged with the crimes, and was convicted of five rapes and two murders.

Bigamy

Bigamy is the offence of marrying someone whilst legally married to someone else, and can be punished with a maximum of seven years imprisonment, although prosecutions are relatively rare these days. In 1983 in England and Wales 92 cases of bigamy were known to police; 10 years later, the number was 90. The lowest number of cases in the intervening years was 66 in 1987.

Such a marriage is declared void, and if *both* partners in the illegal marriage *knew* it to be bigamous, any resulting children would be illegitimate. But it can be a defence against a charge of bigamy if the person alleged to have committed it can show that he or she genuinely believed that his or her former marriage partner was dead, or if that partner had not been heard of for seven years and was not *known* to be alive.

Fact

Johann Hoch, a German immigrant hanged for murder in Chicago, Illinois, in February 1906, was known as the 'Stockyard Bluebeard'. He was believed to have illegally married at least 55 women, promptly deserting most of them when he had obtained their possessions. But no less than 15 of his 'wives' died from arsenic poisoning.

A more celebrated defence was offered at the Old Bailey in 1719 by one Catherine Jones, who had married Constantine Boone at Southwark whilst her first husband, John Rowland, was still alive. Mr Rowland was abroad at the time, and when he returned to England he instituted proceedings against his wife. Catherine Jones freely admitted her second marriage, but denied that it could be bigamous as the second husband was a hermaphrodite. A witness testified that Boone had been brought up in girls' clothing and trained in needlework until the age of 12, when he "turned man, and went to sea". He (or she) had been exhibited at fairs as a hermaphrodite, and it was stated that the female sexual characteristics were predominant over the male ones. The jury acquitted Catherine Jones of bigamy.

It is recorded that a man named Miller was sentenced to stand in the pillory in 1790 for bigamy, having been convicted of marrying 30 different women in order to plunder them. And lesbian women have on numerous occasions married other women while disguised as men. Ann Morrow was sentenced to three months in prison and exposure in the pillory after being convicted of impersonating a man and marrying three different women. When she stood in the pillory at Charing Cross, a mob consisting mainly of women pelted her with missiles so severely that she was blinded in both eyes.

In April 1776, Elizabeth Chudleigh, Duchess of Kingston, a woman renowned for her beauty, was tried in Westminster Hall for bigamy by the House of Lords in the presence of Queen Charlotte and the Prince of Wales. The Duke of Kingston was already in his grave, but the case was brought because the Duke's son-in-law had challenged the validity of the Duke's will, alleging that the Duchess, his stepmother, had unduly influenced its terms. So she was brought before this 'awful tribunal'.

It was alleged that when Elizabeth was married to the Duke at Westminster in March 1769, she was, in fact, already married. Evidence was produced that as a young woman in 1744, she had been secretly married in a midnight ceremony in Hampshire to a naval officer, Augustus Hervey, a son of the Earl of Bristol, and that she had given birth to a child by him. (Five years later Horace Walpole described a masked ball in which Elizabeth had appeared as Iphigenia, "but so naked that you would have taken her for Andromeda".) She had later denied this marriage on oath.

The Duchess was solemnly declared guilty of bigamy and asked if she had anything to urge against judgement being pronounced. The Lord High Steward had acquainted Her Grace with the fact that the death penalty had been abolished for bigamy, but imprisonment and burning in the hand were still prescribed punishments. The Duchess said: "I plead the privilege of the peerage". Their Lordships allowed this traditional plea, which meant that she could not be imprisoned or branded, and the Duchess fainted when told that she would be 'discharged on paying the usual fees', and had to be carried out of the court. The whole procedure had been an elaborate farce for the Duchess had come from France to face trial, and would hardly have done so if she had not been confident in advance of the outcome. But it seems that their Lordships were lenient with the lady, for if they were satisfied that she was a bigamist, and her marriage to the Duke was indeed illegal, then she was not really a Duchess and had no entitlement to the privileges of the peerage. It was only in the following year that her marriage to Hervey was declared valid. As by then Hervey had succeeded his brother as Earl of Bristol, she legally became a countess.

A famous case of bigamy occurred in the Lake District in 1802, when Mary Robinson, teenage daughter of an innkeeper at Buttermere, was married to Colonel the Honourable Alexander Augustus Hope, MP for Linlithgow and brother of the Earl of Hopetoun. Mary was known as the 'Beauty of Buttermere' and had many admirers (among whom were Wordsworth, Southey and Coleridge), and several suitors. But her choice of a husband aroused the suspicions of Coleridge in particular, who had doubts about the Hon. Alexander's lack of deportment and ungrammatical speech. Enquiries revealed that the man was an impostor, for the real Colonel Hope was living in Vienna. Mary's husband was really John Hatfield, a linen draper's salesman who already had a wife and family in Devon. He was well known in the London coffee houses as 'Lying Hatfield'. He had spent time in various prisons and had recently been declared bankrupt. Thus found out, Hatfield made himself scarce, leaving Mary pregnant, but he was soon arrested and brought to trial at Carlisle Assizes on three charges of forgery. This being a capital offence, the bigamous marriage was a mere triviality, and in due course Hatfield was hanged for what the judge described as "crimes of such magnitude as have seldom, if ever, received any mitigation of capital punishment". The sum involved in his forgeries was £50. Hatfield's cruel deception of Mary Robinson led to melodramas on the London stage and still inspires books, Melvyn Bragg being the latest to exploit the story in fiction.

In March 1983 in Phoenix, Arizona, a defendant was given six years imprisonment for bigamy (as well as 28 years for fraud and a fine of $336,000) after being convicted of 104 bigamous marriages in the USA and elsewhere, including Britain, over a period of more than 30 years. Four of his victims were married to him on board ships. Charged under the name Giovanni Vigliotto, one of a large number of aliases, the man's true identity remains uncertain.

Fact

Among the most notorious bigamists in Britain were the murderers George Chapman and George Joseph Smith. (For Smith, see under Murder.) Chapman's real name was Severine Klosovski. He was a Polish immigrant who had left his wife behind when he came to London in 1888. He married another woman and they went to America for two years. When Klosovski came back to England, he left his second 'wife' behind. He then had a series of other 'wives' who died by poison, and Chapman—as he called himself by then—was hanged for murder in 1903.

Part two:
Crimes Against Property

Section 1: Arson

...neither human resources, nor imperial munificence, nor appeasement of the gods, eliminated sinister suspicions that the fire had been instigated.
Tacitus: *The Annals of Imperial Rome*

SETTING FIRE to a dwelling house or other building was a capital offence in Britain from the time of the Anglo-Saxons until 1861, when the Malicious Damage Act reduced the maximum penalty to penal servitude for life. Setting fire to crops could also be punished by a life sentence. Arson in naval dockyards, however, remained a capital offence until 1971, when the Criminal Damage Act abolished the death penalty for that crime. A sentence of life imprisonment can still be imposed on an arsonist, particularly if the fire endangers human life. In practice, arsonists are often judged to be suffering from pyromania, and are sent to psychiatrists rather than to prison cells.

In the past, the *calculating* fire-raiser was often a servant attempting to hide a crime against his master. In 1734 a cook dismissed by his employer, Richard Cantillon, a London banker, returned to the house in Albemarle Street and murdered Mr Cantillon, stole money and valuables, and burned the house down before fleeing to the continent. But the murder was detected despite the blaze, and its perpetrator arrested in The Netherlands.

Other historical motives for arson were resentment by labourers of tithe demands by parish priests or exploitation by wealthy landlords, or arson by poachers who had been severely punished

Fact

The Great Fire of London, which broke out in a baker's shop in Pudding Lane on 2 September 1666, was attributed by many to arson by Papists. A French watchmaker, Robert Hubert, was arrested and confessed to having started the fire and was hanged at Tyburn. But he was an innocent scapegoat; the master of a ship on which Hubert had come to London swore that he did not leave it until the fire had been raging for two days. Nevertheless, the persistent suspicion of arson by Papists found official expression on the Monument, the commemorative column designed by Wren and completed in 1677: the reference to 'Popish frenzy' was not removed until 1830. The fire destroyed over 400 acres of the city, burning more than 13,000 houses, 85 churches, St Paul's Cathedral and many other public buildings. Eight people lost their lives, and 100,000 were made homeless. In all probability, the conflagration started accidentally with an overheated oven.

by magistrates. Burning down the barns, hayricks or stables of the rich was easy revenge for perceived injustices, with little risk of being caught. In 1844 an East Anglian arsonist left a note near a fire he had started: "You bluddy farmers could not live if it was not for the poore, tis them that keeps you bluddy raskells alive". Other common motives have been political sabotage and insurance frauds. In the winter of 1979—80 there was a spate of arson attacks by Welsh nationalist extremists when 32 fire-raising incidents took place against English holiday homes in North Wales. In recent years, arson has been employed by animal rights campaigners.

One of the most famous of British arsonists was Jonathan Martin, the brother of John (known as 'Mad Martin'), the painter of apocalyptic landscapes. A religious fanatic, Jonathan tried to burn down York Minster in 1828 after hiding himself behind the organ-pipes. He conceived this act as a contribution to church reform! The fire caused great damage, especially to the cathedral's choir and roof. Martin was confined to a lunatic asylum.

Arson was among the weapons adopted by the militant Women's Social and Political Union, led by Mrs Emmeline Pankhurst, in support of women's suffrage. She was several times arrested and imprisoned for less serious offences, but a sustained campaign of arson by the suffragettes in 1913, including a bomb attack on Lloyd George's home as well as burning houses and setting fire to pillar-boxes and empty railway carriages, resulted in her receiving a sentence of penal servitude for three years, and she was sent to Holloway Prison. She was, however, released within 12 months.

Men and women arrested for arson have often ended up being charged with murder. H.H. Holmes (also known as Herman Mudgett), the American multiple murderer of young women and girls, tried to burn down his house in Chicago, the so-called 'Torture Castle', where police eventually discovered the remains of 200 victims.

Case Histories

John the Painter

Fact

A boy of 8 years was hanged for arson at Abingdon in the 17th century. He was convicted of setting fire to two barns with 'malice, cunning and revenge'.

On 7 December 1776, a serious fire broke out in the ropehouse of the Royal Navy dockyard at Portsmouth. The authorities suspected arson. Six weeks later, on 16 January, dockside warehouses were set ablaze at Bristol. At first, no connection could be made between the two fires, but then baffled investigators began to suspect that the fires might have been started by American agents intent on damaging English shipping to aid the colonists in their war of independence. This was strongly denied by the Americans, who countered by accusing Tory *agents provocateurs* of causing the blazes.

At length a 24 year-old man named James Aitken, known as 'John the Painter', was arrested. He was an itinerant house-painter, born in Edinburgh, who had come to London; failing to make a living at his trade, he had turned to highway robbery and shoplifting. He had been in America for a time and had taken part in the Boston Tea Party. He returned to England in 1775, supporting the American Revolution, and sought to promote its success by attacking the shipping that was vital to the British government's cause. At Bristol his intention had been to burn not only the shipping but the whole city. He was not, it appeared, in the pay of the Americans but acting purely on his own initiative, although he may have been encouraged in his plan by Silas Deane, a member of Congress whom he had met in Paris.

"I spent two days in the contemplation of this malicious design", Aitken admitted, "and promised myself immortal honour in the accomplishment of it. I beheld it in the light of a truly heroic enterprise, such as never would have been equalled to the end of time. I was persuaded it would entitle me to the first rank in America, and flattered myself with the ambition of becoming the admiration of the world".

No such distinction followed his crimes: Aitken was brought to trial at Winchester in March 1777. Convicted and sentenced to death, the disillusioned fire-raiser was executed by hanging at Portsmouth on 10 March, and his body hung in chains at the harbour mouth.

Fact

During the anti-Catholic Gordon Riots of June 1780, Newgate gaol was set on fire and 300 prisoners set free. They included three highway robbers who were due to be executed at Tyburn next morning. The house of the gaol-keeper, Richard Akerman, was also burnt down. Newgate had to be extensively rebuilt and repaired at a cost of more than £20,000. The rioters also burned down the house of Lord Mansfield, the Lord Chancellor, and several other buildings, including the King's Bench and Fleet prisons.

The Incendiary Nanny

In August 1982, a young Scottish woman employed as a nanny by an Italian family living on the island of Elba was arrested for arson and attempted murder. Carol Compton, 20, from Aberdeen, was alleged to have started two fires and endangered the life of a three year-old child named Agnese who was in her care. She was also suspected of starting three fires at Ortiséi on the mainland where she had worked as an *au pair* for Signora Emanuela Ricci before coming to Elba.

Because of the snail's pace of Italian justice, it was over a year after her arrest before Miss Compton was brought to trial at Livorno on five charges of arson and one of attempted murder. The dock in which she stood was a locked cage built to accommodate accused terrorists. For the journalists and *paparazzi* besieging the courtroom, this drama of a common-or-garden arsonist had an irresistible sub-plot—the accused woman was popularly supposed to be a witch. Unhampered by any constraint such as contempt of court in Italian law, reporters freely aired this accusation. There were stories that strange things happened in her presence, such as plates and pictures inexplicably falling to the floor. Professor Vipolo Nicolo, a forensic expert from Pisa University, testified that fires Miss Compton was accused of starting were the strangest he had ever investigated, and were "created by an intense sort of heat, but not by flames".

Fact

In 1789, the King's Theatre in London's Haymarket was burnt down. It was one of the capital's finest theatres, designed by Sir John Vanbrugh and opened in 1705 under the management of William Congreve. A theatre employee named Carrivalli is said to have confessed on his deathbed to arson. In January 1792, the Pantheon in Oxford Street was also burnt down. This fire occurred 20 years almost to the day after the opening of the building described by Horace Walpole as "the most beautiful edifice in England". There was £60,000 worth of damage. Rumour attributed the fire to friends of the rival King's Theatre, rebuilt in 1791.

Fact

One of the most notorious cases of arson in the present century was the burning of the Reichstag in Berlin on the night of 27 February 1933. Even while the parliament building was ablaze, the Nazi leaders were blaming the fire on the Communists whom they alleged were unleashing a revolution in Germany. A feeble-minded Dutch Communist and pyromaniac, Marinus van der Lubbe, may have started the fire, but whether he did or not, he became the scapegoat for Hitler and his lieutenants, and was probably a well-prompted dupe. Other Communists were arrested and tried at Leipzig for arson and treason, but were acquitted. Van der Lubbe was convicted and executed by beheading. It is virtually certain that Nazi leaders—notably Goering and Goebbels—staged the fire themselves and used it as a reason for expelling left-wing political enemies, thus clearing the way for Hitler to exercise dictatorial powers. He promptly made acts of arson and sabotage subject to the death penalty.

Both defending and prosecuting counsels did their best to dismiss all consideration of paranormal events from the case. The public prosecutor said that Miss Compton had probably started the fires so that she could leave and join her boyfriend in Rome. He demanded a sentence of seven years, and advised the two professional and six lay judges that they should only acquit Carol Compton "if in conscience you believe that today you would entrust your child to her".

Nevertheless, Miss Compton was acquitted of one of the arson charges and found not guilty of attempted murder. But she was convicted on four charges of arson and sentenced to two and a half years imprisonment after a trial in which difficulties of translation added to the chaos of the case.

Because of the time she had already spent in detention, Miss Compton was released at once, and on 18 December 1983 she was formally expelled from Italy and returned to Britain. An appeal to have the conviction overturned was unsuccessful.

Section 2: Robbery and Theft

Im as prigs what isn't 'isn,
When 'e's cotched'll goo t'prison.

Hertfordshire dialect verse

THIS SECTION INCLUDES ALL CRIMINAL ACTS of taking away someone else's property with the intention of permanent deprivation. It thus covers everything from picking pockets and shoplifting to burglary and bank raids. Robbery is distinguished from theft by being accompanied by actual or threatened violence in the course of stealing. Burglary and housebreaking are the crimes of entering property illegally with the intention of committing a crime. (Although, technically, that crime is not limited to stealing. Burglary can also be trespassing with intent to commit rape or malicious damage.)

It is a huge subject. Theft and robbery are by far the most common criminal activities in western capitalist societies, and attempts to limit them have led to various extreme measures. In Saxon England, burglary carried a fixed tariff of penalties to compensate the victims. During the reign of King Alfred, breaking into a labourer's home cost the criminal five shillings, but if he broke into the king's palace, the sum would be 120 shillings. (It should not be imagined that the idea of someone breaking into the king's palace was extravagant. Both Windsor Castle and Buckingham Palace have been burgled in modern times.) By the reign of Henry I, a burglar was liable to suffer the death penalty, and this remained the case until 1861. The *Anglo-Saxon Chronicle* records that in 1124, Ralph Basset (who was lord of the manor of Sapcote in Leicestershire and one of the king's thanes) "hanged more thieves than ever before; 44 of them in all were dispatched in no time, and six had their eyes put out and were castrated". (By way of contrast, O.G. Tomkeieff's analysis of about 430 crimes at Lincoln in 1202, including 114 cases of homicide and 89 of robbery—often with violence—shows that only two criminals were hanged. The rest were outlawed, fined or claimed sanctuary in church.)

Burglary was defined in the Tudor period as the crime of breaking in to a dwelling at night, and this was confirmed in the 1861 Larceny Act, when entering a dwelling illegally during daylight hours was defined as housebreaking. The distinction was abolished in 1968. Today, burglary applies to anyone entering any building illegally at any time with the intent to commit an offence. In fact, domestic burglary is now relatively rare at night. Commercial premises are more vulnerable than dwellings during the midnight hours. Afternoons are unpopular with thieves of both persuasions. Nowadays, when both parents in a family are likely to be working—even if only part-time—and the children are at school, weekday mornings are the favourite times for house burglars to operate.

Tobias Smollett said of London in the mid-18th century that thieves and robbers were "now become more desperate and savage than they had ever appeared since mankind were civilized". But in the following century, the efficiency of central London police was said by the Home Secretary, Sir Robert Peel, to be causing criminals to move their activities to other parishes. In 1834 an outbreak of burglaries in Liverpool was blamed on police in the capital who were said to be forcing housebreakers to turn to the provinces! Two years later, people in the fashionable residential area of Headingley in Leeds complained to the local Watch Committee that criminals were being driven out of the city centre into their area! The fact was that burglary was a growth industry, on the increase everywhere. Three-quarters of modern burglars are young single men, and much present-day burglary is committed to finance drug-addiction.

Social and economic circumstances influence the ways in which crimes against property can flourish. Highway robbery was a profitable crime in the 17th and 18th centuries when coaches could be held up on quiet country roads, and England was the only civilized country in Europe which did not have a professional police force. Nowadays, the highest rates of property crime are in urban areas. London, Merseyside and the West Midlands head the list in England. London has more than thrice the national average. It is also the world's chief clearing-house for stolen art and antiquities. Works of art are commonly stolen for ransom and are used to finance drug-deals and money-laundering. (The capital is also, incidentally, the place where the criminal is most likely to get away with his crime. The Metropolitan Police clear-up rate for robberies is currently the lowest in Britain.)

Car theft is a 20th-century crime originating in the use of cars as getaway vehicles after other crimes, such as burglaries and smash-and-

Fact

Possibly the most famous robber in all literature is Barabbas, the criminal whom Pontius Pilate, Procurator of Judaea—acceding to the clamour of the Jerusalem mob—released instead of Jesus of Nazareth. But two small-time thieves have been accorded undreamed-of immortality in the world's great art: Rembrandt van Rijn painted two pictures of 17th century anatomy lectures in Amsterdam in which the subjects being dissected have been identified. Only executed criminals were allowed to be used for demonstrations of anatomy at the time, so surviving Dutch records have enabled the two criminals in Rembrandt's group portraits to be named with confidence. The corpse in the famous Anatomy Lesson of Professor Tulp, *painted in 1632, is that of Adriaan Adriaansz, a 28 year-old thief from Leiden known as* het Kint ('the child'), *who was hanged in January 1632.* The Anatomy Lesson of Johannes Deijman, *painted in 1656, was mostly destroyed in a fire in 1723, but the surviving central portion shows the cadaver of Joris Fonteyn, a thief nicknamed 'Black Jan' who was hanged in January 1656.*

Fact

The Recorder of London in 1581, William Fleetwood, reported to Queen Elizabeth's chief minister, Lord Burghley, that a riverside alehouse keeper, one Wotton, was training boys on his premises to be expert pickpockets and cutpurses. He had a pocket and a purse hung up with little bells attached, and the boys practised taking counters out of them without causing the bells to ring. When practise had made perfect, the boys were qualified to go out as 'foisters' (pickpockets) or 'nippers' (cutpurses).

Fact

After the English Civil War, Captain Zachary Howard, a royalist, set out to 'plague regicides', plundering the house of General Thomas Fairfax and raping Lady Fairfax and her daughter. The unfortunate Lady Fairfax also fell victim to the highwayman John Cottington, who robbed her of a gold watch encrusted with diamonds. Howard was hanged in 1652; Cottington four years later.

grab raids. Scotland Yard's 'Flying Squad' was formed in 1919 to fight the growing crime of car theft. Between that year and the beginning of WWII 20 years later, the number of cars on Britain's roads increased tenfold—from 200,000 to 2 million—and mobile crime increased accordingly. But 'joy-riding' is not theft because the young criminal does not usually intend to deprive the owner of the vehicle permanently. A joy-rider may be convicted of causing damage, dangerous driving, stealing the petrol he has used, and so on, but if he abandons the vehicle he has not stolen it.

Case Histories

To Catch a Thief

Jonathan Wild was a bucklemaker who turned to crime when he failed to make ends meet. Born in Shropshire around 1682, he deserted his wife and went to London to seek his fortune. Newgate Gaol was his college of further education. Imprisoned for debt, he joined the company of cut-throats and highwaymen, pickpockets and prostitutes. When he got out of prison, he promptly opened a brothel.

He also lent his talents to law enforcement. He discovered thieves and pursued them with legendary tenacity, earning sums of money under the Parliamentary Reward system. He became the envy of less efficient sleuths to such an extent that he soon gave himself the grand title 'Thief-Taker General of Great Britain and Ireland'. He wore a lace coat, carried a silver staff, and seemed a minor pillar of society. He was instrumental in bringing some of London's most notorious criminals to justice, including the famed Jack Sheppard.

However, there was not a lot of money to be made from such honest endeavours, and Wild had a fertile imagination and a reservoir of untapped talents which he soon put to profitable use. He presented himself as a 'fence' to the thieves of London, whilst at the same time retaining his role as a 'grass' to the officers of Newgate. He organised the thieves into a huge co-operative enterprise, of which he was the manager and presiding genius. He inspired their crimes and disposed of their loot.

He brought an original touch to these proceedings. Instead of selling the stolen goods to back-street dealers, smugglers and other traffickers, he set up a lost property office and sold it back to the original owners having discovered they would pay more for it than the dealers. He ran this lucrative racket so successfully that he was obliged to expand, and opened new premises in—of all places—Old Bailey. His audacity knew no bounds. He ordered his gangs to discover the identities of those they stole from so that he could—after a suitable interval—notify the victims that their possessions had been 'recovered'.

He paid the thieves a barely living wage, but kept their loyalty by promising rigged trials if they were caught and threatening swift revenge if they dared to double-cross him. They were well aware that he could have them dangling on the end of a rope at Tyburn in no time, and also earn himself the gratitude of upright citizens who wept tears of joy when recovering their stolen property from one of his offices—on payment of a suitable fee.

Wild hoodwinked the magistrates as easily as he browbeat the felons. He had an ingenious device for 'shopping' thieves who did not belong to his organization: when one of his own men was brought to trial, Wild would advise him to turn King's Evidence and obtain a pardon by denouncing the alien crook as an accomplice.

Jonathan Wild was, in effect, both the mastermind of organized crime and the chief of police. But he finally got his comeuppance when he was convicted of receiving stolen goods whilst under arrest in Newgate. Exposed as an iniquitous double-dealer, he was sentenced to death and hanged before a vast crowd in 1725, passing through a noose at Tyburn to a niche in folklore.

Fact

In 1671, Colonel Thomas Blood, an Irish adventurer, gained the confidence of the Jewel-House Keeper in the Tower of London by a ruse which included disguising himself as a clergyman, and talking the keeper, Talbot Edwards, into parting with his pistols. Thus disarmed, the Keeper was easily overpowered when Blood returned later with his accomplices, bound and gagged Edwards and stole the Crown Jewels. But the criminals were soon caught. Colonel Blood, however, was not only pardoned by Charles II, but had his confiscated estate in Ireland restored to him.

Gentlemen of the Road?

Dick Turpin, Claude Duval, Ned Kelly, Ben Hall, Butch Cassidy and the Sundance Kid, et al, are names which legend and the film industry have elevated into romantic heroes when in fact they were, to a man, murderous, thieving villains.

Turpin is easily the most famous of British highwaymen, partly because of the fictitious exploits attributed to him and his mare Black Bess, and the many places fancifully associated with him. But Turpin began his criminal career as a cattle thief when he was a butcher's apprentice, and ended it in 1739 when he was hanged at York for horse-stealing before he was 35 after wantonly shooting his landlord's cockerel and threatening to kill a man who rebuked him for it.

Claude Duval, the Frenchman who terrorized the English highways, threatening the purses of the gentlemen and the honour of ladies, was even younger when he was hanged at Tyburn in 1670. The areas around London where travellers were especially vulnerable to highway robbery were Hounslow Heath and Wimbledon Common, Bagshot Heath and the Great North Road. Holloway was one of Duval's chief haunts, and it was said that Duval's Lane at Highgate (known as Hornsey Lane nowadays) was so infested with highwaymen in the 17th century that "few people would venture to peep into it even at midday".

John Rann, known as 'Sixteen-string Jack' from the silk strings he wore at the knees of his breeches, was hanged at Tyburn in 1774. Nine years later, on 7 November 1783, another highwayman, John Austin, became the last person to be hanged there before the chief place of execution in London was transferred to Old Bailey in front of Newgate prison.

Fact

In 1771 Sir John Fielding, the blind magistrate and co-founder of the Bow Street Runners, asked the actor and director David Garrick to close his production of John Gay's immensely popular The Beggar's Opera *at the Theatre Royal, Drury Lane. He considered that glorification of the play's hero, the highwayman Macheath, and his criminal way of life, would lead to an increase in crime. Such uncorroborated suspicions have been at the heart of much modern censorship of works of art and literature.*

Fact

The character of Fagin in Dickens's Oliver Twist *is commonly believed to have been based on Isaac Solomons, the Jewish pickpocket and 'prince of fences'. Ikey Solomons operated in London's Spitalfields district and the Saffron Hill area until he was arrested for theft in 1827. Two coachloads of stolen property were removed from his house, and he was sentenced to a term of imprisonment but escaped from the Black Maria on the way to Newgate and fled the country. He eventually joined his wife and four children in Hobart, Tasmania, where she had been transported for receiving stolen goods. However, he was sent back to England to face a fresh trial (after trying to save his neck by offering to perform services for the Governor "to the Hutermost of my Obility"). This time he was sentenced to 14 years transportation—to Tasmania!*

Fact

In 1798, James Turnbull, an employee at the Royal Mint in the Tower of London, held up the rest of the staff at gunpoint and escaped with 2,804 newly-minted golden guineas. He was apprehended after nine days at large, and sentenced to death.

The earliest Australian highway robbers were often convicts who had escaped from the penal settlements and been hired as bushrangers. Ben Hall, subject of the famous ballad, was a convict's son. He and his gang robbed mail coaches, stole horses and plundered stores and homes until at the age of 28 he was shot dead by police in 1865. Ned Kelly, the son of an Irish convict, had a price of £8,000 on his head by the time he was 24, and he was hanged for murder in November 1880, in Melbourne.

Robert Leroy Parker ('Butch Cassidy') and Harry Longbaugh ('The Sundance Kid'), are believed to have been killed during a battle with Bolivian troops in 1909, after a career of train and highway robbery in the United States. The man sometimes credited with the 'invention' of bank robbery was Jesse James, the outlaw shot in the back by Bob Ford, a member of the James gang, for the sake of the reward money in 1882.

The Case of Deacon Brodie

One night in March 1788, a lawyer about to enter the General Excise Office in Edinburgh, was startled by a man in black rushing out of the building and disappearing into the night. Shortly afterwards, two more men emerged and quickly vanished. The lawyer, James Bonar, had interrupted a burglary. It was one of a spate of such crimes in the Scottish capital's public buildings and shops. The Royal Exchange and the university library were among the places which had been broken into and robbed. As the men were armed with pistols, Mr Bonar was fortunate not to have been shot.

Some time later, a thief named Brown turned King's Evidence and named two men, Ainslie and Smith, as his accomplices. He then added a third name—that of a leading Edinburgh citizen, William Brodie. Brodie was known as a highly respectable man, the master (or deacon), of one of the local trade guilds, and a member of the city council. This pillar of society, however, made himself scarce before he could be interviewed, having seen posters in London offering rewards for his arrest. He was soon traced to Amsterdam, and extradited to stand trial for armed robbery.

There was some protracted legal argument about the admissibility of evidence against him from known criminals who had a vested interest in appearing to cooperate with the law, but eventually Deacon Brodie and George Smith were convicted on the evidence of Brown and Ainslie, and sentenced to death. They were hanged in front of a crowd of 40,000 spectators on 1 October 1788.

Nearly 100 years later, Robert Louis Stevenson, in collaboration with W.H. Henley, wrote a play about Deacon Brodie's double life—the upright citizen by day and burglar by night—which influenced Stevenson's most famous story, *The Strange Case of Dr Jekyll and Mr Hyde*.

Robbery under Arms

The famous Siege of Sidney Street, which occurred on 3 January 1911, was the result of an attempted jewel robbery in Houndsditch a fortnight earlier. A gang of anarchists, mainly Russians, needing funds to finance their political activities, planned to rob Harris's jeweller's shop by tunnelling into the premises from an empty house at the back. But the noise they made aroused suspicion and the police were called. As officers entered the building to investigate, they suddenly found themselves under fire from the armed robbers. Soon three policemen lay dead and two more were injured as the criminals made their escape. It later transpired that one of the gang's leaders, George Gardstein, had also been caught in the gunfire by accident, and died a few days later whilst in hiding, tended by Sara Trassjonski and Luba Milstein, two of the gangsters' molls.

On 2 January, an informer told police that some of the gang were holed up in a tenement building in Sidney Street, Stepney. They were in a second-floor apartment of No 100, occupied by a Jewish woman, Mrs Betsy Gershon. Armed police surrounded the building during the hours of darkness, but the anarchists did not emerge, and after evacuating the building's tenants, police waited until dawn to alert the criminals to the fact that they were completely surrounded and could not escape. But instead of surrendering, the anarchicsts opened fire, wounding a police officer. Holding Mrs Gershon hostage, they made her take off her skirt and shoes, evidently believing that a devout Jewish woman would never show herself in public in her underwear, but as soon as an opportunity arose, she escaped with alacrity.

Police reinforcements and a detachment of Scots Guards sealed off the street at both ends, and exchanged fire with the gunmen. "Clear the people back!" a police inspector shouted, "Clear 'em right back! We don't want a lot of silly corpses lying round". The Home Secretary, Winston Churchill, arrived and proposed that the front of the house should be blown in with cannon-fire. A troop of the Royal Horse Artillery was sent for, but by the time it arrived the building was on fire. As the blaze spread, and the men were forced to retreat from the flames, one of them, Jacob Vogel, was shot. Another, Fritz Svaars, held out until the burning building collapsed about him, and died, overcome by smoke.

It is not clear whether the fire was accidental or started deliberately by the besieged men. Several other men and women were subsequently arrested in connection with the attempted robbery and the murder of the police officers, but were acquitted, and many of the gang were never caught, including the mysterious 'Peter the Painter', whose real name was possibly Straume. He may have been a Tsarist *agent provocateur,* and is thought to have died in America in 1914. Sara Trassjonski was his mistress. She descended into insanity after the Sidney Street affair, and died soon afterwards in the asylum at Friern Barnet, Middlesex.

The police handling of the affair was something of a shambles. The siege had lasted for six hours during which some innocent spectators were injured by gunfire, and there were casualties among the firemen who fought the blaze, one of whom died later. The government came in for much criticism for calling in the troops.

Fact

The most valuable single object ever stolen was undoubtedly the priceless painting by Leonardo da Vinci known as the Mona Lisa. *Painted in Florence around 1503, it is a portrait of the wife of a Florentine citizen named Francesco del Giocondo. It came to the Louvre Museum in Paris via King Francis I, and has never been valued. On 21 August 1911, it disappeared, and it was nearly two years before it was recovered. Vincenzo Perugia, a burglar, was arrested when he tried to sell the picture to an art dealer in Italy. It turned out that Perugia had stolen the* Mona Lisa *twice! He had been hired by two art forgers, named Chaudron and de Valfierno, to help them steal the picture from the Louvre. The three men, disguised as workmen, concealed themselves in the basement overnight prior to a day of closure for cleaning purposes. Next morning, unnoticed among the other workmen, they simply took the painting off the wall, complete with frame, and walked out. Chaudron and de Valfierno then made several copies of the painting and sold them to gullible Americans for $300,000 a time. Whatever plans they had in mind for the original never reached fruition for Perugia stole it from his erstwhile partners and fled back to Italy, intent on making himself a rich man by selling it. He claimed at his trial to be an Italian patriot committed to returning the portrait to Florence, its true home.*

Fact

One of the most notorious English burglars was Charles Peace, born in Sheffield around 1832. An agile, sanctimonious old reprobate, he went on housebreaking expeditions with his tools in a violin case. After 25 years of burglary in various parts of the country, under an assortment of aliases, he was finally hanged for murder at Armley Gaol, Leeds, complaining on the morning of his execution that "this is bloody rotten bacon".

Fact

The range of theft and robbery is well illustrated by a series of incidents in the spring of 1980. In March of that year, a gang ambushed and hijacked an articulated lorry near Barking, Essex, getting away with silver ingots worth around £4 million. (Most of the ingots were recovered later from a lock-up garage in Enfield.) Soon afterwards, armed and hooded robbers seized employees of a Hatton Garden gems dealer as they arrived for work, handcuffed and chained them together, and made off with diamonds worth about half a million pounds. Between these two robberies, Mervyn Shorthouse was imprisoned for two years at St Albans Crown Court after admitting the theft of 3,540 eggs from the Natural History Museum.

Rail Strike

The quiet countryside of central Buckinghamshire, where the flat agricultural landscape of the Vale of Aylesbury gives way to the Chiltern Hills near the borders with Hertfordshire and Bedfordshire, seems an unlikely scene for a crime which achieved world-wide fame. But it was only two or three miles from a popular local beauty spot, Ivinghoe Beacon, where, during the night of 7—8 August 1963, driver Jack Mills brought the Glasgow to Euston mail train to a stop at a signal gantry which was showing a red light. He sent his fireman to the trackside emergency telephone to find out what the trouble was. Seconds later, he was attacked in his cab by several men who struck him twice on the head during a struggle. Then the locomotive and the first two coaches were separated from the rest of the train and driven forward a short distance to a road bridge. Within minutes, the attackers, using axes and crowbars, had broken into a coach carrying old banknotes to London, and unloaded more than 120 mail bags, passing them down the embankment and into waiting vehicles. They got away with £2.6 million.

The gang that carried out what inevitably became known as the 'Great Train Robbery' had patiently worked out their plan over a period of several months. The 12-man team had been carefully chosen to include specialists who could fix the signals, cut telephone lines and drive the train. It was a commando-like operation carried out with military precision. And it all seemed to have worked perfectly. The men left their temporary HQ, an isolated farmhouse, confident in their alibis and prepared to lie low until the fuss died down before each commenced a new life-style with his share of the profits from the biggest train robbery in history.

As is almost invariably the case, however, it all went wrong. One vital link in the chain broke: when police explored the remains of Leatherslade Farm, the gang's temporary hide-out, they found clues galore. Men hired to burn down the farmhouse had bungled the job of destroying the evidence after the gang's departure. Articles of clothing and various other items remained identifiable and, above all, fingerprints. More than half the gang were in prison within the year, most of them sentenced to 30 years.

Another member was arrested in 1965, and another the following year after returning to Britain from Mexico. The last of the principal gang-members to be caught was Bruce Reynolds, who had also returned from abroad. He was arrested in Torquay in 1968, and was sentenced to 25 years. In the meantime, however, two of the prisoners had escaped. Charles Wilson got out of Winson Green prison in Birmingham after one year, and went first to Mexico and then to Canada. But he was arrested in January 1968 and extradited to serve the rest of his sentence.

The most sensational escape was that of Ronald Biggs, who was 'sprung' from Wandsworth Prison in July 1965 by an outside gang. He had been one of the first of the train robbers to be caught having left his fingerprints on a Monopoly board at the farm, and had been sentenced to 25 years for conspiracy and 30 years for armed robbery, the sentences to run concurrently. He fled to Australia but was constantly pursued until British police came up against a brick wall of obstruction in Brazil, which has, as yet, no extradition agreement with the United Kingdom. Furthermore, when Biggs, who had left his family behind in Australia, got his new girlfriend pregnant, all hope of bringing him back to Britain faded as Brazil's laws did not permit the deportation of the father of a Brazilian child. Biggs remains at liberty, living mainly on the proceeds of his ill-deserved fame.

The train driver, Jack Mills, eventually died of leukemia and, not, as has sometimes been suggested, as a result of the injuries he received during the robbery. That is not to say, of course, that his injuries were not serious and deserving of convictions for grievous bodily harm. Less than £350,000 of the stolen money was recovered, and by 1978, all the captured criminals had been released, no one having served more than 12 years.

Fact

The burglary which had perhaps the world's most far-reaching consequences was committed in June 1972, when six men were found in the US Democratic Party's headquarters in the Watergate building in Washington DC. The intruders were employees of a Republican Party organization, and were caught handling electronic bugging devices. The crime led eventually to the enforced resignation of President Richard M. Nixon—the only US President to resign from office—and to the imprisonment of several of Nixon's aides. Nixon himself, although threatened with impeachment, was pardoned by his successor, Gerald Ford.

The Brink's-Mat Job

A daring raid on a top-security London warehouse resulted in what was then the largest haul of any British robbery. It happened early on the morning of 26 November 1983 at Unit 7 of the Heathrow Trading Estate at Heathrow Airport. Unit 7 was virtually a huge safe, used by Brink's-Mat, the country's leading security firm, as a depository for bullion, currency, jewellery, fine art and other valuable consignments.

Just after 6:30 p.m., a gang of six masked and armed men entered the premises whilst the alarm was switched off to permit the entry of a guard who had arrived late for work. The gang handcuffed and bound five of the guards present, and forced the senior duty guard, Michael Scouse, into submission by dowsing him in petrol and threatening to set him alight if he did not immediately cooperate by giving them the combination to the door of the vault.

Having identified three tons of gold bullion due to be taken that morning to Gatwick Airport, the gang forced the guards to open the doors of the loading bay, brought in a waiting van, and proceeded to load the metal boxes containing the bullion. It took them a quarter of an hour, and when they drove away, they had taken gold, platinum and diamonds worth over £26 million. Police were on the scene within minutes of their departure.

It did not take long to deduce that the robbery could only have been planned and executed with inside help, and the detectives' chief suspect was the guard who had arrived late, Anthony Black. After a thorough grilling, Black admitted giving his sister's partner, Brian Robinson—who had a criminal record—information about shipments and security at the warehouse. He also admitted to letting in Robinson and his accomplices, and named two of the other men as Tony White and Mick McAvoy. All three were quickly picked up.

When the trial of the three commenced at the Old Bailey in October 1984, the chief prosecution witness, Black, had already been tried and

Fact

When a man brought charges of robbery against two prostitutes in Chicago in 1896, alleging that they worked as a team and emptied his pockets at knife-point, the judge dismissed the case with the observation that anyone who went to the Levee, Chicago's red light district, deserved to be robbed!

Fact

The number of burglaries in England and Wales rose from 808,300 in 1983 to 1,369,600 in 1993, an average annual increase of 5.4 per cent. But the rate of increase has tended to slow down since a peak in 1990/91, and the number of burglaries from buildings other than dwellings was slightly lower in 1993 than in the previous year. In 1994 the number of recorded burglaries from dwellings was 680,000, compared with 727,000 in 1993. British insurance companies handled claims for more than £630 million in 1994 resulting from domestic theft and burglary, compared with £740 million in 1993. Shoplifting and theft from vehicles also fell in 1993, probably as a result of increased installation of security systems. The increase in the number of robberies has also slowed down since a peak in 1991, and there were falls in 1994 and 1995 from the previous years' figures.

sentenced to six years. Robinson and McAvoy were found guilty and given 25 years each. But the evidence against White was insufficient to secure a conviction.

The gold bullion had so far not been recovered, but enquiries eventually led police to suspect a known associate of Robinson named Kenneth Noye, a property dealer with a criminal record. His house in Kent was kept under round-the-clock surveillance. In January 1985, two detective-constables, John Fordham and Neil Murphy, entered the grounds to carry out close observation, but were suddenly chased by Rottweiler dogs. Murphy reached the road safely, but Fordham did not follow. When more police officers went in, they found DC Fordham dying on the ground with Kenneth Noye standing over him. "He's stabbed me", Fordham managed to say. Police found 11 gold bars on Noye's premises.

Meanwhile, the trail of clues had led detectives to Avon and Somerset where they raided the homes of Garth Chappell and John Palmer. They also raided the home of Brian Reader, where they found £70,000 worth of banknotes. The chain of disposal had been formed by the initial receiver, Noye, who passed the stolen bullion on to Reader, who passed it on to Chappell. Within six months of the robbery, Chappell had disposed of half the stolen gold. Noye was cleared by the trial jury of murdering DC Fordham; the two officers had gone on to Noye's property dressed in camouflage jackets and balaclava helmets, and would have appeared sinister and menacing to any householder entitled to defend his property. Noye was sentenced to 13 years imprisonment for his part in the robbery; Chappell and Reader to 10 years. Palmer was acquitted. In 1989 a solicitor, Michael Relton, was sentenced to 12 years for his part in the crime—laundering the proceeds of the robbery. Many others suspected of involvement were also arrested. Gordon Parry was convicted and sentenced to 10 years in August 1992. Most of the missing gold has been traced.

Section 3: Fraud and Forgery

Behind every great fortune there lies a crime.
Honoré de Balzac: *L'Histoire de Treize*

IT WAS ALEXANDRE LACASSAGNE, Professor of Forensic Medicine at Lyons University, who said: "Every society gets the criminals it deserves". Each society is responsible for creating the conditions in which certain crimes flourish, and the Georgian proposition that there existed a 'criminal class' was an appalling example of English hypocrisy. Crimes such as housebreaking, malicious damage and armed robbery might be the preserve of the lower classes, punishable by the upper classes which find those crimes offensive and inconvenient. As C.E.M. Joad once put it: "The man who makes the laws...can see to it that he has no incentive to break them. Thus we have the majestic impartiality of the modern law which forbids rich and poor alike to sleep in doorways". But the upper classes have a monopoly in crimes such as large-scale financial fraud and evils which go largely unpunished, like exploitation.

Fraud and forgery are 'white-collar crimes'. They are the educated variants on robbery and theft. The law does not recognize any illegal act under the name of fraud, although the word is used a good deal in the media. What is commonly called fraud is, in law, deception committed in order to obtain some benefit. The difference between fraud and forgery, both criminal acts of deception, is that in a case of fraud the defendant must have obtained some material thing by deception in order to be convicted, whereas in a case of forgery it is a criminal offence to falsify a document whether it has been used to obtain something by deception or not. Thus, a person who forges a doctor's prescription in order to obtain drugs is guilty of a crime even if he has not obtained the drugs, but a person who falsely claims to be collecting money for a charity is not guilty of a crime unless someone has been deceived into giving him money. Until he has profited from the deceit, he is merely a liar. Arthur Ferguson, the Scottish con man who persuaded rich Americans in the 1920s that he was authorized to sell Big Ben and Nelson's Column, was imprisoned for five years because some of them believed him and paid up. (Perhaps it was the Americans who should have been jailed!)

Copying a famous painting is not forgery, because a painting is not a document, but selling it to someone who has been led to believe that it is the original is obtaining money by deception.

One of the most famous cases of forgery in British history was brought to light in 1824 when Henry Fauntleroy, a private banker, was convicted of forgery with intent to defraud the Bank of England of more than £250,000. He is sometimes said to have raised forgery to the level of an exact science, but as he was found out, this is a debatable conclusion. There was, perhaps surprisingly, much public sympathy for this 'gentleman', who owned a Thames-side villa and a house in Brighton, and kept a string of mistresses. A hundred thousand people are said to have gathered to witness his execution outside Newgate prison on 30 November 1824—the largest crowd ever known for such an event. Not since Earl Ferrers in 1760 had an English gentleman suffered death in public at the hands of the common hangman.

Alphonse Capone, the gangster notorious for racketeering during the prohibition era in Chicago, was finally brought to justice in 1931 not for murder, 'bootlegging' or gambling rackets, but for fraud in the form of tax evasion. Al 'Scarface' Capone, America's Public Enemy Number One, was charged with non-payment of taxes and sentenced on conviction to 11 years imprisonment and a fine of $50,000. It was the heaviest sentence ever handed down for tax evasion in America. Capone had been boss of the Chicago underworld for only six years, and the sentence finished him. He was 32, and suffering from syphilis.

Fact

A passionate affair led Robert Franklin into temptation and eventually to the gallows. He forged banknotes to finance the expensive life he led with his mistress, Mary Jones, fearful that he would lose her to one of her other admirers if he could not maintain their life-style. Well aware that he would forfeit his life if he were found out, he joined the navy thinking he would be safe at sea, but when he heard that Mary was pining away without him, he came home on leave. His leave over, he was returning to his ship when he was robbed at an inn in Rochester. When the unsuspecting thieves tried to spend the stolen money, they were arrested for passing forged notes. Bow Street Runners traced the notes to Robert Franklin, by then aboard HMS Hydra. *He was tried for forgery, convicted and hanged at Tyburn in 1798.*

Fact

In 1841 two men named Wallace attempted a type of insurance fraud that was, perhaps surprisingly, not at all uncommon. One of them was a merchant and the other an ordinary seaman. When their brig Dryad *ran on to rocks near Santa Cruz in fair weather, they claimed that the cargo had included clothes and cotton goods, beef and pork, earthenware and butter, as well as the recorded freight of the company which had commissioned the voyage. But it was proved in court that the Wallaces had not only taken out additional heavy insurance on non-existent cargo, but that the ship had been wrecked deliberately. Both men were sentenced to transportation for life. They admitted to five other intentional shipwrecks for fraudulent reasons.*

Fraud comes in many guises. On the same day in October 1995 that a doctor and a chemist in Leeds were imprisoned for defrauding the National Health Service of £1 million by claiming for false prescriptions, a cattle dealer in Devon was fined £30,000 for making false declarations about beef cattle sent for slaughter and breaking the important rules made to protect the meat market from BSE ('mad cow' disease). In the Leeds court, the judge told the defendants that they had treated the NHS as a milch cow. In the Exeter court, prosecuting counsel said the defendant had, for "a few pieces of silver... betrayed the farming community, and put a substantial industry in jeopardy".

Case Histories

Art and Craft

In June 1837, William Macready, the great tragic actor, accompanied his friends Charles Dickens and John Forster on a visit to Newgate where Dickens was intent on research for a story. In one cell they saw a man quietly reading, and Macready suddenly cried out, "My God! There's Wainewright!"

The prisoner he had recognised was Thomas Griffiths Wainewright, and Macready was one of many famous writers and artists who had once dined at his table. The convict numbered among his acquaintances such men as Charles Lamb, William Hazlitt, Thomas de Quincey, William Wordsworth, John Clare and Sir David Wilkie. Wainewright was himself a painter, and had exhibited at the Royal Academy where his work had been admired by William Blake. He was also an art critic who was to be quoted approvingly by Oscar Wilde. Now he was known as 'Wainewright the Poisoner', although he was never convicted of murder. It was as a forger that he was in Newgate, awaiting transportation.

Wainewright was born at Chiswick in 1794, but his mother died giving birth, and his father not long after. His grandfather became his guardian, but he, too, soon passed away. When Thomas eventually married, he found himself short of money, and when his trustees refused him permission to sell stock held in his name, he forged all four of their signatures on a document with which he defrauded the Bank of England of more than £2,000. In 1829 he apparently poisoned his uncle, George Griffiths, with strychnine, inheriting by his death the house at Turnham Green where he had spent his childhood.

Meanwhile Wainewright had become an accomplished writer on art and other matters, contributing regularly to the *London Magazine* and using facetious pen-names such as 'Janus Weathercock' and 'Van Vinkvooms'. But the possibility of making easier money by poisoning people seems to have held an irresistible appeal for him, and he murdered his mother-in-law, Mrs Abercrombie, and his young sister-in-law, Helen, after insuring the latter's life for £18,000. The insurance company, however, refused to pay up. Wainewright was never brought to justice for the murders he was suspected of committing, but eventually admitted to at least one of them. When someone reproached him later for the murder of Helen Abercrombie, he is said to have replied, "Yes, it was a dreadful thing to do, but she had very thick ankles".

Wainewright went abroad, where he is alleged to have committed another murder by poison, but rather foolishly returned to England, was recognised by a Bow Street Runner and arrested for his forgery of 13 years earlier, being charged with "forging and uttering a certain power of attorney for £2,259, with intent to defraud the Governor and Company of the Bank of England". He pleaded guilty on two indictments, and was sentenced to transportation for life. He was sent from Newgate to the hulks at Portsmouth, and from there shipped to Van Diemen's Land. "There is..." Oscar Wilde wrote, "something dramatic in the fact that this heavy punishment was inflicted for what, if we remember his fatal influence on the prose of modern journalism, was certainly not the worst of all his sins".

In Tasmania the convict continued painting. One of those whose portrait he painted was Henrietta Heathorn, a brewer's daughter in Hobart who married the biologist T.H. Huxley and was the grandmother of Aldous and Julian Huxley. Dickens based the character of 'Slinkton' in his story *Hunted Down* on Wainewright, and Lord Lytton also based a character in his *Lucretia* on him. Wainewright also undoubtedly had some influence on Oscar Wilde's *The Portrait of Dorian Gray*. Wilde knew the story of Lady Blessington receiving from her brother in Hobart a portrait of a young woman, painted by Wainewright, in which the artist had "contrived to put the expression of his own wickedness into the portrait of a nice, kind-hearted girl". Wainewright took to opium, and died in Hobart at the age of 53, in 1847.

The Railway Clerk

Edmund Beckett Denison, chairman of the Great Northern Railway Company, was standing on a station platform in 1856, talking to a peer of his acquaintance, when his company's registrar of shares, a man named Redpath, passed by and raised his hat to the chairman. Hardly had Denison acknowledged his underling before the peer—much to Denison's surprise—grasped Redpath by the hand and greeted him warmly. When Redpath had passed on down the platform, Denison turned to the peer:

"What do you know of our clerk?", he asked.

"Only that he is a capital fellow", his lordship replied, "who gives the best dinners and balls in town".

When they heard of the incident, this astonishing revelation prompted the board of the Great Northern to examine the company's books, and soon a massive fraud was brought to light. Leopold Redpath, who was about 40 years old, had spent 10 years in the company's

Fact

Probably the greatest confidence trick of all time was perpetrated by Victor Lustig, a Czech, and Robert Tourbillon, a Frenchman. In 1925 they persuaded five French businessmen that they were acting for the government in selling the Eiffel Tower which was to be demolished as it was unsafe. Swearing the tycoons to secrecy because of the expected public outcry when the government announced the planned demolition, they invited bids for the 7,000 tons of scrap metal. Lustig accepted the tender of one André Poisson who—suspecting nothing fishy—handed over a large cheque to smooth 'Count' Lustig's negotiations with government officials on his behalf. By the time Poisson realised he had been duped, Lustig and Tourbillon had fled the country. But they returned later to France and repeated the trick, obtaining money from another gullible scrap merchant. The con men fled once again, and were never brought to justice for their crimes.

Fact

The largest forgery of banknotes on record was carried out by Nazi Germany during WWII: 'Operation Bernhard' was conceived with the aim of undermining the British economy. According to William Shirer in The Rise and Fall of the Third Reich, *the idea came from Alfred Naujocks, an SS officer, who proposed that counterfeit Sterling banknotes should be dropped by air over Britain. The man in charge of the forgery was Major Bernhard Krüger, a security officer in Berlin who recruited a Jewish forger from the concentration camp at Mauthausen and several other prisoners with expert knowledge. The team eventually produced notes of various denominations with an estimated value of £134 million. Only a tenth of this was actually distributed, however, and that chiefly in neutral countries. The whole operation proved an expensive failure. Near the end of the war, some of the forged currency was found by the Allied liberators of the concentration camp at Sachsenhausen; in 1959 more was discovered in a lake in the Austrian Alps. An interesting sidelight was that notes from Operation Bernhard were used to pay the spy 'Cicero', the British Ambassador's valet in Ankara, Turkey, who photographed secret documents for the Germans. The Germans gained little from the documents, and 'Cicero' little from the £300,000 he received in banknotes. The Germans paid for worthless information with worthless money.*

employment cooking the books, forging signatures and creating artificial stock to the tune of at least a quarter of a million pounds, though the exact figure was never established. Redpath's audacity was breathtaking. He was enjoying a rich life-style on the proceeds of his crimes, owning land and works of art, as well as a house near Regent's Park and a country home at Weybridge. He had become well known as a generous host and a philanthropist. He was a governor of Christ's Hospital and gave freely to the poor. And this was a man who had been taken on by the Great Northern after failing as an insurance broker and being declared bankrupt.

By the time a warrant was issued for Redpath's arrest, he had already resigned and fled temporarily to Paris, but he was arrested immediately on his return to London and committed to Newgate. The Stock Market, meanwhile, had been seriously affected by the news. In 1857 Redpath was brought to trial at the Old Bailey for embezzlement and forgery, and sentenced to transportation for life.

A recent case bore some remarkable similarities to the Redpath fraud. In 1991, Rosemary Aberdour was sentenced to four years imprisonment after being found guilty on 17 charges, including two of theft and seven of obtaining property by deception. Posing as 'Lady' Aberdour, she had stolen £2,700,000 of charity money whilst raising funds in her position as deputy director of the National Hospital Development Fund.

A doctor's daughter from Essex, Aberdour had studied book-keeping and become an expert. She began working for the National Hospital charity in 1986, and started using donations as her own money (including, ironically, a donation from Robert Maxwell). She moved to a lush apartment in Kensington, and indulged her taste for lavish society parties. She was careful, however, always to leave parties early so as to avoid any danger of *in vino veritas*. By the winter of 1990-1 she was spending an average of £15,000 a day. The respect in which 'Lady' Aberdour was held was no doubt much increased when she herself made a generous donation to the hospital fund! But in June 1991 the charity's director found documents bearing signatures that he knew were forged. By this time the bird had flown—to Rio de Janeiro. But at her family's request, she returned to face the music. She was released after two years in prison.

The Tichborne Claimant

In April 1854, the ship *La Bella* set sail from Rio de Janeiro for England. Among its passengers was Roger Charles Tichborne, rightful heir to the estates of Sir James Frances Doughty Tichborne, Baronet, of Tichborne House, Hampshire. News soon reached England that the ship had been lost at sea, but there was a report that some of the passengers and crew had been picked up by a vessel bound for Australia. Roger Tichborne's mother, the Dowager Lady Tichborne, refused to accept that her eldest son was dead. Instead, she advertised for news of his whereabouts, offering a substantial reward for information and welcoming any merchant seaman to her home who might be able to give her any hope or clue that he was still alive. Sure enough, after 11 years, she received a letter from him:

My dear Mother,
The delay which has taken place since my last letter dated April 22nd, 1854, makes it very difficult to commence this letter. I deeply regret the truble and anxiety I must have cause you…

Well, Roger had never been good at spelling.

The writer was living at Wagga Wagga, New South Wales, under the name Thomas Castro. He was married, with one child, and made his living as a butcher, though he was on the point of bankruptcy. At length, he decided to come home and claim his inheritance, arriving in England on Christmas Day, 1866. Lady Tichborne was in Paris, and he went there within a few days to seek her acknowledgment. Accompanied by a solicitor, the old lady was brought to meet him at a hotel. Roger Tichborne had been a tall, slim young man who, despite being somewhat frail, had served in the 6th Dragoon Guards. The man on whom Lady Tichborne's eyes alighted as she entered the Paris hotel room was fat and coarse-featured. But after looking at him for a few moments, she said that he was indeed her son, despite putting on so much weight—which he had already warned her about from Australia—and just like his father.

The early death of Sir Alfred Tichborne, the 11th baronet, and the presumed death of his elder brother, had led to the title passing to Sir James's nephew, Henry, a 2 year-old boy. Mr Castro would have to prove his right to the title in a court of law. Lawyers acting on the 12th baronet's behalf set about resisting the claim.

He had passed the first hurdle with his acceptance by Lady Tichborne, but no one else in the family would entertain the idea that this 171.5 kg (27-stone) stranger was the long-lost heir. Nevertheless, Guards officers, former pupils of his old school, Stonyhurst College, and others who had known him, were prepared to testify that Castro was Roger Tichborne.

But when the civil case came to court on 11 May 1871, to determine if there was any reasonable doubt that the claimant was the man he said he was, it was easily demonstrated that there was *plenty* of doubt—in spite of his considerable knowledge of Sir Roger's background. By this time the Dowager Lady Tichborne had died, leaving sworn affidavits. The family's lawyers spent 22 days cross-questioning Castro about his past life. Roger Tichborne had received a classical education and had spoken French fluently, but this man could not tell Latin from Greek and claimed to have forgotten all the French he had learnt. A school friend referred to Roger's tattoo on his left arm; this man had none. Worse still, he did not know his mother's Christian names. He had made a wild guess from her initials that her names were Hannah Frances. In fact, she was French-born, and they were Henriette Félicité. In August, after 102 days, Serjeant Ballantine, representing the claimant, sought leave to withdraw the suit.

Fact

In 1983, the German magazine Stern *announced serialization of the recently-discovered diaries of Adolf Hitler. Newspapers and magazines in other countries, including the French* Paris-Match *and the English* Sunday Times, *rushed to obtain rights in the sensational find made by* Stern's *Gerd Heidemann, who said the diaries—in 62 separate volumes—had survived an air crash near Dresden in 1945. The historian Hugh Trevor-Roper (Lord Dacre of Glanton), author of* The Last Days of Hitler, *pronounced his satisfaction as to their authenticity in an article in the* Sunday Times *on 23 April 1983. But other experts did not believe them to be genuine, and it was found after lengthy investigation that the paper and ink were of post-war manufacture. Lord Dacre withdrew his original view, admitting that he had not been sufficiently thorough in his examination. The diaries had, in fact, been written by one Konrad Kujau, a dealer in Nazi memorabilia in Stuttgart with whom Heidemann had conspired to fake the Führer's journals. Heidemann had also kept for himself a good deal of the money which* Stern *thought it was paying to Kujau. The two chief editors of* Stern *resigned. Kujau and Heidemann both got sentences of four and a half years in prison.*

Fact

Computer fraud is the modern growth area in crimes of deception. Stanley Rifkin was sentenced to eight years imprisonment in 1980 for manipulating a computer system to defraud a bank in Los Angeles, California, of over $10 million. L. Benjamin Lewis, a Los Angeles manager of the Wells Fargo National Bank, was sentenced to five years imprisonment in 1982 for embezzling more than $21 million by the manipulation of computerized accounts—known as electronic kiting.

Fact

There was an average annual increase in cases of fraud and forgery in England and Wales of 2.9 per cent in the 10 years from 1983, but the numbers fell in both 1992 and 1993 from the 1991 peak of 174,700 cases. There was a further drop in 1994, with 146,000 cases, compared with 163,000 in 1993.

The next chapter in the saga was the arrest of Castro on 23 charges of perjury and forgery. The criminal trial began at the Central Criminal Court before the Lord Chief Justice, Lord Cockburn. The prosecution abandoned the forgery charges, aware that they would complicate matters for the jury and lead to an even longer trial than was already anticipated. The Crown, faced with proving that Castro was an impostor, produced over 200 witnesses against him, many of whom had to be brought from Australia and South America at public expense. The claimant produced 300 witnesses on his own behalf, among whom was a man who testified that he had been a ship's steward on a vessel which had rescued survivors from the sinking *La Bella* in 1854. This sensational witness was quickly exposed, however, as a confidence trickster.

Lawyers acting for the infant 12th baronet had had Castro followed when he landed in England in 1866. He had gone straight to a house in Wapping to visit a butcher and his family, named Orton. A private investigator had then ascertained that a son of this family, named Arthur, had left the country while still a youth. Ending up in Australia, he had assumed the name Castro from friends in Chile, which he had visited when he was a merchant seaman. Already in his teens he had been nicknamed 'Bullocky' Orton on account of his size. The man now claiming to be Sir Roger Tichborne was, the prosecution alleged, none other than Arthur Orton.

The criminal trial occupied 188 days, at the end of which the jury found Thomas Castro, otherwise called Arthur Orton, guilty of perjury for his bogus claim to the Tichborne title and estates. He was sentenced on 28 February 1874 to two consecutive terms of imprisonment with hard labour. The whole case had taken up 1,025 days, and was, until recently, the longest trial in British legal history. It cost the public an estimated £150,000, and the Tichborne family £70,000.

Orton served 10 years, mainly at Dartmoor, where he was called 'Sir Roger' by his fellow convicts. After his release, he returned to Australia and confessed his imposture in a Melbourne newspaper. It is believed that old Lady Tichborne may have acknowledged him as her son to get her revenge on the family with whom she had quarrelled. But many have remained unconvinced that this man was really Arthur Orton, a butcher from Wapping.

Beautiful for Ever?

The sport of taking money from gullible women ranges from the relatively harmless, such as fortune-telling and some advertising, to the positively evil, as in the 'brides in the bath' murders. But rarely has it been raised to such an art form as the deception practised in London in the 1860s by Sarah Leverson, who became famous as 'Madame Rachael', the owner of a beauty parlour in fashionable Bond Street.

Mrs Leverson came from Lancashire, where she was born to a poor Jewish couple named Russell. They named her Sarah Rachael. By the time she set up her successful business in Bond Street, she had been married three times. Her third husband, Philip Leverson, had left her. She had tried making a living by telling fortunes, dealing in old clothes, and selling fried fish, and had ended up in a debtors' prison for a time.

For her new venture, despite being practically illiterate, she drew on a hitherto untapped reservoir of native cunning approaching genius. With some literary assistance from a colleague, whose identity is unknown, she launched her new beauty parlour in 1863 with a seductive publication entitled 'Beautiful for Ever'. This slogan also appeared above the entrance to her shop. She advertised all manner of potions and ointments which she claimed to have imported from the mysterious East—or the Sahara Desert—which would restore colour to greying hair and beauty to "persons of considerable antiquity". The advertising copy made much use of the imagery of harems, and Madame claimed to have exclusive rights to magic rock dew from the Sultan of Morocco, and to count the Sultana of Turkey among her grateful customers. As well as buying exotic cosmetics, women would indulge themselves in luxurious-sounding beauty treatments, and even arrange for a touch of romance on the premises.

By exploiting the empty-headed vanity of ageing women, Madame Rachael soon became wealthy. But her rapacious money-making exploits were not limited to selling fake oriental beauty treatments; she added other types of fraud, including blackmail, to her repertoire. She would threaten to expose her clients' peccadillos if they hesitated to pay her exorbitant bills.

It all came to a head with a vain middle-aged widow named Mary Borradaile. Seduced by Madame Rachael's extravagant promises of rejuvenation, she became a client, but after a time expressed some disappointment with the results. Anxious to retain her custom, Madame then informed Mrs Borradaile that she had a secret admirer: a nobleman, Lord Ranelagh, had seen her on the premises and fallen in love with her. In due course the flattered client was briefly introduced to this gentleman, and promptly paid £1,000 for a further course of beauty treatment in order to please him. She began to receive love letters from him, signed 'William' for discretion, in which he said that he slept with her letters pressed to his heart, and urged her to do everything that Madame Rachael asked of her in order that their secret romance could reach fruition. He explained that for family reasons he must woo her by correspondence only—until the day of their wedding.

At his lordship's request, Mrs Borradaile surrendered her jewellery to Madame Rachael as he said its quality was unworthy of her and he would replace it with better jewellery when they were married. Mrs Borradaile also sold property she owned in order to save her fiancé from some temporary financial embarrassment. In due course she had been stripped of everything she possessed except her pension. Madame Rachael tried to get her hands on that, too, by having her erstwhile customer imprisoned for debt.

But though she might have been a 'self confessed idiot' (as *The Times* later called her), the disillusioned scraggy-faced widow with rouged cheeks and yellow wig, had a human instinct—a desire for revenge. She had Madame Rachael arrested and charged with obtaining money by false pretences.

Fact

Köpenick was a little known Berlin suburb until it was put firmly on the map by an enterprising shoemaker in 1906. Wilhelm Voigt acquired a Prussian officer's uniform and, taking full advantage of the native respect for uniformed authority, commandeered two genuine soldiers and marched them to the burgomaster's office where he informed the startled burgomaster and the town's treasurer that they were under arrest for suspected misappropriation of public funds. When they obeyed the officer's command to open the safe for inspection, Voigt quickly removed all the money and absconded. The shoemaker was afterwards immortalized as the 'Captain of Köpenick'.

Fact

Capitalist societies breed an acquisitiveness in people of all classes that sometimes leads even the famous and comparatively well-off into temptation, though they usually gain little and often, in the end, lose everything. The Welshman Ivor Novello was the idol of theatre matinée audiences in the 1930s and 40s, famous as an actor, dramatist and composer. His romantic shows such as Perchance to Dream, The Dancing Years *and* King's Rhapsody *filled West End theatres by the coach-load. But in April 1944, Novello was sentenced to eight weeks in prison and a fine of £100 for a fraud against the petrol-rationing law by using a false permit to obtain petrol for his Rolls-Royce. He served one month in Wormwood Scrubs and came out a broken man. The affair possibly cost him a knighthood, and in 1951 he died of a heart attack when he was 58.*

The trial took place at the Old Bailey in September 1868. The defence easily made a laughing-stock of the plaintiff. Lord Ranelagh himself went into the witness box and declared that he had met this woman only twice, which was true. His name was Thomas, not William, and he was embarrassed by the very idea that he had corresponded with her, let alone asked her to marry him. But this was not enough to protect Madame Rachael, who was referred to by counsel as a "most filthy and dangerous moral pest". She was found guilty and sentenced to five years penal servitude. One of her assistants let the cat out of the bag with regard to the precious ointments: Madame's famous and luxurious 'Royal Arabian' baths consisted of hot water with bran added. The much sought-after 'Jordan Water' consisted of water *without* bran added!

Released in 1872, the incorrigible woman picked up more or less where she had left off, this time in Great Portland Street. But this time she fell foul of a young woman, Mrs Pearce, who had her arrested again, and in April 1878 she was once more brought to trial and sentenced to five years. On 12 October 1880, Sarah Rachael Leverson died in Woking prison, aged around 74.

The Charlatan

Horatio Bottomley was born in the East End of London in 1860, and brought up in an orphanage. He began his working life as an errand boy, but his ambition was to be rich and famous and he used his gift for journalism to make his first fortune, founding a local newspaper, the *Hackney Hansard*. He supplemented his earned income by buying worthless properties and selling them to his own publishing company at large profits. In 1891 he was charged with fraud, but his legal skill and gift of the gab helped him to secure an acquittal. Meanwhile, he had been a co-founder of the *Financial Times*, and was soon making money out of Australian gold mines.

In 1906, Bottomley founded the weekly *John Bull*, and in the same year became Independent Member of Parliament for South Hackney. He promoted competitions in *John Bull*, but invented non-existent prize-winners, thus defrauding the ordinary people whose champion he claimed to be. Charged again with fraud in 1909, he conducted his own defence as before, and once more walked free from the court. He resigned as an MP in 1911 by applying for the Chiltern Hundreds because of bankruptcy, but at the end of WWI, he was discharged as a bankrupt and resumed his seat in the House of Commons as one of the most popular journalists and orators in Britain, rivalling even Lloyd-George. It was long-rumoured that Bottomley was the illegitimate son of the atheist MP Charles Bradlaugh and the birth control pundit, Annie Besant, but although Bottomley never denied it, there is no truth in the story; his father was a poor East End tailor.

He launched new prize schemes such as the Premium Bond Scheme, pocketing most of the subscriptions and spending money lavishly on horse-racing, champagne, and a string of mistresses. Then he launched his Victory

War Bond scheme in *John Bull*, and again pocketed a large proportion of the subscriptions and again invented imaginary prize-winners. When a pamphlet exposed Bottomley's fraud, he could not sue the author for libel because what had been written was the truth. So he set up a conspiracy whereby a hard-up printer was paid to reprint the pamphlet and then pleaded guilty to libelling Bottomley. This effectively prevented repetitions of the accusations in print. By this time, however, the Court of Chancery was investigating the intermittent millionaire's business affairs.

In March 1922 he was committed for trial at the Old Bailey. When asked if he pleaded guilty or not guilty to the charges against him, he replied, "Most decidedly not guilty". But this time his self-assurance was ill-founded: he was convicted of fraudulent conversion and sentenced to seven years penal servitude. He had siphoned off £150,000 of subscriptions to his Victory Bond Club, and had spent a tenth of it on horse-racing. He was expelled from the House of Commons and served five years, mostly at Maidstone. When he was released in 1927, he again tried—unsuccessfully—to make money from journalism, and indulged his taste for seeking damages in libel actions. He sued Woolworths, for instance, for selling an out-of-date American magazine which referred to him as a swindler and a scoundrel. He was awarded £250, but had to pay the costs. Horatio Bottomley was finally reduced to appearing in music-halls for pitiful wages, and died penniless on Derby Day in 1933.

Fact

Cyril Joad was a philosopher, popularly but incorrectly known as 'Professor' Joad, who was widely known through his frequent broadcasts on the radio programme, 'Brains Trust'. He was a great popularizer, though not distinguished for original thought. (When Bertrand Russell was asked to contribute a foreword to one of Joad's books, Russell excused himself in a brief note to the publisher, saying "Modesty forbids".) Joad was notoriously tight-fisted with money. In April 1948, he was taken to court for defrauding the Great Western Railway of 17s 1d by travelling to the West Country without a ticket. He made matters worse by saying that he had boarded the train at Salisbury, when in fact he had travelled from London. It turned out that he had done it before, and he was fined £2 plus costs of 25 guineas. This affair ruined his career and he turned to religion. He died in 1953, at the age of 62.

The Art of Embarrassment

In 1945, at the end of the war in Europe, the Allied Art Commission was set up to investigate art treasures plundered by the Nazis with the aim of returning them, as far as possible, to their rightful owners. The most voracious of the Nazi collectors had been Reichsmarschal Hermann Goering, and one of the paintings in his possession was *Christ and the Adulteress* by the 17th-century Dutch master, Vermeer. The picture was found hidden in the Alt-Aussee salt mine, near Salzburg, but records proved that Goering had come by it honestly, paying the equivalent of £165,000 to an agent named van Strijvesande in October 1942.

Van Strijvesande had acquired the painting from one Han van Meegeren, an Amsterdam artist and collector. At the end of May, two officers of the Netherlands Field Security Service called at van Meegeren's house on the Keizersgracht. In view of the rarity of paintings by Vermeer, and its discovery among the property of one of the top members of the Nazi hierarchy, it was necessary to trace its movements with particular care. But when the officers politely enquired of van Meegeren where *he* had acquired the painting, he refused to answer. He would say only that he had bought it from an Italian family before the war, and that it was a condition of the sale that the seller's identity should remain secret. In the circumstances, this answer was considered unsatisfactory. Van Meegeren was arrested on suspicion of collaborating with the enemy, and imprisoned to await trial.

Fact

One of the most famous literary forgeries of recent years was the autobiography of Howard Hughes. In 1971 an American author, Clifford Irving, offered his publisher, McGraw-Hill, the ghost-written autobiography of Hughes, one of the world's richest men, a former aviator and holder of air-speed records, oil millionaire, Hollywood producer, promoter of Jane Russell's voluptuous charms, aircraft designer, and latterly, a reclusive mystery man. The book was bound to be a sure-fire bestseller. McGraw-Hill gave Irving a contract, and Life *magazine paid to publish extracts from the book. But then lawyers acting for Howard Robard Hughes, who had apparently been countersigning cheques paid out by the publishers, said that neither the book nor the story of their client's life was genuine. It turned out that the signature 'H.R. Hughes' was that of Irving's wife who had opened a Swiss bank account in the name 'Mrs Helga R. Hughes', and that Irving had obtained most of his information not directly from Hughes as he claimed, but from unpublished memoirs by a freelance journalist. Irving was charged and sentenced to two and a half years in prison.*

An ailing 56 year-old drug addict, van Meegeren maintained his stubborn silence for six weeks until 12 July, when he suddenly broke down, calling his interrogators fools. "You are fools like the rest of them!" he said. "I sold no great national treasure—I painted it myself!" The astonished officers then listened with mounting disbelief as van Meegeren added that he had painted not only *this* supposed work by Vermeer, but several others by the artist, including *Christ and the Disciples at Emmaus,* bought for the Boymans Museum in Rotterdam for £58,000 in 1937, and *The Washing of Christ's Feet,* recently purchased by the Dutch State for £130,000.

The immediate assumption was that this man was out of his mind—inventing an outrageous fantasy to try and save himself from conviction for a wartime crime which could carry the death penalty. After all, *The Christ and the Disciples at Emmaus* had been certified as a genuine Vermeer by no less an expert than Dr Abraham Bredius, the world's most distinguished contemporary authority on Dutch art, who had been director of the Mauritshuis Museum in The Hague and now lived in Monaco.

"It is a wonderful moment in the life of a lover of art", Dr Bredius had written in 1937, "when he finds himself suddenly confronted with a hitherto unknown painting by a great master, untouched, on the original canvas and without any restoration, just as it left the painter's studio!"

Bredius was proud to claim that he had discovered this masterpiece: "I am inclined to say *the* masterpiece of Johannes Vermeer of Delft, and moreover one of his largest works, quite different from all his other paintings and yet every inch a Vermeer".

Van Meegeren, however, was speaking the plain truth. In the course of about 10 years he had painted 14 pictures accepted as the works of Dutch artists: one by Franz Hals, one by Gerard Terborch, two by Pieter de Hooch, and the rest by Vermeer. After scientific tests on *The Adulteress* had aroused suspicions that van Meegeren's claim might have some substance, van Meegeren offered to paint a new 'Vermeer' before the very eyes of the authorities. In the constant presence of Field Security officers, he spent two months painting a *Young Christ Teaching in the Temple,* and was able to demonstrate a complete command of 17th-century techniques and pigments. A commission of experts was set up to carry out chemical and other tests on eight paintings which had been sold by van Meegeren as 17th-century works. By March 1947, the experts had concluded that all of them were, in fact, modern.

The charge of collaborating with the enemy was withdrawn and charges of fraud and forgery substituted. After many postponements, van Meegeren finally came to trial in Amsterdam in October 1947. The State was anxious to play down the affair. It had, after all, paid out a large sum of taxpayers' money for a fake, and several reputable men besides Bredius had been made fools of. Moreover, it could be argued that van Meegeren had done the State a service, for Goering had paid for *The Adulteress* in kind, returning in exchange many genuine and valuable paintings which the Nazis had stolen during their occupation of The Netherlands. If van Meegeren had only limited his confession to faking that one painting, he might have been seen as a national hero.

The trial occupied one day. Van Meegeren was found guilty of obtaining money by deception and of forging signatures. He was sentenced to one year in prison, the minimum sentence possible, due to the state of his health. But van Meegeren, arguably the cleverest of all art forgers, was to cheat the authorities once more. Before he had even commenced the sentence, he collapsed and was admitted to hospital. He died of a heart attack on 30 December 1947.

Fact

Peter Clowes of Barlow Clowes International was arrested by Fraud Squad officers in June 1988, after the £190 million collapse of the investment company of which he was chairman. He was charged with diverting up to £100 million of investors' money into his personal business empire. An estimated 18,000 people had lost substantial savings—their life savings in some cases. The British government later agreed to compensate most of the investors for 90 per cent of their losses.

Home Maintenance

When taxi-driver Leslie Harvey turned up at his widowed mother's home in Rhyl in May 1960, his intention was to redecorate the house while she was away. Sarah Harvey, 65 years old, had gone into hospital for a period of observation.

Mr Harvey's first task was to assess what needed doing and what materials he would require. On the first floor landing of the terraced house there was a cupboard which had been securely locked ever since Leslie himself had lived there as a small boy. Now he had the opportunity to satisfy his curiosity. Having no key, Leslie used a screwdriver to prise open the double wooden doors. Instead of the piles of dusty old rubbish he was expecting, he found a mummified corpse.

The doubled-up body was that of an elderly woman in a nightdress and dressing-gown. It was covered in dust and cobwebs, and a fly-paper hung above it. How long had the corpse been there? Leslie Harvey thought the face looked familiar. It was: the body turned out to be that of Mrs Frances Knight, a semi-invalid his mother had taken in as a lodger many years ago. But as far as Leslie knew, she had left the house by 1940.

When they interviewed her, Sarah Harvey told police that Mrs Knight had died in the house in 1939, and she had hidden the body because she did not know what to do with it. Pathologists confirmed that the corpse could have been in the cupboard for more than 20 years. Freak circumstances had preserved it from putrefaction as dry warm air had circulated round the cupboard. But round the woman's neck they found the remains of a knotted stocking. Furthermore, local enquiries led to the discovery that Mrs Harvey had been regularly collecting £2 a week to which the divorced Mrs Knight had been entitled under the terms of a court order. Police appeared to have a case of murder on their hands. Sarah Jane Harvey was arrested.

When the case came to trial, however, the prosecution's allegation that Mrs Harvey had strangled her lodger in order to benefit financially could not be made to stick. In the first place, it was impossible to say with certainty how Mrs Knight had died. She was known to have suffered from multiple sclerosis, and could have died of it. As for the stocking, it was common for ailing old women to wear socks or stockings round their throats to keep chills and sore throats at bay. The trial was stopped and Mrs Harvey was acquitted of murder by the judge's direction. But she was sent to prison for 15 months for fraudulently claiming Mrs Knight's maintenance money for 20 years as if her housebound lodger were still alive.

Fact

The self-styled Reverend Jim Bakker, 'televangelist' superstar in the United States, was convicted in 1988 on 22 counts of fraud and sentenced to 45 years imprisonment. Bakker's real god was Mammon, and he had unashamedly fleeced his admiring 'congregation' of their money and used it to finance a lavish life-style for himself and his wife Tammy.

Disappearing Act

In November 1974, James Charlton, a British company director on a business trip to Miami, Florida, reported to local police that his business partner was missing. He was referring to John Stonehouse, the 48 year-old Member of Parliament for Walsall North, and former Postmaster General, who had gone for a swim the day before, leaving his clothes on the beach, but had not come back for them. British newspapers were soon telling the nation that John Stonehouse was presumed drowned, and that he had committed suicide, leaving behind a mountain of debts as well as a wife and two children.

Some time later, police in Melbourne, Australia, began watching a well-spoken Englishman about whom suspicions had been raised by an observant bank teller. The Bank of New South Wales knew their customer as Mr Mildoon; the Bank of New Zealand knew the same man as Mr Markham. Police thought he might be Lord Lucan, the missing earl wanted in connection with the murder of his children's nanny, Sandra Rivett. Mr Markham, alias Mildoon, was arrested, and turned out to be, not Lord Lucan, but John Stonehouse. In the summer of 1975 he was extradited back to Britain, and in April of the following year his trial began at the Old Bailey on charges of theft, forgery and fraud.

Stonehouse had planned his disappearing act with great care, and the only person who was in on the plot was his mistress and former secretary, Sheila Buckley, 20 years his junior. Aware that an imminent Department of Trade investigation into his various companies would lead to his ruin, Stonehouse and Buckley had decided to start a new life together with what money he could salvage from his collapsing businesses. Stonehouse cleverly assumed the identity of a dead man, Joseph Markham, and obtained a passport in Markham's name by forging the signature of an MP, Neil McBride, to certify that a photograph of himself was a true likeness of Joseph Markham. (Stonehouse knew that Mr McBride was dying of cancer.) He went to elaborate lengths to establish the credibility of Joseph Markham and his other alias, Donald Mildoon, which he intended to use to cover his tracks even further when he left Australia to settle in New Zealand.

The preliminary hearing and trial stretched over five months, at the end of which Stonehouse was found guilty on 14 counts of forgery, fraud and embezzlement, and sentenced to seven years imprisonment. Sheila Buckley, tried as an accessory, got a two-year suspended sentence.

Stonehouse was released from Brixton Prison in 1979, having served only three years, but he had suffered two heart attacks and came out ill and bankrupt. He married Sheila Buckley in 1981, but died seven years later.

Fact

The rock star Chuck Berry was sentenced to imprisonment for 100 days in California in 1979 for tax evasion. Sophia Loren, the beautiful Academy Award-winning Italian actress, had an international film career and was famous for such films as The Millionairess, Two Women, *and* Marriage Italian Style. *She was married to wealthy producer Carlo Ponti. But in 1982 she served 18 days in prison for tax irregularities.*

Fact

Lester Piggott, one of the greatest English jockeys, had 30 winning mounts in the classic races, including nine Derby winners, and was champion jockey 11 times. He eventually retired from riding to become a trainer, but in 1987 he was sentenced to three years imprisonment for tax evasion. He served one year before being released on parole, and was stripped of his honours award, the OBE.

God's Banker

On the morning of 18 June 1982, a postal clerk crossing Blackfriars Bridge over the Thames in London saw a man's body hanging by the neck from a rope attached to the bridge's sub-structure. The pockets of the man's suit were weighted with bricks and lumps of masonry, and in his wallet was a large sum of money in various currencies. The passport in his pocket bore the name Gian Roberto Calvini. The body was examined by Professor Keith Simpson, and identified as that of Roberto Calvi, 62 year-old chairman of Italy's Banco Ambrosiano. It appeared that he had committed suicide, and this was the verdict at the inquest.

Calvi had worked his way up through the Banco Ambrosiano in Milan to become its chairman in 1975, and had acquired a vast financial empire. By 1982, however, the bank was on the verge of financial collapse. It was saved, temporarily at least, by help from the Vatican's bank, known as the Instituto per le Opere di Religione (Institute of Religious Works!), which was run by the Pope's financial adviser, Archbishop Paul Marcinkus. Calvi and Marcinkus had perpetrated some shady business transactions involving Vatican finances. When Pope John Paul I died of a heart attack in September 1978, only a month after being chosen as pontiff, a rumour grew that he had been poisoned because he had opposed some of the Vatican bank's activities and was intent on driving the money-changers out of the temple. Fuel was added to these suspicions by the Vatican's refusal to allow an autopsy.

Calvi had also been named as a member of Propaganda Due, or P2, an illegal Freemasonry group run by Licio Gelli in which Members of Parliament, leading financiers and other Italian VIPs were implicated—among them former Prime Minister Giulio Andreotti. P2 was believed to have links with the Mafia via Gelli's friend, the Sicilian financier Michele Sindona who was wanted on fraud charges in both Italy and the USA. (Sindona was subsequently sentenced to 25 years.)

Calvi had provided the money with which Sindona had acquired a controlling interest in the Franklin National Bank, but the Arab oil crisis in 1973 had helped to bring about the Franklin's collapse—reputedly the biggest bank failure in US history. In 1981, Calvi was indicted and arrested, with 10 others, for illegally exporting several billion lire to Switzerland. During the trial, he attempted suicide by swallowing an overdose of barbiturates and cutting one of his wrists, but the attempt was half-hearted. On 20 July 1981, he was convicted and sentenced to four years imprisonment and a fine of 16 billion lire. He was released pending his appeal. When Calvi's deputy and general manager, Roberto Rosone opposed Calvi's remaining as chairman (he was the only one of Ambrosiano's directors to do so), an attempt was made on Rosone's life, but he was only wounded while the would-be assassin was shot dead.

In May 1982, the Bank of Italy demanded explanations for loans of billions of lire made by Banco Ambrosiano to companies registered in Panama which were owned by the Vatican bank. On 11 June, Calvi was

Fact

Britain's biggest tax fraud cost the Inland Revenue £97 million in lost corporation tax when nearly £140 million of Nissan UK's profits were siphoned off into a Swiss bank account. Michael Hunt, Nissan's 61 year-old deputy chairman, was among those convicted of the fraud, and was imprisoned for eight years in 1993.

Fact

When two paintings by Turner, worth £20 million, were stolen from a Frankfurt art gallery where they were on loan from the Tate Gallery in London, a man calling himself 'Rothstein' demanded £30,000 for their return—to be paid in cash or postal orders! The hoax caller was later arrested and convicted of attempted deception.

Fact

The longest sentence for fraud in British legal history was passed on Abbas Gokal, a Pakistani shipping tycoon. On 8 May 1997, Mr Gokal was sentenced at the Old Bailey to 14 years imprisonment for his part in the collapse of the Bank of Credit and Commerce International from which he had siphoned £750 million.

reported missing after flying to Rome the previous day. His corpse was found a week later.

Calvi's family challenged the inquest verdict, believing that he had been murdered—a view also held by both British and Italian police. Among the speculation and rumour surrounding his death was the possibility that he had been killed by the Mafia, or ritually killed by the Freemasons (hence the chunks of symbolic masonry in his pockets). Calvi's wife believed the Vatican was responsible for his murder. In June 1983, a jury at a second inquest returned an open verdict.

Much of the mystery still remains, but what is certain is that Calvi was involved in massive financial frauds in which the Vatican bank was implicated, laundering money from illegal transactions which included proceeds from the sale of arms and drugs. It seems that help from the Vatican bank finally dried up when Calvi attempted to blackmail Archbishop Marcinkus by threatening to reveal that the Vatican was subsidizing Solidarity, the Polish trade union led by Lech Walesa.

On 11 June 1982, the day Calvi disappeared in Rome, he had jumped bail and driven to Austria, and a day or two later had flown to London from Innsbruck. His wife and children were already safely abroad in America and Switzerland. On 17 June in Milan, the Ambrosiano directors decided to sack Calvi. Signor Rosone was appointed as the new chairman. Later that day, Calvi's secretary, Graziella Corrocher, died after falling from one of the building's windows, apparently in a suicidal jump. Soon after Calvi's death, the Banco Ambrosiano was declared insolvent. In September, Gelli, the head of P2, was arrested in Switzerland, but a few months later he was apparently abducted from his prison cell.

In 1984, after two years of negotiations, the Vatican bank—in recognition of its 'moral involvement'—agreed to pay around $250 million in final settlement of the Ambrosiano collapse having owned 10 per cent of the dummy South American companies to which Ambrosiano had lent $1.2 billion. Archbishop Marcinkus remained under suspicion of fraud. The whole truth about Vatican and Mafia involvement with Banco Ambrosiano is yet to be told.

Section 4: Body-snatching

Who shall conceive the horrors of my secret toil, as I dabbled among the unhallowed damps of the grave...?
Mary Shelley: *Frankenstein*

BODY-SNATCHING as an underworld activity grew up almost exclusively in Britain and Ireland because unlike the governments of other civilized European countries, the British government failed to make adequate provision for a supply of corpses to the medical profession for dissection—despite the increased demand for trained surgeons brought on by the Napoleonic wars in the late 18th century. Body-snatching also occurred in the United States, though not on the same scale.

Recognition of the need for surgeons to practise their skills on dead bodies—before risking the lives of their patients—had resulted in the surgeons of Edinburgh being granted the corpse of one executed criminal a year since 1505. English surgeons were similarly granted the corpses of four criminals a year during the reign of Henry VIII, when the Company of Barber-Surgeons was incorporated. But this source of bodies could not keep pace with demand. Moreover, the acquisition of such corpses was exclusive to the Barber-Surgeons, and as private medical schools were established, the competition for corpses led to many unseemly scenes at Tyburn, the chief place of execution in London. Medical students took to stealing freshly-buried bodies from graveyards to supply their teachers with subjects for dissection.

In 1752 an act decreed that *all* executed murderers were to be either publicly dissected or hung in chains. This new law was not introduced as an aid to medical research; it was principally a move to distinguish the crime of murder with peculiarly horrific penalties, and thus act as a deterrent. But the government doubtless expected that it would go some way towards satisfying the anatomists' demands. It did not. By the first quarter of the 19th century, when pre-eminence in medical science had passed from the leading continental schools such as Padua and Leiden, to Edinburgh and London, there were more than 1,000 students in each of these British cities—to say nothing of those studying at the rising provincial schools—whilst the number of criminals executed annually throughout the country was less than 80. The requirement for cadavers so far outstripped the capabilities of both students and the early professionals to keep pace with it, that an import trade started from France and Ireland, where corpses were cheap and plentiful. They could be bought from Irish body-snatchers for 10 shillings each. The Home Secretary, Sir Robert Peel, turned a blind eye to this trade.

Initially, the stealing of dead bodies was not regarded as a serious crime. Stealing a shroud or a coffin was a felony, but a corpse was not held by the law of the land to be anyone's property, so removing one from a churchyard did not rank high on the list of offences punishable by law, however outraged the public might be by such activities. Even

Fact

Strictly speaking, 'resurrection man' is a more precise term than 'body-snatcher' as it clearly implies raising a body from the grave. A body-snatcher may sometimes have stolen a corpse which had not yet been buried. Two London operators, Cornelius Bryant and Israel Chapman, became known as specialists in this method. They would steal bodies awaiting funerals, and do deals with undertakers, gravediggers, etc., in order to obtain corpses before they were committed to the earth.

Fact

Two Scottish medical students dug up a man's corpse at Leven and took it to an inn for the night, intending to return to Edinburgh across the Firth of Forth in the morning. But the rifled grave was discovered sooner than expected, and when two constables called at the inn to make enquiries, the students fled, leaving the corpse behind. They did not know that the body was that of the former innkeeper. His widow found her husband in bed several days after she had seen him buried.

when the practice grew in frequency, it was regarded only as a misdemeanour. Hence, the experienced body-snatcher always stripped a corpse naked before removing it from a churchyard so as to be convicted only of the lesser offence if apprehended. But magistrates would sometimes convict body-snatchers for trespassing or causing a disturbance. By this time, the criminal fraternity had caught-on to the potential money-making opportunities that existed. One could easily get the impression from some books that body-snatching in Britain was largely confined to London and Edinburgh. In fact, it went on in towns and villages all over the country, from Plymouth to Aberdeen.

The arrival of professional body-snatchers on the scene led to increasingly sophisticated methods. Medical students had often outraged public opinion—particularly in Scotland—by digging up coffins and leaving them lying empty in churchyards beside the open graves. Professional criminals took more care to hide their tracks and protect their trade by perfecting a method of extracting a corpse from a grave without digging up the coffin. Digging down to the head end, they could either drive an outsize corkscrew through the lid, or use a crowbar to heave it upward until it split open, then extract the corpse by means of a rope around the neck. They then restored the grave to its original state before making off with their booty, and the robbery would often remain undiscovered. The body-snatchers thus left themselves free to visit the same churchyard again.

Body-snatching as a profitable crime was brought to an end by the passing of the Anatomy Act of 1832, rushed through Parliament as a reaction to the case of Burke and Hare and other cases which showed that the high prices being paid for anatomical subjects were operating as an incentive for murder. The Act provided for a legal supply of dead bodies, such as those given by executors to licensed surgeons and teachers of anatomy. It also abolished the practise of dissecting executed murderers, and thus ended the long-standing association of anatomical studies with criminal activity. Henceforth, bodies unclaimed by relatives came from hospitals and parish workhouses, and from individual bequests.

Fact

Several methods of protecting graves against nocturnal marauders were introduced at different times. Volunteers from the community, akin to today's 'neighbourhood watch', would take it in turns to spend nights in watch-huts erected in churchyards. Spring-guns and other booby-traps were sometimes set on fresh graves. Churchyard walls were heightened and gates locked at night. Huge slabs of stone were sometimes laid over coffins until they were safe (for anatomists would only purchase fresh corpses). Some people went to the expense of having their loved ones buried in sealed lead coffins. The method most favoured in Scotland was the iron 'mort-safe'—a strong and heavy iron grille which formed a cage round a grave until the danger of disinterment was past. The contraption could then be removed and employed by the next customer. However, none of these methods of protection was fool-proof.

Case Histories

Doctor Pattison's Raw Materials

In December 1813, only a few days before Christmas, an angry mob in Glasgow broke windows at the home of Dr James Jeffrey, Professor of Anatomy at Glasgow University. The crowd had got wind of the fact that the body of a Mrs McAlister had been stolen from the kirkyard at Ramshorn. A law officer had seen the resurrectionists, who were medical students, but they had escaped him, making off in the direction of the medical college.

The subsequent search for Mrs McAlister's corpse led to the

Fact

One of the earliest recorded indictments for body-snatching in England was in 1777, when two men were convicted of removing the body of Mrs Jane Sainsbury from her grave in the churchyard of St George the Martyr, in London's Queen Square.

dissecting rooms of a newly-appointed lecturer, Dr Granville Sharp Pattison. Peace officers armed with a search warrant, and accompanied by the dead woman's former dentist, searched the premises and found parts of a female human body in a tub of water. The dentist, Mr Alexander, identified teeth in a jawbone as Mrs McAlister's, and a severed finger was recognised by someone else as her wedding-ring finger. Dr Pattison was arrested, together with another lecturer, Andrew Russell, and two students who were present, Robert Munro and John McLean. As they left the building, stones thrown by the crowd outside rained down on them. Officers continued their search of the premises, and further human remains were discovered under the floorboards.

Dr Pattison and his fellow-defendants were brought before the High Court of Justiciary in June 1814, charged with stealing the corpse of Mrs McAlister, conveying it to the dissecting room and mangling the body to prevent its recognition. Counsel for Dr Pattison immediately requested that the case be heard in camera as some of the evidence he would present was of a somewhat delicate nature. The request was refused, but their lordships instructed the newspapermen in court to give as little publicity to the case as possible as the details would "only tend to inflame the minds of the vulgar". The result of the trial was that Russell and McLean were declared not guilty by direction of the Lord Justice Clerk, and the case against Pattison and Munro was found Not Proven.

The *Glasgow Herald*'s report stated simply that medical witnesses had found it impossible to say whether the parts of the body alleged to be Mrs McAlister's were hers or not. In fact, the defence had lost no time in playing its trump card: Mrs McAlister, it was pointed out, had been a mother, but a significant part of the body claimed to be hers was that of a virgin!

Fact

Body-snatchers were often quite indignant at being arrested and charged with crimes, considering (with some justice) that they were agents acting in the interests of medical science. A magistrate sitting when two resurrectionists were brought before the bench in June 1830 was treated to a speech by one defendant complaining that the police would be "much better engaged in looking after thieves and house-breakers than apprehending respectable men who lived by supplying the faculty with subjects for dissection". There were other remarkable defences. A Hertfordshire man accused of digging up and selling the body of his own grandmother entered a plea in mitigation that it was surely more fitting that he, rather than some complete stranger, should have the money!

The Hope Street Gang

In the autumn of 1826, dock workers at Liverpool's St George's Dock complained about an intolerable stench rising from three casks marked 'Bitter Salts', which they were required to put on board a smack bound for Leith. The shipping note read: "Please ship on board the *Latona* three casks of Bitter Salts, from Mr Brown, Agent, Liverpool, to Mr G.H. Ironson, Edinburgh". Investigation of the casks' contents revealed 11 human corpses. There were six male and five female bodies. All were naked, pickled in brine and packed in salt. A police surgeon examined them, and said they all appeared to have died from natural causes, and had been dead six or seven days.

Officers soon traced the carter who had delivered the casks to George's Dock Passage. George Leech said that a Scotsman had hired him to collect the casks from a cellar at 12 Hope Street, Liverpool, and take them to the dock. When police went to this address, they found the house belonged to a clergyman, Rev. James McGowan, who ran a school on the premises. McGowan explained that he had let the cellar since

Fact

Four men tried at Exeter for digging up two bodies in 1830 were given a fortnight's imprisonment for what the judge described as "a gross outrage on the feelings of our nature and punishable as a misdemeanour". But one of the corpses was that of a woman, and the men had carelessly taken the shift in which she was buried. For this crime they got seven years transportation.

Fact

A well-known London body-snatcher, James May, gained some celebrity in the criminal underworld for his successful defence when brought before the Middlesex Sessions in 1825. He and a colleague had been chased by a watchman in the churchyard of St Leonard, Shoreditch, and arrested in possession of a spade, a pick-axe and a body in a sack. The two got off by protesting that they were not the men who had dug up the body, but public-spirited passers-by who had come to the aid of the watchman in chasing the real culprits, who had abandoned their tools and booty when they fled.

Fact

Body-snatching was not entirely a male preserve. In January 1832, Eliza Ross was hanged for the murder of an old woman named Walsh who sold laces and cotton in the streets around London's Aldgate. Ross was a drunken Irish woman who was said to have been well known as a body-snatcher for 12 years. Even the cats in the neighbourhood were reputed to have disappeared because she killed them to sell the skins. Her own corpse was duly dissected after its delivery from the gallows to the Royal College of Surgeons, where a formal incision was made 'from sternum to pubis' before the corpse was donated to the London Hospital.

January of that year to a man named Henderson, who had said he was a cooper. Some of McGowan's pupils had complained of an offensive smell coming from the cellar, but he had merely told them to open a window.

The officers gained entry to the cellar and found themselves in a veritable charnel house. There were 22 corpses—nine men, five women, five boys and three girls. The police surgeon, Thomas Davis, supposed all the bodies to have been disinterred from the evidence of a thread on one of the women's toes—commonly used before burial to hold the feet of the deceased together. Some of them had been raised from the parish burial ground, where three graves had been found empty. Also found in the cellar was a brass syringe which had probably been used to inject hot wax into the veins of the corpses as a preservative. Nevertheless, some of them were in an advanced state of decomposition, and orders were given by the coroner for their immediate re-burial.

The first man to be brought to justice in connection with this outrage was a young Scot named James Donaldson. He was identified by several local witnesses as one of a number of men who came to the cellar frequently with a hand-cart bearing casks. He was charged with having conspired "with divers other persons, lately, at Liverpool, and unlawfully, wilfully, and indecently disinterred, taken and carried away, divers dead bodies, which had lately before that time been interred". One witness testified during the trial that a tierce of brine in the cellar had been found to contain the bodies of babies, and this evidence made the foreman of the jury feel so ill that he had to leave the court to recover. Prosecuting counsel told the jury that "the disinterring of dead bodies, for the purpose of disposing of them, was unquestionably a crime, even if for the purposes of anatomy alone; but, when done with the cool calculating object of gain, the delinquency was greater..." Donaldson was found guilty and sentenced to 12 months in the Kirkdale House of Correction, as well as being fined £50.

Two more resurrectionists, Patrick McGregor and John Ross, were arrested a few days later. They were also identified as members of the Hope Street gang, and given terms of imprisonment and fines of £25 each. They claimed that they had been hired by medical students of various universities and had been driven to the work by their poverty. One of them was recognized by the carter, Leech, as the man who had hired him to transport the casks, but none of the three convicted men was the 'Mr Henderson' who had rented the cellar from Rev. McGowan. He was never traced.

The Perowne Case

In 1838 (six years after the Anatomy Act became law), James Maxey, a blacksmith, died at Norwich. On 9 July, the day after his death, Mr Maxey's former employer, the veterinary surgeon George Perowne, called on the widow, and assured her that he would pay for her late husband's proper burial as 'a Christian and a gentleman'. He arranged for a coffin to be delivered to the house.

Two days later, whilst Mrs Maxey was out, Mr Perowne entered her house and took the coffin away with the body inside it. Mrs Maxey soon demanded the return of her husband's body, but Perowne told her that it was quite safe and that the funeral would take place from his premises on the following day.

At the appointed time, Mrs Maxey turned up with the bearers, and found the coffin lid already nailed down. She said she wanted to see her husband, and her friends supported her in this request. Perowne, however, flew into a rage, fetched a gun, and threatened to shoot the lot of them if they did not get off his premises.

Out in the street, Mrs Maxey and her friends thought they could hear the coffin lid being removed and large stones being handled. Eventually, they were let in again, and were shown the open coffin with Mr Maxey's corpse in it. But, they said later, it had been 'cut and hacked', and looked as if it had been anatomized.

Perowne was brought before the local magistrate, but appeared in court drunk and was kept in a cell for the night. Next morning, he claimed that he had done a deal with Maxey, 16 years earlier, for possession of the blacksmith's body after his death. He said that dissection had showed that Maxey had died of ossification of the heart. The magistrate pointed out that the law did not recognise any ownership in a dead body, and that Perowne was not, in any case, licensed for anatomical studies on humans. He committed Perowne for trial at Norwich Assizes. When the day of the trial came, however, Perowne was formally discharged. It seems that influential friends must have been at work on his behalf.

Fact

Some famous men have reputedly been stolen from their graves (knowingly or otherwise) and delivered to anatomists for dissection. They include Dick Turpin, the notorious highwayman hanged at York for horse-stealing in 1739, and Laurence Sterne, celebrated author of The Life and Opinions of Tristram Shandy, *who was buried originally in St George's churchyard, Hanover Square, in 1768. Turpin's body was rescued by the local populace before dissection and re-buried. The dissection of Sterne's corpse had already commenced (at Cambridge University) when a former friend of his recognised the face and fainted. The body was hastily re-interred.*

Latter-day Resurrection Men

Although the Anatomy Act made professional body-snatchers redundant, grave-robbing is not entirely a thing of the past. The idea persists that a dead body is not without value in the right hands. In 1876 an American gang attempted to steal the remains of President Abraham Lincoln. They intended to use them as a bargaining tool for the release of a convicted forger, Ben Boyd. But the culprits were caught in the act.

In 1878, Benjamin Harrison, a future US President and son of a former Senator, John Scott Harrison, had occasion to visit the Medical College in Cincinatti. There he came across the corpse of his own father, who had been buried some days earlier at North Bend, Ohio.

In 1881, the body of Alexander Lindsay, 25th Earl of Crawford and Balcarres, was stolen from the family vault at Dunecht. The thieves demanded a ransom of £6,000. After six months, the corpse was found in a shallow grave on the family estate. A rat-catcher named Soutar was sentenced to five years penal servitude for this crime, but his accomplices were never caught.

In 1888, the grave of the great Spanish artist Francisco Goya was

Fact

A man named William Clarke confessed in court in 1825 to having raised 45 corpses in five months from the churchyard at Walcot, a suburb of Bath.

opened in Bordeaux—where he had died 60 years earlier—in order to return the remains to his native soil. But when the coffin was opened, the skeleton was found to be headless. The bones were duly re-buried in Madrid, but the skull has never been found. The reason for its theft remains a mystery.

In March 1978 the corpse of Charles Chaplin, the comedian and film director, was stolen from his grave at Vevey, in Switzerland. The thieves demanded 600,000 Swiss francs for its return, but they were soon arrested. Roman Wardas, a Pole, and Gantcho Ganev, a Hungarian, wanted the money to start a garage business. Wardas got four and a half years imprisonment and Ganev an 18-months suspended sentence. The great man's remains were recovered from a shallow grave in a cornfield.

A Score of Professional Body-Snatchers

Name	Chief area of activity	Comments
Robert Armstrong	Liverpool	Associated with Dr William Gill, surgeon and teacher of anatomy. Jailed. Home Secretary Peel rejected appeal for mitigation of sentence.
John Bishop	London	Asked by police for his trade or profession, replied: "I'm a bloody body-snatcher". Hanged for murder, 1831.
Cornelius Bryant	London	Specialist in snatching corpses before burial.
Tom Butler	London	Former dissecting room porter. Member of Crouch gang. Sentenced to death in Edinburgh for theft, but reprieved.
Israel Chapman	London	Specialist in snatching corpses before burial.
Ben Crouch	London	Former prize-fighter. Leader of gang operating from Southwark. Bought hotel on proceeds, but died in poverty. Known as 'Corpse King'.
Bill and Jack Harnett	London	Bill was former pugilist; Jack was his nephew. Members of Crouch gang. Bill died of TB, Jack became wealthy.
Thomas Head, aka Williams	London	Married Bishop's sister and lived in same house, working as team. Hanged for murder, 1831.
John Craig Hodgson	Leeds	Solicitor's clerk. Earned living as 'legal adviser' in London after several convictions. Died 1868.
'Praying Howard'	Edinburgh	Associate of Merrilees. So called from habit of posing as pious mourner at funerals in order to spy out fresh burials.
Tom Light	London	Former 'gentleman's gentleman'. Clumsy worker who saw error of his ways and turned to religion.
James May	London	Associated with Bishop and Williams. Sentenced to death in 1831, but reprieved. Collapsed from shock and died soon after.
Andrew Merrilees	Edinburgh	Former carter. Known as 'Merry Andrew'. Sold corpses to Dr Knox, including, possibly, his own sister's.
Geordie Mill	Dundee	Gravedigger at parish burial ground known as the 'howff'.
William Millard	London	Superintendent of dissecting room at St Thomas's Hospital. Died of gaol fever at Coldbath Fields prison, 1823.
Patrick Murphy	London	Succeeded Crouch as gang-leader. Once made £144 for 12 corpses in one day. Invested in property.
Joshua Naples	London	Naval rating under Nelson, then gravedigger. Member of Crouch gang. Given job in dissecting room at St Thomas's, but died of drink.
Thomas Stewart	Liverpool	Partner of Armstrong. Likewise refused mitigation of prison sentence after conviction for lifting bodies from local churchyards.
Tom Vaughan, aka Goslin	London	Member of Crouch gang. Transported for 7 years in 1830 for stealing grave-clothes at Devonport.

Section 5: Poaching

About this matter, the law of the land does not square with the moral law as it is written in the heart of the peasant.
W.H. Hudson: *A Shepherd's Life*

POACHING IS THE OFFENCE OF TRESPASSING with the intent of killing or taking game. A landowner does not own the wild animals and birds that inhabit his land, but he has the exclusive right to hunt and kill game (in season), and when it is dead, it is his property. We generally take an indulgent view of the poacher today, thinking of the popular image of a poor countryman with his ferret on the squire's estate, catching a rabbit for his family's dinner, and being arraigned before the whole might of the law for his abominable crime. But the time was when poaching was the greatest obsession of the criminal law in England, and savage retribution was enacted against the poacher as if he were the most heinous of monsters.

The origins of this legal terrorism were repressive forest laws dating back to William the Conqueror. The preservation of game for the king to hunt in his royal forests, and the landed gentry to pursue on their estates, was a jealously guarded priority over the desperate need for cheap food among poverty-stricken peasants.

King James I said: "It is not fit that clowns should have these sports", and in the year of his accession, 1603, the selling of hares, partridges and pheasants was prohibited in an attempt to reduce poaching. The gentry of the 17th century were practically unanimous in seeing the purpose of anti-poaching laws as preventing 'persons of inferior rank from squandering that time which their station in life requireth to be more profitably employed', and the laws became ever more Draconian.

The preservation of game—deer, hares, rabbits, pheasants, grouse and partridges—for the rich man's sport reached almost the status of a religion with some wealthy landlords. In Wychwood Forest in the Oxfordshire Cotswolds, a statute of 1662 authorized the chief ranger, Richard Legge, to confiscate all guns and setting dogs within a compass of 10 miles, and until the end of the 19th century, gamekeepers had the right to search any cottage in the forest for hidden venison. An act of 1670 made it a criminal offence for anyone with an income of less than £100 a year from a freehold estate to kill game *even on his own land.*

In May 1723, the Black Act was rushed through Parliament as a stern response to increased poaching and damage in royal forests, especially in Berkshire and Hampshire. 'Blacks' was the name under which gangs of poachers, armed and in disguise, hunted and killed deer. Walpole's government branded this activity as a Jacobite conspiracy. In fact, it was just a crime wave in which country folk, refusing to accept that wild animals were anyone's property, pursued an illicit but profitable trade in venison. The rural poor had only contempt for the law, and thought they had scriptural authority on their side, for when God gave men dominion over 'the fish of the sea, and over the fowl of the air, and over every

Fact

The original 'Waltham Blacks' were seven men who had been caught poaching deer on Waltham Chase in Hampshire, with their faces blacked to avoid recognition. They were convicted at Winchester and brought to London, chained together in irons, to be hanged at Tyburn. One of them, Edward Elliott, was 17 years old and had been arrested while trying to catch a live fawn as a present for his girlfriend.

Fact

Poaching can still lead to serious consequences. In January 1982, an unemployed man was caught shooting pheasants on the Broadlands estate in Hampshire—home of the late Earl Mountbatten of Burma. The poacher fired at the gamekeeper, peppering him with lead shot. He was charged at Winchester Crown Court with attempted murder. The judge ruled that a sufficient case had not been made out for attempted murder, but the man was convicted of grievous bodily harm with intent to resist arrest, and imprisoned for three years.

Fact

There was a tradition in Wales for some law-breakers to disguise themselves in women's clothes. They were known as 'Rebeccas'. There were many fierce clashes between these men and the police and water-bailiffs when the Rebeccas went out at night with torches and spears to poach salmon from the local rivers.

Fact

At the Hampshire Midsummer Sessions in 1821, Rev. John Clerk, JP, sentenced Charles Grist to three months in jail for having 'kept and used a certain dog called a lurcher to kill and destroy game'. Henry Hickman was also imprisoned for 'having had unlawfully in his possession five partridges'. Grist was 14 years old; Hickman was 12.

Fact

In 1779, Thomas Bell, a cobbler by trade, was hanged for his part in a shoot-out between poachers and gamekeepers in Norfolk, though no one died in the affray.

living thing that moveth upon the earth', there was no Biblical injunction that deer and pheasants were specifically excluded from this bounty. Poaching even became a symbol of virility: Rev. Gilbert White recorded in his *Natural History of Selborne* that "towards the beginning of this century, all this country was wild about deer-stealing. Unless he was a *hunter*, as they affected to call themselves, no young person was allowed to be possessed of manhood or gallantry".

Justices of the Peace would sometimes order poachers' dogs (usually lurchers—a cross between a greyhound and a collie) to be hanged in grotesque parodies of the Tyburn executions. And it was regarded as 'justifiable homicide' for a keeper to kill a poacher who resisted arrest. Determined poachers kept up running battles with landowners and their gamekeepers, and arson and threats of physical violence were common. Gamekeepers who brought poachers to justice were seen as traitors to the common people. They had their jobs to do, however, and among other deterrents, they took to setting man-traps with names such as 'The Crusher' and 'The Thigh-Cracker', which could result in such mangling of the victim's limbs that amputation was the only option. In 1776, a fine for a first offence and transportation for a second were substituted for the death penalty for killing deer. But in Suffolk in 1785, four poachers were killed in one night by man-traps and spring-guns.

The grossly inequitable game laws which were, as Mary Russell Mitford said, a "fertile source of crime and misery", were gradually modified, but only to the extent that society was eventually outraged by the disproportionate suffering inflicted on rich and poor alike by maiming, arson and violence, not to mention death sentences resulting from the excessive measures to protect game for the sporting aristocracy. A late 18th-century writer put poachers on a level with prostitutes as one of the lowest forms of human life, and as G.M. Trevelyan expressed it, "...there was never a truce to the poaching war in old England".

It was illegal for anyone except a landowner or a gamekeeper to be found in possession of any of the common implements of poaching—guns, dogs, snares, nets, etc. In 1803, a new act made death the punishment for any poacher who threatened a gamekeeper with a gun, and in 1816 the Night Poaching Act made transportation for seven years the penalty for anyone caught with a net or a stick with intent to take game or rabbits. Two years later it was made illegal to *buy* game, as well as to sell it.

"For every pheasant that flutters in a wood", Rev. Sydney Smith observed, "one English peasant is rotting in gaol". In 1823, William Cobbett found that out of 77 prisoners in gaol in Berkshire, 22 had been committed for poaching—some sentenced by clergymen acting as Justices of the Peace, and "in many cases punished with more severity than theft..." As often as not, the aggrieved landowner and the local magistrate were one and the same man.

The Victorian Game Acts helped to curb poaching by giving additional powers to rural constables, but by then the economic incentives of poaching by organized gangs had largely gone. The railway age made poaching common among the itinerant 'navvies', who substituted free fresh rabbit for the expensive meat they could not afford in the local shops. Fishermen also indulged in poaching in the winter months when they could not put to sea, while gypsies commonly fed their families by poaching. But even in the 20th century, it has been considered quite proper under the law of the land that a poor man should be heavily fined for being caught trespassing with a ferret whilst King Edward VII and his noble friends conducted wholesale massacres of wildfowl purely for pleasure.

Fact

An incensed gamekeeper who apprehended a poacher in Staffordshire testified that the defendant "gave me Very Roof langwag, beding me to kiss his Bakside..."

Fact

In 1933 a farmer named Rose encountered five poachers on his land near Beverley in the East Riding of Yorkshire. He fired a shot over their heads with his double-barrelled 12-bore shotgun, but the men attacked him, and one of them, named Waudby, was shot in the ensuing struggle and died later from the injury. The poachers swore that the farmer had deliberately shot their friend while standing facing him, but the ballistics evidence did not support this allegation and the farmer was released.

Case History

Cunning as a Fox

Among the most celebrated poachers of modern times were two brothers from Stevenage, Hertfordshire, named Albert Ebenezer and Ebenezer Albert Fox. They were identical twins, the sons of a local Baptist preacher, and were active in the years around the turn of the century. They eventually notched up nearly 200 convictions between them, but often got off with their two standard defences.

Working as a team, but never close together, they would provide each other with virtually unchallengeable alibis. One would make his apparently innocent presence known in a public place whilst the other was busy at his nocturnal trade. Then if the poacher happened to be caught and arrested, he would claim that it was a case of mistaken identity—*he* had actually been in the place where his brother had been seen, and the police or gamekeeper had arrested the wrong man. If that ruse failed, the defendant would claim that he had only been looking for mushrooms. In one such case before the Hitchin Petty Sessions, Sam Hoare, a gamekeeper, testified that he found two pheasants caught in wires in a hedge at Langley, in the parish of Hitchin: "The next day", he told the court, "he resumed his watch on the wires, and at 10 a.m. defendant Ebenezer Albert Fox came and went straight to the pheasants. Witness, who was only 10 yards away, asked him why he was searching for game. Fox said he was after mushrooms. Witness replied: "What, mushrooms with feathers on? I'll give you mushrooms!" Fox, on oath, said that he was 20 yards off the pheasants, and he did not handle them. He had permission to go into the meadow next to the wood, and he went over the fence separating the wood and the meadow to get some mushrooms, and then the keeper spoke to him. He had some mushrooms in a handkerchief in his hand. He did not see the pheasants until the keeper pointed them out..."

"You're a clever man, Fox", said the magistrate, Squire Delmé-Radcliffe, "but we think you're a little too clever. You'll be fined £2 or one month".

The Fox brothers eventually fell foul of the new method of identification by fingerprinting. They died in the 1920s.

Fact

Many people suspected that 'General Ludd' or 'King Ludd', who ostensibly ordered machine-breaking raids from his headquarters in Sherwood Forest, was Gravenor Henson, leader of the illegal Union Society of Framework Knitters. Henson strongly denied it, and in fact criticized the Luddites, who prejudiced his chances of obtaining better pay and conditions by regulation of the trade through Parliament.

Section 6: Other Crimes

Machine-breaking

MACHINE-BREAKING is a type of malicious damage specially associated with the so-called Luddite Rebellion of the early 19th century, although it had been employed by disgruntled workers long before that. London weavers had smashed looms in the 17th century, and machine-breaking was first made a capital offence in 1727. The Luddite movement had its origins in the cottage industry of the Midlands, and spread northward through those counties which were engaged in textile manufacturing. It was due to economic distress aggravated by the Napoleonic Wars. Midland stocking workers in the formerly prosperous hosiery industry were victims of exploitation which often left them starving or in the workhouse.

Legend ascribes the spark which caused the flare-up of machine-breaking to a half-witted youth at Anstey, Leicestershire. Ned Ludd is said to have smashed his stocking frame in resentment against some punishment he had received. In fact, a mob in Leicester had destroyed a newly-invented machine which they believed would deprive them of work as early as 1773, and in 1787 a riot occurred when an angry mob broke up a new worsted spinning machine, attacked the homes of its owners, Coltman & Whetstone, and stoned the mayor so severely when he tried to pacify them that he subsequently died from his injuries.

A disastrous harvest in 1795 rocketed the price of bread, and the new men's fashion of wearing trousers drastically reduced demand for stockings so that the hosiery trade seemed to be crumbling under an avalanche of burdens. The introduction of wide frames, which could knit several stockings at once, seemed the last straw to poor and illiterate men who saw increasingly efficient machinery taking out of their families' mouths what little bread they could afford. In March 1811, framework-knitters smashed machines in Nottingham. In April, stocking-makers at Hinckley went on a rampage through the town, breaking windows and plundering and burning houses.

By the end of that year, the destruction of machinery was at its height in Nottinghamshire and had also spread to Derbyshire, Cheshire, Lancashire and Yorkshire. About 1,000 stocking frames were destroyed in the Midlands in the 12 months up to February 1812.

Seven Nottinghamshire Luddites were sentenced to transportation in March, some for seven years and some for fourteen. The foreman of the jury that convicted them soon received a threatening letter signed 'General Ludd'. When five Luddites were killed at Middleton, Lancashire, during their attempt to wreck power-looms, their fellow-workers burned down the house of the mill-owner, Mr Burton. Soon there were riots in Manchester as well.

The government, mindful of the recent consequences of revolution in France, set up a 'Secret Committee on the Disturbed State of Certain

Counties'. There was much talk of sedition, political insurrection and subversive elements, and in due course, 12,000 troops—more than Wellington had under his command in the Peninsular War—were deployed in suppressing the Luddites. At length, the Secret Committee concluded that the source of all the trouble was—a secret committee! It was true that the Luddites had taken on all the ridiculous appurtenances of a secret society, with passwords and a mythical leader, 'General Ludd', who was supposed to issue his commands from the depths of Sherwood Forest. But there was little recognition in government circles of the simple economic facts of life, that the textile workers—forbidden by Pitt's Combination Act to form a union or any kind of legal common voice—were trying to save themselves from starvation. The government decided to enforce the death penalty for machine-breaking.

Lord Byron had seen the pitiful state of the knitters in Nottinghamshire, and on 27 February 1812 made his impressive maiden speech in the House of Lords against this Draconian measure. He ended with a challenging peroration, picturing a starving man breaking the law in an effort to feed his wife and children: "...suppose this man...dragged into court, to be tried for this new offence, by this new law; still there are two things wanting to convict and condemn him; and these are, in my opinion, 12 butchers for a jury, and a Jeffreys for a judge!" Byron's eloquence was lost on their Lordships, however.

There was a lull in machine-breaking for a time, but it was only temporary, and there were soon fresh outbreaks in the Midlands. Thomas Morley, of Greasley, Nottinghamshire, testified that five or six persons woke him and his family at 2 a.m. on 4 April 1814, broke into his house and smashed five frames and damaged the work on them. Machines were also destroyed at Kimberley. All these frames belonged to Messrs. Needham & Nixon, who had resolutely refused to increase the wages of stockingers by two pence a pair, though other manufacturers had agreed to do so. These fresh outbreaks, which were followed by others in Nottingham, Mansfield and elsewhere, culminated in a dramatic climax in Leicestershire on the night of 28 June 1816, when a number of men with blackened faces broke into the lace factory of Heathcoat, Lacy and Boden at Loughborough. They smashed 53 bobbin-net machines, valued at £6,000, and during the raid they shot and wounded a watchman. On 17 April 1817, six men were hanged in front of Leicester Gaol for this crime, and three others sentenced to transportation.

Physical violence on a large scale subsided after this incident, although the hardships of the textile workers continued for many years, and in 1826 there were sporadic outbreaks of destruction of power-looms in Manchester and other Lancashire towns, by which time the main cause of discontent had become the factory system rather than the earlier exploitation of individual framework-knitters.

Damage to machinery today, as with malicious damage to any property, would be prosecuted under the Criminal Damage Act, the offender being liable to a sentence of 10 years imprisonment.

Fact

One of the most serious incidents of the Luddite campaign occurred at Middleton, Lancashire, in April 1812, when a mill belonging to Daniel Burton was attacked. Mr Burton had introduced power-looms, which had enabled him to cut his workforce by half. A crowd of several thousand gathered at the site and threw stones at the windows. The military dispersed the crowd, but not before three rioters were killed. Next day, the crowd assembled again, many armed with hammers, picks and muskets. This time they set fire to Mr Burton's house, but five more were killed when the military arrived to restore order. Burtons decided to stop operating their looms.

Fact

The Rawfolds Mill incident forms the background to Charlotte Brontë's novel Shirley, *in which Cartwright was the model for the mill-owner Robert Moore, who "did not sufficiently care when the new inventions, which he employed in his mill, threw the old people out of employ: he never asked himself where those to whom he no longer paid weekly wages found daily bread..."*

CASE HISTORIES

Rawfolds Mill

During the night of 11–12 April 1812, about 150 Luddites, armed with muskets and axes, hammers and other weapons, marched towards Rawfolds Mill at Liversedge in Yorkshire's West Riding, and attempted to break in. The mill was owned by William Cartwright who had installed shearing machinery which the local wool dressers or 'croppers' objected to because the machines threatened these skilled hand-workers with unemployment.

Cartwright, however, was fully aware of the danger and had taken extensive precautions against such an attack. A guard dog was kept on the ground floor, and an alarm bell on the roof. There were spiked rollers on the staircase and a vat of acid at the top. And Mr Cartwright and some of his loyal employees regularly slept in the mill, reinforced by armed soldiers.

So when the attackers attempted to force an entry by breaking down the door, the defenders opened fire, and in the exchanges of gunfire in the dark, two of the Luddites were seriously wounded and the assailants retreated without having achieved their purpose, which was to enter the building and smash the machines. The two wounded Luddites were soon attended by a surgeon, but both died from their injuries. Their deaths were attributed to Justifiable Homicide.

The machine-breakers were now more incensed than ever, and notices soon appeared demanding 'vengeance for the blood of the innocent'. A few days after the attack, Cartwright was shot at as he rode home, but he escaped unhurt.

The Luddites then turned their attention to William Horsfall, another mill-owner who was using machinery, and who was so antagonistic to the Luddites that he had declared publicly that he was ready to "ride up to his saddle-girths in Luddite blood".

As he was riding home from Huddersfield market on 28 April, shots were fired at him from a small wood beside the road, and Horsfall was fatally wounded. Before he died, he was able to say only that he had seen four men with firearms. A witness who had come to Mr Horsfall's aid also spoke of four men running away from the scene of the crime.

Eventually, one of the four, Benjamin Walker, turned King's Evidence and named his accomplices as George Mellor, William Thorpe and Thomas Smith. These three were hanged for murder at York Castle, after a trial by a Special Commission which also sentenced 14 others to death and several more to transportation for assorted crimes, which included machine-breaking and the attack on Cartwright's mill. Some of those condemned did not work in the woollen industry at all, and were convicted only of burglary, but all those tried were treated as Luddites by association in what was always planned as a show trial.

Organized Crime

The Mafia, or 'La Cosa Nostra', is usually regarded as originating from a Sicilian underground movement which in 1282, at Easter, massacred French troops and civilians in Palermo in a vendetta that became known as the 'Sicilian Vespers', and succeeded in raising a rebellion which drove the French rulers from the island. The secret society grew in Italy and Europe and was taken to America by Italian immigrants in the 19th century. It gradually transformed itself into the biggest business in the United States, and the world's most profitable criminal organization.

There were many other early criminal gangs in America besides the Mafia, however. Among them were the 'Bowery Boys' of New York, who were anti-Irish and supported the repatriation of Irish immigrants. In a street battle with rival Irish criminals in 1857, gangsters on both sides were killed.

The early American Mafia 'families' thrived on running protection rackets in the immigrant ghettoes of large cities, but the advent of Prohibition in 1920 gave the 'Mob' a major boost. It profited hugely from bootlegging and speakeasies, particularly during the Depression, and by the time the market for illicit liquor had dried up with the repeal of federal prohibition in 1933, the rich Mafia racketeers had moved in on illegal gambling, loan-sharking, prostitution and extortion right across the Unites States, from New York and Chicago to Reno and Las Vegas. The next big area for the 'Mafiosi' to move into was obviously the growing drugs market.

The early years of open gang warfare on the streets eventually gave way to the low-profile organization of crime on a more cooperative basis, although the elimination of rivals and informers did not entirely disappear, and has hardly done so even today. In 1976, the dismembered corpse of Johnnie Roselli, a Mafia boss, was found in an oil drum floating in the Atlantic off the Florida coast. Roselli had told the CIA that the murder of Lee Harvey Oswald by Jack Ruby was part of a Mafia conspiracy, and that Ruby was "one of our boys". Roselli was due to give evidence to a Senate Investigating Committee. In July 1979, 50 years after the St Valentine's Day Massacre in Chicago, Carmine Galante, the self-appointed New York Godfather, was shot dead in a hail of bullets whilst enjoying a meal of spaghetti and Chianti in a restaurant. Frank Tieri, whose Genovese family Galanti had tried to take over, was voted Godfather in his stead.

The profits of the Mafia's enormous criminal conspiracy were estimated at $48 billion in the late 80s, and even their *legitimate* business was reckoned to produce profits five times higher than those of Exxon, America's largest industrial corporation.

In Britain, the most notorious gangland empire was that of the Kray twins, Ronald and Reginald. Former professional boxers, the twins moved in on London's criminal activity in the East End during the 1950s and established 'the Firm', modelling themselves on the Chicago 'Mob'. Their original HQ was the Regal Billiard Hall in Mile End Road, and they soon had interests in the protection racket, illegal gambling and

Fact

Latin American drug barons are among the greatest beneficiaries of organized crime in today's world. The economic viability of one or two countries, most notably Bolivia, depends on the cultivation and trafficking of narcotics. Hence, drug barons have been involved officially in government, and others unofficially control police and politicians. Hugo Ganzer, who became President of Bolivia in 1971, was a drug-trafficker, and was deposed seven years later. Luis Arce Gomez, arrested in December 1989 for drug trafficking, was Bolivia's Minister of the Interior. General Manuel Noriega, the Panamanian dictator, was tried in the USA in 1992 for drug-trafficking, and imprisoned for 40 years.

drinking clubs. Gang warfare went with the territory; the Richardson gang was the Krays' chief rival.

Ronnie Kray, a homosexual psychopath, got three years imprisonment in 1956 for grievous bodily harm after attacking a street trader with a bayonet. At Winchester prison he was diagnosed as a paranoid schizophrenic and certified insane. Reggie got him out by changing places with him, but eventually realized that his brother did need professional help, and had him sent back to prison. In 1959, however, Ronnie Kray was released, having served his time and apparently recovered.

By the mid-60s, the Kray twins were well in with the Canadian Mafia, and coveted the American gangsters' life-style, but the London scene seemed a bit down-market by comparison. Diana Dors and Barbara Windsor were hardly substitutes for the likes of Clark Gable, George Raft and Frank Sinatra when it came to being seen in the company of famous show-business personalities.

The Krays sheltered Ronald Marwood, who was eventually executed for the murder of a policeman; and 'sprang' Frank Mitchell, the so-called 'Mad Axeman', from Dartmoor prison. They were strongly suspected of murdering Mitchell later, but were convicted and sentenced for two other killings after police had overcome the reluctance of potential prosecution witnesses to testify. As Ronald Kray put it in their joint autobiography: 'I went down for murdering George Cornell and being an accessory in the McVitie killing. Reg went down for murdering McVitie and being an accessory in the Cornell killing'.

In July 1968, both twins were sentenced to life imprisonment with a recommendation that they should serve not less than 30 years. The twins' elder brother Charles was also convicted and imprisoned, along with other members of the Kray gang. Ronald Kray died in Broadmoor in 1995; Reginald Kray remains in prison.

Fact

'Murder Incorporated' was an American underworld assassination squad, which got its name from a massacre of potential informers against powerful members of the New York Mafia in 1936. Legend ascribes a thousand murders to this gang of professional hit-men, but the true figure is probably much lower. Among Murder Inc's best-known killers were 'Bugsy' Siegel, who was himself shot dead in 1947; Albert Anastasia, known as the 'Lord High Executioner', who was also murdered, in a Manhattan barber-shop in 1957; and Louis 'Lepke' Buchalter, who was executed by electric chair at Sing Sing Prison in March 1944. Buchalter was known as 'The Judge', and was labelled by the FBI at the time as the most dangerous criminal in the United States. He was the only leading mobster to be legally executed.

Part three:
Crimes Against the State

Section 1: Treason

Treason doth never prosper; what's the reason?
For if it prosper, none dare call it treason.
Sir John Harington: *Epigrams*

LAWS AGAINST TREASON in the United Kingdom date from the reign of Edward III. The Statute of Treasons of 1351 made it an offence punishable by death (formerly hanging, drawing and quartering), to plot against the life of the king, queen or heir to the throne; to make war against the king in his realm; to give aid to the king's enemies, etc. This definition has been expanded at various times to include other acts conceived as crimes against the State. Under Henry VIII, for instance, the definition of treason embraced refusal to take the oath of supremacy, and Sir Thomas More was executed under this law. In the reign of Elizabeth I, it was a treasonable offence to introduce papal bulls from Rome. Jesuit priests could be charged with treason if they failed to leave the country after an act of 1585 ordered them to do so within 40 days. Judicial decisions in the 16th century made it treason to riot against the enclosure of land. Treason against the State was called 'High Treason' to distinguish it from 'Petty Treason'—formerly the killing of a man by his wife, or a master by his servant.

Among the most famous victims of the treason laws since the Tudor period in England were

Fact

The five leaders of the Cato Street conspiracy, publicly executed by hanging in front of Newgate Gaol on 1 May 1820, were the last traitors to be sentenced to the ritual reinforcement of the State's punishment for treason. After their bodies had been left hanging for an hour, the heads of Arthur Thistlewood and his fellow-conspirators—who had planned to assassinate the entire cabinet and take over the government—were speedily cut off by a masked man in a seaman's jersey. He is believed to have been a body-snatcher named Parker, who was paid £20 to do the job by the Under-Sheriff of London. The mob, however, observing the efficiency of the decapitations and grasping at a rumour that the man had come from Argyll Street, assumed him to be the surgeon Thomas Wakley, subsequently founder of the medical journal The Lancet. *That night a few remaining conspirators set fire to his house and the surgeon was seriously injured.*

Mary Queen of Scots in 1587; Guy Fawkes and his fellow-conspirators in 1606 (see under Sedition and Conspiracy); Sir Walter Raleigh, executed in 1618 after being accused of plotting against James I; King Charles I, beheaded in 1645; and the captured noblemen who supported Bonnie Prince Charlie's rebellion in 1745.

Throughout the ages charges of treason have been levelled at persons who appear to pose threats to those holding power. In 1483 the Protector, Richard, Duke of Gloucester, ordered the instant execution of William, Lord Hastings, the Lord Chamberlain, for his alleged treachery, and swore he would not dine until Hastings's head had left his body. Thus he removed one obstacle on his path to the throne as Richard III.

More than 400 years later, Joseph Stalin resorted to similar tactics in the Soviet Union. The infamous 'treason trials' of the 1930s were stage-managed show trials of leading Bolsheviks seen as possible rivals to Stalin, and heralded the 'Great Purge' of 1936-38, when many associates of Lenin, members of the Politburo, senior officers of the NKVD, and high ranking army officers were accused of treason and executed as 'enemies of the working class' and 'betrayers of the motherland'. The charges against them included having pro-German sympathies and plotting against the life of the paranoid Comrade Stalin.

In America during the Civil War, the punishment for treason was altered from a mandatory death sentence to either death or imprisonment with hard labour, plus a fine and disqualification from holding office. In the UK the death penalty remains on the statute book as a punishment for treason, although the last person to be executed for treason was William Joyce (see case history) in 1946.

Case Histories

The Dreyfus Affair

In September 1894, a cleaning-woman at the German Embassy in Paris found in a waste-paper basket a note referring to some items of military information which an anonymous Frenchman was willing to sell to the Germans. Suspicion fell on a Jewish officer on the French General Staff—Captain Alfred Dreyfus—and he was arrested and tried for treason by a secret court martial.

Dreyfus was convicted by witnesses who were unashamedly anti-Semitic, and by evidence that was forged. His protestations of innocence did not save him from being sentenced to ritual military degradation and transportation. Stripped of his insignia in front of jeering troops, the former artillery captain was manacled in an iron cage and shipped to the notorious and dreaded Devil's Island off the coast of French Guiana, there to "expiate his abominable crime in merited torments", as the novelist Emile Zola later expressed it.

Whilst Dreyfus was incarcerated on Devil's Island, however, it became clear that the spying for which he had been convicted was still going on. A campaign was mounted to free Dreyfus, but when a counter-espionage officer suggested to his superior that a mistake had been made, the general's response was: "If you keep silent, no one need know". But Lieutenant-Colonel Picquart did not keep silent. He became convinced that the real spy was a Major Esterházy, but Picquart was dismissed from his post for voicing his suspicions, and Esterházy was cleared by a court martial set up at his own request.

France was now divided by this *cause-célèbre*. Zola wrote his famous open letter to the President of France in defence of Dreyfus. Entitled 'J'accuse', it denounced the court martial of Esterházy as an army cover-up. Zola was charged with libel, and in a long speech—ostensibly in his own defence—he returned to the attack, declaring over and over again with passionate conviction that Dreyfus was innocent. Zola was convicted of criminal libel and sentenced to a year's imprisonment and a large fine. When his appeal failed, he fled to England and continued his campaign on behalf of Dreyfus from across the Channel.

After prolonged investigation, it was at last decided that the conviction of Dreyfus should be annulled and a retrial ordered. Major Hubert Henry, the chief of military intelligence who confessed to forging documents to implicate Dreyfus, committed suicide in prison, cutting his throat with a razor. In the summer of 1899, Dreyfus—bearded, grey and looking considerably older than his 39 years—was brought back to France. Then, to the astonishment and outrage of millions in France and throughout Europe, a fresh trial *again* found him guilty, and he was sentenced to 10 years in prison. Ten days later, however, President Loubet, recognising a feeble attempt by the army at damage limitation, announced a free pardon for Dreyfus, and seven years afterwards, he was fully exonerated and his army commission restored.

The guilty Esterházy, who had been paid DM12,000 a month for passing military information to the Germans, had long before fled the country. Dreyfus's greatest champion, Zola, was found dead at his Paris home shortly after returning from England in 1902. He had been suffocated by fumes caused by a blocked chimney. Some thought it had been blocked deliberately by Anti-Dreyfusards to cause his death by carbon monoxide poisoning.

Dreyfus fought gallantly for France in WWI and was awarded the Légion d'honneur. He died in 1935.

Fact

In Paris, towards the end of WWII, four plain-clothes policemen armed with sub-machine-guns entered the hotel bedroom of P.G. Wodehouse, the world-famous author of the 'Jeeves' stories, and arrested him and his wife for treason. Wodehouse had been resident in Le Touquet when the Pétain government surrendered, and was interned by the Germans. American representations obtained his release, and he went to Berlin where he naïvely fell for a CBS offer to broadcast to his American fans. German radio naturally exploited the broadcasts for Nazi propaganda purposes, and an hysterical campaign against Wodehouse began in Britain, led by Duff Cooper, the wartime Minister of Information, and 'Cassandra' of the Daily Mirror, *who absurdly accused Wodehouse of "selling his country" and "worshipping the Führer". Wodehouse was banned from the British airwaves by the BBC, and there were demands for his trial on treason charges—hence his arrest by French police. The furore gradually died down when it was realized that Wodehouse had been merely a political innocent abroad, and his broadcasts silly but harmless and entirely without malice. Instead of being hanged as a traitor in 1945, he was knighted 30 years later, shortly before his death.*

Sir Roger Casement

Roger David Casement was an Irishman in the employment of the British Foreign Office. He won fame, honour and respect by his thorough exposure of the unspeakable atrocities being suffered by the natives of the Belgian Congo and in the Putumayo basin of Peru, and was knighted for his services in 1911.

Fact

In December 1945, the month before William Joyce was executed in Britain for high treason (see case history), John Amery, the disowned son of Conservative politician Leo Amery (a member of Churchill's wartime government) was hanged for making pro-Nazi speeches and broadcasts in Europe during the war. Among those Amery had recruited to Hitler's cause was Kenneth Edward, a practically illiterate 17 year-old internee in France, who subsequently attempted to recruit young British prisoners of war into what Amery had called the 'Legion of St George'. Handed over to the Americans by the Red Army at the end of the war, Kenneth Edward was sent back to Britain and tried for treason. He was given nine months imprisonment—the lightest sentence passed on any convicted traitor.

However, at the outbreak of war in 1914, his devotion to the cause of Irish freedom took him to Germany, where he attempted to persuade Irish prisoners of war to form an Irish Brigade on the side of the Kaiser. He also tried to persuade the German government to send an expeditionary force to aid Ireland in the imminent rebellion. Both efforts failed, but at the eleventh hour the Germans did send arms and ammunition, just before the Easter Rising of 1916. On Good Friday, 21 April, Casement was arrested by a local constable as he was put ashore on the coast of County Kerry by a German U-boat. He was sent back to London where he was charged with high treason. A Tory MP promptly asked the Prime Minister, amid cheers in the House of Commons, if he could assure the nation that "this traitor will be shot forthwith". Mr Asquith replied that there was no question of such summary methods being used. Casement was moved from Brixton Prison to the Tower of London to await trial, but conditions in the Tower were so unhealthy that he was eventually returned to Brixton.

The trial of Sir Roger Casement began in the Royal Courts of Justice on 26 June. He was the first knight of the realm to be put on trial for treason for hundreds of years. Much of the trial was taken up with legal argument as to whether Casement was a traitor within the meaning of an unpunctuated indictment in a 500-year-old statute. Casement, resigned to his fate, commented in a letter on legal antiquaries who would "hang a man's life upon a comma, and throttle him with a semicolon". The trial occupied four days, ending in his conviction and sentence of death. Next day, the *London Gazette* announced that the king had been "pleased to degrade Roger David Casement from the Order of Knights Bachelor".

Several petitions were got up on Casement's behalf, chief of which was addressed to the Prime Minister by Sir Arthur Conan Doyle, who had also contributed to Casement's defence costs. It bore the signatures of many eminent people, including Arnold Bennett, G.K. Chesterton, John Galsworthy, Sidney and Beatrice Webb, the Bishop of Winchester and the President of the Royal College of Physicians. Another was drawn up by Bernard Shaw who had advised Casement before his trial to admit all the facts and demand to be treated as a prisoner of war. To this suggestion Casement had objected that he would never plead to be "let off" by an English jury. They could hang him and be damned.

Meanwhile, a disgraceful smear campaign was being carried out against Casement on behalf of the government by the circulation of his private diaries to influential people, including newspaper editors. The diaries contained references to Casement's homosexual practices, and the campaign was organized to prevent his execution from making a martyr of him in Ireland and America, and alienating those countries from the British cause. Asquith is alleged to have told the American ambassador, who had seen the diaries, "you need not be particular about keeping it to yourself". The diaries were subsequently shown to President Wilson, and even to King George V lest His Majesty should feel inclined towards clemency. This campaign was masterminded by Basil Thomson (later Sir Basil Thomson), Assistant Commissioner of Metropolitan Police and Head of the Criminal Investigation

Department, and Captain Hall (later Admiral Sir Reginald Hall), Director of Intelligence at the Admiralty. The Archbishop of Canterbury was one among several who would have appealed for clemency if they had not seen the diaries.

Casement was hanged by the executioner John Ellis at Pentonville on 3 August 1916. It was the first execution for treason in Britain for nearly 100 years. Ellis recalled later that "Casement may have been a traitor, but he died like a soldier".

"Don't let my body lie in this dreadful place", Casement had pleaded in Pentonville. But his remains did lie there for nearly half a century until, in February 1965, Prime Minister Harold Wilson agreed to allow their return to Ireland, where they were reburied in Dublin's Glasnevin Cemetery.

Fact

Among other Cold War traitors to Britain—in addition to Klaus Fuchs, Burgess and Maclean, Philby and Blunt—was Dr Alan Nunn May, a physics lecturer at London University who was sentenced to 10 years imprisonment in May 1946 for what the judge called his "crass conceit and wickedness" in betraying the country's atomic secrets. He was released in December 1952.

'Lord Haw-Haw'

Barely a fortnight after Britain had declared war on Germany in September 1939, radio listeners in the UK were treated to the plummy and drawling tones of a Nazi propaganda broadcast beginning, "Jairmany calling... Jairmany calling..." The broadcasts which followed were designed to spread alarm and despondency among the population by predicting the inevitable defeat of Britain at the hands of the superior German forces, and by announcing seemingly accurate details about the country which suggested that the Nazis had spies everywhere.

The speaker, who continued to be heard throughout the war in Europe, was William Joyce, a scar-faced Irish-American who had spent much of his life in England, and carried a British passport. He had been well educated in London at Birkbeck College and King's College, studying history, psychology and English. He was quickly nicknamed 'Lord Haw-Haw', becoming generally regarded in the UK as more comic than menacing. Nevertheless, the fact remained that the *intention* of the broadcasts was to assist Germany in Britain's defeat, and that Joyce—a former member of the British Union of Fascists—was a willing collaborator in that object.

Arrested in Germany at the end of the war, he was arraigned on a charge of treason and tried at the Old Bailey in September 1945. The charge was that he had committed high treason, 'being a British subject, owing allegiance to His Majesty the King...contrary to the Treason Act, 1351'.

Joyce was *not* a British subject, however, and there was much soul-searching about Britain's right to try him for treason. William Joyce was an American citizen, born in New York in 1906, and his 'offences' had been committed on foreign soil, not within the realm. He had acquired a British passport in 1933 by falsely claiming that he was born in Ireland. But this passport had expired in 1940. Moreover, he had been granted German nationality in September 1940. He had been appointed chief English-speaking commentator on German radio, and had been

Fact

The 80 year-old Simon Fraser, Lord Lovat, executed for treason after the Jacobite rebellion, was the last person to be executed in Britain by beheading. His head was severed by one blow of an axe in the Tower of London in April 1746. The axe and block believed to have been used on this occasion can still be seen at the Tower.

honoured by Hitler. How could this alien be accused of being a traitor to Britain?

It was ruled that Joyce, as a holder of a British passport between September 1939 and July 1940, had the right of protection by the British Crown, and therefore owed it his allegiance. The jury convicted him of treason and he was sentenced to death.

The trial established the important precedent that an alien holding a British passport could be guilty of treason in respect of an act committed outside the realm. It seemed to some as if Britain had changed the law ('moved the goalposts' is the current phrase) so that it could execute Joyce, who was—as war criminals go—relatively harmless. Joyce was, in effect, condemned to death for the fraudulent acquisition of a British passport. But the Law Lords upheld the verdict on appeal, and William Joyce, amid continuing controversy, was hanged at Wandsworth prison on 3 January 1946. He was the last person to be executed in Britain for treason.

The Cardinal

The execution of Sir Thomas More for high treason in 1535—for refusing to acknowledge Henry VIII as head of the Church in England—found something of a modern parallel in eastern Europe more than 400 years later when Cardinal Jósef Mindszenty, Primate of Hungary, was arrested in December 1948 and charged with treason.

Some years earlier, as Bishop of Veszprém, he had been a national hero. His courage in openly defying the Nazis had led to his arrest and imprisonment by the Germans, and he had made defiant gestures to the last, insisting on wearing full canonicals when being taken to prison from which he was released by the Red Army at the end of the war. But the cardinal was equally uncompromising with Hungary's new Communist regime, refusing to leave the country and warning his people in advance not to believe any "confessions" that might be forced out of him. His trial in February 1949 in Budapest was a travesty of justice, and he was sentenced to penal servitude for life. In the wake of the short-lived Hungarian Rising of 1956 he was freed by the insurgents. But the Soviet suppression of the uprising led him to seek asylum in the American Legation, where he remained for nearly 15 years, stubbornly refusing to acknowledge the reconciliation which had been achieved between the Vatican and the Hungarian government.

The case inspired Bridget Boland's drama *The Prisoner*, in which Alec Guinness starred on both stage and screen in the 1950s.

Eventually, Cardinal Mindszenty was allowed to leave Hungary and go to Rome where he was persuaded by Pope Paul VI to resign his primacy. He went to live with a religious community in Vienna where he died in 1975 at the age of 82.

Klaus Fuchs

Klaus Emil Julius Fuchs, born in 1911 at Russelsheim, near Darmstadt, came to England in the 1930s to escape Nazi oppression. He had been a radical university student at Kiel and Leipzig, and a member of the Communist Party in Germany when Hitler had begun his purge of Communists for allegedly burning down the Reichstag.

Fuchs obtained a doctorate of philosophy in mathematics and physics at Bristol University, and a doctorate in science at Edinburgh. After a spell in Canada as an internee during the early years of the war, he joined physicists doing atomic research at Birmingham University and became a naturalized British subject. In 1943, Dr Fuchs went to Los Alamos in New Mexico to work on the atomic bomb project under Dr Robert Oppenheimer. When he returned to Britain, he became head of theoretical physics at the Atomic Energy Research Establishment at Harwell.

Despite his well-documented Communist past, it was not until 1948 that Dr Fuchs was suspected of being a Russian agent. The general excuse for ignoring his Communist affiliations in Germany was that this information came from the Gestapo and, as the Prime Minister, Clement Attlee, stated in the House of Commons, "the Gestapo accused everybody of being a Communist". But information passed by the Americans to British Intelligence led to the arrest of Klaus Fuchs in February 1950.

He had been passing secret information to the Soviet Union for several years. He had given them details of atomic bomb development at Los Alamos, and of a plant producing bombs at Knoxville, Tennessee, as well as information about his work at Harwell and the nuclear reactor plant at Windscale in Cumbria. Fuchs was charged under the Official Secrets Act with communicating information that might be useful to an enemy. This was a lesser charge than high treason, for which he could have been hanged.

During the trial at the Old Bailey, Lord Chief Justice Goddard characteristically made no secret of his opinion that the death sentence would have been appropriate for Fuchs's crimes. He had imperilled the good relationship between Britain and the USA by revealing American secrets; he had betrayed the work of other scientists which could have brought *them* under suspicion; he had caused other refugees working in Britain to lose their jobs and endangered their right of asylum. But above all, he could have brought the disaster of nuclear war on Britain and America, for he had, as he admitted, told the Soviets how to make the atom bomb and perhaps saved them years of research and enormous sums of money.

Fuchs pleaded guilty to four charges of spying on dates between 1943 and 1947, and the trial was over in an hour and a half. He was sentenced to 14 years in prison, and stripped of his British citizenship. Released in June 1959, having served nine years and earned full remission for good behaviour, he chose to go to East Germany where he worked on nuclear research at Rossendorf, near Dresden, until his retirement in 1979. Klaus Fuchs died in 1988. It could be argued that one of the worst offences he committed against the British people was forcing them to pronounce his name.

Fact

George Blake, a diplomat of Dutch-Jewish origin, was captured by North Koreans while serving as British vice-consul in Seoul, and may have been brainwashed. Tried in camera *at the Old Bailey in 1961 for passing secrets to the USSR, he was given a sentence of 42 years imprisonment, the longest fixed sentence ever imposed by a criminal court in Britain up to that time. But Blake escaped from Wormwood Scrubs in 1966 and fled to Moscow.*

Fact

Sir Thomas More, the former Chancellor of England, refused to take the oath required by the Succession Act of 1534. This would have required him to repudiate the Pope, which among other things, his conscience would not permit him to do. Henry VIII had More committed to the Tower and beheaded under a new law enacted that same year—the Treasons Act.

Rosenbergs

The Klaus Fuchs case led to much examination in Britain and the USA of the efficiency of their security services, and in America, hysteria about the 'Red menace' was encouraged and exploited by Senator Joseph McCarthy, later chairman of the Senate Committee for Un-American Activities. Described by Harry Truman, the former president, as a "pathological character assassin", McCarthy—contemptuous of what he called "twisted-thinking eggheads"—wildly accused the State Department of harbouring prominent Communists, and the Democratic Party and the US Army of being "soft on Communism".

It was during this period that Julius and Ethel Rosenberg were tried and sentenced to death for passing atomic secrets to the Soviet Union during the war. Julius Rosenberg, the son of Russian immigrants, had been discharged from the army for belonging to the Communist Party. He was working for an engineering company in Brooklyn. His wife's brother, David Greenglass, also worked there, and in June 1950, Greenglass was arrested by the FBI for betraying information which had come into his possession whilst a soldier at the Los Alamos base.

Greenglass implicated his sister, Ethel Rosenberg, and his brother-in-law, and the Rosenbergs were arrested and charged. They denied any knowledge of espionage. Julius said that he knew nothing about the atomic bomb until it was dropped on Hiroshima. But in order to save his own life, Greenglass agreed to testify against them. He told the court that he had been lured into espionage by Julius, who had sent Ruth Greenglass to Los Alamos to urge her husband to become a spy, and that Ethel Rosenberg had typed information for passing to the Russians.

The Rosenbergs' attorney begged the jury to believe his clients rather than Greenglass, who was "willing to bury his sister and her husband to save his own life... Any man who will testify against his own flesh and blood, his own sister, is repulsive, revolting, and is violating every code of civilization that ever existed. He is lower than the lowest animal I have ever seen". Nevertheless, the jury found the Rosenbergs guilty, and they were sentenced to death by a judge who declared that millions of innocent people might have to pay the price of their treachery, and that they had "altered the course of history to the disadvantage of our country".

Successive appeals were made on behalf of the couple. It was pointed out in letters to the press that there was evidence of a family feud between the Greenglasses and the Rosenbergs, and many people, including Albert Einstein, felt uneasy that the Rosenbergs were being sent to their deaths on the evidence of a man who stood to profit by it. The justice of the conviction was also doubted by some on the grounds that the spying had been done at a time when the USSR was a United States ally, not an enemy. Appeals on the couple's behalf also came from Europe. The Rosenbergs refused to save themselves by "co-operating" with the government. Julius said history would record that "we were the victims of the most monstrous frame-up in the history of our country"; and Ethel claimed that they were the "first victims of American fascism".

Direct petitions to President Eisenhower were abortive, and the executions were carried out by electric chair at Sing Sing Prison on 19 June 1953. Ten witnesses watched Julius go to his death first, and were then horrified to see Ethel's violent contractions, and smell burning flesh as she was given repeated shocks before her life was pronounced extinct. Their deaths were the only American executions of civilians for espionage during peacetime. Ethel Rosenberg was the first woman to suffer the death penalty for a federal offence since Mary Surratt was hanged in 1865 for complicity in the assassination of Abraham Lincoln.

David Greenglass, jailed for 15 years, was freed in 1960. Documents released into the public domain years afterwards showed that he had secured immunity from prosecution for his wife, Ruth, by agreeing to testify against the Rosenbergs; and that J. Edgar Hoover, Director of the FBI, had engineered the charge against Ethel in order to put additional pressure on her husband.

Fact

During the French Revolution, treason was the charge used to justify the beheading of nearly 1,200 noblemen and women, as well as the king, Louis XVI, and the queen, Marie Antoinette. Altogether, over 400,000 people died by the guillotine. When Danton and Robespierre, two of the creators of the 'Terror', were themselves executed, the exploitation of vague charges of treason rebounded against them.

Aleksandr Solzhenitsyn

Treason is defined differently according to the kind of society one lives in. You cannot be charged with treason in Britain simply for criticizing the government. But in Russia, persistent attacks against the system under Soviet Communism were always seen as treasonable, especially under Stalin.

One Tuesday afternoon in February 1974, Natalia Svetlova, second wife of the great Russian novelist and dissident, Solzhenitsyn, told her husband that two men from the prosecutor's office were at the door wanting to see him to "clear something up". Aleksandr went to let them in, and as he took the chain off the door, they and six other men burst in and ordered him to accompany them to the prosecutor's office immediately.

The KGB officers took him to Moscow's Lefortovo Prison, where he was stripped and searched and put in a cell with two other men. After about an hour, he was taken to the office of the USSR's deputy Prosecutor General, Mikhail Malyarov, and told that he was being charged with treason.

Solzhenitsyn was 56. As a younger man, he had served eight years in a corrective labour camp for criticizing Stalin's conduct of the war, and spent a further three years in exile in Siberia, suffering from cancer. His novels were banned in the Soviet Union, and the award of the Nobel Prize for Literature in 1970 had provoked much criticism from the Soviet authorities, especially when he had used the opportunity of his acceptance speech for yet another of his well-known denunciations of the Soviet system. *The Gulag Archipelago*, his great factual account of the Stalinist terror, published abroad, had brought him more criticism inside the USSR. He was expecting to be arrested, but his world-wide fame and the respect in which he was held abroad now protected him from a death sentence or further long-term incarceration.

Fact

Lord George Gordon was tried for high treason in 1780 after leading the so-called Gordon Riots in London, which caused a breakdown of law and order in the capital for several days. Fifty thousand people marched to present a petition to Parliament against concessions to Roman Catholics; Newgate Prison, the house of the Lord Chief Justice, Lord Mansfield, and many Catholic houses and chapels were destroyed in the ensuing rioting. Hundreds of people were killed. Nevertheless, Gordon, who was undoubtedly eccentric, was declared 'not guilty'. He was skilfully defended by his cousin, Thomas Erskine, who persuaded the jury—in front of Lord Mansfield himself—that Lord George, far from inciting the riots, had tried to prevent them and had only wished to influence the government by peaceable means.

The day after the charge was read to him, Aleksandr Solzhenitsyn was taken from his cell after breakfast and told that he was to be deported. The order read: 'By decree of the Presidium of the Supreme Soviet of the USSR, for the systematic execution of actions incompatible with Soviet citizenship and harmful to the USSR, Solzhenitsyn A.I. is to be deprived of Soviet citizenship and evicted beyond the borders of the Soviet Union, today 13 February 1974'.

That afternoon he was put on board a scheduled Aeroflot flight to Frankfurt which left Moscow three hours late. The other passengers were told that the delay was due to fog. In fact, the aircraft had been held up in order to get Solzhenitsyn on board. The West German Chancellor, Willi Brandt, had stated publicly that Solzhenitsyn would be welcome and free to work in the German Federal Republic, but until the plane landed and he saw the name on the airport buildings, Solzhenitsyn had no idea where he was being taken. He eventually settled in the USA and did not return to Russia until 1994, after publication of *The Gulag Archipelago* in the USSR and the subsequent collapse of the Soviet Communist system.

The Professor

Public disclosure of the long tunnel of treachery dug by assorted moles through the British security services began in 1951 when Guy Burgess and Donald Maclean, both civil servants working for the Foreign Office, fled to Moscow during the night of 25 May. Their defection was prompted by the imminent interrogation of Maclean, who was suspected of passing secrets to the USSR. It soon became clear that a third man was involved in the conspiracy. It turned out to be Harold Philby, known as 'Kim', who was First Secretary at the British Embassy in Washington. It was he who had tipped off Maclean and organized his escape. Philby in turn defected to Moscow in January 1963.

Meanwhile, a former KGB officer, Anatoli Golitsin, who had defected to the USA, made it known to the CIA that there was a ring of *five* high level traitors in Britain, which had originated among Communist sympathizers at Cambridge in the 1930s.

The fourth man was not publicly unmasked until 1979, when it was revealed by the Prime Minister, Margaret Thatcher, that he was none other than the distinguished art historian Sir Anthony Frederick Blunt, KCVO, Fellow of Trinity College, Cambridge, Surveyor of the Queen's Pictures, former director of the Courtauld Institute of Art, former Slade Professor of Fine Art at both Oxford and Cambridge, leading authority on the work of the 17th-century French painter Poussin, and holder of many academic honours from both British and foreign universities.

It became clear that the treachery of Blunt (code-name Johnson) had been known to the authorities since 1964, soon after Philby's defection, when Blunt had confessed after several interrogations to spying for the Soviet Union while an MI5 officer during the war. He was granted immunity from prosecution by the Attorney-General, Sir John Hobson, without the knowledge of the then Prime Minister, Sir Alec Douglas-Home. The Queen, however, was told, but agreed to keep Blunt in her service in the interests of national security because if he were publicly exposed it would almost certainly lead to other spies taking prompt evasive measures before they could be brought to justice.

In 1979, Blunt was stripped of his knighthood and other titles. He died in disgrace in 1983, a brilliant and celebrated scholar who had betrayed his country and would undoubtedly have been hanged for high treason if his exploits had been known immediately after the war. But one incident that may have worked in his favour—part of the reason why there was "a tendency to treat Mr Blunt with kid gloves" as former Prime Minister James Callaghan later expressed it—was Blunt's accomplishment of a delicate mission in 1946 on behalf of King George VI. He had gone to Germany to recover some sensitive documents. Security officers interrogating Blunt were asked to steer clear of this little matter. The documents were possibly records of potentially embarrassing discussions between the Führer, Adolf Hitler, and the King's brother, the Duke of Windsor, formerly Edward VIII, during the Duke's controversial visit to Berlin in 1937. Blunt had been made a Commander of the Royal Victorian Order in the following year.

The fifth member of the 'Cambridge Circus' was identified by another KGB defector as James Cairncross. These men did enormous damage to Britain's national interests, but not one of them was ever brought to justice in a court of law.

Fact

In 1819 Sir Francis Burdett, a Leicestershire fox-hunting squire and radical MP, sent an open letter to the press deploring the 'Peterloo Massacre' at Manchester at which 11 people were killed and 400 injured by troops during a peaceful political gathering. He was arrested and charged with seditious libel, being a 'seditious, malicious, and ill-disposed person' who had excited dis-affection and sedition among the king's subjects and hatred of the government. He was found guilty at Leicester Assizes, fined £2,000 and imprisoned for three months in the King's Bench Prison. Sir Francis had demanded in his letter that English gentlemen should not stand by doing nothing but fattening bullocks and planting cabbages when unarmed men had been killed and women "disfigured, maimed, cut down, and trampled on by Dragoons!" They could not "stand tamely by as lookers-on", he insisted, "while bloody Neros rip open their mother's womb". Outrage at the Peterloo Massacre led to a great many published protests which the authorities did their best to suppress. In 1819 there were 63 prosecutions in Britain for seditious, blasphemous and defamatory libels—far more than in any other year.

Section 2:
Sedition and Conspiracy

They determined to put down the multitude. They thought they were imitating Mr Pitt because they mistook disorganization for sedition.
Benjamin Disraeli: *Coningsby*

SEDITION is the crime of agitating against the authority of the State. Words or actions liable to lead to insurrection or a breakdown of public order are seditious. Prosecutions for sedition are rare in modern democratic countries such as Britain. The principles of free speech and sedition seem diametrically opposed. So-called 'gagging laws' designed to limit the freedom of the press—particularly in regard to political matters—have always been, on the whole, counter-productive for as everyone knows, the best way to ensure that people want to read something is to ban it. But up to the 18th and 19th

Fact

The arrest of Henry Hunt, the radical agitator popularly known as 'Orator Hunt', was the objective of the Manchester magistrates who had sent in the troops on the day of the 'Peterloo Massacre'. Hunt was arrested and lodged in Manchester's New Bailey prison to await trial, which took place at York in March 1820. Hunt conducted his own defence, but was convicted and sentenced to two years imprisonment for sedition. He passed his sentence in the damp old Somerset county gaol at Ilchester. His allegations of cruel treatment of prisoners led to questions in the House of Commons and to an enquiry which resulted in condemnation of the governor who, Hunt said, had put female prisoners in the stocks and turned a blind eye to their sexual exploitation by the turnkeys.

centuries, trials for sedition were common, and conspiracy was the handmaiden of sedition. Sedition is a lesser crime than treason, but it can still carry heavy penalties.

When the Puritan lawyer William Prynne published *Histrio Mastix; The Players Scourge, or, Actors Tragoedie,* in 1632, this attack on the theatre was taken, by implication, as an insult to the Queen, Henrietta Maria, who was an enthusiastic participant in masques. Prynne had said that women acting in plays and masques were no better than whores. He was prosecuted for sedition and committed to the Tower, fined £5,000 and expelled from Lincoln's Inn. That was not all. The Earl of Dorset, presiding over the court of Star Chamber, asked his fellow-judges whether Prynne ought to have his nose slit or his forehead burnt, adding: "I should be loathe he should escape with his ears". In the event, Prynne had his nose slit and his ears cropped whilst standing in the pillory. Three years afterwards, what was left of his ears was cut off and both cheeks were branded with the letters SL (for 'seditious libeller').

The most famous conspiracy in history was that of the Roman generals Cassius and Brutus and their supporters against the demagogue Julius Caesar, which resulted in Caesar's assassination in 44 BC. No action was taken by the senate against the conspirators, who according to the Roman biographer, Suetonius, numbered more than 60.

Conspiracy can, of course, be a crime on its own. A plot by two or more people to carry out a serious crime can result in punishment for conspiracy as well as for the crime it led to (as happened, for instance, in the case of the Great Train Robbery). The famous Tolpuddle Martyrs (see case history) were condemned for both conspiracy and sedition.

Conspiracy was one of the charges brought against the four men accused in the Guinness illegal share-support scandal in 1990. Anthony Parnes, Gerald Ronson and Sir Jack Lyons were sentenced to terms of imprisonment and/or large fines. Ernest Saunders, Guinness's chief executive, was given five years for conspiracy and three and a half years for false accounting, the two sentences to run concurrently. Saunders, who had appeared arrogant and paranoid during the trial, did not serve either sentence. He was released on grounds of his apparent illness.

Case Histories

The Gunpowder Plot

The most famous conspiracy in British history began in 1604, when a group of disaffected Roman Catholics led by a Warwickshire gentleman, Robert Catesby, plotted to blow up the Palace of Westminster on the opening day of Parliament, when the King and Queen and the Prince of Wales, as well as the Privy Council and both Houses of Parliament, would be present. The cause of the conspirators' malice was that the King, James I, had promised to improve the position of Catholics in

England, but far from keeping his word by increasing religious tolerance, he had allowed a new wave of Catholic repression.

The men who formed the nucleus of the conspiracy were Catesby's relatives and friends: his cousins Robert and Thomas Winter; John Wright and Francis Tresham; Thomas Percy, heir of the great northern noble family which had come to England with William the Conqueror; Sir Everard Digby; and Guy Fawkes, a Catholic convert from Yorkshire. The plot was carried through with considerable skill and admirable patience. In May 1604, Lord Percy hired a house adjacent to the Palace of Westminster. The conspirators then spent six months digging a passage from the cellar of the house to a point beneath the House of Lords. In March 1605 they rented another cellar next door and made a passage joining the two cellars. This enabled them to store more than 30 barrels of gunpowder, hidden under heaps of fuel, directly beneath the palace. In charge of this part of the operation was Fawkes, who used the name Johnson.

Meanwhile, Catesby and Digby had formulated a plot to bring about a Catholic uprising in the Midlands, capture the other royal children, Prince Charles and Princess Elizabeth, and, after the success of the murderous explosion, to place one of the children on the throne.

The plot was betrayed, apparently by Tresham, who wrote anonymously to his brother-in-law, Lord Monteagle, warning him not to be in the House on 5 November. Monteagle showed the letter to the chief minister, Lord Salisbury, who informed the King. On the day before the opening of Parliament, search parties discovered Guy Fawkes at his post, as well as the gunpowder. Under torture in the Tower, Fawkes named his fellow-conspirators. Catesby and Percy were shot dead a few days later while resisting arrest near Kingswinford in Staffordshire. Tresham died in prison. Eight men were tried in January 1606 and executed. The last of them was Guy Fawkes. Stretching on the rack had rendered him incapable of mounting the scaffold unaided.

Fact

Daniel Defoe, subsequently the author of Robinson Crusoe *and* Moll Flanders, *was charged with sedition in 1703 after publication of* The Shortest Way with the Dissenters, *a pamphlet satirizing extremist ideas. Defoe ironically proposed a new St Bartholomew's Day massacre as the only way of getting rid of nonconformists, of whom he himself was one. He was sentenced to a fine and a term of imprisonment in Newgate, and made to stand in the pillory on three occasions, in Cheapside, Cornhill, and at Temple Bar.*

That Devil Wilkes!

John Wilkes, Member of Parliament for Aylesbury and, although a somewhat disreputable character, undoubtedly one of the great champions of English liberty, was arrested and locked up in the Tower in 1763, under Lord Bute's government, charged with seditious libel. (Wilkes, ever the mischievous wit, requested that he should be confined in a room where no Scotsman had been imprisoned, and when asked why, explained that he was afraid of catching the itch.) He had published in his journal *The North Briton* (the famous 45th edition), an allegation that the King's Speech from the throne contained lies put into His Majesty's mouth by his ministers. Such an attack on the royal speech was unprecedented. It was ordered that *The North Briton* No 45 should be publicly burnt by the common hangman. The symbolic execution was to take place in front of the Royal Exchange on 5 December.

Fact

When Thomas Paine published the second part of his book The Rights of Man *in 1792, which supported the French Revolution and advocated the overthrow of the English monarchy, the government promptly issued a proclamation against seditious writings and began legal proceedings against Paine, but he escaped to France before he could be brought to trial. A clergyman, Rev. Winterbottom, got two years imprisonment for sedition two years later after preaching a sermon in which he praised revolutionary France.*

At noon on the appointed day, a small bonfire was lit in the presence of the Sheriff of London and a large crowd. The executioner, Thomas Turlis, received the offending literature from one of the officials. But between the sentence and the execution, the government which had condemned the publication had fallen, and the mob was on the side of Wilkes. As Turlis stepped forward to drop *The North Briton* into the flames, the incensed mob surged forward, pelting law officers and the hangman with mud and stones, and wrecking the Sheriff's coach. Turlis, bruised by the barrage of missiles, stood his ground long enough to do his duty, but no sooner had he consigned the publication to the flames than someone snatched it out again, and Turlis fled for cover.

Wilkes had been released from the Tower on grounds of Parliamentary privilege, but the House of Commons passed a resolution that the privileges of Parliament 'do not extend to the case of writing and publishing seditious libels'. By this time, however, "that devil Wilkes", as George III called him, was safely abroad.

The Commons, meanwhile, voted the article in *The North Briton* a 'false, scandalous and seditious libel', which would, according to Lord North, disaffect the people towards the King, instil disobedience to the law, and incite insurrection against the government. The courts confirmed this view, and Wilkes was declared an outlaw and expelled from the House of Commons.

In due course, he returned to face the music. He was sentenced to 22 months in prison and a fine of £1,000. He served his time in the King's Bench Prison, where he lived in relative luxury, receiving gifts of salmon, game and wine from his supporters, who, at one point, threatened to free him in a disturbance which became known as the 'St George's Field Massacre', when several people were killed by troops called in to quell the riot.

The Tolpuddle Martyrs

William Pitt's government acted in 1799 against trade union agitation by bringing in a law forbidding any combination of workers to pressurize employers for higher wages or shorter working hours. It reinforced an earlier act forbidding secret oaths to be administered to union members.

In 1834, six Dorset farmworkers were arrested for forming a branch of the Labourers' Union at Tolpuddle, near Dorchester, and administering an oath. They had met under a sycamore tree at the village centre and raised a joint protest against a reduction in their already pitiful wages. At a meeting presided over by the vicar of Tolpuddle, their employers had previously agreed to wages of 10 shillings a week, but then cut them to nine shillings, then eight, with further reductions threatened. George Loveless and his brother James organized their fellow-workers to protest at wages which made it "impossible to live honestly". The law against trade unions had been repealed in 1824, and more than 40 labourers joined Loveless and his friends. But the oath of secrecy made their meeting, in the eyes of the law, a conspiracy for seditious purposes.

Six men were brought before Judge Williams at the Shire Hall in Dorchester on 18 March 1834. They were the Loveless brothers, James Brine, Thomas Standfield and his son John, and James Hammett. Convicted, they were sentenced to transportation for seven years, and shipped in chains to Australia.

Protests and petitions were organized in England against the savagery of the sentence while the six men suffered as convicts. James Brine was assigned to work for a magistrate as a labourer. Set to dig postholes with bare feet, and wash sheep while standing up to his chest in water, Brine asked for shoes and a blanket. The magistrate's reply was: "I understand it was your intention to have murdered, burnt and destroyed everything before you, and you are sent over here to be severely punished, and no mercy shall be shown you". He threatened Brine with frequent flogging if he had the nerve to ask for anything again.

After two years, the six were granted a pardon and their free passage back to their native land, but George Loveless had already served three years of his sentence by the time he returned in June 1837, and four others did not return until the following year.

Fact

Thomas Cooper, a leader of the Chartist reform movement from Leicester, was arrested on charges of conspiracy and sedition in 1842 after lecturing on political reform in the Potteries, and was sentenced at Stafford to two years imprisonment.

Section 3: Piracy

Go tell the King of England,
Go tell him this from me- –
If he reign King of all the Land,
I'll reign King at Sea.
17th-century ballad: *Captain Ward and the Rainbow*

PIRACY on the high seas consists of any act committed in peacetime conditions beyond the State's jurisdiction which, if it were committed on land, would be regarded as a felony. Thus Sir Francis Drake was a pirate, but instead of being hanged as a criminal, he was honoured as a popular hero and rewarded for carrying out robbery and plunder on behalf of the State.

Although the Royal Navy virtually eliminated piracy on the world's oceans in the 18th century, and kept them free of pirates for over 100 years, piracy is far from being a thing of the past. Just before midnight on 23 August 1981, for example, a British-registered ship named *Corsicana* was sailing eastward in the Strait of Singapore when she was boarded by three men armed with knives and axes. They seized the ship's master, and whilst two of them cut telephone lines and guarded the other officers on the bridge, the third forced the master at knife-point to open the safe in his cabin. The pirates escaped with about £4,000. Two

Fact

In the days of public executions, those convicted of piracy in London and sentenced to death were traditionally hanged at Execution Dock on the Thames shore at Wapping Old Stairs. Their bodies were customarily left chained to a stake until three tides had washed over them so that they should serve as a deterrent to the crews of all ships using the Pool of London. Captain David Ferguson, brutal master of the merchant ship Betsey, *was convicted at the Admiralty Sessions at the Old Bailey of murdering his cabin boy and was hanged at Execution Dock on 4 January 1771.*

Fact

Sir Henry Morgan, one of the most famous of British pirates, was born around 1635 in Glamorgan, and was reputedly kidnapped as a youngster in Bristol and shipped to Barbados, where he joined the buccaneers. But he was knighted by Charles II for his exploits against the Spaniards, and ended up as a Deputy Governor of Jamaica, dealing out rough justice to the class of criminals to which he had formerly belonged. He died in 1688.

Fact

The pirate known as Blackbeard was Edward Teach or Tache, whom Daniel Defoe described as "altogether such a figure that imagination cannot form an idea of a Fury from Hell to look more frightful". He operated in the Caribbean and off the eastern coast of North America, until his capture in 1718 by an English naval vessel. He was beheaded on board, and his head affixed to the ship's bowsprit.

years later, the master of a British-registered bulk carrier was attacked in a similar raid, this time with firearms, in the Brazilian port of Santos, and £2,300 was stolen.

Nor has the legendary pirates' emblem, the 'Jolly Roger', entirely disappeared. When eight armed men attacked a Malaysian fishing boat off the Natuna Islands between Malaysia and Borneo in 1982, it was reported that their boat was flying a flag bearing a skull and crossbones.

The Spanish Main, scene of most of the romantic tales about swashbuckling pirates, was the Caribbean Sea and the coastal waters of Colombia and Venezuela. Pirates could get rich pickings from the fleets of galleons bringing cargoes of precious merchandise from the Spanish colonies to Europe. Ships laden with the treasures of Peru and Mexico had to risk fire and sword to get their hoards of riches back to Spain.

The other great scene of piracy in the western world was the Barbary Coast—the western Mediterranean coast of north Africa. But the modern 'black spots' for piracy on the world's oceans are the South China Sea, the Pacific around the Philippine Islands, and the Atlantic off the West African coast.

One of the greatest hauls of the old-time pirate fleets was made in 1695, when a squadron of five ships led by Henry Every, known as 'Long Ben', attacked a Mogul fleet in the Indian Ocean. One of these vessels was described as "the greatest in all the Mogul dominions", and had 400 soldiers on board. But the pirates easily overcame them, raped the women and stole a great quantity of jewels and other valuables, sufficient to pay every man of the pirate crew £1,000 each. There were possibly 400 of them on the five ships. 'Long Ben' was never caught.

In reality, piracy was always a very different affair from that depicted in so many romantic tales and films. The real pirates were filthy, often drunken maritime desperadoes, riddled with syphilis and liable to torture prisoners by slicing off their noses. They plundered and pillaged the ocean trade in worm-eaten and stinking ships, and ate cats and dogs when they could not steal anything better.

Among the unfortunate modern victims of pirates have been the famed Vietnamese 'boat people'. In the early 1980s, more than three quarters of the boats carrying refugees from Vietnam to Thailand were attacked at sea. Fleeing Vietnamese families had their women raped, their daughters abducted and their valuables stolen. It was reported in 1985 that pirates around the coast of Thailand had killed 1,376 people, raped 2,283 women, and abducted 592. Some of those abducted were bartered in exchange for fish. On 26 March 1989, pirates killed 26 men and abducted more than 30 women in an attack on Vietnamese refugees in the South China Sea; less than three weeks later, more than 130 boat people were massacred in another attack when pirates set the refugees' boat on fire and shot and clubbed to death those who jumped overboard. The pirates numbered seven and were armed with shotguns and hammers. Before setting the Vietnamese boat ablaze they raped women and girls, including one who was 12 years old.

Case Histories

William Kidd

Born in Greenock, Kidd left his native land and went to New York. While engaged in legitimate trading, he gained a detailed knowledge of the pirates and their methods. When King William III conferred the government of New England on the Earl of Bellamont, the Earl approached Captain Kidd with a plan to suppress the rapacious pirates then swarming the waters of the West Indies and making huge profits from their booty in New York. The Earl and some other public-spirited noblemen raised £6,000 between them to purchase and man a privateer, the *Adventure Galley*, and in 1696 Kidd was given a commission to sail and seize pirates on behalf of the King of England and bring them to justice. He was to be rewarded with a fifth of the profit, the remainder of which was to be shared by the promoters of the enterprise, with 10 per cent going to the Treasury.

Kidd, however, plundered instead of protecting the vessels that were not pirate ships, thus becoming a pirate himself. Cruising between the West Indies and Madagascar, he attacked ships without regard to their nationality—Portuguese, French, Dutch and English alike. Within the space of a week, a third of his original crew had died of scurvy or cholera forcing him to take on 50 replacements. Eventually he left one of his captured vessels in the care of an Englishman named Bolton, who sailed to Boston and informed Lord Bellamont about what had happened. It became known in England that the *Adventure Galley*, launched to free the seas of buccaneers, was itself the terror of the Indian coast. Kidd was declared a pirate by the English government, and colonial governors ordered to seize him on sight. There were accusations that the noble promoters, who included the Lord Chancellor, the Duke of Shrewsbury and the Earls of Romney and Orford, were guilty of complicity with the criminals. The Whig cabinet was lampooned as 'a Corporation of Pirates'. Meanwhile, Kidd lost his temper with one of his gunners and killed him with a blow to the head with a bucket. One merchant testified that Kidd had robbed him of £60,000 in the Persian Gulf, and the pirate's effects were afterwards valued at nearly a quarter of a million pounds.

Kidd, of whom it was reported that 'there was never a greater liar or thief in the world', was arrested in New York at the first opportunity, clapped in irons, and sent back to England in February 1700, where he was tried at the Old Bailey for piracy and murder. The latter charge, tortuously worded, said that, 'being moved and seduced by the instigations of the Devil he did make an assault upon William Moore upon the high seas with a certain wooden bucket bound with iron hoops, of the value of eight pence', and that, holding the bucket in his right hand, he 'did violently, feloniously, voluntarily, and of malice

Fact

Captain Bray, a revenue officer at Deal, Kent, apprehended a noted pirate, one Brown, as he was landing illegal spirits on a local beach in 1784. It was reported that Brown "presented a blunderbuss to Bray's breast, both of them not being half-a-yard distance from each other. The captain was undaunted. One of his men seeing his brave master in this situation, with a cutlass cut Brown's cheek clean off. Bray seconded the stroke, and with his cutlass severed his head from his body and put a period to this pirate's life".

Fact

Following the abolition of slavery throughout the British Empire in 1833, the continuing slave trade (abolished in Britain itself in 1807) was classified as piracy. The importation of slaves into the United States was declared to be piracy in a law of 1808, but the law was not enforced until March 1862, when one Nathaniel Gordon was hanged in New York after his ship had been captured with a cargo of nearly 1,000 negroes. Gordon was the last white man to be executed for piracy.

Fact

As editor of The Freethinker, *George William Foote was sentenced to a year's imprisonment for publishing a blasphemous libel in 1883, along with its printer and sales manager, H.A. Kemp and W.J. Ramsey, who got three and nine months respectively. These three men, and not Holyoake, as is often claimed, were the last to be imprisoned for blasphemy in Britain. The journal had contained a cartoon of the Hebrew Deity, and the defendants were indicted at the Old Bailey for scandal to the Christian religion, 'the high displeasure of Almighty God', and injury to 'the peace of our Lady the Queen, her Crown, and dignity'. The trial jury could not agree, and was dismissed. A second jury was selected with some care, and agreed on a verdict of guilty within two minutes of the judge concluding his infamously partial summing-up.*

aforethought, beat and strike the aforesaid William Moore a little above the right ear, then and there upon the high sea and within the jurisdiction of Admiralty of England, giving the said William Moore one mortal bruise of which he did languish and die'.

William Kidd was sentenced to death, and conveyed from Newgate to Execution Dock on 23 May 1701, practically senseless from drink. The first attempt to hang him failed when the rope broke, and the 55 year-old naval veteran had to be hanged again before being left for the tides to wash him physically—if not morally—clean. He left behind him rumours of buried treasure which has never been recovered.

Section 4: Blasphemy

All great truths begin as blasphemies
George Bernard Shaw: *Annajanska*

HISTORICALLY, BLASPHEMY was regarded in England as an offence against Church and State, and it could be tried in both ecclesiastical and secular courts. Openly expressed anti-Christian sentiment became more common after the Reformation, and several laws attempted to curb what was seen as a threat to the stability of society.

The Blasphemy Ordinance of 1648 made it a punishable offence to deny there was a God, reject Christ and the Holy Ghost, or cast doubt on the scriptures. A Blasphemy Act followed in August 1650. Abiezer Coppe, a Warwickshire man who became leader of the sect known as Ranters, was committed to Newgate in 1650 after his *Fiery Flying Rolls* had been burnt by the public hangman as containing 'many horrid blasphemies'. Jacob Bauthumley, a Leicestershire shoemaker, was bored through the tongue in the same year as a result of his blasphemous book *The Light and Dark Sides of God*. Blasphemy was among the charges levelled at George Fox, founder of the Society of Friends, who was imprisoned on numerous occasions, but only on account of his unorthodox pronouncements. His disciple James Nayler, a Yorkshireman, committed a much more dramatic act of blasphemy: in 1656 he was imprisoned at Exeter and after his release made his way to Bristol where he rode into the city on a donkey, with women strewing palm leaves in his path. The hysteria this action provoked was so frenzied that many MPs, instead of questioning his sanity, demanded the death sentence for him. He was tried and convicted of blasphemy, and sentenced to be branded, whipped and imprisoned. He was flogged through the streets of London with such brutality that he never recovered; his forehead was branded and his tongue bored through with a red-hot iron; then he was sent to Bristol where he was also flogged.

Released from prison in 1659, he died the following year, aged 43.

William Bond, a weaver of Lacock, Wiltshire, was charged in 1656 with atheism and blasphemy after declaring publicly that "there was no God or power ruling over the planets", and "no Christ but the sun that shines upon us". In Scotland, in the same year, Alexander Agnew was sentenced to death for denying the existence of the Holy Ghost or that Christ was God, and broadcasting his opinions "to the entangling, deluding and seducing of the common people".

An 'act for the effectual suppressing of blasphemy and profaneness' became law under William III in 1697. It made any person "educated in or having made profession of the Christian religion", who spoke or published any denial of the central truths of Christianity, liable to three years imprisonment. It was not, in theory, a law against atheism, but in practice it has been seen as such, and George Jacob Holyoake (see case history) believed—with good reason—that he had been condemned for his atheism.

The law has only rarely been enforced in modern times. It was originally a crime against the common law to deny the existence of God, but an act of 1813 toned down the interpretation of blasphemy, and it came to be held that it was not blasphemous to deny the truth of Christianity provided it was expressed in reasonable language which would be unlikely to lead to a breach of the peace. Today, blasphemy is usually regarded as an attack on the Christian religion in language calculated to outrage Christians.

Blasphemy is treated much more harshly by the Islamic world than in Christian countries. A 12 year-old boy was recently condemned to death for blasphemy in Pakistan, though the sentence was subsequently lifted. The publication in 1988 of *The Satanic Verses* by Salman Rushdie, which resulted in a *fatwah* (death sentence) being pronounced on the author by the Iranian Ayatollah Khomeini, led to strong argument from some quarters in favour of extending Britain's blasphemy law to protect other religions as well as Christianity. Another school of thought maintains that it would be preferable to abolish the law against blasphemy altogether, and there is a strong argument for such abolition. It would be difficult to extend the law of blasphemy to *all* professed religious beliefs, some of which are bizarre to say the least.

Fact

Most 19th-century prosecutions were brought against 'literary blasphemy'—that is, against the publishers or sellers of works judged to be blasphemous, rather than against those who openly expressed anti-Christian views. Such a victim was Richard Carlile, who spent several years in prison for blasphemous libel. Matilda Roalfe suffered two months in prison in 1844 for selling in her Edinburgh shop books she considered worthy, 'whether they did or did not bring into contempt the Holy Scriptures and the Christian religion'.

Fact

Thomas Woolston, a well-known freethinker, was sentenced to a fine and imprisonment in 1729 for blasphemy in his Discourses on the Miracles of Our Saviour, *in which he argued that the gospel narratives, if taken literally, were absurd.*

Case History

George Jacob Holyoake

Holyoake was born in Birmingham in 1817 and taught mathematics at the Mechanics' Institute there. He was also the founder of the Secular movement, and despite a sensitive nature and a fairly severe speech impediment, lectured on social reform. In May 1842, after delivering a lecture at Cheltenham, a question from the audience allegedly drew from him the statement: "I do not believe there is such a thing as God". He was said to have added that he would "place Almighty God on half-

Fact

In 1979 a private prosecution for blasphemy was brought by Mrs Mary Whitehouse against the editor of Gay News, *Denis Lemon, who had published a poem by James Kirkup which described sexual interference with the body of Christ after his crucifixion. It was the first prosecution for blasphemy for more than 60 years. Mr Lemon was given a suspended sentence of a year's imprisonment.*

Fact

Charles Southwell was among those who preceded Holyoake to prison in the 19th century. In his case, it was for making offensive remarks on the Bible, which he called an "odious Jew production".

pay". The local paper, the *Cheltenham Chronicle,* reported that this 'poor misguided wretch' addressed the audience with 'blasphemous and awful remarks, which we cannot sully our columns by repeating...'

He was called a 'monster', and after his arrest, one police official declared that he was "only sorry the day is gone by when we could send you and Owen of Lanark to the stake instead of to Gloucester gaol". Holyoake wrote afterwards that Cheltenham, owing to priestly and conventional influences, would "furnish a jury who would, under direction, bring in any man guilty of blasphemy who boiled his tea-kettle on a Sunday".

After being made to walk through Cheltenham with his wrists in irons, Holyoake was transported to Gloucester by train. He had to pay his own train fare and those of the two policemen accompanying him, otherwise he would have had to walk the nine miles to Gloucester in chains. He was put in a prison cell infested with lice, and dared not lie down to sleep. He spent two weeks in jail awaiting trial. Tried for blasphemy at Gloucester Assizes, Holyoake was described in the indictment as a 'labourer' and a 'wicked, malicious, and evil-disposed person', charged with 'wickedly and profanely devising and intending to bring Almighty God, the Holy Scriptures, and the Christian religion into disbelief and contempt among the people of this kingdom...' The jury consisted of seven farmers, two shopkeepers, a poultry dealer, a miller and a maltster.

Holyoake, though frail in health, undertook his own defence. The court tried to charge him 8s 6d for a copy of the indictment, which consisted of one sheet of paper. His habitual stammer virtually disappeared as he addressed the court with conviction and eloquence for more than eight hours. Parts of his speech reduced women in court to tears, and Holyoake was afterwards congratulated on what some regarded as 'the very best appeal for liberty that has yet been heard within those halls called Courts of Justice'.

Mr Justice Erskine, summing-up, told the jury that if they were convinced that the defendant's words were "uttered with levity, for the purpose of treating with contempt the majesty of Almighty God", then they must find him guilty. They did, and Holyoake was sentenced to six months in the town gaol. "The arm of the law", the judge said, "is not stretched out to protect the character of the Almighty; we do not presume to be protectors of our God, but to protect the people from such indecent language".

Little in the way of Christian charity attended Holyoake's period in prison. His cell was damp and filthy, and the food almost uneatable. He had scant opportunity for exercise, and was permitted hardly any visitors, nor was he allowed to receive letters or write to his wife. He was not allowed his mathematical instruments lest he used them to commit suicide. He heard at length that his two year-old daughter, Madeline, had died, enfeebled by poverty. He had last seen the child waving him goodbye as he set out from Cheltenham for his trial.

When the prison chaplain remarked to him that he could not *really* be an atheist, Holyoake retorted: "And you say this who have been a party to imprisoning me for being one! If you believe yourself, go and demand my liberation". But Holyoake had to serve his full term, and was released in February 1843.

Freethinkers were apt thereafter to doff their hats as they passed the prison at Gloucester as a mark of respect to this champion of free speech who had suffered for his beliefs and who worked afterwards, though in vain, for repeal of the law against blasphemy. Holyoake was not the last person to go to prison in Britain for blasphemy, but he was the last person to be sentenced to imprisonment for expressing his atheism.

Fact

It is said that a trial for blasphemy contributed to the death of Lord Ellenborough, the notorious hanging judge. Presiding over the trial of William Hone, he directed the jury to find him guilty, but they refused and Hone was acquitted. The shock of being contradicted by a jury hastened Ellenborough's end.

Section 5: Witchcraft

I pray you all, tell me what they deserve
That do conspire my death with devilish plots
Of damned witchcraft, and that have prevailed
Upon my body with their hellish charms?
William Shakespeare: *Richard III*

THE SUPPOSED USE OF MAGIC to bring about both malevolent and beneficial effects is as old as mankind. Witches are alleged to produce their supernatural effects by forming compacts with the devil. Laws against witches in England can be traced back as far as the reign of King Cnut (Canute) in the 11th century. Those accused of witchcraft were mostly dealt with by ecclesiastical courts, sanctioned by scripture: 'Thou shalt not suffer a witch to live'. Trial by ordeal was the common medieval method of justice, but the crime was also indictable under common law, witches sometimes being accused of treason. Henry V's stepmother, Joan of Navarre, was alleged to have 'compassed and imagined the death and destruction of our lord the king' by means of magic, and 22 years later Joan of Arc was accused of witchcraft, sorcery and heresy, and burnt at Rouen on 30 May 1431. In 1441, the Duchess of Gloucester, Eleanor Cobham, was accused of conspiring with others to cause the death of Henry VI by means of magic.

Fact

The first important English witchcraft trial after the passing of the 1563 Act was that of the so-called Chelmsford Witches in 1566. One of them, Agnes Waterhouse, was the first convicted witch known to have been hanged under this Act.

It was during the 16th and 17th centuries that the religious campaign against witchcraft reached its climax throughout Europe. Fear of witchcraft as a perceived threat to Christendom grew slowly at first. It is significant that it followed the devastating effects of the Black Death and the Hundred Years War. There were less than 50 trials of witches in Europe in the half-century to 1375. A hundred years later, the number in the preceding half-century had more than doubled. The witch craze was instigated by the Roman Church. A bull issued by Pope Innocent VIII in 1484 called upon the Inquisition in Germany to stamp out witchcraft, for "these wretches", the holy father wrote, "do not shrink from committing and perpetrating the foulest abominations and excesses to the peril of

Fact

A petty criminal named Mainwaring-Knight conned gullible Christians in Sussex not only into believing that he was possessed by the devil, but also into parting with £250,000 for his redemption, only possible—he persuaded them—by purchasing expensive satanic regalia. The village rector raised the money from the wealthiest among his flock. Mainwaring-Knight spent the money on fast cars and prostitutes, and was eventually imprisoned for obtaining money by deception. This was in 1986.

their souls, whereby they offend the Divine Majesty and are a cause of scandal and dangerous example to very many". Protestants quickly joined the campaign and raised the persecution to a frenzy. Martin Luther called witches "the Devil's whores", and John Calvin reminded his followers that "God expressly commands that all witches and enchantresses shall be put to death". The terror spread like wildfire from Germany to Switzerland and France, Austria and Poland, Sweden and The Netherlands, Spain and Italy, England and Scotland.

The Catholic persecution was in the hands of the Holy Inquisition, but there was no inquisition in Britain where, in 1542, witchcraft was made a common felony under secular law. It was a capital offence to invoke spirits for any unlawful purpose. After 20 years, the law was revised to make a witch liable to the death penalty only if a human victim died as a result of his or her actions.

The sudden eruption of terror and the consequent persecution of witches may have been a form of mass hysteria, but it was not confined to the poor and ignorant. It affected all sections of society, and learned men lent their voices to the condemnation of witches. A little over 100 years after Joan of Arc was executed, Henry VIII remarked of Anne Boleyn after she miscarried a male child that he had been seduced by witchcraft into marrying her against his will.

Supposed witches were often elderly widows or spinsters living alone in country villages, with cats or other animals for company. They were apt to mutter to themselves and were usually regarded as eccentric or quarrelsome by their neighbours. Their accusers were often idle children and malicious gossips. James I stated in his book *Daemonologie,* in 1597, that the sex ratio among witches was as high as 20 women to every man. Of 99 witches burnt to death at Geneva in 1571/2, only eight were men.

Witches throughout Europe, including Scotland, were—in theory—generally burnt alive, though in practice, if they were fortunate they were mercifully strangled at the stake before the flames consumed them. The exceptions were Spain and Italy, where burning alive meant exactly what it said. In England and America witches were hanged, but there was some uneasiness about this method of execution in England. An account of the trial of six witches at Maidstone in 1652 says that members of the public wanted them burnt, not hanged, because it was firmly believed that if the body of a witch was burnt her blood was thereby prevented from 'becoming hereditary to her progeny in the same evil, which by hanging is not'.

The use of torture to extract confessions was forbidden in English law, but in practice, accused persons were often deprived of sleep, intimately searched for 'witch marks', and pricked to draw blood. They might also be subjected to the ordeal of 'swimming'—being ducked in ponds in the belief that if they floated they were guilty and if they sank, innocent. (The logic of this trial by ordeal is sometimes thought to be that witches were light in weight, which is why they could fly. But ordeal by swimming was a test for *all* crimes in late Saxon and early Norman England. Furthermore, in ancient Babylon, it was *sinking,* not floating, that established guilt in charges of black magic.)

The massacre of witches reached a crescendo in the first half of the

17th century. It was a holocaust akin—in mindless savagery if not in scale—to the Nazi destruction of Europe's Jews in the present century. In Germany, where more witches were executed than in any other country (often after torture to extract confessions), nearly 400 witches were burnt in the Trier district between 1587 and 1593. In 1583 alone, 121 convicted witches were burnt at Osnabrück; 38 at Weil de Stadt between 1615 and 1629; 24 witches at Coblenz in 1629. The town of Würzburg burnt 900 witches in the eight years to 1631. In Bamberg, another 600 were put to death at the stake in a similar period. In the 20 years to 1635, 5,000 witches were burnt in Strasbourg; 133 witches in one day in 1589 at Quedlinburg, near Leipzig. An executioner at Neisse, south of Breslau, anticipated the Nazis by burning women and children accused of witchcraft in a specially constructed oven.

In Switzerland, more than 300 convicted witches were burnt in the Lausanne area in one ten-year period, and in France, 400 witches were consumed by fire at Toulouse in 1577. In 1595, 23 witches went to their deaths at the stake in Aberdeen, and 68 were hanged at Bury St Edmunds in 1645. It was in that year, during the Commonwealth, that the peak of witchcraft executions was reached in England.

The lead in abandoning the persecution of witches was given by the enlightened and tolerant Netherlands. No witch was executed in Holland after 1597, and there were no trials of witches after 1610.

The capital crime of witchcraft was removed from the English statute book by an act of 1736 which repealed the Witchcraft Act passed under Elizabeth I in 1563, but made it an offence punishable by one year's imprisonment to pretend to employ witchcraft, tell fortunes, etc. Centuries-old fears and superstitions were not easily eliminated, however, and people sometimes took the law into their own hands. In 1751 at Gubblecote in Hertfordshire, an elderly couple suspected of witchcraft became victims of mob violence. John and Ruth Osborn were dragged out of the village church where they were hiding, stripped naked, tied up and dragged through a pond. The woman was dead when she was pulled out, and her husband died soon afterwards. The leader of the popular clamour against the couple, Thomas Colley, was hanged for murder.

Superstitions and delusions about witchcraft persist. In 1977, a 39 year-old woman from Stevenage was sentenced to life imprisonment for the murder of an elderly spinster at Hitchin. The defendant described herself as a witch, and was said to frighten local children by threatening to turn them into toads.

Fact

It has been estimated that at least 200,000 people condemned as witches were executed during the European witch craze of the 16th and 17th centuries. Probably between 6,000 and 7,000 were executed in Britain, mostly in Scotland, although more than 1,000 witches were executed in England.

Fact

The earliest recorded trial for witchcraft in a secular court in the British Isles was that of Dame Alice Kyteler in 1324, at Kilkenny in Ireland. The first such trial in England occurred later in the same year, when 27 people at Coventry were charged with engaging necromancers to bring about the death of King Edward II.

Fact

The last-known witch-burning in Europe occurred in Poland in 1793. It was illegal, witch trials having been abolished in Poland in 1787. The last legal *execution of a witch is believed to have occurred in Switzerland, when Anna Göldi was burnt to death at Glarus on 18 June 1782.*

Case Histories

The Witches of Belvoir

Sir Francis Manners, 6th Earl of Rutland, employed among his staff at Belvoir Castle in Leicestershire two sisters named Margaret and Philippa Flower. Margaret, who worked in the laundry, was dismissed

Fact

Among the most famous of English witch-trials were those of the so-called Lancashire Witches in 1612 and 1634. In the first trial, 21 defendants were brought before Mr Justice Bromley at Lancaster, accused of bewitching 16 people in the Pendle Hill vicinity 'by devilish practices and hellish means'. All except one were convicted, and 10 were hanged. In the second trial, 17 women were found guilty of witchcraft but subsequently acquitted.

Fact

Matthew Hopkins, the self-appointed 'Witchfinder General' operating in the eastern counties of England around 1645, was responsible for the execution of 68 persons known to us by name, and probably many more whose records have not been preserved. He would arrest old women and swear to the court—as he did in the case of Elizabeth Clarke at Chelmsford—that with this own eyes he had seen four familiars come to her in the form of two dogs, a polecat and a black imp. On this evidence, Elizabeth Clarke was convicted and hanged.

after she was found to be pilfering. Her mother, Joan Flower, who lived near Bottesford and was reputed to be a witch, threatened revenge on the Earl and Countess. Among items stolen from the castle were gloves belonging to the Earl's two young sons by his second marriage to Cecilia Hungerford. One of these gloves was allegedly dipped in hot water by the Flower women and pierced with pins. Within a week, Lord Henry Rosse, the Earl's heir, died. Then his younger brother's glove was buried in a dunghill and he, Lord Francis, also died. The boys' step-sister, Katherine, the Earl's daughter by his first wife, also suffered fits and strange maladies, but recovered. Next, a curse was put on the Earl and Countess, rendering them sterile.

Five years elapsed after the deaths of the Manners boys before the Flower women and three local accomplices were arrested. Joan Flower protested her innocence before the trial, and challenged her inquisitors to give her bread, declaring that if she were guilty it would choke her. Bread was duly brought and, no doubt as much to her own surprise as to anyone else's, she instantly choked and died. This startling occurrence so alarmed the other accused women that they could hardly wait to incriminate one another. The trial of the remaining 'Witches of Belvoir' took place at Lincoln in 1619. Bizarre details of their rituals poured forth in an astonishing account of Flower power. They described orgies and meetings in their covens on a hill below the castle, and spoke of familiar spirits which sucked beneath their breasts. Philippa confessed that she had heard her mother "often curse the Earle and his lady, and thereupon would boil feathers and blood together using many devilish speeches and strange gestures". Philippa herself was reputed to have been 'lewdly transported with love' for a man named Simpson, and to have bewitched him when he rejected her advances.

The five women were convicted and sentenced to death. On 11 March 1619, they were hanged at Lincoln Gaol. Sir Francis Manners died in 1632 without further issue, and the earldom passed to his brother, George. The ornate tomb of the 6th Earl in Bottesford church still bears a rare inscription to his 'two sonnes, both who dyed in their infancy by wicked practice and sorcerye'.

The Witches of Salem

In the spring of 1692 at Salem, Massachusetts, two young cousins, Abigail Williams and Elizabeth Parris, aged 11 and 9 respectively, began to exhibit strange gestures. It was said that they were bitten and pinched by invisible agents, and were sometimes 'taken dumb' and their limbs 'wracked and tormented' in apparent convulsions. It was soon feared that they had been bewitched, especially when other young women began to display similar symptoms. The two cousins claimed they were possessed by the devil, and accused three local women—Sarah Good, Sarah Osburn and Tituba, a slave from Barbados in the Parris household. In no time, the population of Salem felt besieged by demons.

Elizabeth Parris's father was a minister of religion, and he and Rev. Cotton Mather were the chief prosecutors of those who fell victim to the sudden local hysteria.

Tituba was threatened and beaten, and other women were pressurized into making confessions in which they incriminated yet more alleged witches. The number of those accused steadily mounted. They included a Congregationalist minister, George Burroughs, and Rebecca Nurse and Martha Carrier. They and many others were brought before a magistrate in a special court convened at the behest of the clergymen, and imprisoned to await trial.

Before Judge Jonathan Corwin, Tituba confessed that she and the two women named Sarah had signed pacts with Satan, bewitched the two girls, and had flown through the air. A witness testified on oath that a woman had floated in through his bedroom window and "laid her body on his". In July, six convicted witches were hanged. Rev. Mather said that Martha Carrier was a "rampant hag" who had been chosen by Satan to be "Queen of Hell". She was executed on 19 August. Reasonable people were prevented by fear from protesting against these goings-on. By October, 19 people had been hanged. Giles Corey, who was 80 years old, had been pressed to death for refusing to plead, and many others had been imprisoned, two dying in gaol. John Proctor wrote from prison that his young son William, for refusing to confess his guilt, had been tied by 'the neck and heels till the blood gushed out at his nose...' The hundreds of accused included the wife of the Governor of Massachusetts, William Phips, the President of Harvard University, and Judge Corwin's mother-in-law. These people of rank, however, were not prosecuted.

Gradually, the hysteria began to subside. The sheer extravagance of this sexually charged episode forced public opinion back to reason. Boston clerics petitioned the governor to exclude 'spectral evidence'. The governor then dissolved the court and released the remaining prisoners. It became apparent that the two girls had been stimulated by Tituba's stories of voodoo in Barbados, and by Cotton Mather's accounts of supposedly bewitched girls in Boston some years earlier. What had begun as a prank had got out of control. Tituba herself was kept in prison without trial until May 1693, when she was sold as a slave.

Twenty years after the affair, the Massachusetts legislature annulled all the convictions and granted compensation to the families of those who had been executed. The episode inspired Arthur Miller's famous play, *The Crucible.*

The Pittenweem Witches

In 1704 Beatrix Laing, wife of a former treasurer of Pittenweem on the Firth of Forth, went to the local blacksmith for some nails. The smith, Morton, asked his son Patrick to make them for her, but the 16 year-old youth said he was too busy. Mrs Laing, losing her temper, threatened

Fact

The last execution of a convicted witch in England was in 1685, when Alice Molland was hanged at Exeter. But she was not the last woman to be condemned to death for witchcraft in this country. This was Jane Wenham in 1712 (see case history). The last burning of a convicted witch in Scotland was in 1722, when Jenny Horn was executed at Dornoch. Although the last witchcraft trial in Ireland took place in 1711, the law against witchcraft was not repealed there until 1821.

Fact

The last trial in an English civil court of anyone accused of witchcraft under the old law took place at Leicester in 1717. Jane Clarke of Wigston Magna and her son and daughter were the defendants. Despite the hostile testimony of 25 witnesses, all the accused were acquitted.

Fact

The last execution for witchcraft in France occurred in 1745, when Father Louis Debaraz was burned alive at Lyons for saying sacriligious masses.

Fact

Queen Christina of Sweden banned witch trials in her country in 1649, saying that women who confessed to making pacts with the devil were suffering either from delusions or female internal disorders. But there was a brief revival of hysteria and executions until prosecutions for witchcraft were finally banned by Charles XI.

revenge. Patrick soon had fits and breathing problems and lost his appetite, becoming weak and emaciated. He accused Beatrix Laing and another woman of practising witchcraft on him. They were imprisoned, and Laing was tortured until she implicated others, and was then put in solitary confinement in a dungeon for five months. She was eventually freed with a fine, but had to leave the area because of the danger from the local populace, and soon died from the effects of her treatment.

Janet Cornfoot, one of those she named, was flogged by the Presbyterian minister himself, and tortured, but was eventually set free only to be lynched by a mob who beat her and crushed her to death under a door piled with rocks.

Patrick Morton's sham was eventually exposed, but not before a third victim of his accusations died. Thomas Brown, named by another of those implicated, Isobel Adam, died in prison of starvation.

Fact

One of the most famous instances of a man being executed for witchcraft was that of Father Urbain Grandier, a parish priest in Loudun, near Tours in France. He was held responsible for the demonic possession of Ursuline nuns at the local convent. They were consumed by sexual hysteria and the Mother Superior, Sister Jeanne des Anges, swore that the amorous Grandier had bewitched them by throwing a bouquet of roses over the convent wall. Father Grandier was burned alive after torture in 1634. The story was the subject of Aldous Huxley's book The Devils of Loudun *(1952); John Whiting's stage play* The Devils *(1961); and Ken Russell's film of the same title (1971).*

Jane Wenham

Jane Wenham, a 70 year-old wise-woman who lived at Walkern in Hertfordshire, was the last person in England to be condemned to death for witchcraft. She was accused in 1712 of bewitching a 16 year-old girl named Ann Thorn. The girl, a servant of the village parson, complained that cats scratched and mewed at her door and appeared at her bedside. She said she had seen Jane Wenham in the shape of a talking cat, which urged her to kill herself and offered her a knife for the purpose. The old woman was also accused of causing the girl to run half a mile and jump over a five-bar gate, even though she had a dislocated knee at the time.

Jane Wenham was arrested and brought to trial before Sir John Powell, whom Jonathan Swift described as "the merriest old gentleman I ever saw". The hostile witnesses included Rev. Francis Bragge, the fanatical vicar of Hitchin who had earlier published a popular pamphlet against witches. Witnesses swore that attempts to draw blood from the defendant's arm by running a pin into it had failed. They testified that she could not say the Lord's Prayer. She was accused of being able to fly. "There is", observed Mr Justice Powell, "no law against flying". But feelings were running high, and despite a summing-up which left no doubt that the judge expected an acquittal, the jury found Jane Wenham guilty. Sir John had no alternative but to pass the death sentence on her. He took the opportunity to say that "the same ignorance and superstition which had instigated her accusers to apprehend her, operated in the minds of 12 men, sworn to do justice; and they, to their eternal shame, found her guilty".

Judge Powell did not let matters rest there, however. He interceded with Queen Anne on the old woman's behalf, and she was granted a reprieve. She lived until 1730, though she had to move away from her native village for her own safety. It was said afterwards that Ann Thorn was an idle hussy whose malicious accusations ceased when her sweetheart turned up and married her. The furore created by this case contributed to the abolition of the death penalty for witches.

Section 6: Other Crimes

Fact

The entire cast of a play about the revolutionary hero Che Guevara was arrested in New York in 1969. They were charged and convicted of public lewdness and obscenity, but the director replaced the cast and continued the production until he was eventually forced to close when he ran out of actors.

Obscene Publications

ALTHOUGH we tend to think of obscene publications in terms of pornographic books or pictures, by no means all prosecutions under this heading have been brought against novels like *Lady Chatterley's Lover,* or indecent paintings and photographs masquerading as works of art.

Under the Obscene Publications Act of 1857, Charles Bradlaugh, the atheist MP, and Annie Besant, the birth control propagandist, were prosecuted in 1877 for republishing a pamphlet entitled *The Fruits of Philosophy*, which advocated birth control and was written by an American doctor, Charles Knowlton. It had been condemned as 'lewd, filthy and obscene'. The case was tried before Lord Chief Justice Cockburn, with the Solicitor General, Sir Hardinge Giffard, prosecuting. Lord Cockburn himself had defined obscenity in 1868 as "the tendency of the matter charged...to deprave and corrupt those whose minds are open to such immoral influences, and into whose hands a publication of this sort may fall". Bradlaugh said that he denied "the right of anyone to interfere with the full and free discussion of social questions affecting the happiness of the nation". The jury found that the pamphlet in question was "calculated to deprave public morals", but that the defendants did not have corrupt motives in publishing it. Nevertheless, they were sentenced to six months in prison, and fines of £200 each. The Court of Appeal, however, quashed the convictions on a technicality.

The Cockburn ruling, which remained on the English statute book until 1959, was also adopted in the United States. In 1895 a US citizen in Kansas was charged with sending obscene matter through the mail. It turned out that the offending literature consisted of quotations from the Bible. Three years later a bookseller was prosecuted for having in his possession a copy of the acclaimed medical work *Sexual Inversion,* by Havelock Ellis; and Dr Marie Stopes, the English pioneer of birth control, came close to being prosecuted for obscene libel when her book *Married Love* was published in 1916. The book was banned in the USA.

Nevertheless, it is mostly creative fiction rather than educational literature that falls foul of the law. The publication of a pornographic book or picture was first made a misdemeanour in 1824, but there had been prosecutions under the common law before that as—for example—in 1770 when John Wilkes was charged with obscene libel for his *Essay on Woman,* a salacious parody of Pope's *Essay on Man*. Found guilty, Wilkes was eventually sentenced to a year's imprisonment and a fine of £500. The case also led to his expulsion from the House of Commons, although it is very doubtful if he was the sole or even the principal author of the poem.

In 1888, a London publisher was fined £100 and bound over for 12 months for publishing Emile Zola's *La Terre* in an English translation; and in 1915, the publishers Methuen were prosecuted for publishing D.H. Lawrence's *The Rainbow*.

Fact

Ralph Ginzburg, editor of a magazine called Eros, *was imprisoned in 1963 for publishing obscene matter which included prints by Degas, poems by Ovid and Burns, and Hindu temple sculpture. The items which most offended the United States District Court in Philadelphia, however, were apparently photographs of a naked black male embracing a white woman.*

The more celebrated modern trials for obscenity in Britain date from 1928, when the Director of Public Prosecutions instigated action against the publishers of Marguerite Radclyffe Hall's novel *The Well of Loneliness,* which deals sympathetically with lesbianism. A journalist, James Douglas, had announced that he would rather give a phial of prussic acid to a child than put this book in its hands. (Someone—was it Bernard Shaw?—promptly offered to provide Douglas with a child and prussic acid so that he could demonstrate his sincerity to the world, but Douglas declined the offer.) The publishers, Jonathan Cape, were defended by Norman Birkett, KC, who argued that treatment of the theme of female homosexuality in the book could not possibly offend against either the law or good taste. "It is done out of a sense of duty, with a high-minded desire to deal with it as a fact of life. I submit that the theme of the book is a theme which ought to be discussed in order that it may be understood". The magistrates did not agree, and gave an order for the book to be destroyed. Their decision was upheld on appeal.

The next stage in the law regarding obscenity came with the prosecution of Stanley Kauffmann's novel *The Philanderer* in 1954. The book had been published without any trouble in the USA, and the English publishers, Secker & Warburg, elected when charged to go for trial by jury. The enlightened Mr Justice Stable directed the jury members to read the whole book, and base their view on that complete reading, and not by picking out what he called "the highlights". This was a different ruling from the view expressed by the Attorney-General during the *Well of Loneliness* appeal. Sir Thomas Inskip had said then that even though the majority of a book may be beyond criticism, "one passage may make it a work which ought to be destroyed as obscene". The defendants in the *Philanderer* trial were acquitted, and a change in the law came five years later with the new Obscene Publications Act, which laid down that a work was only to be deemed obscene if, *taken as a whole,* it tended to 'deprave and corrupt persons who are likely, having regard to all relevant circumstances, to read, see or hear the matter contained or embodied in it'.

The trial of Penguin Books for publishing the first unexpurgated edition of *Lady Chatterley's Lover* followed in 1960 as a test case in the wake of the new law. Even at the time, this supposedly solemn exercise in criminal law at the Old Bailey took on an air of pantomime as a motley procession of 'experts' was marshalled into the witness box by defence counsel to testify that this indifferent novel by D.H. Lawrence was "a work of genius" (Walter Allen); one which had "educational merit" (Rev. Donald Tytler); and one which "every Catholic priest...would profit by reading" (Norman St John Stevas). The spectacle of distinguished churchmen, academics, writers, publishers and Members of Parliament testifying on oath to the literary and moral value of Lawrence's worst book seemed grotesque. But of course the real point at issue for many of the witnesses was not the merits or otherwise of *Lady Chatterley's Lover* in particular, but the principle of freedom from prosecution for serious authors in general. Thirty-five witnesses were called and there were more in reserve in what amounted to a well-orchestrated chorus of approval conducted by Gerald Gardiner, QC, as the celebrities replied in turn to prosecuting counsel's charge that this was an obscene book, 'Oh no it isn't!'

Mr Justice Byrne in his summing-up reminded the jury that one of the "relevant circumstances" to which the new Act referred was, in this case, the price of the book—three shillings and sixpence. The trial was largely a question of whether the working classes should be allowed to read what the rich could read. "Is it a book that you would even wish your wife or your servants to read?" Mr Mervyn Griffith-Jones innocently enquired of the jury of nine men and three women.

The defendants were acquitted, and the book went on sale boosted by the most expensive State-sponsored advertising in literary history. But the management of one of W.H. Smith's warehouses still made sure that women packers did not handle the book.

In 1962, a successful prosecution was brought against the publisher of the *Ladies' Directory,* a sort of catalogue of prostitutes with their telephone numbers and the services they offered. The defendant was convicted of conspiring to corrupt public morals, publishing an obscene article, and living on the earnings of prostitution (because the prostitutes paid for their advertisements to be in the book). He was sentenced to nine months in prison.

Other famous cases followed, such as that in 1964 of the novel *The Memoirs of a Woman of Pleasure*, better known as 'Fanny Hill', by John Cleland. Although written in the mid-18th century, this work had been the subject of the first prosecution in America for the sale of obscene literature. In 1819—20 in Massachusetts, two booksellers were convicted, one being fined and the other imprisoned. The 1964 prosecution in England was brought against a paperback edition for sale at three shillings and sixpence. Mr Griffith-Jones once more found himself cross-questioning a parade of distinguished intellectuals and critics, but this time enjoyed a minor success. The magistrate, Sir Robert Blundell, ordered the destruction of 171 copies seized by police.

There have been other widely publicized prosecutions, such as that of the magazine *Oz* in 1971, (in which the conviction was quashed because of the judge's misdirection of the jury), but in recent years attention has tended to concentrate on film and videotape rather than on the written word.

In 1968, the Theatres Act abolished the powers of the Lord Chamberlain to exercise control of theatre productions. The Lord Chamberlain's duty of licensing public performances in theatres had existed since the 16th century, formerly for political reasons but latterly as a form of moral censorship. One of the most vociferous opponents of the system was George Bernard Shaw who said of the then Lord Chamberlain: "It is a frightening thing to see the great thinkers, poets and authors of modern Europe—men like Ibsen, Wagner, Tolstoy and the leaders of our own literature—delivered into the vulgar hands of such a noodle as this amiable old gentleman". Shaw's own play *Mrs Warren's Profession* had been banned by the Lord Chamberlain for 32 years, and Ibsen's *Ghosts* was not licensed for public performance in Britain until 1914, 33 years after it was written. Among other plays which ran the risk of prosecution for obscenity were Shelley's *The Cenci*, and Oscar Wilde's *Salome*.

Fact

The celebrated novel Lolita, *by Vladimir Nabokov, was first published in Paris in 1955, 33 years after James Joyce's* Ulysses *had been published there. Vigorous attempts were made to suppress both books, and copies were seized by British Customs.* Lolita *was not published in Britain until 1959, after the passing of the Obscene Publications Act.*

Fact

The 'Marquis' de Sade (actually the Comte de Sade) was sentenced to death at Aix in 1772 for unnatural sexual practices, but escaped. Imprisoned later in the Bastille, he wrote some of his most notorious works before being removed in 1789 to an asylum at Charenton, where he died.

Fact

The innocent-looking Talland Bay Café not far from Polperro, one of Cornwall's most popular tourist villages, became an object of intense Scotland Yard and Customs interest in 1979, when a gang was watched as it unloaded 2.5 tonnes (two and a half tons) of cannabis resin with a street value of more than two million pounds, from a yacht, and his it under the floor of the café. Customs and Excise officers intercepted the yacht as it attempted to put to sea again, and several drug dealers were arrested in Cornwall and in London.

The 1968 Act made theatre productions subject to the same laws of the land as other allegedly obscene publications, and the self-appointed guardian of the nation's morals, Mrs Mary Whitehouse, took advantage of this fact to bring a private prosecution against Howard Brenton's *The Romans in Britain* at the National Theatre. Three days into the trial at the Old Bailey in March 1982, however, the prosecution was dropped.

Use and Trafficking of Illegal Drugs

"Which is it today", I asked, "morphine or cocaine?"
He raised his eyes languidly from the old black-letter volume which he had opened."It is cocaine", he said, "a seven-per-cent solution. Would you care to try it?"
Sir Arthur Conan Doyle: *The Sign of Four*

'Drug addiction', a popular encyclopaedia was able to assert in 1950, 'does not present a serious problem in the United Kingdom, addicts numbering less than 400'. Half a century on, the situation has changed dramatically. The trafficking of illegal narcotics is big international business, and the increasing use of drugs, especially by young people, is a major social problem which has made its own jargon part of the common language, from 'junkie' and 'pusher' to 'chasing the dragon' and 'cold turkey'.

In the 19th century opium was the world's largest single commodity trade, and Britain had established a monopoly in it after the opium war with China which ended in 1842. Morphine had been refined from opium in the 1820s, but it was only with the introduction of the modern hypodermic syringe in the 1860s that it came into common use. The wife of Dr Alexander Wood, the syringe's perfector, was the first person who is known to have died from an injected overdose.

Victorian and Edwardian drug use in Europe was largely restricted to opium, hashish and morphine, and well known addicts such as Coleridge and De Quincey, Wilkie Collins and Robert Louis Stevenson, were exceptional. No moralist raised a storm of protest when Conan Doyle gave his popular hero, Sherlock Holmes, the habit of injecting himself with drugs three times a day. At the time it did not pose a threat to society.

In the inter-war years, the use of cocaine and heroin became more common. Billie Carleton, a young actress, died of cocaine poisoning in 1918 during the victory celebrations at the end of the war, and her boyfriend, Reggie de Veuille, was charged with her manslaughter. Four years later, a depressed dancing-teacher, Freda Kempton, committed suicide by taking cocaine in water. She had obtained the drug from a Chinese restaurateur named Chang, who was well known in the London underworld and to the Metropolitan Police as 'Brilliant' Chang, an arch-fiend with a profitable sideline in drug-trafficking. He was believed to have a hideout in Limehouse, and to be smuggling drugs ashore by concealing them in the soiled linen brought off ships in dock by innocent laundry-women. Police could not prove anything against

Chang in the Kempton case, but he was subsequently deported in 1924.

Britain had come to be recognized as a country with an enlightened attitude towards drug addiction, but it led to a good deal of complacency, even in the years after WWII, by which time one foreign addict had stated publicly that London was "a junkie's seventh heaven".

In 1960, the number of *registered* drug addicts in Britain was 437. Within 10 years the number had risen to 2,657, and by 1980 it was 5,107. In the next three years, this figure more than doubled. These figures, of course, were only a small proportion of the real numbers of addicts in the country.

Events in the autumn of 1979 illustrated the scale of the problem as it then existed in Britain. On 11 September police discovered LSD tablets worth £5 million in a Bedfordshire wood. One week later, 4.4 tonnes (four and a half tons) of cannabis resin, with an estimated street value of £10 million, were seized in a police raid on a garage in south-east London following a Customs surveillance of a converted fishing boat near Polperro in Cornwall. On 1 October, police uncovered Scotland's biggest illicit laboratory for producing amphetamines. Jan Stuurman, of Dutch nationality, was imprisoned for 12 years by the Edinburgh High Court.

In June of the following year, two Malaysians, Goy Kok Poh and Tan King To, were jailed for 14 years, and a third, Khoo Boon Pin, for eight years for attempting to smuggle heroin worth around £6 million into London Docks concealed in the rear inner tubes of a car's tyres.

The estimated value of drugs illegally entering Britain each year had reached about £6 million by 1985, and a huge increase in other crimes was following the need of addicts to pay for their fixes. It was estimated that drug-related crime amounted to nearly one and a half billion pounds a year in the UK and $20 billion in the USA, and an American study concluded in 1984 that almost half the bank robberies in the country were being carried out by drug users to finance their addiction.

Modern celebrities who have broken the law by assorted drug offences—including rock stars Paul McCartney and Grace Jones; actors Robert Mitchum and Stacy Keach; comedian Lenny Bruce and athletes David Jenkins and Ben Johnson—have been regarded much more seriously as setters of unacceptable standards than their Victorian and Edwardian counterparts.

English Common Law is unwritten law which has become recognised by long and universal custom and practice. Statute Law is written law made by legislation. Thus, murder and theft are crimes under common law, but the possession and use of drugs are crimes because the government has made them so. All attempts to stem the explosive increase in drug use and trafficking, however, have been unsuccessful, despite the vigilance of police and Customs. For instance, the law against possession of cannabis for personal use has become virtually unenforceable as police do not have the resources to control the problem. It was announced by the Home Secretary in 1984 that a new Criminal Justice Bill would introduce life imprisonment, instead of the previous 14 years, as the maximum sentence for trafficking in dangerous (Class A) drugs.

Fact

The pop music industry has a bad public record in the use of illegal drugs. Among others, Mick Jagger and Keith Richards of the Rolling Stones spent a night in jail in London in 1967 on drugs charges; Paul McCartney of the Beatles was sentenced to nine days imprisonment in Tokyo in 1980 for possessing marijuana; John Phillips of The Mamas and the Papas got 30 days for possession of cocaine at Los Angeles in 1981; Grace Jones got four days in Jamaica in 1989.

Fact

The phenomenon of widespread drug use among young people in modern western society had its origins in the smoking of 'pot' (cannabis) among devotees of the US 'Flower Power' cult in the 1960s. LSD (lysergic acid diethylamide), a much more addictive and dangerous substance, was soon replacing the relatively harmless pot or marijuana, and society was on its way to the alarming escapist youth culture which the Law struggles to contain.

In 1988 a US grand jury indicted General Manuel Antonio Noriega, the former dictator of Panama, on charges of drug trafficking, and he was arrested by troops sent into Panama by President Bush. Noriega was sentenced in 1992 to 40 years imprisonment.

In 1989, the world's largest seizure of drugs on record up to that time was made in Los Angeles, California, when police acting on a tip-off discovered in a warehouse parcels of cocaine with a street value estimated at between six and seven billion dollars. Cocaine worth £160 million was seized on the Thames in London in November 1992, when a Panamanian-registered ship, *Fox Trot Five,* was searched on arrival from South America. The largest haul in Britain was made in January 1994, when cocaine worth around £250 million was seized at Birkenhead from a Polish-American vessel, *Jurata*. The 1.3 tonnes (1.3 tons) of cocaine were hidden in a cargo of bitumen.

The number of drug-trafficking offences known to police in England and Wales in 1983 was 4,994. By 1993 the number had risen to 14,840, an average annual increase of 11.5 per cent.

Such statistics are, however, short-lived, and all the latest records will no doubt have been broken by the time this book is published. It is sometimes said in mitigation of drug abuse that the smoking of tobacco causes far more disease and death than all the dangerous drugs put together. That may be so, but it does not seem a very good reason for letting up in the war against dangerous drugs. Instead, it surely argues for a stepped-up campaign against smoking.

Smuggling

Smuggling is a form of fraud—the criminal offence of importing or exporting any item with intent to evade the Customs duty applicable to it, or of importing prohibited goods. Thus, the most serious form of smuggling in recent decades is the importation of illegal drugs. But of course smuggling has a much longer history than drug-trafficking. As far back as the 13th century, English 'owlers' were known to supply wool to French and Flemish weavers at prices below the legitimate rates, which included tax levied by Edward I.

A proclamation was made by Charles II in 1649 against "a sort of lewd people called 'Smuckellors' who made it their business to steal and defraud His Majesty of His Customs". By the 18th century, smuggling had reached epidemic proportions. In 1724, Daniel Defoe saw Customs officers searching Romney Marsh for owlers, and observed that smuggling was "the reigning commerce of all this part of the English coast, from the mouth of the Thames to Land's End of Cornwall".

Although place-names throughout coastal England, from Frenchman's Creek in Cornwall to Robin Hood's Bay in Yorkshire, conjure up romantic images of smugglers and adventure, the reality was very different from the legend. Smugglers were often coarse and lecherous cut-throats, and what we now regard as quaint villages, like Mousehole, were dens of iniquity.

Smuggling frequently led to other crimes in defending the illicit trade, such as arson and murder. William Galley, a revenue officer, was buried in a hole (possibly still alive) by a gang in Sussex in 1748, after being severely beaten and having his nose and testicles cut off. Anyone who informed the authorities about smuggling activities was especially liable to be murdered if found out.

It has been estimated that 20,000 people were engaged in full-time smuggling in the 18th century. At this time, when tobacco and spirits were the chief contraband, a smuggler could be sentenced to seven years transportation, but by the middle of the century smuggling had been made a felony punishable by death, and harbouring smugglers, or assembling with the intention of running contraband, were also capital offences. Smuggling was a wide-ranging criminal activity. In Scotland, smugglers aided the Jacobite cause by landing arms in the Highlands. English smugglers later supplied gold to France, earning the gratitude of Napoleon for enabling the country to pay its troops.

The counties of Kent and Sussex accounted for around a quarter of all contraband smuggled into England when there were heavy import taxes on items such as brandy and tobacco, sugar and spices, silk and calico, tea and coffee. Less than half the huge quantity of tea consumed annually had the required duty paid on it. Prime Minister William Pitt eventually solved the problem by reducing the import duty so drastically that tea was no longer worth smuggling.

Smuggling in Cornwall had its origin in the tin mines, where tinners would secrete some of the tin they had dug before it was taken away to be weighed and stamped. They could supplement their incomes by selling it to foreign seamen. They called it 'fair-trading', a euphemism that has stuck in the region.

One of the most successful smuggling enterprises on the Cornish coast was run by the Carter family of Prussia Cove. John Carter, nicknamed the 'King of Prussia', and his three sons, John, Henry and Charles, outwitted the authorities for many years whilst trading in spirits and other contraband.

Polperro was one of many coastal villages where the whole community was engaged in smuggling in one way or another, as well as the more legitimate business of fishing. Excise men following up information received about a 'run' there would usually find a reception committee of armed and hostile villagers awaiting them, and would wisely retreat. Robin Hood's Bay in Yorkshire was another place where the entire population thrived on smuggling. Among the cobbled passages and flights of stone steps, an alley called 'The Bolts' was planned specially to facilitate escape from the Excise officers. Nevertheless, the Court Leet of Fylingdales dealt out plenty of death sentences.

Among the most notorious smugglers of that period were members of the Hawkhurst Gang, so-called because they operated from the town of that name near Hastings. They also had temporary bases all along the south coast from Kent to Devon. At one point this large and well-organized gang threatened to burn down the whole town of Goudhurst and kill its population. The leaders of the gang became wealthy on the

Fact

In April 1736, a popular smuggler, Andrew Wilson, was executed in Edinburgh for robbing the Custom House at Pittenweem. Some in the crowd that gathered threw stones in anger at the authorities, and John Porteous, Captain of the City Guard, ordered his men to fire at the mob. Four people were killed and 11 wounded. Captain Porteous was sentenced to death for murder, but reprieved by Queen Caroline. On 7 September the Edinburgh mob seized him from the Tolbooth and hanged him from a pole in the Grassmarket.

Fact

Dick Turpin was involved in smuggling in his early career as a criminal. He fell in with a gang which operated from the ruins of Hadleigh Castle above the Thames marshes in Essex, and they kept inquisitive locals at bay by illuminating the supposedly haunted castle with ghostly lights. Even the law officers kept their distance.

Fact

It has been estimated that in the mid-18th century in England, out of a total population of 8 million, around 20,000 people were making their living as full-time smugglers.

Fact

A House of Commons Committee of Enquiry into Frauds and Abuses in the Customs to the Prejudice of Trade and Diminution of Revenue, appointed in 1733, came to the conclusion that if all the goods smuggled into the country at Falmouth, Cornwall, in one year had been imported legally with the necessary dues paid, the Crown would have collected more than double the annual land-tax for the whole kingdom.

proceeds of their activities, but most of the gang were finally hanged and gibbeted after an armed gang war.

Smuggling was not confined to what was then thought of as the 'criminal class', and there was a great deal of hypocrisy throughout society. Corrupt revenue officers were often in league with the smugglers, turning a blind eye for a consideration. And in coastal towns throughout Britain the squire and the parson were as likely as the poorest parishioners to be sympathetic towards local smugglers. The mayor of Fowey in Cornwall was evidently one of those who saw nothing to be ashamed of in 'fair-trading'. Sir Robert Walpole, the Prime Minister, whilst introducing Draconian measures to suppress smuggling, brought his own smuggled French wines up the Thames on an Admiralty barge. Lady Holderness, whose husband was Governor of the Cinque Ports, ran a private trade at Walmer Castle in silk gowns smuggled in from Paris.

The heyday of smuggling as a local illegal activity in Britain may have passed by the late 19th century after the Coastguard Act of 1856 had made the Admiralty responsible for guarding the coasts. But it has never disappeared, since there are always profits to be made by evading Customs duties, and always prohibited imports which someone requires, for good reasons or bad. In the years after WWII, high import duties and a scarcity of certain types of goods encouraged a revival of smuggling. Watches, cameras and nylon stockings were among the chief commodities smuggled into Britain in large quantities, and the 'black market' provided an easy outlet for the goods brought *in* illegally, whilst the smuggling of currency *out* of the country also became common. A former naval vessel, *Dawn Approach,* captured at Beaumaris on the Isle of Anglesey in 1951, was found to have brought 13,000 watches into the country hidden in a false bulkhead.

The smuggling associated with some of the most attractive coves and harbours of the west country is not a thing entirely of the romantic past. When a fishing boat, the *Ann Lynn,* was found by Customs officers to have landed a large quantity of cigarettes and spirits at Teignmouth, Devon, in 1964, the skipper and another man were fined £1,392 each and given six months imprisonment. A local appeal was organized to pay the fines by public subscription since it was felt that the men had contributed to the town's popular image since it regularly featured in publicity campaigns as a 'smuggler's cove'.

In September 1978, Talland Bay near the tourist magnet of Polperro in Cornwall, was the scene of a dramatic haul by police and Customs of 2.5 tonnes (two and a half tons) of cannabis resin with an estimated street value of £2,250,000. Plain clothes officers watched as the crew of a yacht, *Guiding Lights,* brought the drugs ashore. Several men were arrested in the west country and in London, and given prison sentences of between two and 10 years, as well as fines totalling £675,000. One of the ringleaders of the gang, however, escaped justice: despite police opposition, Ronald Taylor was given bail and absconded to Spain before the trial.

It is organized international crime on a large scale, dealing in drugs and diamonds and so forth, with which the law enforcement authorities are chiefly preoccupied nowadays.

Wrecking

A one-time accompaniment of smuggling was the crime of wrecking. This was the deliberate luring of ships on to rocks or shallow water by means of showing false lights in order to plunder the distressed vessels; or the pillaging of ships which had come to grief in storms. It was associated particularly with Cornwall, where it had the tacit sanction of whole local populations, but it occurred elsewhere too, and despite the severity of the law against such savage crimes, the coastal communities—long used to pillaging as a way of life—considered that the laws of the land, and not their evil habits, were wrong.

Sailors escaping from shipwrecks were at the mercy of wreckers, and were often stripped of all their clothes, and sometimes murdered by the barbarians who waited like voracious spiders for victims to fall into their traps. When the *Charming Jenny* was lured on to the Anglesey coast in 1774, only the master and his wife made it to the shore, but when the captain went in search of his wife on the beach, he found only her half-naked and plundered corpse.

In Cornwall, wrecking was taken so much for granted as a gift from God that even local magistrates and parsons were apt to join the gangs of fishermen and tin miners who would descend like vultures on a stranded vessel, and there are tales of congregations rushing out of church when news of a wreck was brought in. Even when a ship was intact, and only waiting to be refloated on the next tide, she would be considered fair game. Tales of undamaged ships being plundered come from Carmarthen Bay and Goodwin Sands, the Cornish coast and the Shannon estuary.

Raiders were not content to steal valuables from ships' cargoes and crews' quarters. Often they would strip a vessel of its very timbers and rigging. Defoe described coastal settlements in Norfolk where there was scarcely a stable, barn or pigsty that was not built of old planks from wrecked ships.

The government was powerless to put an end to this community crime, and the best the authorities could do was to mount military guards on wrecks with valuable cargoes with orders to open fire on anyone who attempted to plunder them. Nevertheless, an armed guard of 35 men on a wreck at Helston in 1722 was overpowered by a gang, even though several wreckers had been shot dead at Dartmouth only the year before by soldiers guarding an East Indiaman. Wrecking continued around the British coasts until the middle of the 19th century, when better standards of law enforcement, improved ships and navigational aids gradually brought it to an end.

Fact

Daniel Defoe wrote that the Isles of Scilly were 'inhabited by a fierce and ravenous people; for they are so greedy, and eager for the prey, that they are charged with strange, bloody, cruel dealings… especially with poor distressed seamen when they come on shore by force of a tempest, and seek help for their lives, and where they find the rocks themselves not more merciless than the people who range about them for their prey'.

Part four:
Crime and Punishment

Section 1: Death

Must we kill to prevent there being any wicked? This is to make both parties wicked instead of one.
Blaise Pascal: *Pensées*

DEATH BY HANGING was the penalty for serious crimes in England from the time of the Anglo-Saxon invaders. Before then, the Romans employed decapitation by the sword, and the death penalty was exacted by earlier societies in blood-revenge—the Biblical principle of an eye for an eye. The evidence of well-preserved remains found in peat bogs suggests that the method common throughout northern Europe was strangulation with hemp rope, possibly by hanging, possibly by a form of garrotting. But there is evidence that drowning and stoning to death were also used.

William the Conqueror was sparing in his use of the death penalty, employing it only against traitors. But Henry I reintroduced it for murder and other crimes, and for more than 800 years thereafter, murderers at least were almost automatically sentenced to be hanged by the neck until dead. Modern society, troubled by the idea of the State formally exacting mere revenge, deluded itself that capital punishment was a deterrent. The evidence was entirely against it. Any *individual* contemplating murder might, of course, be deterred by fear of the consequences, but if the murder rate as a whole goes up rather than down, any supposed deterrent is clearly a failure. When the

Fact

When Charles I was due to be beheaded on a scaffold erected in front of the Banqueting House in Whitehall on 30 January 1645, there was much speculation about the identity of the executioner. It was rumoured that Richard Brandon, the common hangman, had refused the job. It was said that two troopers named Hulet and Walker had volunteered to do it. When the executioner and his assistant appeared on the scaffold, they were masked and heavily disguised. After the King's head had been severed with one crashing blow of the axe, other rumours circulated. Some said the executioner was the Earl of Stair, a Scottish judge; others favoured Captain Joyce, a soldier in Cromwell's army. There was even speculation that it was Hugh Peter, an army chaplain. A French report went so far as to assert that Cromwell and Fairfax had done the job themselves. There is little real doubt, however, that the two men were Richard Brandon and a ragman called Ralph Jones, who often assisted Brandon. Many years later, in an attempt by Charles II to avenge his father's death, William Hulet was condemned for executing the King, but witnesses swore that it was Brandon, who was himself dead by that time.

death penalty was imposed for theft, pickpockets had field days among the crowds which gathered to watch the public execution of thieves.

From time to time throughout British history, hanging has been supplemented by alternative means of causing death for specific crimes. Until the mid-18th century, noblemen sentenced to death for treason were executed by beheading. This was supposed to be the privilege of their class, akin to dying in battle. But it was often a gruesome business. Any half-wit could put a rope round a man's neck and hang him from a tree or a beam to strangle him to death. (And any half-wit often did; there was a long tradition that criminals could obtain pardons if they agreed to serve as common hangmen. In 1731 at York, one Matthew Blackbourn, convicted of a capital offence, 'had his Pardon, being made Hangman'. It was a tradition, mentioned by Shakespeare in *Measure for Measure*, that lasted into the 19th century in Yorkshire.) But to sever a man's head with one strike of an axe required a greater skill and a steadier nerve, and not all common executioners possessed *either* of those qualities. When the notorious Jack Ketch attempted to decapitate the Duke of Monmouth on Tower Hill in 1685, the first blow missed the target and wounded the Duke, who half rose and looked at the executioner before resuming his position. Ketch's arms swung over and the blade flashed down again. Blood gushed and the body twitched, but the head was still not off. Again Ketch took aim, and again he failed. Shouts of horror rose from the crowd. Ketch threw down the axe. "God damn me, I cannot do it", he cried. "Take up the axe, man!" the Sheriff ordered. Ketch did so, but he had to strike twice more before the Duke's body stopped quivering, and even then, the head was still attached to the trunk and Ketch had to separate it with a knife. ('Jack Ketch' became a common nickname for subsequent hangmen, and indicates the abhorrence in which they were generally held by the populace.)

Beheading was used for common criminals in some parts of the kingdom at different times. The 'Scottish Maiden' and the 'Halifax Gibbet' were both decapitating machines which preceded the introduction of the guillotine in France. John Hamilton, executed for murder in Scotland on 30 June 1716 by means of the 'Scottish Maiden', was the last man to be done to death with such a gadget in Britain.

The last persons to be publicly beheaded in Britain were the Cato Street conspirators in 1820, but this was an exemplary punishment for treason, the five men having already been executed by hanging before it was carried out. It was a relic of drawing and quartering for traitors. The deranged Arthur Thistlewood and his crazy henchmen had plotted to assassinate the Cabinet and take over the country, but the government had been watching them and had a spy in their midst.

Another special method of execution was burning to death. It was, of course, the common punishment for religious heresy, but we are not concerned with that in the present context. Burning at the stake was used well into the 18th century in Scotland for those convicted of witchcraft, but in England it was reserved for women guilty of 'petty treason'—the murder of a man by his wife—or of coining (counterfeiting coin of the realm or clipping gold and silver coins, etc.). In theory, the condemned were strangled at the stake before the flames reached them, but in practice this did not always happen. When Catherine Hayes was sentenced to be burnt for murdering her husband in 1726, the hangman, Richard Arnet, was unable to strangle her first either because he was drunk or because the fire forced his premature retreat. Spectators were appalled to see the woman shrieking with terror as the flames licked round her, and she was burnt alive.

For a brief period in the 16th century, boiling to death was specified for poisoners, and 'William Boilman' became another temporary nickname for the public executioner. This savage law was in force for only 17 years until 1547, but in 1531 a servant girl was boiled to death at King's Lynn for the murder of her mistress.

These refinements apart, hanging was the statutory mode of execution for criminals in Britain from the 12th century to the 20th, and until 1868 it was carried out in public, often in front of rowdy and drunken mobs. Charles Dickens witnessed the execution of Francis Courvoisier outside Newgate in 1840, and commented that he did not see "one token in all the immense crowd; at the windows, in the streets, on the housetops, anywhere; of any one emotion suitable to the occasion. No sorrow, no salutary terror, no abhorrence, no seriousness; nothing but ribaldry, debauchery, levity, drunkenness, and flaunting vice in 50 other shapes. I should have deemed it impossible that I could ever have felt any large assemblage of my fellow-creatures to be so odious..."

Throughout most of English history, the death penalty was reserved for the most serious of crimes against the State and against the person—treason, murder, rape, etc. But in 1723 the Black Act was rushed through Parliament as a response to increased poaching and damage in royal forests. It heralded a period of legal terrorism when almost every trivial crime seemed to be suspected by the government as part of a devilish Jacobite conspiracy. The Act was continually extended to cover a multitude of crimes against property. The Black Act remained in force for 100 years, and became commonly known as the 'Bloody Code'. By the end of the 18th century, there were well over 200 capital crimes on the statute book, the majority of them crimes against property. People could be hanged for shooting rabbits or stealing turnips, setting fire to haystacks or consorting with gypsies, impersonating a pensioner of Greenwich Hospital or appearing on a public highway with a sooty face!

The tender age of a culprit was no protection against the rigours of the law. Children were hanged as readily as hardened professional criminals, often for stealing items of paltry value. The poet Samuel Rogers recalled seeing a "cartload of young girls, in dresses of various colours, on their way to be executed at Tyburn". In 1801, 13 year-old Andrew Brenning was hanged for breaking into a house and stealing a spoon. A girl of seven was hanged at King's Lynn in 1808, and as late as 1831, William Calcraft hanged a boy of nine at Chelmsford for setting fire to a house.

"There is no country on the face of the earth", Sir Samuel Romilly declared, "in which there have been so many different offences according to law to be punished with death as in England". But when he proposed that the death penalty should be abolished for shoplifting, the

Fact

William Kemmler, executed at Auburn Prison, New York, on 6 August 1890, was the first person to be done to death by means of an electric chair. Kemmler had murdered his mistress, Tillie Zeigler. The execution did not go smoothly. When the current was switched off, witnesses saw the 'dead' man's chest heave and he strained at the straps. There was some panic before the current was switched on again. Kemmler was pronounced dead after four more minutes. The bungling of the first execution by this new-fangled method led newspapers to predict confidently that it would not be used again. But despite these teething troubles, New York State had no intention of returning to the 'barbarism of hanging', and other states speedily followed suit. In the next 15 years, more than 100 executions by electrocution were carried out in the United States. The first woman to be executed by electric chair was Martha Place, convicted of the murder of her step-daughter, Ida. Her execution took place at Sing Sing prison on 20 March 1899.

Fact

When Thomas Dun was arrested for multiple murder in Bedfordshire during the reign of King Henry I, and taken for summary execution without a trial, he fought and struggled with his executioners, escaping several times from the scaffold before they succeeded in chopping off the exhausted man's hands, feet and head for public exhibition as a deterrent, and burning his trunk.

Lord Chief Justice, Lord Ellenborough, indignantly retorted that no man would be able to "trust himself for an hour out of doors without the most alarming apprehensions, that, on his return, every vestige of his property will be swept off by the hardened robber".

So the judicial killing went on. It was not until the mid-19th century that the Bloody Code began to be watered down. "It is impossible to conceal from ourselves", the Home Secretary, Sir Robert Peel, said in 1829, "that capital punishments are more frequent and the criminal law more severe on the whole, in this country, than in any country in the world". But even Peel thought abolition of the death penalty for theft a "most dangerous experiment". Nevertheless, by 1838, the death penalty had been abolished for forgery and coining, burglary and theft from dwelling houses, sacrilege and returning from transportation. The last execution for forgery was in 1829. By 1861, when the last execution for *attempted* murder took place at Chester, the number of capital offences had been reduced to the four which remained on the statute book for the next 100 years—murder, treason, piracy with violence, and arson in naval dockyards.

In the latter decades of capital punishment in Britain and the Commonwealth, defenders of hanging as a *method,* particularly the hangmen themselves, were fond of claiming that it was the most efficient means of exacting the supreme penalty, resulting in instantaneous death—when carried out properly. But that was certainly not always the case. Until William Marwood introduced the 'long drop' in the 1870s, victims of hanging were invariably strangled to death, dangling on the ends of ropes while their weight caused the nooses to tighten round their necks. They could take many minutes to die, and sometimes their agonies would be relieved only by pulling hard on their legs. The long drop was devised to cause death by fracture of the cervical vertebrae, and in time executioners came to have an almost scientific knowledge of how to produce this effect by varying the length of drop according to the weight and build of the victim.

Executioners and prison governors were strictly forbidden to reveal details of executions. (Major Blake, former governor of Pentonville, was prosecuted under the Official Secrets Act in 1926, after revealing in his reminiscences in the *London Evening News* that Frederick Bywaters had sworn to him that Edith Thompson was innocent of murder. He was fined £250.) But truth will out, and numerous instances are known when execution by hanging—even with the long drop—was far from efficient or instantaneous. The celebrated case of John Lee at Exeter in February 1885 was due to mechanical failure: the trapdoors repeatedly failed to open when the lever was operated, and attempts to hang the man had to be abandoned. But more botched jobs have been due to human error. The hangman James Berry collapsed and had to be revived with brandy when he gave Robert Goodale too long a drop at Norwich, and tore the man's head off. A similar incident occurred at Liverpool when Berry hanged John Conway in August 1891. There are other cases where *suspicions* of inefficient execution have been raised.

Other countries favoured their own methods. The guillotine was used throughout France after its successful employment during the

Revolution, until the death penalty was abolished in 1981. Germany, Austria and Belgium also favoured decapitation. The first person executed in France by the newly-designed guillotine was Nicholas-Jacques Pelletier, who was publicly beheaded in Paris on 25 April 1792. The Sanson family of France (see under Executioners) easily exceeded, in public executioners, British family firms like the Billingtons and the Pierrepoints.

Breaking on the wheel was another form of capital punishment used in France and Germany in earlier times, as well as in The Netherlands. The victim was bound spread-eagled to a horizontal wheel and had his limbs smashed with iron bars before receiving the *coup de grâce*. Breaking on the wheel was not abolished in France until 1788, and in Germany it remained until early in the 19th century. Perhaps the most notorious case of breaking on the wheel was the execution of the 64 year-old Huguenot, Jean Calas, at Toulouse in 1762. Calas had been accused and convicted of murdering his eldest son, Marc-Antoine, to prevent him from turning Roman Catholic. The other members of his family were accused of complicity and also punished, though not by death. The philosopher Voltaire took up the case and conducted a lengthy one-man campaign which resulted in a tribunal of the Court of Petitions in Paris nullifying the accusations against Calas and his family three years later. Marc-Antoine Calas had committed suicide, but the family had concealed the fact to avoid the public disgrace and confiscation of property that automatically followed cases of suicide. Of course, as with all miscarriages of justice when the death penalty is involved, the official reversal was too late to save the chief victim, Calas *père*.

Spain's official mode of execution was garrotting until its abolition in the 1970s. The victim was bound, seated in a chair, with a cord or metal collar round his neck. The collar could be tightened through the back of the chair by means of a lever or screw, or by twisting with a bar so as to cause death by strangulation. The Spaniards naturally bequeathed this method to their subject-peoples in South and Central America. Atahualpa, the Inca ruler, was executed by garrotting in the Peruvian city of Caxamalca in 1533. A late refinement of this method projected a spike into the back of the neck to sever the spinal cord.

As for the United States, they have adopted methods of execution from other countries and invented their own, employing noose, electric chair, gas chamber, firing squad and lethal injection in a veritable riot of judicial killing. Many states have abolished the death penalty at some time, only to reintroduce it later as a reaction to rising murder rates. (Some states have also executed those convicted of rape, aggravated assault, etc., particularly when committed by black men in the southern states.)

Although firing squads have normally been reserved for military executions in western countries (German spies were shot in the Tower of London during both world wars), the murderer Gary Gilmore was put to death by this method in the USA in 1977. An habitual criminal, Gilmore was released on parole from the federal penitentiary at Marion, Illinois, after serving 11 years, during which he and another convict had almost killed another prisoner in a knife attack. Within months of his

Fact

Charlie Brooks, a black American convicted of the murder of a second-hand car salesman, was the first person to be executed by means of a lethal injection. He was put to death at Huntsville Prison, Texas, on 7 December 1982. It might be thought that the method of lethal injection, which uses drugs to first render the victim unconscious and then to paralyze his heart and lungs, is a clean and painless way of causing death compared with the horrors of the electric chair and the gas chamber. But this procedure can be botched like any other. It has been known for a man to take 20 minutes to die by lethal injection. When Stephen Morin was executed by this method in Texas in 1985, it took the executioners 40 minutes to find a suitable vein owing to the fact that Morin had a long history of injecting drugs.

Fact

On 7 April 1995, Nicholas Ingram, from Cambridge, became the first British citizen in the 20th century to suffer the death penalty by electric chair in the USA. He was executed at Atlanta, Georgia, after being held on death row for 12 years, following his conviction for a brutal murder.

Fact

It has been estimated that more than 500 people a year were being executed at London's Tyburn during the Tudor period, and that around 50,000 may have been executed there by the time the last hanging took place. The last person to be executed at Tyburn was John Austin, who was hanged on 7 November 1783. Tyburn was abandoned because of increasing traffic in and out of London, and because the West End was becoming a fashionable residential area. The chief place of execution in the capital north of the Thames became Old Bailey, in front of Newgate gaol.

Fact

The last woman to be burnt at the stake in Britain was Christiane Murphy, who was convicted in 1789 of coining. She was tied to a stake outside Newgate Prison, standing on a stool. Then the stool was pulled away so that she strangled to death before faggots were heaped around her and set alight. This execution took place on 18 March 1789. In the following year, the penalty of burning for women convicted of coining and petty treason was abolished.

release, Gilmore had committed two murders in Utah in the furtherance of theft, shooting a service station attendant and a motel manager in the backs of their heads while they lay at his mercy on the ground. Gilmore demanded the death penalty, and refused to have appeals made on his behalf for a stay of execution. The states of Idaho and Utah use firing squads and lethal injection as alternative methods of capital punishment, and Gilmore chose the former. On 17 January 1977 he was strapped into a chair in an industrial building and shot dead by a firing squad aiming at a white mark pinned over his heart.

Gilmore's insistence on being executed set the ball rolling again in the United States, after a short period in which capital punishment was suspended, the Supreme Court having ruled in 1972 that the death penalty was a cruel and unconstitutional punishment.

A long campaign to abolish the death penalty in the United Kingdom achieved its aim in 1965, when Parliament suspended capital punishment for murder for an experimental period of five years, and finally abolished it at the end of 1969. The final campaign inside Parliament had been led by Sydney Silverman, MP, and outside by the publisher Victor Gollancz and Gerald Gardiner, QC (later Lord Gardiner), as joint chairmen of the National Campaign for the Abolition of Capital Punishment.

The last executions in Britain were carried out on 13 August 1964, when Peter Anthony Allen (21) and John Robson Welby (alias Gwynne Owen Evans, 24) were hanged at Walton prison, Liverpool, and Strangeways prison, Manchester, respectively. They had been convicted of the murder of a laundry-van driver, John Alan West, at his home in Workington. The Liverpool execution was carried out by Robert L. Stewart and the Manchester one by Harry B. Allen. These two men were the last British hangmen, and not Albert Pierrepoint, as is often said. Stewart died in 1988; Allen and Pierrepoint in 1992. (The last execution in Scotland took place in August 1963, when 21 year-old Henry John Burnett was hanged at Aberdeen for the murder of his lover's husband, a merchant seaman.)

However, as the death sentence remains on the statute book for treason, and there is a fully operational scaffold at Wandsworth—where more executions have been carried out than in any other British prison—it follows that there is, somewhere in this country, a fully trained executioner waiting for an opportunity to demonstrate his efficiency as a government-approved killer.

Section 2: Transportation

Come all you gallant poachers that ramble void of care,
While walking out one moonlit night with gun
and dog and snare,
With hares and lofty pheasants in your pocket and your hand,
Not thinking of your last career upon Van Diemen's Land.
Convict ballad

TRANSPORTATION began in the 17th century as an alternative punishment to imprisonment. An Act of Elizabeth I in 1597 had allowed for rogues and vagabonds to be 'banished out of this Realm', and if any one returned to his native land without permission, he was to be hanged. The earliest destination of those so banished was the New World.

The system was extended by an Act of 1718 which provided for offenders who would normally be flogged and branded, and those whose death sentences were commuted, to be shipped to the American colonies for seven and 14 years respectively. In the following year, deer-poachers were made liable to transportation for seven years. Large-scale transportation suddenly seemed a wonderful new solution to a major problem. It got rid of a large part of what the governing gentry regarded as the 'criminal classes', without the need to keep them in prisons at public expense, and it provided what amounted to slave labour for economic exploitation of the colonies. Justices at Bristol, Britain's chief slave port, often had vested interests in supplying labour for the American colonies, and were apt to threaten criminals with death so that they would pray for the mercy of transportation. Criminals were shipped out by government-paid merchants, who made large profits by selling convicts as labourers to the owners of American plantations. In the 15 years from 1760 to 1774, more than two thirds of all those criminals convicted at the Old Bailey received sentences of transportation.

Tens of thousands of British and Irish felons were banished to Virginia, Maryland and Massachusetts, as well as Jamaica and Barbados, until the American colonies rebelled. By 1770, the only colony still accepting regular shipments of convicts was Maryland. The new republic was prepared to build its wealth on the backs of African slaves, but not on social outcasts from Britain, which had to seek a new dumping ground. It considered the Falkland Islands, Canada, Gibraltar, and the west coast of Africa. But it settled in 1783 on a land 11,000 miles away, whose eastern coast had been charted by Captain Cook only 13 years earlier—Australia. The first fleet of ships carrying criminals sentenced to transportation from Britain to Australia sailed from Portsmouth on 13 May 1787. It had 736 convicts on board 11 vessels. The oldest of them was 82 year-old Dorothy Handland, sentenced to seven years transportation for perjury. The youngest was John Hudson, a nine year-old chimney sweep, convicted of stealing clothes, and also

Fact

Estimates of the numbers of Soviet convicts banished to Stalin's camps vary. What Aleksandr Solzhenitsyn has called 'exterminatory labour camps' existed throughout the Soviet Union by the 1930s, but among the most notorious were the arctic camps along the Kolyma River basin in eastern Siberia. Ordinary criminals and political prisoners, called 'enemies of the people', made up the populations of settlements where the condemned died in conditions of slave labour in the frozen wastes. Robert Conquest estimated that there were around 12 million deaths among those sent to convict settlements in the years 1936-50, and this figure does not include the huge number of people executed for their crimes.

Fact

Between 1788 and 1852, 24,000 women were among the 168,000 transported to the antipodes. Between 1841 and 1850, nearly 30,000 men and women were transported from Britain to Van Diemen's Land. During the whole period of transportation, 825 shiploads of prisoners were sent out from England and Ireland to Australia. Many convicts died during the voyage.

Fact

The Town of Ramsgate inn in London's Wapping High Street has cellars which were once used as temporary dungeons for criminals awaiting transportation to Australia. The riverside inn overlooks the spot known as Execution Dock, near Wapping Old Stairs, where pirates were regularly hanged.

Fact

Eighty per cent of the criminals sentenced in Britain to transportation were those convicted for crimes against property. A great many of Russia's transportees, sent to Sakhalin and Siberia under the Tsars, were—as under the Soviet regime—political prisoners. Among the chief destinations of those condemned to forced labour before the October Revolution were the silver mines at Nerchinsk, near the Chinese border.

Fact

Between 1717 and 1775, about 40,000 people were transported to the American colonies from Britain and Ireland.

transported for seven years. The fleet anchored at Botany Bay on 20 January 1788. Dorothy Handland became Australia's first known suicide in the following year when she hanged herself from a tree. Botany Bay was soon a name to arouse fear in the British criminal mind.

The penal settlements multiplied rapidly. Van Diemen's Land (Tasmania) was added to the settlements on the eastern coast of the mainland, and the shipping of convicts there continued after transportation to Sydney ceased. Western Australia also received convicts from 1850. The notorious Norfolk Island, nearly 1,000 miles out in the Pacific, became a source of special terror for those who, having been transported from Britain, were then transported from Australia.

Norfolk Island was an 'ugly, brutal and sex-perverted' place. No women or free settlers were allowed on it. Convicts sentenced to a spell there were chained together in a dark and filthy ship's hold for a voyage that could take two weeks, and arrived on the island to face rape, flogging and torture. Prisoners worked in chain-gangs, in quarries or at road-building, from sunrise to sunset every day, with an hour's break at midday for a meal of cornmeal and salt beef.

Convicts were flogged with the cat-o'-nine-tails to within an inch of their lives for the slightest misdemeanour, and received no medical attention afterwards. Sometimes they were strapped in straitjackets to their iron bedsteads, unable to relieve their bleeding backs. Their putrefying flesh, infested with maggots, reeked of decomposition. One man received 100 lashes for singing, and another for 'Smiling while on the Chain'. Men were sometimes forced to stand for hours naked in chains, with their arms stretched upwards; or confined in a dark subterranean cell up to their waists in salt water, unable to sleep for fear of drowning. And all this was done in the name of the British government.

Transportation to New South Wales ceased in 1840, and to Van Diemen's Land in 1853. The system was finally abolished altogether in 1868, when the last convict vessel arrived at Fremantle in Western Australia. But just as Britain was abandoning a policy which had succeeded only in degrading and brutalizing Queen Victoria's subjects, France and Russia were jumping on the bandwagon with their own forms of compulsory exile. France's first shipment of *transportés* arrived in French Guiana in 1852, and the first Russian forced labour camp on the island of Sakhalin was set up in 1857.

Both places were quite as horrific as Britain's penal settlements in Australia. French Guiana was made worse by the climate. Convicts on the mainland worked in chains in the tropical forest, at the mercy of mosquitoes and deadly snakes. The camps at Cayenne and St Laurent had an 80 per cent mortality rate from disease, murder and suicide. In one year alone more than 2,000 Frenchmen died of malaria, dysentery, scurvy or typhus.

The French equivalent of Norfolk Island was one of the Iles du Salut (Islands of Salvation) off the coast. The escape-proof Ile du Diable, surrounded by strong currents and patrolled by sharks, was originally a leper colony, but was utilized as a maximum security area and became notorious throughout the civilized world as Devil's Island. At one time, the French also considered the possibility, advocated by some experts, of colonizing Algeria with delinquents, orphans and prostitutes. It was not until 1938 that the government of France abolished transportation, and the last convict was not repatriated from French Guiana until 1953.

The chief Russian settlements on Sakhalin, a large island off the eastern coast of Siberia in the Sea of Okhotsk, were at Dué, Aleksandrovsk and Voyevodsk. While French criminals died in the tropical heat, Russian convicts died in the subarctic cold. Here, men in the prime of life succumbed to tuberculosis or pneumonia. The doctor and author Anton Chekhov spent three months on Sakhalin studying life in the convict settlements. He called the place a hell, and said that here he had seen the ultimate in human degradation.

Fact

The most famous prisoner of Devil's Island, after Dreyfus (see under Treason), was Henri Charrière, nicknamed 'Papillon'. Convicted at the age of 25 of the murder of a pimp and police-informer, he was sentenced to transportation en perpétuité, *and arrived on the Ile du Diable in 1941 after periods in other settlements in French Guiana. He eventually made his escape by throwing himself into the ocean strapped to a makeshift raft of sacks of coconuts, and finally reached Venezuela where he won his freedom 12 years after leaving Paris as a convict.*

Section 3: Imprisonment

The faculties for getting into jail seem to be ample. We want more organizations for keeping people out.
Charles D. Warner: *Backlog Studies*

IT COMES AS A SURPRISE to many people to learn that the idea of committing common criminals to terms of imprisonment as a punishment is a relatively recent one. Because prisons are constantly in the news nowadays, it is easy to imagine that they have always been with us. But the familiar dungeons of history, in which heretics were tortured and traitors languished, were not for the common criminal. If his crime was a felony, he was executed or transported. If it was a mere misdemeanour, he was whipped, or put in the stocks or pillory. Locking him away was not on the regular agenda before the 19th century. The old bridewells (gaols) were conceived to provide work for the unemployed, whilst local lock-ups were merely for temporary safe custody while awaiting trial. Although gaols such as Newgate had existed since the early Middle Ages, only a very small proportion of sentences were for terms of imprisonment before the late 18th century, when 70 per cent of criminals convicted at the Old Bailey received sentences of transportation, and only about 2.5 per cent were sent to prison. Sentences were never for longer than three years, and the Home Secretary in 1837, Lord John Russell, remarked that imprisonment for 10 years would be "a punishment worse than death". London had its debtors' prisons—the notorious Fleet, Marshalsea and King's Bench prisons—but separate prisons for debtors were rare elsewhere in Britain.

A crisis in the system of transportation, caused by the American War of Independence, led to the temporary solution of using old ships as prisons. Within 10 years of the Act of 1776 which authorized this use of redundant ships, 2,000 convicts were living on rotting hulks moored in the Thames at Woolwich and at Chatham, Portsmouth and Plymouth.

Fact

The most costly prison to operate over a long period in the western world was Alcatraz, the island prison in San Francisco Bay, California. This fortress of steel and concrete became a federal maximum security prison in 1933. It could accommodate 302, but was never filled to capacity. The average population was 260. The US government decided to abandon Alcatraz, commonly known as 'the Rock', in 1963. Its maintenance and running costs had been at least double those of any other federal prison in the USA. Alcatraz is now a national park and museum.

Fact

The total prison population of England and Wales was 24,000 in 1952—a peak year in the post-war period. By the late 80s, the number of people in prison in Britain, in proportion to the total population, was higher than in any other major country in Europe. The average population in custody (including police cells) in England and Wales during 1993 was 44,600. Although this figure was the lowest since 1984, it was not exceeded by any country in Europe except France. In 1994 the figure was 48,600.

Fact

The biggest mass-escape from a prison in the UK was made on 25 September 1983, when 38 IRA prisoners escaped from Block H-7 of the Maze Prison, near Belfast in Northern Ireland. Ten of the escapees were still at large after five years. Two were recaptured in the USA in 1992. In August 1996, James Smyth was extradited from the USA to Northern Ireland to serve the remainder of his 20-year sentence. The Maze, formerly known as Long Kesh, already held the previous record: on 6 November 1974, 33 Republican prisoners escaped, but all but one of them were recaptured on the same day.

The ships included men-o'-war of Nelson's fleet at Trafalgar, the *Leviathan* and *Bellerophon*, and Captain Cook's *Discovery*. They soon became floating slums, alive with vermin and stinking with the foetid air of overcrowding and lack of ventilation. Convicts died of typhus and cholera and suffered from scurvy and scrofula, dysentry and diarrhoea. In 1798 two ships at Portsmouth had more than 50 boys under the age of 12 among their prisoners. The homosexual rape of young convicts was a matter of course, and venereal disease was almost universal. The hulks remained in use until large-scale transportation to Australia had relieved the problem, and convict ships were finally abolished in 1857.

From the mid-19th century, however, when transportation was suspended, a national system of imprisonment for major crimes was initiated, and a huge prison-building programme got under way. Soon imprisonment passed from being a novelty to appearing a self-evident solution to one of society's major problems. Detention of the criminal—depriving him of his liberty for a prescribed period—has now become so much taken for granted that it is difficult to think of modern society without it. It is the necessary evil of industrial civilization. There is, it seems, no alternative to it.

The early principles of confinement came to be represented by two American approaches—the Auburn system and the Philadelphia system. In the first, prisoners worked, fed and exercised together, but there was a strictly enforced rule of silence, as in medieval monasteries, and at night they were locked up in individual cells. In the Philadelphia system, prisoners were kept in strict isolation all the time. The idea of the penitentiary, where the aim would be psychological reform of the criminal rather than physical punishment, gradually took hold. The idea, advocated by Quaker reformers, was that neither seeing nor hearing others the convict would be forced to come to terms with his own conscience. Even the great prison reformer John Howard thought that 'solitude and silence are favourable to reflection; and may possibly lead to repentance'. The rivalry of the 'silent' system and the 'separate' system lasted for decades.

Coldbath Fields House of Correction, built as a local bridewell in the late 18th century but converted to use as a prison run on the silent system, was closed in 1887. The first prison in Britain to be built and run by the State, instead of local authorities, was Millbank Penitentiary, completed in 1821. It was the largest prison ever built in this country, with a capacity of 1,500, and was run on the separate system. It proved an expensive failure, being closed in 1890 and demolished in 1903. Pentonville, opened in 1842, had taken its place. It was called the Model Prison at first, and was also run on the separate system. Wandsworth—originally the Surrey House of Correction—became its counterpart for London south of the Thames. But experience in Britain and elsewhere was showing that the main achievement of the well-intentioned Philadelphia system was a tenfold increase in mental illness among the inmates. Within eight years of the opening of Pentonville, six prisoners had hanged themselves in their cells, 22 had been declared insane, and another 26 were said to be suffering from delusions.

The early prison regimes included flogging with the cat-o'-nine-tails for insolence or misdemeanour; confinement in dark cells on a diet of bread and water; and compulsory work on treadwheels or crank machines. Oakum picking was generally a communal activity in prisons run on the silent system. Prisoners sat in large workshops, occupied with the painful task of unravelling old rope, which was often tarred and cut and blistered their fingers and broke their nails. Anyone caught talking might be flogged or sent to solitary confinement. The sewing of mailbags duly became another common prison occupation.

It was only in the late 19th century that the gratuitous cruelty practised in British prisons in the early Victorian period began to be relaxed. This followed a series of scandals like the one at Birmingham's Winson Green prison in 1854, when a series of suicides culminated in Edward Andrews, a 15 year-old prisoner, hanging himself after suffering two months of the sadistic regime of the governor William Austin. Austin, a former naval officer, was eventually dismissed and imprisoned for six months for abusing the system.

Among those who criticized relaxation of the prison regime were Charles Dickens and Thomas Carlyle. Dickens thought prisoners were too well treated at Pentonville, and Carlyle called it a 'palace for felons'. Among these felons was a boy of 14 who had been sentenced to four years penal servitude for stealing a handkerchief worth a shilling.

In the 20th century, another source of stress among both prisoners and staff has replaced the old physical hardships and raised fresh controversies. Severe overcrowding and squalor became characteristic of British prisons as more criminals were sent to them and successive governments failed to modernize old buildings or build new ones. Princetown prison on Dartmoor, originally built in 1806-9 as barracks to house French prisoners of war, has repeatedly been rumoured since the 1930s to be due for closure, but it still survives and has recently undergone some ominous refurbishment. There was a proposal to close Pentonville in 1939.

By 1984, more than 11,000 prisoners in British gaols were living two to a cell, and more than 4,000 were living three to a cell. The official report of Her Majesty's Chief Inspector of Prisons for that year described how more than 14,000 inmates of gaols in England and Wales had to use chamber pots whilst sharing cells, and queue up for the ritual of 'slopping out' every morning.

Prison riots and rooftop demonstrations have become a commonplace of modern life in Britain and elsewhere. The riot at Strangeways, Manchester, in April 1990, resulted in one prisoner's death and a great deal of damage. The protest in this case was said not to be against the 'screws' or the system, but against one group of prisoners, but it did undoubtedly serve to accelerate long-overdue modernization.

It is surely self-evident that prisons are colleges of further education in criminal activity, and that men and women sent to them, particularly long-term prisoners, come out better qualified for lives of crime than when they went in. The more people sent to prison, it can be argued, the more criminals are eventually let loose on society. But the British Tory government's response to the problem of overcrowding has not been to lock up less people, but to build more prisons. Thus the criminal

Fact

A quarter of a century after John Howard had found women in Middlesex gaols kept "almost naked, with only a few filthy rags almost alive with vermin, their bodies rotting with distemper, and covered with itch, scorbutic and venereal ulcers", Elizabeth Fry saw in Newgate "disorderly, dram-drinking, half-naked women, vagrants and felons, convicted and unconvicted alike, some with little children clinging to their skirts, penned up promiscuously in crowded wards and yards, reeking with filth and infested with vermin". Newgate was calculated to hold 427 prisoners at this period, but it sometimes held as many as 1,200.

Fact

In terms of capacity, the largest prison in Britain is Wandsworth. Its official capacity is 965, but this has long been exceeded. In August 1990 the actual occupancy of the prison was 1,556. This figure had fallen to 1,027 by 1994. Among Wandsworth's inmates in 1872, when Queen Victoria had been on the throne for 35 years, was William Towens, a 12 year-old boy sentenced to a month's hard labour for stealing two tame rabbits.

Fact

The chief criminal prison in France before the Revolution, the fortress of Grand Châtelet near the centre of Paris, had a dungeon known as the Oubliette—a deep hole into which prisoners were lowered with ropes through a trap-door, and from which they might never emerge alive.

fraternity multiplies, and crime escalates.

In 1988 the government published a Green Paper entitled *Private Sector Involvement in the Remand System,* proposing the privatization of prisons, and the implementation of its proposals is now under way, reversing the system which has been in force, and considered the best method, for nearly 200 years.

Some of Britain's Principal Surviving old Prisons (more than 100 years old)

Note the number built in the 1840s and 1850s, when transportation was ending

Prison	Date of original building	Notes
Wakefield, West Yorkshire	17th century	There was a House of Correction on the present site in 1611, though little of that building remains.
Gloucester	1792	The model for 19th century prisons prior to Pentonville, and the first prison to instal a treadwheel.
Parkhurst, Isle of Wight	1799	Converted to maximum security prison, 1838
Dartmoor, Devon	1809	Converted to civil prison, 1850
Maidstone, Kent	1819	
Brixton, London	1820	Taken over by state as women's prison, 1853
Leicester	1828	Subject of scandal, 1862
Pentonville, London	1842	Originally known as the 'Model Prison'
Reading, Berkshire	1844	
Armley, Leeds	1847	
The Verne, Portland	1848	
Wandsworth, London	1849	
Winson Green, Birmingham	1850	Subject of scandal, 1862
Holloway, London	1851	Became women's prison in 1902
Walton, Liverpool	1855	
Strangeways, Manchester	1868	
Wormwood Scrubs, London	1874	Built by convicts under supervision
Barlinnie, Glasgow	c 1896	

Section 4: Torture and Mutilation

...much the most important evils that mankind have to consider are those which they inflict upon each other through stupidity or malevolence or both.

Bertrand Russell: *Unpopular Essays*

MOST OF THE WORLD'S judicial systems have at some time employed torture as a means of extracting confessions or evidence, and Britain's is no exception, despite the fact that torture has never been recognized as legitimate under common law. Torture was widely practised during the religious persecutions of the Tudor period, and trial by ordeal was common during the European witch-craze, when accused women were 'pricked' or 'swum'. Only English hypocrisy could deny that this was torture.

Dr John Fian, a schoolmaster, was implicated in an alleged plot to kill James VI of Scotland by means of sorcery, and was arraigned in December 1590 on 20 charges of treason and witchcraft. He was supposed to have conspired with Satan to wreck a ship carrying the King to Norway by throwing a dead cat into the sea. To get a confession out of him, his interrogators first thrawed his head, which meant binding it tightly with a rope and jerking it in different directions. Then he was put in the 'boots'—a vice-like mechanism designed to crush the victim's legs. Then the torturers stuck pins into his tongue. At last, Dr Fian succumbed and confessed, implicating the Earl of Bothwell in the conspiracy. But Fian afterwards withdrew his confession, and was tortured again. Needles were sunk into his fingers under the nails, and the nails pulled off, and his legs crushed in the 'Spanish boots' until blood and marrow spurted out, but he refused to confess again, and was finally burnt at the stake on Edinburgh's Castle Hill in January 1591. Rack, thumbscrews, witch's bridle, Spanish boot and other devices were used in Scotland until judicial torture was abolished in 1708, but branding and burning at the stake continued throughout the kingdom.

In the well-known cases of torture by the rack and other means in places like the Tower of London, licences to employ such methods were obtained from the monarch or the court of Star Chamber, to override the prohibition of torture under common law. Thus, the rack, 'Skevington's gyves', and the water dungeon were authorized in a country which purported to be above the use of torture. As Lord Macaulay put it: "Those rulers who had occasionally resorted to it had, as far as was possible, used it in secret, had never pretended that they had acted in conformity with either statute law or common law, and had excused themselves by saying that the extra-ordinary peril to which the state was exposed had forced them to take on themselves the responsibility of employing extra-ordinary means of defence".

This political manipulation of the law permitted the Irish rebel Thomas Miagh to be tortured in the Tower with Skevington's irons; the Protestant Anne Askew to be stretched on the rack 'till her bones and

Fact

Joan of Arc, held for several months on charges of heresy and witchcraft, and interrogated by the Papal Inquisition in a cold stone dungeon in the castle at Rouen in 1431, was taken at last to a tower where Pierre Cauchon, Bishop of Beauvais, awaited her with other inquisitors.'The instruments of torture were shown to her, and next to them the torturers, Mauger, Leparmentier, and his assistants. Also present was the usual array of greffiers de douleurs *and the* notaires d'angoisse, *trained in the indispensable art of picking confessions from the incomprehensible shrieks of the victims. Monsieur de Beauvais gave her sufficient time to take in the nature of the assembled implements, the pullies and cords, the winches and the rack, the mallets and the funnels, the hooks, the gridirons, the knives, the spikes, the boot, the pincers, and the braziers glowing in the shadows'. Faced with such threat of imminent torture, Joan was interrogated again, with what result we are only too familiar.*

Fact

The last person to be pressed to death is believed to have been Matthew Ryan in Ireland in 1740. Charged with highway robbery, he affected dumbness, and was pressed to death in the market-place at Kilkenny.

joints were almost plucked asunder'; and the Jesuit priest John Gerard to be suspended by his wrists in a dark, underground chamber where he saw 'every device and instrument of human torture'.

It was not only in the State prisons, however, where torture was employed. Nor was it very secret. Since there was no right of silence in earlier times, accused persons who refused to plead were subjected to the *peine forte et dure,* or pressing to death. Stretched out on the bare floor, almost naked and tightly bound, prisoners would have heavy weights of stone or iron loaded on their chests until they either submitted or expired, a process that could take several days. The Press Yard at Newgate was notorious, but *peine forte et dure* was practised throughout the land. Walter Calverly, charged with the murder of his wife and children in 1605, was pressed to death at York Castle for refusing to plead. A murderer at Kingston bore the pressure of nearly 200 kg (4 cwt) for an hour and a quarter in 1726 before begging for mercy, after which he was convicted and executed. And a man accused of murder at Nottingham was pressed to death in 1735 for his failure to plead—he was deaf and dumb. It was not until 1772 that this punishment was finally abolished.

Mutilation was a common punishment for various crimes in medieval England. Thieves would have their hands cut off; forgers might have their ears cropped; others were liable to have their noses slit, or to be branded. A convicted blasphemer might have his tongue bored through with a red-hot iron. Sometimes convicted men were castrated.

Branding was a primitive means of establishing a person's criminal record, as well as being a painful punishment. Criminals were branded on their cheeks, foreheads or hands with the letters T for thief, SL for seditious libeller, FA for false accuser, etc. Branding prevented abuse of the system of 'Benefit of Clergy', by which any reasonably literate felon could avoid rigorous civil punishment by reading or reciting a verse from the Bible and getting himself handed over to the ecclesiastical court instead. But Benefit of Clergy was a one-off privilege. Branding ensured that no one could claim it twice.

When John Howard toured the prisons of Britain and Europe in the 18th century, the conditions he discovered in British prisons were bad enough, but he found that torture was still used extensively in prisons in France and Germany, Belgium and Denmark, Spain and Italy. In Liége he learned that officers patrolled the *outside* of the prison to prevent members of the public from stopping to listen to the shrieks of prisoners in the torture chamber.

The treadwheel was a form of unproductive hard labour called by convicts the 'everlasting staircase'. The first prison to instal a treadwheel was Gloucester in 1811. But five years later the engineer William Cubitt invented an improved version, and within a few years his machines were installed in more than 50 prisons throughout the country. The treadwheel was a huge cylinder with slatted steps along its length, varying in size to accommodate anything from six to 18 prisoners working side-by-side in separate stalls. In most cases, it was simply a form of torture with no end-product, though in some prisons it was used to raise water or grind corn, or to supply power to other machinery. The government thought the treadwheel an 'excellent instrument of corrective discipline', and it became an alternative source of terror to the gradually abandoned horrors of solitary confinement. The labour of 'grinding the wind', as convicts called it, was extremely exhausting because, as a warder explained, "the men can get no firm tread, like, from the steps always sinking away from under their feet..." Henry Mayhew described a treadwheel as having the appearance of "the stalls of a public urinal", and its male operators had a sensitive reason for hating it. They called it the 'cockchafer'. Worse still, convicts subjected to it sometimes fell into the machinery and were mangled to death. Pregnant female convicts had miscarriages, and men suffered from ruptures and respiratory illnesses.

The crank machine was a small iron drum with a handle, which could be screwed tight or weighted to resist turning. Its great advantage as an instrument of torture was that it could be installed in individual cells, whereas the treadwheel was a communal machine. The crank machine was thus admirably suited to those prisons run on the separate system. Convicts were required to complete a fixed number of revolutions per day, and this useless labour was described as 'very distressing and severe'. The average rate at which a crank could be turned by reasonably fit men was about 1,200 revolutions per hour. At Coldbath Fields prison, convicts were required to achieve 10,000 revolutions per day, equal to about eight and a quarter hours of labour. Governor Musson at Leicester prison instituted a system in 1848 in which adult male convicts had to achieve 14,000 revolutions a day—equivalent to eleven and a half hours' labour—in order to earn their meals. The severity of the work and deprivation of food led to numerous cases of a dropsical disease called 'crank oedima'. Juvenile prisoners were also put to work on cranks, and were sometimes required to achieve as many as 12,000 revolutions a day. The chief warder at Leicester told an enquiry that the youngest boy he could remember doing crank labour was 8 years old.

As well as the crank machine and the treadwheel, another form of torture employed in some British prisons was 'shot drill'. It was in use at Lancaster Castle, for instance, until 1878, when the State took over the responsibility of administering county and borough gaols. Prisoners had to stand in concentric circles, each man with a 11 kg (24 lb) shot at his feet. At the order to move, each man had to lift the heavy shot waist high, step forward six paces, put the shot down, and return to his starting point where he found another shot waiting for him deposited by the man behind him in the next circle. This exhausting, painful and demoralizingly useless process could go on for four hours at a time, and had an obvious tendency to cause ruptures.

Flogging and birching were universal forms of torture employed well into the 20th century in the UK. It was only in 1820 that the flogging of women was abolished in Britain. The abolition of flogging of men *in public* followed. In 1938 the Home Secretary, Sir Samuel Hoare, announced the abolition of the cat-o'-nine-tails following controversy surrounding the flogging of the so-called 'Mayfair men', Harley, Wilmer, and others, for a violent jewel robbery in one of London's most

Fact

A tough young Irish convict named Frayne, sentenced on Norfolk Island to 100 lashes, told the island's governor, Lieutenant Colonel Morisset, that he was as great a tyrant as Nero. Morisset thereupon sentenced him to a further 100 lashes, and ordered that he was to be kept in his cell in irons for the rest of his life, and never to be allowed to see daylight again. This part of the inhuman sentence was not enforced, but Frayne was frequently flogged so mercilessly that his only relief from his agony was to pour his meagre water ration on the floor and lie on his back in the puddle, which he increased by urinating into it.

Fact

The last recorded case of the flagellation of a woman in Britain was in 1817, when a woman was flogged at Inverness for being drunk and disorderly.

Fact

Although the courts could no longer order flogging after the 1948 Criminal Justice Act, Boards of Visitors to prisons could still do so. During 1954, 10 prisoners were flogged with the cat-o'-nine-tails in British prisons, two of them receiving 18 lashes each.

Fact

The treadwheel and crank machines were abolished as instruments of hard labour in Britain's prisons in 1899.

Fact

Whipping 'at the cart's tail' involved tying the criminal (man or woman) by the wrists to the tail of a cart, which was then drawn through the streets whilst the victim, stripped to the waist, was lashed with a whip of five or six knotted cords. The order of the court was customarily that he or she should be whipped 'until his back be bloody'. The last instance of whipping at the cart's tail occurred in Glasgow in 1822.

prestigious hotels. But because of the war, it was 10 years before the main elements of his Criminal Justice Bill became law. Corporal punishment inside prisons continued until its final abolition, after much soul-searching, in 1967. There are still loud demands from some quarters for the reintroduction of birching.

The history of the punishment of crime shows only too clearly, alas, that those appointed to enforce the laws have often been as degraded as the criminals who have passed through their hands. Punishment, as Freud pointed out in *Totem and Taboo,* 'will not infrequently give those who carry it out an opportunity of committing the same outrage under colour of an act of expiation. This is indeed one of the foundations of the human penal system and it is based, no doubt correctly, on the assumption that the prohibited impulses are present alike in the criminal and in the avenging community'.

The 'third degree' methods of interrogation by police were being practised in the United States long before the world became familiar with the physical and mental torture known as 'brainwashing' in use behind the Iron Curtain. Prisoners would be put in solitary confinement and deprived of food and sleep, then questioned interminably until they confessed through hunger and exhaustion. And the scene with the sadistic Nazi dentist in the film *Marathon Man* was not a mere figment of a Hollywood scriptwriter's imagination. A New York journalist, Emanuel Lavine, reported in the early 30s that he had seen an accused man put in a dentist's chair and 'held there, while the dentist, who seemed to enjoy his job, ground down a sound molar with a rough burr'.

A Deputy Commissioner of the NYPD wrote, somewhat ingenuously, in *Police Magazine* in 1925: 'There was never such a thing as the 'third degree'. You simply get a man into a mental corner, provided he is really guilty, and then he will wilt every time, that is, if you get a wedge in as a start. It's pretty hard to get a confession unless you have some little clue to start with on your line of questioning. But, having found that weak spot, the discrepancies in the man's story begin to widen until finally he becomes so confused and befuddled that he sees the game is up. All his defences have been beaten down. He's cornered, trapped. That's when he bursts into tears. The torture comes from his own mind, not from outside'.

Section 5:
Exemplary Punishments

Now behold
This grievous torment, thou, who breathing go'st
To spy the dead: behold, if any else
Be terrible as this.
Dante Alighieri: *The Divine Comedy*

MAKING A TERRIFYING example of a criminal guilty of a particularly abominable crime was long held to be the best possible deterrent—a grim warning to others of what could happen to them if caught in a comparable act. The French had a good expression for it—the *amende honorable*. When François Ravaillac killed the popular king of France, Henri IV, in 1610, the assassin was made an 'example of terror' that would, it was believed, 'convert all bloody-minded traitors from the like enterprise'. Ravaillac was first bound supine on the scaffold and the hand which had gripped the murderous knife was burnt with flaming brimstone. Then the executioners used red-hot pincers to sear his nipples and tear out chunks of flesh from his thighs, arms, and other fleshy parts, and poured scalding oil, pitch and brimstone into the wounds, all the while exhorting the screaming regicide to reveal the names of his accomplices. Finally, they tied his limbs to four horses, and drove them away so that he would be dismembered, but had to sever the sinews with a knife before the horses were able to tear the arms and legs from the trunk.

But the lasting effectiveness as a deterrent, even of this terrible punishment, was limited. In 1757 Robert François Damiens attempted to kill Louis XV, and even though the King was only wounded and soon recovered, the would-be assassin was condemned to the same torments as Ravaillac had suffered. A similar appalling death had been the fate of Balthazar Gérard, who murdered William the Silent at Delft in 1584.

Hanging, drawing and quartering was an exemplary punishment reserved in England for high treason, a crime considered more heinous than murder. In theory, the victim was supposed to be cut down from the gallows while still alive, and have his bowels ripped out and burnt before his eyes, before being decapitated and divided into quarters, usually for exhibition in various parts of the kingdom. Visitors to London would be welcomed to the city by the heads of traitors stuck on pikes above Temple Bar, London Bridge, or Westminster Hall.

The common exemplary punishments for ordinary criminals were dissection and hanging in chains. Hanging the corpses of executed malefactors on gibbets near the scenes of their crimes was a practice of ancient origin. A gibbet was a post, often with a cross-beam, on which the corpses were suspended either in chains or in an iron cage, as exemplars of the wages of sin. This form of government terrorism was legalized in 1752 and lasted for nearly a century.

Highway robbers and others were hung in chains as well as murderers, and it was not unknown for men to be *executed* by that

Fact

Helen Torrence and Jean Waldie were hanged in Edinburgh in 1752 for the murder of a boy, whose corpse they had sold to a surgeon for two shillings and sixpence. By the time they were brought to justice, an act had been passed decreeing that all executed murderers were to be either publicly dissected or hung in chains, and the two women's bodies were duly delivered for dissection in a classic case of 'the biter bit'.

Fact

On 31 January 1945, Private Edward Donald Slovik from Detroit, Michigan, serving in G Company, 109th Infantry, became the first and only American soldier since the Civil War to be executed for cowardice in the face of the enemy. Forty-nine death sentences were decreed by US Army courts martial during the WWII, but Slovik's was the only one to be carried out. The order for execution was confirmed by General Eisenhower, and Slovik was shot by firing squad in a garden at Ste-Marie-aux-Mines, France.

means, being suspended alive until they died from exposure or starved to death. Holinshed's *Chronicles* record that a man convicted of wilful murder might be 'either hanged alive in chains near the place where the act was committed (or else upon compassion taken first strangled with a rope) and so continueth till his bones consume to nothing'. A notorious northern highwayman, John Whitfield, is said to have been hung alive on a gibbet at Wetheral, near Carlisle, around 1777. He remained alive for several days until a mail-coachman, passing that way and taking pity on the wretched moaning felon, shot him.

Corpses ordered to be hung in chains were usually enclosed in iron hoops or cages with the heads tarred, and left to rot as a grim reminder of the horrible fate in store for those who transgressed the law. Samuel Pepys, riding along the Dover road in 1661, passed "the man that hangs upon Shooter's Hill, and a filthy sight it is to see how his flesh is sunk to his bones". Corpses would sometimes remain on gibbets for years—black masses of putrefying flesh half eaten by birds and vermin.

The practice had no authority under the law until 1752, when it was officially sanctioned by the 'Murder Act'—along with dissection by teachers of anatomy—as alternative additional punishments for crimes of peculiar magnitude, such as premeditated homicide. 'It is become necessary', the *Act for Preventing the horrid Crime of Murder* stated, 'that some further Terror and peculiar Mark of Infamy be added to the Punishment'.

Until the Anatomy Act of 1832 repealed the law ordering bodies of executed criminals to be either hung in chains or handed over to surgeons for dissection, the latter punishment, in particular, had been for 80 years a cause of riots at places of execution as friends and relatives of those executed fought with law officers to prevent their loved ones from being carted off to Surgeons' Hall—even though the Murder Act had prescribed transportation for anyone obstructing the law in this way. In the late 18th century William Wilberforce was among those who wanted dissection to be extended to rapists, arsonists and robbers, as well as murderers. The surgeons, always short of fresh corpses, would have been only too pleased to have these additional sources of raw materials, but no such change in the law was made.

Dissection was feared more than any other punishment because it appeared to preclude the possibility of bodily resurrection on Judgement Day. When constables arrested Vincent Davis, a Smithfield butcher, for stabbing his wife to death in 1725, he confessed immediately, saying: "I have killed the best wife in the world, and I am certain of being hanged, but for God's sake, don't let me be anatomized". His friends managed to protect his corpse from the surgeons, and buried it at Clerkenwell.

Section 6: Other Punishments

Stocks and Pillory

In 1376, Edward III decreed that every village in the kingdom was to maintain a set of stocks for the punishment of offenders. These contraptions were generally set up on village greens or in town squares, and were sometimes equipped with wheels so that they could be moved easily to specific sites for the effective humiliation of wrongdoers. They remained in use for nearly 500 years. In 1860, John Gambles was sentenced at Pudsey, near Leeds, to sit in the stocks for six hours for gambling on the Sabbath. Stocks were often combined with whipping posts, with iron clamps by which an offender could be held by his wrists while he was flogged for his crime. As well as punishing offenders against public order, the stocks were used by the Church courts for moral offences such as fornication or failing to attend church services. The last recorded use of stocks was in 1865.

If the local people approved of the punishment, the more aggressive among them would gather to throw missiles such as rotten vegetables at the victim, and it was nothing for the village adults and children to see one of their neighbours punished and humiliated by being bound to the post and whipped on his bare back until the blood ran.

George Fox, founder of the Society of Friends, or 'Quakers', knew what it was like to sit in the stocks at the mercy of the local rabble. At Mansfield in Nottinghamshire, he was put in the stocks after being beaten with sticks and fists, and remained there 'some hours', during which the locals threw stones at him and threatened to whip him with dogwhips and horsewhips.

The pillory was a similar device, except that the hinged boards with holes were raised on a post so as to grip the standing malefactor's head and hands instead of his feet. The pillory, more common in towns, was more dangerous than stocks because it was intended for more serious offences. Stocks were used to punish local drunks, brawling and other disorderly rustic conduct, but the pillory was used in the Middle Ages to punish cheating tradesmen, such as bakers who sold their customers loaves of short measure. They would usually be banished from the town after spending a specified time in the pillory.

When Daniel Defoe was pilloried at Temple Bar in 1703 (see under Sedition and Conspiracy), he was treated as a hero by the London populace, and people gathered round to drink to his health. But many offenders were seriously injured, or even killed by the fury of an unrestrained mob while standing in the pillory. Being pilloried in a large town was somewhat akin to having one's photograph splashed all over the front pages of modern tabloid newspapers. One was permanently marked as a guilty man. As Dr Johnson remarked to Boswell: "People are not very willing to ask a man to their tables who has stood in the pillory".

When Anne Marrow was pilloried at Charing Cross for marrying

Fact

Several old gibbet posts survive in England. The unusually tall Combe Gibbet on Inkpen Hill in Berkshire, which was destroyed by vandals in 1991, was originally erected in 1676 to hang George Broomham and Dorothy Newman who had murdered the widow Newman's two children. The gibbet close to the crossroads of the A14 and A45 near Caxton, Cambridgeshire, is said to have been put up in 1753 to expose the corpse of a highwayman named Gatwood, hanged for robbing mail coaches in the vicinity. At Steng Cross, Northumberland, between Elsdon and Morpeth, a gibbet post stands where a murderer named Winter was hung in chains in 1791. This post, however, is a 19th-century replica. The post in Gibbet Lane, half a mile south of Bilstone in Leicestershire, was used in March 1801 (not February 1800, as the sign on it states) to expose the corpse of John Massey who had been hanged for murdering his wife.

Fact

Many sets of wooden stocks survive in situ *throughout Britain, mainly on village greens where local malefactors would have been subjected to punishment by the lords of the manors. One of the few remaining pillories stands at the bottom of Church Hill at Coleshill in Warwickshire, between Birmingham and Coventry.*

three times whilst disguised as a man, she was blinded by the missiles of the hostile crowd. Pillorying for sexual deviancy was an effective method of exposing the culprit to the contempt of the majority. This was justice being seen to be done. Several men found guilty of homosexual acts came close to death in the pillory.

John Waller, pilloried at Seven Dials for robbery and perjury in 1732, died from his injuries when his head was repeatedly struck by various missiles. And when four men convicted of highway robbery and conspiracy in a 'thief-taking' scam were sentenced to the pillory in 1756, they were pelted with stones, potatoes and dead cats. Although constables attempted to control the savage mob, one man, James Egan, was already dead when taken out of the pillory. His skull had been smashed by a huge stone. The other three, Stephen MacDaniel, John Berry and James Salmon, died from their injuries soon afterwards in Newgate.

The pillory had fallen into disuse by the early years of the 19th century, and was finally abolished in 1837.

Section 7:

Justice and Human Frailty

Chief Justices of England

THE MOST NOTORIOUS of all English chief justices was, of course, George Jeffreys, appointed by King James II to try for treason the alleged followers of the Duke of Monmouth in the failed rebellion of 1685. Judge Jeffreys, ordered by the King to show no mercy, presided over the trials held in the west country at Dorchester, Exeter and Taunton, which became known, with good reason, as the 'Bloody Assizes'. Regaling the courtrooms with such impartial observations as, "Was there ever such a villain on the face of the earth?", and, "There is not one of these lying, snivelling, canting Presbyterians but, one way or another, had a hand in the rebellion", the ferocious 37 year-old Chief Justice showed his impatience in no uncertain terms if the juries even felt it necessary to leave their seats to consider their verdicts, and he would be beside himself with fury if the 12 good men hesitated to pronounce an accused guilty. Jeffreys, as Macaulay tells us, 'stormed, cursed and swore in language which no well-bred man would have used at a race or a cockfight'. In a few weeks of judicial savagery, he sentenced 74 alleged rebels to be executed in Dorset, and 233 to be hung, drawn and quartered in Somerset, as well as condemning a further 800 to be transported to the American colonies. Jeffreys afterwards boasted that he had "hanged more traitors than all his predecessors together since the Conquest", and in recognition of these services to the Crown, the King made Baron Jeffreys of Wem his Lord Chancellor.

Edward, Baron Ellenborough, Lord Chief Justice from 1802 until his retirement in November 1818, presided during that period of legal barbarity known as the 'Bloody Code', and soon gained a reputation for uncommon severity, especially after he opposed abolition of the death penalty for shoplifting. "My lords", he said, "I conjure your lordships to pause before you pass a Bill which will have the effect of increasing the number of crimes, and adding to the enormous catalogue of offences, which now disgrace the criminal records of the country". So the death penalty for shoplifting remained for a few years more. Ellenborough also opposed abolition of the pillory in 1815—a punishment he considered "particularly suited to perjury and fraud". Ellenborough sentenced Daniel Eaton in 1812 to 18 months in prison, merely for publishing Tom Paine's *The Age of Reason,* and added to the severity of this sentence the medieval punishment of standing in the public pillory for two hours in each month. The poet Shelley published an indignant open letter to Lord Ellenborough in which he said that, if the burning of heretics had not been abolished, 'I conceive that, from the promise held out by your lordship's zeal, we need not despair of beholding the flames of persecution rekindled at Smithfield'. It was Ellenborough, too, who sentenced Leigh Hunt and his brother James for libel (see under Defamation). Lord Ellenborough's illness and death were said to have been hastened by the shock of being defied by a jury which he had directed to return a guilty verdict, but which refused to do so.

The last of the so-called 'hanging judges' was Rayner Goddard, Lord Chief Justice from 1946 until his retirement in 1958. Lord Goddard remained a stern believer in both capital and corporal punishment at a time when the civilized world was changing its attitudes. A proposal before Parliament in 1948 to suspend the death penalty for an experimental period of five years was described by Lord Goddard in the House of Lords as 'gambling with the lives of the people', and he successfully opposed a proposal to raise the age limit for liability to the death penalty from 18 to 21 years. He spoke once of the need to 'destroy' murderers. When he appeared before the Royal Commission on Capital Punishment in 1950, Lord Goddard made it clear that he thought too many condemned criminals were being reprieved, and that he was in favour of hanging both women and the insane.

Nothing in all the evidence given to the Royal Commission makes more chilling reading than the words of Lord Chief Justice Goddard. Fortunately, he was a man out of step with his times, and the law was changed in spite of him. He showed contempt for psychiatrists and anyone else who sought to show mitigating circumstances when an accused was on trial for his life, and ended his career as an irascible octogenarian reactionary, inflexible and unloved.

Fact

In 1825, the body of Margaret Savage was found in a river in County Waterford. It became obvious that she had been murdered by her husband, Daniel, but it was over eight years before her death was avenged when a man calling himself Edmond Pine was recognized as Savage. He was convicted and executed. But the man was not Daniel Savage. Several witnesses at the trial testified that he was not, and only one positively identified him. Edmund Pine was a painfully shy and nervous man who was incapable for speaking up for himself, and no one in authority did anything to save him from being hanged for a crime he did not commit.

Fact

Among one-time policemen who turned to other careers were Dennis Nilsen, the English serial killer; Josef Locke, the Irish tenor who left England to escape the Inland Revenue; Errol Flynn, the film star charged with statutory rape but acquitted; and James Berry, the Yorkshire executioner who hanged 134 men and women in eight years and sought to relieve his conscience first through drink and then through religion.

Bent Cops

Since Home Secretary Sir Robert Peel established the Metropolitan Police in 1829, the British police force has maintained a proud overall record of service. But the counties and boroughs of England were at first very slow in following the lead of the capital in properly organized crime prevention and law enforcement. Yorkshire was slowest of all in establishing a regular police force. By mid-19th century, London had roughly one policeman to every 450 inhabitants, but some boroughs had only one to every 4,000. The constables were recruited from the lowest levels of society and very poorly paid, so it is hardly surprising that large numbers of these early officers were dismissed for assorted misdemeanours, especially drunkenness. One constable was sacked for urinating on an office desk; another for raffling a watch he had stolen from a murder victim. The Chief Constable of Wigan, John Whittle, was discharged for 'misconduct' with a woman he was supposed to be arresting.

In 1877 three senior detectives were given sentences of two years hard labour after being convicted at the Old Bailey of corruption. They were found to be in the pay of a confidence trickster, Harry Benson, who was operating gambling frauds and was always forewarned when the police were intent on arresting him. The occasional bad apple has continued to turn up ever since. In 1950 PC James Robertson was hanged for murder in Glasgow after deliberately running over his pregnant mistress, Catherine McCluskey. In 1957, the Chief Constable of Worcestershire was imprisoned for fraud, and in 1972, two senior Scotland Yard detectives were convicted of corrupt association with criminals. In 1976, ex-Detective Chief Superintendent William Moody, former head of the Met's Obscene Publications Squad, was imprisoned for 12 years for his involvement—with 11 other officers—in corruption charges arising from their regular receipt of money from Soho pornographers who were paying the officers £200 a week to secure immunity from prosecution.

In December 1979, three Metropolitan Police detectives were convicted of conspiracy to obtain £6,000 corruptly from Mrs Soraya Khashoggi, then reputed to be the world's richest woman. Det. Supt. John Colligan got two and a half years, and DCs Bryan Smethurst and John Follows two years each.

After the major disturbances at Wapping in January 1987 arising from the sacking of 5,000 staff of Rupert Murdoch's News International, 24 police officers were charged with various offences which included perjury and conspiracy to pervert the course of justice.

Police corruption is not a male prerogative. Even as I write, a policewoman in New Orleans—currently the 'murder capital' of America—has been sentenced to death for murder committed in the course of a robbery, and two young Lancashire WPCs have been jailed for 12 months for possessing and supplying drugs. Elizabeth Hartley and Liza Wilkinson, both 25, were sentenced at Liverpool Crown Court on 10 October 1995, after pleading guilty to possessing cannabis and amphetamines and supplying them to friends at cost price.

Few British cops, however, can compete with J. Edgar Hoover—head of the American FBI for nearly half a century before his death in 1972—for sheer hypocrisy. His well-known persecution of liberal activists was carried on whilst he was apparently engaging in homosexual activities and cross-dressing, and pulling his punches in the war against organized crime because of Mob threats to expose him.

Racial tensions are an ever-present factor in the policing of heavily-populated urban areas in some countries, including Britain, but American cities are especially vulnerable to charges of police brutality against black criminals. Los Angeles exploded into riots in 1991 when four white police officers were released after being seen by millions on TV violently beating a 25 year-old black suspect, Rodney King, whilst he lay on the ground. Ten were killed in the ensuing violence. Mr King was subsequently awarded $3 million damages in a civil action against the LAPD.

Fact

The last man to be executed in public in Britain was Michael Barrett on 26 May 1868. He was a young Fenian, sentenced to death for his part in causing an explosion at Clerkenwell when a wall in the local House of Detention was blown up in an attempt to free Irish prisoners. Several innocent people, including children, were killed. The last woman to suffer public execution was Mrs Frances Kidder, hanged for murder at Maidstone on 2 April of the same year. The hangman in both cases was William Calcraft, the longest-serving executioner in British history. In the same year, on 13 August, he carried out the first execution inside prison walls when he hanged Thomas Wells, also at Maidstone. Wells, who was 18, had murdered the station-master at Dover.

Executioners

Albert Pierrepoint referred in his autobiography to his pride in what he claimed was his family's 'unique tradition of service to the State'. It was hardly that. There have been numerous 'family firms' of executioners in the past, and Shakespeare refers in *Coriolanus* to 'hereditary hangmen'. The Billington family preceded the Pierrepoints in Britain, and earlier there had been the Brandons in London and the Ormistons in Scotland (both father-and-son teams) and the Otways of Somerset. The record in family businesses, however, belongs to France, where the Sanson family supplied executioners through several generations, from 1688 to 1847. Most famous of them was Charles-Henri Sanson, commonly known as 'Monsieur de Paris', who dispatched nearly 3,000 victims during the 'Terror' of 1793-4 in revolutionary France. His six brothers were also executioners, and Sansons carried out the executions in Rheims and Tours as well as in Paris during the Revolution. Charles-Henri's victims included the King and Queen, Louis XVI and Marie Antoinette, as well as Charlotte Corday, Madame du Barry, Madame Roland, and finally, the architects of the massacre themselves, Danton and Robespierre.

Two men convicted of stealing livestock were sentenced to death at York in 1800 and at Lancaster six years later; John Curry had stolen five sheep at Hewarth, near York, and Edward Barlow had stolen a horse at North Meols, near Hoylake. These were serious capital crimes—the legendary Dick Turpin had been hanged at York for horse-stealing in 1739—but neither Curry nor Barlow was executed. The reason was that they were the hangmen for Yorkshire and Lancashire respectively, and their usefulness as public servants outweighed their crimes. Barlow, in particular, was as great a villain as any of those he hanged, and was said to be guilty of 'nearly every vile act'. This Welshman, commonly known as 'Old Ned', executed Lancashire's condemned for about 25 years. He died in Lancaster Castle, having had his death sentence commuted to life imprisonment on condition that he continued to execute the other local felons. Curry was little better. He had already been condemned for

Fact

In France, the last public execution by guillotine took place on 17 June 1939, when Eugen Weidmann, convicted of murder, was executed before a large crowd at Versailles. The executioner was Henri Desfourneaux. The last person executed before abolition of the death penalty in France in September 1981 was 28 year-old murderer Hamida Djandoubi, who was decapitated at Baumettes prison, Marseilles, on 10 September 1977.

sheep-stealing once before, seven years earlier. He hanged the criminals of Yorkshire for about 30 years, and died in the parish poor-house at Thirsk. Many hangmen were rogues, and several of them *did* end up at the wrong end of ropes themselves.

The longest-serving hangman in British history was William Calcraft, who was in office from 1829 to 1874. But few executioners have been so desensitized to man-to-man killing that they could do it for 45 years. A good many, indeed, have ended up executing themselves. An Australian hangman cut his own throat in 1924; a German executioner, Schweitz, committed suicide in 1926 and an American one, Hulbert, in 1929. Schweitz's successor in Germany, Paul Spaethe, died by his own hand, soon to be followed by an Austrian executioner named Lang in 1938. In Britain, George Ormiston, an Edinburgh hangman, threw himself over a precipice to his death in 1702. It seems that he had been driven to despair by the execration and loathing of his fellow citizens.

John Ellis was an executioner from 1901 to 1924. A barber by trade in Rochdale, Lancashire, his sideline took him all over the country, and among those he 'put away', as he liked to express it, were Dr Crippen, George Joseph Smith, Sir Roger Casement, and Edith Thompson. In 1924, a few months after his retirement, Ellis shot himself, but succeeded only in fracturing his jaw. Charged with attempting to commit suicide, he was dismissed by the magistrate on an undertaking not to repeat the attempt and to give up intoxicating drink. It was widely rumoured that the distressing experience of hanging Mrs Thompson had unhinged his mind, even though he had hanged another woman afterwards. Social ostracism had taken its toll, as well as the act of killing. 'Conversations cease suddenly when I am about', Ellis wrote later, 'and I can feel people eyeing me as if I am some exhibit in the chamber of horrors'. Ellis went

Principle Hangmen of England (from late 18th Century to late 20th Century)

Name	Place of birth	Operative dates	Reason for replacement	Notable victims
William Brunskill	London	1786 - 1815	Suffered a stroke	John Bellingham
John Langley	London	1815 - 1817	Died, aged 51	Elizabeth Fenning
James Botting	Brighton, Sussex	1817 - 1824	Imprisoned for debt	Cato Street conspirators
James Foxen	London	1824 - 1829	Died, aged 61	William Corder
William Calcraft	Baddow, Essex	1829 - 1874	Pensioned off	Frederick and Maria Manning
William Marwood	Horncastle, Lincs	1874 - 1883	Died, aged 63	Charles Peace
James Berry	Bradford, Yorks	1884 - 1892	Resigned	Dr Cross, Mrs Pearcey
James Billington	Bolton, Lancs	1884 - 1901	Died, aged 54	Amelia Dyer
William Billington	Bolton, Lancs	1901 - 1904	Resigned	George Chapman
Henry Pierrepoint	Clayton, Yorks	1905 - 1910	Resigned	Arthur Devereux
Thomas Pierrepoint	Clayton, Yorks	1906 - 1946	Retired	Mahon, Rouse
John Ellis	Rochdale, Lancs	1907 - 1924	Resigned	Dr Crippen, Roger Casement, G.J. Smith
Albert Pierrepoint	Clayton, Yorks	1940 - 1956	Resigned	William Joyce, John Christie, Ruth Ellis
Harry Allen	Manchester	1956 - 1965	Redundant	Peter Manuel, James Hanratty
Robert Stewart	Edinburgh	1956 - 1965	Redundant	Norman Harris

Note: This list does not include all qualified executioners in the period. There were always two or more hangmen, trained and approved by the Home Office, whom county sheriffs could choose to employ. The dates given are those served as 'No 1' hangmen, and do not include preliminary periods as assistants.

into show business for a time, arousing controversy by acting the part of hangman in a melodrama about Charles Peace, and touring fairgrounds and seaside resorts to deliver lectures illustrated by demonstrations on a model scaffold. In 1932, the slump had so affected Ellis's hairdressing business that he was reduced to selling counter-cloths to public houses. He suffered from neuritis and drank heavily. On 18th September, 1932, he committed suicide by cutting his throat with a razor, after threatening to cut off the heads of his wife and daughter.

The stress of being paid killers has troubled the minds of many other executioners who have often been led into the business through youthful bravado and then been too proud to admit, on mature reflection, that the experience has been something they would have been better without, and in the end have sought release in religious absolution or cerebral abdication. The concept of 'The Law' is supposed to absolve a jury that pronounces an accused guilty from all responsibility for a criminal's fate ; the judge who sentences him to death; the Home Secretary who refuses a reprieve; and the executioner who carries out the sentence. But it is the hangman who commits the final *physical* act of putting a rope round the criminal's neck and pulling the lever. As Bernard Shaw said: "Criminals do not die by the hands of the Law. They die by the hands of other men".

Hangmen are not intellectuals at home with abstract concepts. What they reflect on as they grow older is that they have killed men and women (and children, too, in earlier times) for blood money. One of the most important questions about the death penalty is whether the State should have the right to expect any of its citizens to carry out such a task. As the consultant psychiatrist, A. Hyatt Williams, put it in 1969: "The long-term ill-effects upon the character balance of those who participate in legal homicide are not to be underestimated". One modern British executioner was rumoured to go home and burn all his clothes after each job. Even Pontius Pilate would have found that a bit extreme.

Fact

Richard Brandon, the man who beheaded King Charles I, was the son of Gregory Brandon of Whitechapel, who was himself an executioner. Gregory had been convicted of manslaughter in 1611, but pleaded 'benefit of clergy', and got away with being branded on his thumb. Richard, who succeeded his father as common hangman in 1640, is said to have prepared himself for his career by decapitating cats and dogs.

The Defenders

Some famous criminal lawyers achieve their reputations chiefly as remarkable and successful defence counsels rather than as prosecutors, and among the best in British history have been Sir Edward Marshall Hall and Sir Patrick Hastings.

Marshall Hall was born at Brighton in 1858 and called to the bar in 1888. His outstanding advocacy resulted in some sensational verdicts in the first two decades of the 20th century. In 1907, he secured the acquittal of Robert Wood, a young artist accused of the murder of a prostitute, Phyllis Dimmock, who had been found on her bed with her throat cut. The case came to be known as the 'Camden Town Murder'. Wood had been in the victim's company several times during the last week of her life, including the night before her death. Furthermore, he had asked Ruby Young, an artist's model who had been his lover, to provide him with an alibi for the night before Phyllis's murder. Everything seemed to

Fact

The novelist Henry Fielding, author of Tom Jones *and co-founder of the Bow Street Runners, was also a justice of the peace, and told the story of a judge, Sir Francis Page, who had a horse-thief brought before him under the Black Act. The thief claimed that he had* found *the animal. "Thou art a lucky fellow," the judge said, "I have travelled the circuit these 40 years, and never found a horse in my life: but I'll tell thee what, friend, thou was more lucky than thou didst know of; for thou didst not only find a horse, but a halter too, I promise thee".*

point to his guilt, but Marshall Hall's eloquence brought both public and jury round in Wood's favour. Wood was the first defendant to be acquitted of murder in a trial under the Criminal Justice Act of 1898, by which the accused had the right to give evidence on his own behalf.

Marshall Hall believed his greatest victory was his successful defence of Edward Lawrence in 1909. A man known for violence, Lawrence was charged with the murder by shooting of a barmaid, Ruth Hadley, with whom he had had an affair. Marshall Hall persuaded judge and jury that the woman had been shot accidentally during a struggle.

In 1920, Hall won an unexpected acquittal for Ronald Light, a schoolmaster from Leicester accused of the 'Green Bicycle Murder'. Bella Wright, a factory worker, had been shot and left by a roadside near Little Stretton, a village in Leicestershire. She had been seen with a stranger who was riding a green bicycle, and when a green BSA bicycle was recovered from a local canal and traced to Ronald Light, even though the number had been carefully filed off, police were sure they had their man. But Light said that he had disposed of it after realizing that he would be suspected of the murder, which he had read about in the newspapers. And Marshall Hall persuaded the jury that this claim was true. (Although it formed no part of Marshall Hall's case, the ballistics expert, Robert Churchill, testified that a dead crow had been found not far from the body. The bird had been shot, and it was possible that Bella Wright had been shot accidentally at the same time, and not murdered at all.)

Even Edward Marshall Hall's unrivalled advocacy was not enough to save *all* his clients from the gallows. They included, for instance, George Joseph Smith (see under Murder). But he has rarely been matched, and never surpassed, in the eloquence and persuasiveness with which he represented defendants whose fates seemed already sealed when their trials began. He occasionally got himself reprimanded for unprofessional conduct, but he was the supreme actor who could reduce those in court to tears at the very thought that they could have suspected the innocent in the dock of such an abominable deed.

Patrick Hastings, born in 1880, was called to the bar in 1904, and was made a King's Counsel in 1919. His greatest triumph, perhaps, was in securing the acquittal of Elvira Barney in 1932 (see under Murder). "Members of the jury" he said in beginning his closing speech on that occasion, "I shall not indulge in flights of oratory or dramatic surprises such as are supposed to be the attributes of an advocate. They may be amusing, but we are not in this court to amuse". This struck exactly the right note at that juncture. Hastings had already enjoyed his dramatic moments in the case, as when he had suddenly ordered Mrs Barney to pick up the fatal revolver, so proving that she was right-handed. But Hastings's method was the keen, incisive, intellectual approach, not the high-powered emotional appeal.

Sir Norman Birkett (later Lord Birkett) was another brilliant defender who has already appeared in these pages. His successful defence of Toni Mancini, tried in 1934 for the murder of his mistress Violette Kaye whose corpse was found in a trunk in Mancini's lodgings at Brighton, was little short of a minor miracle in view of Mancini's criminal record and all the circumstantial evidence.

Clarence Darrow, the American attorney born in 1857, was a powerful advocate of similar mould to Marshall Hall, his contemporary. His long summation at the trial in August 1924 of Leopold and Loeb, the wealthy Chicago teenage boys who had confessed to kidnapping and killing Bobby Franks 'for kicks', undoubtedly saved them from the electric chair in the face of a determined prosecution demand for their execution.

In the following year, Darrow defended John Scopes, a Tennessee biology teacher who had defied the state's ban on teaching Darwinian evolution. The journalist H.L. Mencken, weighing up local feeling before the trial, related how one local woman denounced the reading of books and another, offered a glass of Coca-Cola, uttered a 'gurgle of terror'. The local preacher had prohibited Coca-Cola as a 'levantine and Hell-sent narcotic'. From this community was drawn the trial jury. Clarence Darrow was identified as the beast with seven heads and 10 horns described in the Book of Revelation.

Darrow's chief opponent in what became known as the 'Monkey Trial' was William Jennings Bryan, a zealous defender of fundamental Christianity, a born orator, Secretary of State under Woodrow Wilson, and thrice a Democratic presidential candidate. The clash between them revolved round Bryan's stubborn opposition to all common sense and decency, and his insistence that every word in the Bible was literally true. Darrow repeatedly exposed the absurdity of such Fundamentalist beliefs and had Bryan writhing and sweating with pent-up hatred and resentment. John Scopes was unquestionably guilty of breaking the state law, and was fined $100, but when the Tennessee Supreme Court considered his appeal, he won on a technicality. The morality of the state's reactionary law was not brought into question, but the moral victory in the trial was undoubtedly Darrow's.

Fact

Early in 1831, a judge at Salisbury sentenced a farmer, Isaac Looker, to transportation for life for writing a letter to a neighbour threatening that his farm would be 'burnt down to ground, and thy bluddy head chopt off'. Looker denied writing the letter, but the half-sheet of paper on which it was written matched a half-sheet found in Looker's house, with the watermark torn through. "You will be sent", Justice Alderson told him, "to a country where you will find very few worse than yourself". Then Mr Looker's 18 year-old son, Edward, confessed that he had written the letter. He had two cousins in prison awaiting trial, and believed that the neighbouring farmer would be deterred by the threat from giving evidence against them. Isaac Looker was acquitted, and his son transported for seven years instead.

Miscarriages of Justice

Now that is the power of logic for you. For 1,000 years prosecutors and accusers have never even imagined that the fact of arrest might in itself be a proof of guilt. If the defendants were innocent, then why had they been arrested? And once they had been arrested, that meant they were guilty!
Aleksandr Solzhenitsyn: *The Gulag Archipelago*

Several acknowledged miscarriages of justice from the past have been included among the case histories in this book—Alfred Dreyfus, Sacco and Vanzetti, Oscar Slater and Timothy Evans for example, as well as cases in which some reasonable doubt persists about the safety of the convictions, such as Walter Graham Rowland, Edith Thompson and James Hanratty.

Since 1989, when the so-called 'Guildford Four' were released after being convicted of pub bombings in 1975, based on confessions signed under duress, a spate of miscarriages in British courts has been revealed. In March 1991, the 'Birmingham Six' were released after 17 years in

Fact

Stefan Kiszko was sentenced to life imprisonment in 1976 for the murder of a schoolgirl, Lesley Molseed. Sixteen years later, he was released when forensic evidence, which had been available at the time of his trial, proved that he could not have been the girl's murderer. Mr Kiszko died soon afterwards.

prison. In June, the 'Maguire Seven' were released after convictions on bomb-making charges. In November, three convicted prisoners were cleared of the murder of PC Blakelock at the Broadwater Farm Estate, Tottenham, in 1985. In February 1992, Stefan Kiszko was released from prison after serving 16 years for the murder of a schoolgirl. Scientific evidence that he could not have been the killer was not produced at his trial. In the same year, forensic evidence judged unsafe led to the release of Judith Ward, sentenced to life for the 1974 coach bombing on the M62, in which 12 people were killed. In December 1992, the life sentences passed on three men convicted of the murder of a Cardiff prostitute in 1988 were overturned.

The quashing of convictions by the Court of Appeal does not necessarily mean that the accused have been proved innocent. It means that the proof of guilt has been flawed, falling short of the highest standards of justice under which a criminal may be properly sentenced. Many suspected cases remain unacknowledged. Some of them have resulted from the defects of the jury system, in which ordinary men and women chosen at random are expected to arrive at correct decisions on the basis of highly technical evidence which they are ill-equipped to judge. This possibility of human error remains one of the most powerful arguments against capital punishment. If the death penalty were still in force in Britain, possibly as many as 18 of those listed in the previous paragraph would have been hanged on the strength of false or unsafe evidence.

On 21 March 1815, Elizabeth Fenning, 21, who had been employed only a few weeks as a cook in the Turner family's home in London's Chancery Lane, served steak and dumplings for dinner. Within minutes, Robert Turner, his wife Charlotte, and his father Orlebar, were suffering from stomach pains and vomiting. So was Eliza Fenning, who had naturally sampled her own cooking, and Roger Gadsden, an apprentice, who had eaten some dumpling. A doctor was called, and in due course, all of them recovered.

Old Mr Turner, however, had remembered that a packet of arsenic kept in a drawer for use on mice had disappeared, and he had the contents of a pan in which the dumplings had been cooked examined by physicians. Arsenic was found, and Eliza Fenning was arrested. A magistrate committed her to Newgate to await trial for attempted murder.

The trial was a disgraceful parody of justice. The evidence was entirely circumstantial, but the Turners, especially Charlotte, were very hostile towards Eliza. It was implied that she was resentful and bent on vengeance because she had been caught going to the apprentices' room one night and threatened with dismissal. The judge virtually instructed the jury to convict her.

Eliza wrote to her fiancé from prison: 'They have, which is the most cruellest thing in this world, brought me in guilty'. She added, 'I may be confined most likely six months at least'. In fact, she was sentenced to death. Hysterical with disbelief, she protested her innocence continually until the morning of her execution, when she was hanged by John Langley, appeals for clemency to the Prince Regent, the Home Secretary and the Lord Chancellor having fallen on deaf ears. Elizabeth Fenning's father had to pay 14 shillings and sixpence before he was allowed to take his daughter's body away for burial. This sum was called the 'executioner's fee'. It turned out that Robert Turner had suffered from a mental derangement and had threatened to kill both his wife and himself. It was he who had bought the arsenic.

An old lady in Hertfordshire some years ago was telling a local journalist that she could remember when 22 year-old Mary Ansell was hanged at St Albans in 1899. She had been convicted on circumstantial evidence of murdering her sister Caroline, a patient in the Leavesden Asylum at Watford, in order to claim £10 of insurance money. "I remember feeling sorry for the victim", the old lady said, "but I think we all felt she must be guilty as they were hanging her". But there was a history of serious mental illness in the family, and Mary's mother said that she had been "silly from the time she was at school". Even if Mary *did* send a poisoned cake to her sister through the post, as alleged, it seems clear that she had little understanding of the gravity of what she had done, and it is said that her brother afterwards confessed to the murder on his deathbed.

Although the consequences of miscarriage are obviously most serious in capital crimes because execution is irreversible, such errors are by no means confined to cases of murder. In 1896, Adolph Beck, a man of Norwegian origin, was brought to trial at the Old Bailey and convicted of theft and fraud, having been recognized in a London street by a German woman, Ottilie Meissonier, as a man who had tricked her out of jewellery and wrist-watches. Other women came forward and identified Beck as the man who had practised confidence tricks on them too. Furthermore, police witnesses identified him as a man who had been convicted of fraud under the name 'John Smith' in 1877 and sentenced to five years imprisonment. Beck was convicted and given seven years penal servitude.

Beck could prove that he was not Smith. Records showed that Smith had been circumcised, and Beck had not. Moreover, whilst Smith was serving his sentence, Beck had been in South America. Nevertheless, Adolph Beck served five years before being released from prison in 1901, and was then arrested again on similar charges in 1904, and again convicted on the evidence of women who identified him. But then another man, William Thomas, who looked remarkably similar to Beck, was arrested after a further series of deceptions, and he confessed not only to these crimes, but also to the earlier ones. He was the man imprisoned as 'John Smith'. Beck was released and awarded £5,000 in compensation for wrongful imprisonment, and it was largely as a result of this classic case of mistaken identity that the Court of Criminal Appeal was established in 1907.

Fact

Sounds familiar?

French and Saunders: *Mary French and John Saunders were convicted as accessories of Charles Schmid in the rape and murder of 15 year-old Alleen Rowe in California in 1965. Saunders got life imprisonment and French four to five years.*

Ken Barlow: *Kenneth Barlow was a male nurse who was given a life sentence for the murder of his wife Elizabeth in 1957.*

Bernard Shaw: *He was the bodyguard who married heiress Patty Hearst after the sensational kidnapping affair in the USA (see under Kidnapping and Abduction).*

Norman Schwarzkopf: *He was the senior New Jersey police officer in charge of the Lindbergh kidnapping case (see under Kidnapping and Abduction).*

John le Mesurier: *A carpet dealer, he was one of those accused with Jeremy Thorpe in 1979 of conspiring to murder Norman Scott, a male model. He was, like the other defendants, acquitted.*

Margaret Thatcher: *One of those accused of witchcraft in the 1692 witch hysteria in Salem, Massachusetts (see under Witchcraft). She was Judge Corwin's mother-in-law, and was not prosecuted.*

Fact

One of the most spectacular acquittals in a murder trial at the Old Bailey occurred in 1923, when Sir Edward Marshall Hall defended Marguerite Fahmy against the charge of shooting her husband, Prince Ali Kamel Fahmy Bey at London's Savoy Hotel. She had met the millionaire Egyptian playboy in Paris and they were soon married, but the marriage was disastrous. The Prince was physically and mentally abusive—and a homosexual—and treated his wife with degrading cruelty. The final quarrel in the suite at the Savoy resulted in Madame Fahmy levelling a pistol at her husband—to frighten him, she claimed. Marshall Hall cast the Prince as a monstrous pervert, and at the climax of his speech pointed the pistol at the foreman of the jury in imitation of his client. "And to her horror," he said, "the thing went off". After a moment's silence, he dropped the weapon to the floor, as Madame Fahmy said she had done. "I ask you to open the gate and let this western woman go back into the light of God's great western sun", he concluded. And they did. Madame Fahmy was acquitted of both murder and manslaughter. But the manner of the defence brough a diplomatic protest from the Egyptian Embassy in London.

Old Bailey

The 'Old Bailey', whose very mention has sent shivers down the spines of criminals and followers of great criminal trials, is actually a little street in the City of London, 183 m (200 yards) west of St Paul's Cathedral. In the 16th century John Stow called it the "Old Bayly, or court of the chamberlain of this city". At its northern end it joins Newgate Street, and at the junction stood Newgate prison until its demolition in 1902 to make way for the new Central Criminal Court, which retained part of the centuries-old prison's outer wall.

Public executions were carried out in the street in front of Newgate from the demise of Tyburn in November 1783 until the abolition of executions in public in 1868. Underworld lingo used 'Dancing in Bailey's ballroom' as a euphemism for being hanged there. In 1831, when the murderers Bishop and Williams were hanged by William Calcraft, 30,000 people are said to have assembled, all trying to pack into Old Bailey to get a good view of the scaffold. Many were injured in the crush, including several policemen, and some had to be taken to Bart's Hospital for treatment.

The name Old Bailey has long been popularly identified with the court itself. The new building was designed by Edward Mountford and completed in 1907, when it was officially opened by King Edward VII. It is a baroque building of Portland stone. Originally it contained four court rooms, but extensions in the 1960s and 70s added 15 more. There are 70 cells for prisoners in custody. The dome above is surmounted by a symbolic figure of Justice, the work of Frederick Pomeroy, RA. The female figure holds a sword in one hand and scales in the other, and its head is 65 m (212 ft) above ground level.

One of the essential English rituals attending sessions here is the carrying of posies of fragrant flowers by the judges on opening days. This custom survives from the need to disguise the noxious smells that used to greet them from Newgate prison, rife with gaol fever. Inside, among the statues of various monarchs, is one of Elizabeth Fry who did a great deal to alleviate the awful conditions of prisoners in the old gaol.

Many of this century's greatest trials for capital crimes have taken place within these walls. Among those who have faced the judges—as black caps were placed on their heads for sentences of death to be pronounced—were Dr Crippen, Sir Roger Casement, George Joseph Smith, Edith Thompson, William Joyce, Timothy Evans, John Christie and James Hanratty.

Index